LEARNING
Excel 2000®

275 Madison Avenue, New York, NY 10016

Acknowledgements

To Mom, who proves to me over and over again what a great mother she is as well as a great friend.
Jennifer Fulton

Project Managers

Emily Hay
Monique Peterson

English Editors

Robin Drake
Emily Hay

Technical Editors

Robin Drake
Howard Peterson

Design and Layout

Shu Y. Chen

Cover Design

Amy Capuano

Acquisitions Manager

Chris Katsaropoulos

Editorial Assistant

Jacinta O'Halloran

ISBN: 1-56243-705-4
Cat No.: Z39

DDC Publishing Inc. Printing

10 9 8 7 6 5 4 3 2

Contents

Contents

LESSON 9:
Create and Modify Charts   247

Introduction

How We've Organized the Book

Each lesson in **Learning Microsoft Excel 2000** is made up of several exercises for using Excel 2000 in real-life settings. Every exercise (except for the Critical Thinking Exercises) is made up of seven key elements:

- **On the Job**. Each exercise starts with a brief description of how you would use the features of that exercise in the workplace.

- **Exercise Scenario**. The Excel tools are then put into context by setting a scenario. For example, you may be the manager of computer store putting together a monthly sales report or a weekly payroll form.

- **Terms**. Key terms are defined at the start of each exercise, so you can refer back to them quickly. The terms are also highlighted in the text.

- **Notes**. Concise notes describe and outline the computer concepts in each exercise.

- **Procedures**. Hands-on mouse and keyboard procedures teach all necessary skills.

- **Application Exercise**. Step-by-step instructions put your skills to work.

- **On Your Own**. Each exercise concludes with a critical thinking activity for you to work through on your own. You are challenged to come up with data and then additionally challenged to use the data in a workbook. The *On Your Own* sections can be used as reinforcement, for practice, or to test skill proficiency.

- In addition, each lesson ends with a **Critical Thinking Exercise**. As with the *On Your Owns*, you need to rely on your own skills to complete the task.

Working with Data Files

As you work through the exercises in this book, you'll be creating, opening, and saving files. You should keep the following instructions in mind:

- Many exercises instruct you to open a file from the CD-ROM that comes with this book. The data files are used so that you can focus on the skills being introduced — not on creating lengthy workbooks. The files are organized by application in the **Datafiles** folders on the CD-ROM.

  ✓ See **What's on the CD** for more information on the data files.

- When the application exercise includes a file name and a CD icon 💿, you should open the file provided on CD.

- The Directory of Files lists the exercise files (from the CD-ROM) you will need to open to complete each exercise.

- Unless the book instructs otherwise, use the default settings when creating a file. If someone has changed the default software settings for the computer you're using, your exercise files may not look the same as those shown in this book. In addition, the appearance of your files may look different if the system is set to a screen resolution other than 800 x 600.

- All the exercises instruct you to save the files created or to save the exercise files under a new name. You should verify the name of the hard disk or network folder to which files should be saved.

What's on the CD

We've included on the CD:

- **Data files** for many of the exercises. This way you don't have to create lengthy spreadsheets from scratch.

- **Internet simulation** so that you can go to real Web sites to get information — without an Internet connection or modem. Following the steps in the book, you will experience going "online" to locate facts, data, and clip art. You will then use the information in Excel documents.

- **Computer Literacy Basics**. These exercises include information on computer care, computer basics, and a brief history of computers. Once Adobe Acrobat is installed, these exercises can be printed out and distributed.

To access the files:

Data Files

Copy data files to a hard drive:

1. Open Windows 95 Explorer. (Right-click the Start button [Start] and click Explore.)

2. Be sure that the CD is in your CD-ROM drive. Select the CD-ROM drive letter from the Folders pane of the Explorer window.

3. Click to select the **Datafiles** folder in the Name pane of the Explorer window.

4. Drag the folder onto the letter of the drive to which you want to copy the data files (usually **C:**) in the Folders pane of the Explorer Window.

   ✓ *Be aware that if you copy the files to a network drive the file names may be truncated to eight characters. Some networks do not allow the long file names permitted by Windows 95.*

OR

Access data files directly from CD:

1. Be sure that the CD is in your CD-ROM drive. Select the CD-ROM drive letter from the Folders pane of the Explorer window.

2. Click to select the **Datafiles** folder in the Name pane of the Explorer window.

3. Double-click directly on the file to open it or open the file through the application using a File, Open command.

   ✓ *Opening and working with files is covered in the Basics Chapter of the text. The data files do not need to be installed.*

Internet Simulation

Copy Internet simulation to a hard drive:

1. Open Windows 95 Explorer. (Right-click the **Start** button [Start] and click **Explore**.)

2. Be sure that the CD is in your CD-ROM drive. Select the CD-ROM drive letter from the Folders pane of the Explorer window.

3. Click to select the **Simulation** folder in the Name pane of the Explorer window.

4. Drag the folder onto the letter of the drive to which you want to copy the data files (usually **C:**) in the Folders pane of the Explorer Window.

   ✓ *If you copy the Internet simulation to your hard drive, be sure to substitute the correct drive letter in the exercise directions.*

   ✓ *Important note about HTML files: The Internet simulation is made up of HTML files. If you copy the Internet simulation to your hard drive, be sure to **copy the entire HTML folder from the CD**; otherwise the HTML files will not display correctly.*

OR

Access Internet simulation directly from CD:

1. Be sure that the CD is in your CD-ROM drive. Select the CD-ROM drive letter from the Folders pane of the Explorer window.

2. Follow the directions in the Internet activities using the file path provided in the Internet exercises.

   ✓ *If your CD-ROM drive is not D:, you will have to substitute the correct drive letter in the exercise directions.*

   ✓ *The Internet simulation does not need to be installed. The HTML files are simply opened as directed in the Internet exercises.*

Computer Literacy Basic

To access the Computer Literacy Basics files:

1. Locate the Acrobat Reader folder on the CD. (If you have already installed Acrobat Reader, you do not need to go through these steps.)

2. Double-click the Setup icon.

3. Respond to the prompts to install Acrobat Reader 3.0.

After installing Acrobat Reader, you may either:

- Leave the Computer Literacy files on the CD and open, view, and print them from the CD. The Computer Literacy files are located in the **Literacy** folder.

- Copy some or all of the exercises to your hard drive using Windows Explorer (see directions for copying data files above). Once on your hard drive, you can open, view, and print the files. The Computer Literacy files are located in the **Literacy** folder.

Support Material

A complete instructor support package is available with all the tools teachers need:

- Annotated Instructor's Guide includes entire student book with teacher notes, course curriculum guide, and lesson plans.

- Upgraded binder test bank includes pre- and post-assessment tests, mid-term exams, and final exams. Two kinds of tests for each lesson of the student book: conceptual (objective questions) and application (students do the work on their computers). All-new tests.

- Improved visual aids package includes 25 transparencies. A PowerPoint presentation of 25 slides is also available.

- Solutions binder and/or CD of exercise solutions.

Directory of Files

Lesson 1

Excel 2000 Basics

Exercise 1

- ◆ About Microsoft® Excel 2000
- ◆ Start Excel
- ◆ The Excel Window
- ◆ Exit Excel
- ◆ Use the Mouse
- ◆ Use the Keyboard
- ◆ Mouse and Keystroke Procedures
- ◆ Menus and Commands
- ◆ Shortcut Menus
- ◆ Toolbars
- ◆ Dialog Box Options

Exercise 2

- ◆ Change the Size of a Window
- ◆ Set View Preferences
- ◆ The View Menu
- ◆ The Zoom Option

Exercise 3

- ◆ The Office Assistant
- ◆ Other Help Features
- ◆ Help on the Internet

Exercise 4

- ◆ Change the Active Cell
- ◆ Explore the Worksheet with the Mouse or the Keyboard
- ◆ Use Go To
- ◆ Use the Name Box
- ◆ The Excel Keyboard Template

Exercise 5

- ◆ Manage Multiple Workbooks
- ◆ Internet Basics
- ◆ Web Features in Excel 2000
- ◆ Use Web Toolbars

Exercise 1

◆ **About Microsoft® Excel 2000** ◆ **Start Excel** ◆ **The Excel Window**
◆ **Exit Excel** ◆ **Use the Mouse** ◆ **Use the Keyboard**
◆ **Mouse and Keystroke Procedures** ◆ **Menus and Commands**
◆ **Shortcut Menus** ◆ **Toolbars** ◆ **Dialog Box Options**

On the Job

Microsoft® Excel 2000 is a spreadsheet program that makes it easy for you to create, track, and update all sorts of data. Excel's calculating functions are ideal for creating such products as inventories, check registries, or sales invoices.

You've just been hired as an office assistant for the law firm Peterson, Barney, and Smith. Your boss wants you to become familiar with Excel 2000. In this exercise, you'll practice using the mouse by opening and closing your Office programs. You'll also practice controlling the program and workbook windows.

Terms

spreadsheet Also known as a worksheet, a spreadsheet is a grid composed of rows and columns that intersect to form cells. You enter data (text, numbers, and formulas) into these cells, and the spreadsheet performs calculations on the data.

workbook An Excel file that contains one or more worksheets. By default, when you open Excel, a workbook with three blank worksheets appears. You can add or remove worksheets in a workbook.

template A semi-completed workbook on which you can base a new workbook. A template can save you the trouble of creating a commonly used workbook (such as an invoice or a purchase order) from scratch.

program window The window that contains the controls, menus, and toolbars for using Excel.

workbook window The window that frames the workbook's contents.

active cell The cell in which the cursor (or cell pointer) is currently located. A cell must be active in order for you to enter data into it.

mouse A device that allows you to select on-screen items by pointing at them with the mouse pointer. A mouse is connected to the computer by a long, thin cord that resembles a mouse tail—hence the name.

mouse pointer An on-screen indicator, typically displayed as a small thick cross or a small arrow that helps you to select on-screen items. The mouse pointer often changes shape in Excel to give you clues about features you can use.

cell pointer A dark border around a cell in a worksheet, indicating that it's the active cell. Any data you enter will go in this cell. You can move the cell pointer with the mouse or the keyboard.

menu A list of commands. You'll find a program's menus located at the top of the program window, just below the title bar.

toolbar A long bar or row of buttons (small pictures) that represent various commands.

dialog box A box that appears when you select certain commands. A dialog box provides the user with the ability to select options for a command.

Notes

About Microsoft® Excel 2000

- Microsoft® Excel 2000 is a **spreadsheet** program.
  - ✓ *An Excel file is called a **workbook**, which is made up of individual worksheets.*

- You can use Excel to keep track of any data that fits a grid format, such as an address book, quarterly sales report, or order form, although its greatest ability is "number crunching."

- Excel also allows you to create graphs (charts) from your data.

- You can use your Excel data with other Office programs.
  - ✓ *For example, you could import sales data entered in an Excel worksheet into a Word report, or a sales chart into a PowerPoint presentation.*

Start Excel

- There are three ways to start Excel:
  - You can start it with a blank workbook.

  OR
  - You can start it and select a **template** on which to base a new workbook.

  OR
  - You can start it and open an existing workbook at the same time.

- After deciding how you wish to start Excel, select the appropriate command from the Start menu, shown on the right:
  - ✓ *For details on which commands you use to start Excel, see the Procedures section.*

The Windows Start menu

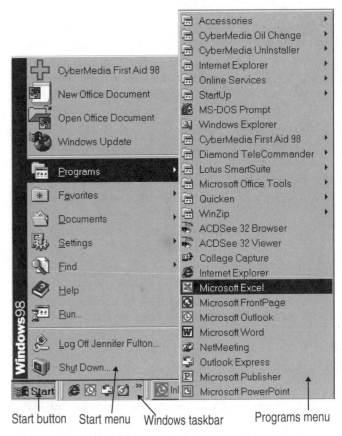

Start button   Start menu   Windows taskbar   Programs menu

The Excel Window

- After you start Excel, the following window appears:

The Excel window

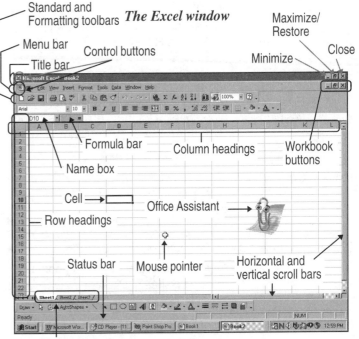

Sheet tabs

- The Excel window contains many parts:

  - *Title bar* — Displays the name of your current workbook.
  - *Menu bar* — Displays a list of drop-down menus from which you can select commands.
  - *Control buttons* — There are two: The button to the left of the title bar contains a list of commands you can use to control the **program window**; the button to the left of the menu bar contains commands for controlling the **workbook window**.
  - *Minimize, Maximize/ Restore, and Close buttons* — There are two sets: The top set controls the program window; the bottom set controls the workbook window.
  - *Toolbars* — Contain buttons you can click to activate commands. At startup, Excel displays two: the Standard toolbar, and the Formatting toolbar.

  ✓ *Initially, the Standard and Formatting toolbars share the same row. You can move the Formatting toolbar underneath the Standard toolbar if you like; see the Toolbars section for help.*

  - *Scroll bars* — Used to display a part of a worksheet that is currently hidden from view—there is a horizontal and a vertical scroll bar.
  - *Name box* — Displays the address of the cell in which the cell pointer is currently located (the **active cell**).
  - *Formula bar* — Provides an area for entering and changing cell data and reviewing cell formulas.
  - *Row headings* — Contain numbers for each row in the worksheet. Rows are labeled 1, 2, 3, and so on.

  ✓ *A worksheet contains 65,536 rows.*

  - *Column headings* — Contain letters for each column in the worksheet. Columns are labeled A to Z, then AA to AZ, BA to BZ, and so on.

  ✓ *A worksheet contains 256 columns.*

  - *Cell* — The intersection of a column and a row. The active cell is marked with a dark outline.

  ✓ *A cell's address is composed of its column letter followed by its row number, as in cell B3.*

  - *Sheet tabs* — A workbook (Excel file) initially contains three worksheets. Click the appropriate sheet tab to access each worksheet.

  ✓ *The tab for the current worksheet is highlighted.*

  - *Status bar* — Displays the current status of the workbook, along with other data, such as the sum of the selected cells.
  - *Office Assistant* — Provides a means for quickly accessing the Help system.

  ✓ *You'll learn more about the Office Assistant in Exercise 3.*

Exit Excel

- You can exit Excel by using the File menu or the Close button.
- If you have made any changes to the workbook, you will be prompted to save the changes.

Use the Mouse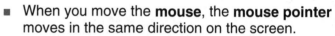

- When you move the **mouse**, the **mouse pointer** moves in the same direction on the screen.

  ✓ *For example, if you move the mouse to the left, the mouse pointer also moves to the left.*

- The mouse pointer's shape will change when you point to or select an object, such as a menu, a chart, or a piece of text. It will also change when you perform specific tasks, such as selecting text.

  ✓ *For example, if you point the mouse at a menu command or a toolbar button, the mouse pointer resembles an arrow.*

  ✓ *If you move the mouse pointer over a cell (the intersection of a row and a column), it changes to a small thick cross.*

- You should use a mouse on a mouse pad, a smooth cushioned pad designed to make moving the mouse easier.

  ✓ *If you move the mouse close to the edge of the mouse pad and need to move it further, just lift the mouse and place it back on the center of the pad and continue moving the mouse.*

Use the Keyboard

- Your keyboard contains many types of keys.

  ✓ *You'll learn the functions of specific keys as you learn how to use Excel.*

- *Function keys* (F1 - F12) can be used to perform certain tasks.

  ✓ *For example, to check spelling in a worksheet, press F7.*

- *Modifier keys* (Shift, Alt, Ctrl) can be used with combinations of other keys to perform actions or select some commands.

- To use modifier keys in combination with other keys, hold down the modifier key while pressing and releasing the other key.

  - ✓ For example, to open a menu with the keyboard, press Alt plus the underlined letter.

- *Numeric keys* appear on keyboards with a 10-key number keypad that will allow you to enter numbers easily.

  - When the Num Lock feature is ON, the number keypad is operational, as are the decimal point and the operation keys (/, *, -, +, and Enter).

  - When the Num Lock feature is OFF, the cursor control keys (Home, PgUp, End, PgDn, and the arrow keys) are active, as well as Ins and Del.

- *Arrow keys* allow you to move the **cell pointer**.

- The *Tab key* allows you to move to the next cell to the right.

  - ✓ For certain Excel operations, the Tab key and arrow keys behave differently.

- The *Escape key* (Esc) allows you to cancel some actions.

  - ✓ For example, to close a dialog box without executing a command, press Esc.

- The *Enter key* allows you to complete the entry of data into a cell.

Mouse and Keystroke Procedures

- Throughout this book, procedures you need to follow in order to complete tasks are listed as shown below.

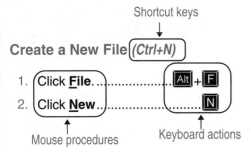

Shortcut keys

Create a New File (Ctrl+N)

1. Click **File**............... Alt + F
2. Click **New**............... N

Mouse procedures — Keyboard actions

- Mouse actions are listed on the left and keystroke procedures are listed on the right.

- Keyboard shortcut keys, when they exist, are listed next to the heading.

  - ✓ A keyboard shortcut, when available, allows you to carry out a command without opening the menu first.

- ✓ In the previous example, the keyboard shortcut, Ctrl+N, is listed next to the heading, "Create a New File." To create a new file, you could simply press Ctrl+N instead of opening the File menu and selecting New.

Menus and Commands

- The menu bar and toolbars provide the means through which you can give commands to a program.

- Initially, when you open a **menu**, only the most commonly used commands are displayed on a short menu.

- After a few seconds this short menu expands to display all available commands.

  - ✓ You can set up Excel so that it displays full menus all the time, if you wish.

Unexpanded menu

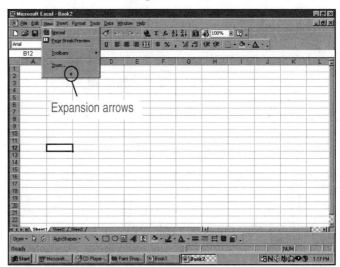

Expansion arrows

The same menu, expanded

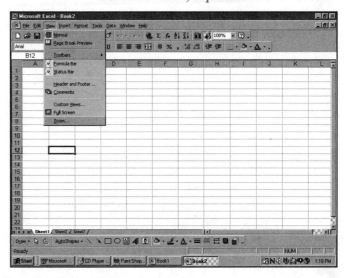

- Excel tracks the commands you use; when you open a menu, Excel displays on the unexpanded menu the commands you use most often.
  - Thus, when you select an infrequently used command from the expanded menu, it appears on the short menu the next time you open it.
- Some menu options are dimmed (grayed).
  - ✓ *Dimmed options are not available for selection because they don't apply to what you are currently doing.*
- A check mark next to a menu item means the option is currently selected or displayed, such as a toolbar.
- A menu item followed by an arrow (▶) opens a submenu with additional choices.
- A menu item followed by an ellipsis (...) indicates that a dialog box will appear when you select that command.

Shortcut Menus

- Shortcut menus offer commands that apply to the current operation. To display a shortcut menu, right-click selected text or a selected object.
- The menu items on the shortcut menu vary depending on the task being performed.
- For example, if you point at a cell containing data and click the right mouse button, a shortcut menu appears with commands for handling data: Cut, Copy, Paste, Delete, and so on.

Toolbars

- When you start Excel, only the Standard and Formatting **toolbars** are displayed.
  - ✓ *The Standard and Formatting toolbars initially share the same row, just underneath the menu bar. You can move the Formatting toolbar underneath the Standard toolbar by dragging its move handle.*

Move handle —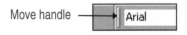

- You can display additional toolbars when needed.
- The Standard toolbar contains buttons for the most common commands, such as opening, saving, and printing files.

Standard toolbar with all buttons shown

- The Formatting toolbar contains buttons that you can use to change the appearance of your data.

Formatting toolbar with all buttons shown

Move handle   More Buttons button

- When you rest the mouse pointer on a toolbar button, a ScreenTip appears, displaying the name of the button.
- You can drag a toolbar to the sides or bottom of the window, or place it in the workbook area.
  - Just click the toolbar's move handle at the left edge of the toolbar, and drag it wherever you want.
  - Toolbars can share the same horizontal area, as the Standard and Formatting toolbars do originally.
    - ✓ *When toolbars share the same area, not all of their buttons are displayed. To display the hidden buttons, click the More Buttons button at the right end of a toolbar.*

Dialog Box Options

- A **dialog box** presents options or choices that let you control what a command does.

Font tab of the Format Cells dialog box

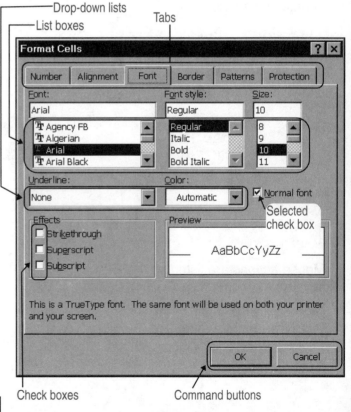

- A list box contains a list of items from which you can select.

  - ✓ *Use the scroll bar (if present) to view hidden items in the list.*

  - ✓ *A drop-down list contains a down arrow. Click the down arrow to open the list so you can select an option.*

- A check box allows you to turn an option on or off.

  - ✓ *A "✔" in the box indicates the option is selected (on).*

  - ✓ *If several check boxes are listed, you can select more than one.*

- Command buttons carry out the action described on the button.

  - ✓ *When a command button includes an ellipsis (…), it will display another dialog box when clicked.*

- A tab allows you to access a different part of the same dialog box with options related to the tab name.

- A text box allows you to type information.

- A combo box gives you a text box into which you can type a value, or use spin arrows to increase or decrease the current value in the combo box.

Print dialog box

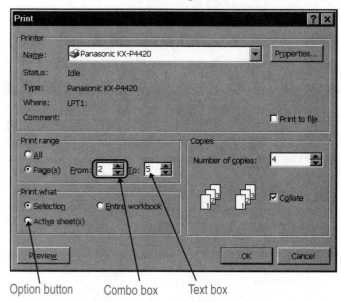

Option button   Combo box   Text box

- Option buttons are small circular buttons that appear in front of a set of options from which you can select.

  - ✓ *You can select only one option from the set. The selected option button appears with a dark circle.*

Procedures

Using the Mouse

To use the mouse, perform any of the following actions:

✓ *In this book, use the left mouse button to perform mouse actions unless specifically told to use the right button instead.*

Point to	Move the mouse pointer over a specific item.
Click	Point to an item and press the left mouse button.
Right-click	Point to an item and press the right mouse button.
Double-click	Point to an item and press the left mouse button twice in rapid succession.
Drag	Point to an item, press the left mouse button, and hold it down while moving the mouse. Release the mouse button to complete the dragging process.

✓ *You must have a Microsoft IntelliMouse in order to perform the following mouse actions.*

Scroll	Rotate the center wheel forward or backward to scroll through a worksheet.
Pan	Press the center wheel and drag the mouse up or down. The farther you drag from where you first clicked, the faster you will scroll through the worksheet.
Auto Scroll	Click the center wheel to scroll down in a worksheet by small fractions. Scroll up by moving the mouse above the point of the first click.
Zoom	Hold down the Ctrl key while you rotate the center wheel to zoom in or out by 15% increments.

Starting Excel with a Blank Workbook

1. Click
2. Click **Programs**.................. P
3. Click **Microsoft Excel**.

Selecting a Template When You Start Excel

1. Click .
2. Click **New Office Document**.
3. Click the **Spreadsheet** tab.

   ✓ *To start Excel with a blank workbook, click the **General tab** and select the **Blank Workbook** icon.*

4. Click the icon that represents the template you want.

   ✓ *For example, click **Invoice**. When you do, a preview of your selection appears in the Preview window on the right, if the template you selected is installed on your computer.*

5. Click .

   ✓ *Excel starts, and a workbook based on that template is displayed.*

   ✓ *If the template is not installed on your computer, you will need to insert the Office CD-ROM into its drive—then Office Setup will install it for you.*

Opening an Existing Workbook When You Start Excel

✓ *If the document you wish to open is a recent one, click **Start**, click **Documents**, and then select the workbook from those listed.*

1. Click **Start**.
2. Click **Open Office Document**.
3. Click the desired file.

   ✓ *You can change to another folder, if necessary, to locate the file you wish to open.*

   ✓ *To change folders, select the folder you wish to change to from the **Look in** list.*

4. Click **Open**.

Controlling the Excel Window

When you click the **Control** button (located just to the left of the title bar), a drop-down menu appears, from which you can choose commands to control the program window.

OR

1. To control the Excel program window, click the appropriate button, located at the right end of the title bar:

   • Clicking the **Minimize** button shrinks the window to a button on the taskbar.

   • Clicking the **Restore** button restores the window to its previous size and causes the button to change to a **Maximize** button.

   • Clicking the **Close** button closes the window.

2. To control a workbook window, click the appropriate button, located at the right end of the menu bar.

   ✓ *If you're displaying more than one workbook in the Excel window, the buttons that control each workbook window will be located on the workbook window's title bar.*

Expanding a Menu

✓ *To display fully expanded menus all the time, open the **View** menu, select **Toolbars**, and then select **Customize**. On the **Options** tab, select the **Menus show recently used commands first** option to turn it off. Then click **Close**.*

1. Click the menu name to open the menu.

   ✓ *For example, click **File** to open the file menu.*

2. The menu displays a short list of the commands you use most often. To expand the menu, perform one of the following:

   ✓ *After you expand one menu, if you slide the mouse across the menu bar to view other menus, you will notice that they are fully expanded as well.*

   • Rest the mouse pointer on the menu for a few seconds.

   OR

   • Slide the mouse pointer to the end of the menu to the expansion arrows.

Select a Menu Command with the Mouse

✓ *To open a shortcut menu, point at the item you wish to work with, and press the right mouse button. Then click a command to select it or press the underlined letter of the command.*

1. Click the menu name.
2. Slide the mouse pointer down the menu.

   ✓ *If a submenu appears, slide the mouse to the right and then down the submenu.*

3. Click the command you want.

Select a Menu Command with the Keyboard

1. Press and hold .... Alt
2. Press the underlined letter in the menu name.
3. Release the letter key and then the Alt key.
4. Then either:
   - Press the underlined letter in the command name.

   OR

   a. Use the up or down arrow key to highlight the command.
   b. Press........................... Enter

Select a Command from a Toolbar

1. Point to a toolbar button.

   ✓ *A ScreenTip appears, displaying the name of the button.*

2. Click the button.

   ✓ *If a button you want is not displayed, click the More*

   Buttons *button* *, and click the button you want.*

Hide/Display Toolbars

1. Click **View** .... Alt + V
2. Click **Toolbars** .... T
3. Select the desired toolbar.

   ✓ *Displayed toolbars appear with a check mark in front of them. When you select an already displayed toolbar, it is hidden.*

   ✓ *Note that not all toolbars can be accessed from the* ***View*** *menu.*

Adding a Button to a Toolbar

1. Click the **More Buttons** button .
2. Click **Add or Remove Buttons** .... A
3. Click the button you want to add or remove.

   ✓ *Buttons currently displayed appear with a check mark in front of them.*

Select Dialog Box Options

1. Select a command with an ellipsis (...) to display a dialog box.
2. Select the options you want:
   - To select a **list item**, click it.
   - To select a **drop-down list item**, click its arrow to open the list, and then click an item.
   - To select a **check box**, click it. To remove the check mark, click the check box again.
   - To change from page to page in a tabbed dialog box, click the **tab** you want.
   - To enter data in a **text box**, click in it and type.
   - To make a selection in a **combo box**, either type the value you want, or use the spin arrows to select it.
   - To select an **option button**, click it. Selecting one option in a set automatically deselects the other options.

3. After making your selections, click OK .

   ✓ *To dismiss the dialog box and not carry out the command, press* ***Esc*** *or click* ***Cancel***.

Closing Excel

1. Click **File**..................... Alt + F
2. Click **Exit** X
3. If prompted, click **Yes** to save changes to your workbook..... Y

   OR

   Click **No** if you want to exit Excel without saving changes .... N

Exercise Directions

1. Start Excel from the Programs menu.
2. Minimize the workbook window.
   - ✓ *Remember that the workbook controls are located on the menu bar.*
   - ✓ *Notice that the workbook is reduced to a button at the bottom of the Excel window.*
3. Maximize the workbook window.
4. Click the workbook window's Restore button.
   - ✓ *Notice that the workbook controls appear now on the workbook's title bar.*
5. Use the vertical scroll bar to scroll down until you see row 40.
6. Scroll back up to view row 1.
7. Use the horizontal scroll bar to view column R.
8. Scroll back to column A.
9. Maximize the workbook window again.
   - ✓ *You can also maximize a window by double-clicking its title bar.*
10. Minimize the Excel window.
    - ✓ *Notice that the window is reduced to a button on the Windows taskbar.*
11. Restore the Excel window.
12. Exit Excel.
13. Start Excel with the Expense Statement template.
    - ✓ *Note that when you select the Expense Statement icon in the New Office Document dialog box, a preview will appear only if the template is already installed. If not, Excel will install it for you when you click OK. (This requires you to insert the Office CD-ROM.)*
14. When prompted, click Enable Macros.
    - ✓ *You should click Disable Macros if you are not sure of the source of a file, and whether or not it is virus-free.*
15. View the partially completed workbook that is based on the Expense Statement template.
16. View the Customize Your Statement worksheet by clicking its tab.
17. Exit Excel.
    - ✓ *If prompted to save the file, click No.*

On Your Own

1. Open Excel using a template of your choice.
2. Click a cell containing text to select it.
3. Click the Bold button on the Formatting toolbar to make the word bold.
4. Open the Print dialog box and print two copies of the workbook.
5. Display a toolbar that's not currently displayed.
6. Add a button or two to a toolbar, and then remove them.
7. Move a toolbar into the workbook area.
8. Close Excel.
   - ✓ *Do not save the workbook.*

Exercise 2

Skills Covered:

◆ **Change the Size of a Window** ◆ **Set View Preferences**
◆ **The View Menu** ◆ **The Zoom Option**

On the Job

When entering data, you may want to change the view of the worksheet. For example, if you have a large worksheet with lots of data, you may want to reduce the size of the worksheet on the screen so you can see more of it. On the other hand, if you have a small worksheet, you may want to enlarge the worksheet so that its data is easier to read. You can also control which window elements (such as scroll bars, sheet tabs, and row and column headings) are displayed on the screen. Hiding the elements you don't need will give you more room in which to work.

To get up to speed using Excel, your supervisor wants you to become more familiar with view options. In this exercise, you'll practice changing your view of the worksheet and setting view preferences.

Terms

zoom A tool that allows you to adjust the relative size of text and graphics on the screen. A zoom level of 100% displays your text and graphics in about the same size as they will appear when printed.

Notes

Change the Size of a Window

- The Excel program window contains the menus, toolbars, and other controls you need to use Excel.

- When you first start Excel, its program window is typically maximized, which means that it fills the screen.

- You can minimize the program (reduce it to a button on the Windows taskbar) or resize it to any size you wish.

  ✓ *You can also resize the workbook window; however, it is usually maximized within the Excel program window.*

Set View Preferences

- You can change your viewing preferences with the View tab of the Options dialog box, shown on the right.

✓ *Remember that a selected check box contains a "✓" and that a selected option button contains a black dot.*

View tab of the Options dialog box

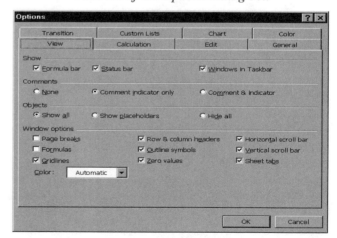

11

- Although the settings you select affect what you view, they do not affect your actual worksheet data.

  ✓ *You can change your viewing preferences as often as you wish without any risk to your data.*

- A few of the options on the View tab require a bit more explanation:

  - *Windows in Taskbar* This option controls whether your workbooks appear on the Windows taskbar. This only affects situations when you have more than one workbook open at a time. (See Lesson 1, Exercise 5 for more information.)

  - *Show placeholders* This option allows you to display objects such as graphics as empty boxes. By not displaying the graphic image, you can speed up the time it takes Excel to display your other worksheet data.

  - *Gridlines* This option allows you to turn off the gray lines that define each cell. Turning this option off gives you a realistic view of your worksheet as it will look if printed without gridlines.

  - *Zero values* With this option, you can control whether a zero (0) appears in a cell whose formula equals zero. This option also affects cells in which you actually type a 0.

The View Menu

- If you don't need to control the display of individual elements on the screen, but rather the entire display of Excel, use the View menu.

  ✓ *The View menu shown here is fully expanded to display all commands—your View menu may initially show only the commands you use most.*

The View menu

- A check mark next to a command on this menu means that the item is selected (shown).

- When you select a checked item (such as Status Bar), its check mark is removed from the menu, and the item is no longer displayed on the screen.

- If you select Toolbars from the View menu, a cascading menu is displayed.

The Toolbars menu

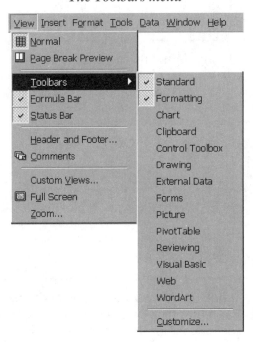

- This menu contains a list of most Excel toolbars. You can use it to control which toolbars are displayed.

- If a check mark appears in front of a toolbar name, it's currently displayed.

  ✓ *To work through the exercises in this text, the Standard and Formatting toolbars must be displayed on your screen.*

- The View menu contains many options:

  - *Normal* This is the default setting; all elements of the screen are displayed (unless they are turned off on the View tab of the Options dialog box.)

  - *Page Break Preview* This view allows you to see where page breaks will occur within the worksheet. (You'll learn more about this option in Lesson 4, Exercise 21.)

  - *Toolbars* Displays a list of common toolbars that you can display (or hide) as needed.

- *Formula bar, Status bar* These commands control the display of these screen elements.

- *Header and Footer* This command allows you to view existing headers and footers or create new ones.

- *Comments* Displays embedded comments.

- *Custom Views* Allows you to save the current view of the worksheet so that it can be recalled quickly.

- *Full Screen* Displays the worksheet minus toolbars, Status bar, and Formula bar.

  ✓ *Full Screen view maximizes the Excel window, even if the window was a different size before you selected this option. Turning off Full Screen view restores the window to its previous size.*

- *Zoom* Displays a dialog box with options that allow you to enlarge or shrink the worksheet data in order to display more or less of the worksheet as needed.

The Zoom Option

- You can change the **zoom** level of a worksheet with either:

  - The Zoom button 100% ▼ (located on the Standard toolbar).

  OR

  - The Zoom command (located on the View menu).

    ✓ *The zoom level in which you choose to work affects the size of text and graphics as displayed on the screen; it does not affect the size of text or graphics when printed.*

- If you zoom to 100%, text and graphics are displayed at approximately the size they will look when printed.

- To zoom in on selected cells, click the down arrow on the Zoom button and then click Selection on the drop-down list.

- You can type an exact percentage into the text box of the Zoom button to change to a custom zoom level.

- You can also enter a custom zoom percentage in the Zoom dialog box, which is displayed when you use the Zoom command on the View menu.

Procedures

Change the Size of the Excel Window with the Mouse

✓ *If the program window is maximized, click the **Restore** button before attempting these steps.*

1. Move the mouse pointer to a corner of the window.

   ✓ *The mouse pointer changes to* ↖.

2. Drag the corner outward to make the window bigger, or inward to make it smaller.

   ✓ *An outline of the proposed window size follows the mouse pointer.*

3. Release the mouse button, and the window is resized.

Change the Size of the Excel Window with the Keyboard

✓ *If the program window is maximized, click the **Restore** button before attempting these steps.*

1. Open the Control menu .... `Alt`+`Space`
2. Select **Size** .... `S`
3. Press an arrow key to stretch the window in that direction .... `↕↔`
4. Press **Enter** .... `Enter`

Set View Preferences

1. Click **Tools** .... `Alt`+`T`
2. Click **Options** .... `O`
3. Click the **View** tab .... `Ctrl`+`Tab`

To set general view options:

1. Select or deselect desired **Show** options:

   a. **Formula bar** .... `Alt`+`F`
   b. **Status bar** .... `Alt`+`S`
   c. **Windows in Taskbar** .... `Alt`+`W`

2. Select or deselect desired **Comments** options:

   a. **None** .... `Alt`+`N`
   b. **Comment indicator only** .... `Alt`+`I`
   c. **Comment & indicator** .... `Alt`+`M`

3. Select or deselect desired **Objects** options:

   a. **Show all** .... `Alt`+`A`
   b. **Show placeholders** .... `Alt`+`P`
   c. **Hide all** .... `Alt`+`D`

To set window view options:

1. Select or deselect desired **Window** options:

   a. **Page breaks** .... `Alt`+`K`
   b. **Formulas** .... `Alt`+`R`
   c. **Gridlines** .... `Alt`+`G`
   d. **Color** .... `Alt`+`C`
   e. Select a color ..... `↕↔`, `Enter`
   f. **Row & column headers** .... `Alt`+`E`
   g. **Outline symbols** ... `Alt`+`O`
   h. **Zero values** .... `Alt`+`Z`
   i. **Horizontal scroll bar** .... `Alt`+`T`
   j. **Vertical scroll bar** ... `Alt`+`V`
   k. **Sheet tabs** .... `Alt`+`B`

2. Click **OK** .... `Enter`

Change to Full Screen View

1. Click **View** ....`Alt`+`V`
2. Click **Full Screen** .... `U`
3. Click **Close Full Screen** .... `Alt`+`C`

Zoom the Worksheet

1. Click **View** menu .... `Alt`+`V`
2. Click **Zoom** .... `Z`
3. Select desired **Magnification** option:

   a. **200%** .... `0`
   b. **100%** .... `1`
   c. **75%** .... `7`
   d. **50%** .... `5`
   e. **25%** .... `2`

   OR

   a. Select **Custom** .... `C`
   b. Type a zoom percentage (10 – 400).

4. Click **OK** .... `Enter`

Use the Zoom Button

✓ *If you're using an IntelliMouse, hold down the **Ctrl** button and roll the center wheel to adjust the view by 15% increments (from 10 – 100%).*

1. Click the down arrow on the **Zoom** button `100%` ▼

   ✓ *The **Zoom** button is located on the Standard toolbar.*

2. Click the zoom percentage you want.

   ✓ *If you do not see the exact percentage you need, just click in the text box of the **Zoom** button and type the percentage you want.*

Exercise Directions

1. Start Excel.

2. Resize the program window so that it takes up about half of the desktop area.

   ✓ *Resize the window horizontally, so that the window is wider than it is tall.*

3. Resize the Program window vertically.

   ✓ *Resize the window so that it is tall and narrow.*

4. Maximize the program window.

5. Zoom the worksheet view to 200%.

6. Change the zoom to 80%.

7. Hide the Formatting toolbar.

8. Display the Drawing toolbar.

9. Hide the Status bar.

10. Redisplay the Formatting toolbar.

11. Redisplay the Status bar.

12. Hide the Drawing toolbar.

13. Exit Excel.

On Your Own

1. Start Excel.

2. Change the color of the gridlines to a bright blue.

3. Change to Full Screen view.

4. Return to regular view.

5. Change the zoom to 125%.

6. Return to Full Screen view.

   ✓ *Notice that you are still at 125% zoom.*

7. Display the Formula bar.

8. Exit Full Screen view.

9. Return to Full Screen view again.

   ✓ *Notice that Excel remembers that you wanted the Formula bar to be displayed in Full Screen view.*

10. Hide the Formula bar again.

11. Exit Full Screen view.

12. Click the workbook window's Restore button.

    ✓ *Notice that the workbook window's controls now appear on its title bar.*

13. Play with the size of the workbook window.

14. When you're through, maximize the workbook window.

    ✓ *Notice that the workbook window fills the program window's screen.*

15. Hide the worksheet gridlines.

16. Close the dialog box so you can view the results.

17. Restore the gridlines to their original color and redisplay them.

    ✓ *Choose Automatic to restore the color of the gridlines.*

18. Exit Excel.

Exercise 3

◆ **The Office Assistant** ◆ **Other Help Features** ◆ **Help on the Internet**

On the Job

If you're working on a worksheet and run into a problem, you can access Help to provide the additional information you need. In Help, you can find out how to change your data, print your worksheet, change Excel options, and perform other tasks. There are a variety of ways in which you can ask for help, so you're sure to find one that suits your style. And if you don't find the answer you want in the Help system, you can connect to Microsoft's Office Update and product support Web sites to locate additional help.

As a new employee at the Peterson, Barney, and Smith law firm, you want to solve as many problems as you can on your own. In this exercise, you'll learn how to use the Help system to answer the questions you may have when using your Office programs. You'll also learn how to find help on the Internet when you need it.

Terms

Office Assistant An animated character that provides an easy way for you to access Office Help.

Internet A worldwide collection of interconnected computers and networks.

World Wide Web (WWW) One part of the Internet. While the rest of the Internet is basically text, on the WWW, information is displayed graphically, with a mix of text, pictures, sound, and animations.

Notes

The Office Assistant

- The **Office Assistant** appears on the screen by default when you start Excel.

  ✓ *Clippit, an animated paper clip, is the assistant that appears by default. However, you can change to a different assistant if you want.*

  ✓ *You can change other options as well. For example, you can silence the Assistant so that it doesn't beep at you. You can even turn off the Assistant, and access Help directly.*

  ✓ *There is only one assistant, so if you change an Assistant option while using Excel, that change is still in effect even when you use another Office program, such as Word.*

- The Office Assistant answers questions, offers suggestions, and provides help whenever you need it.

- After you type a question in the Assistant's balloon, it responds with a list of topics from which you can choose.

  ✓ *If an appropriate topic doesn't appear, you can enter a different question.*

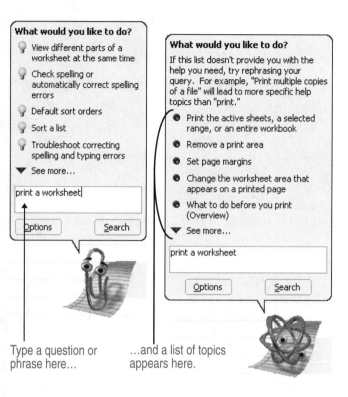

Type a question or phrase here...

...and a list of topics appears here.

- Even when the Office Assistant is hidden, it may display suggestions when you perform some actions.
  - ✓ *For example, if you open the Conditional Formatting dialog box, the Assistant appears, asking whether you need help making selections. You can accept the offer, or select options on your own.*

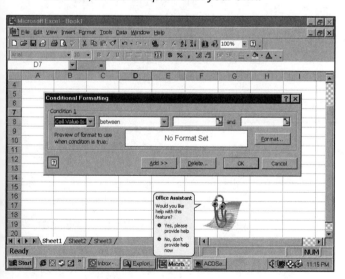

- The Office Assistant also offers tips about features and keyboard shortcuts.
  - When the Assistant displays a light bulb, a tip or hint is available.

- Click the Assistant or the Microsoft Excel Help button ? ▾ (if the Assistant is not currently available) to display the tip.

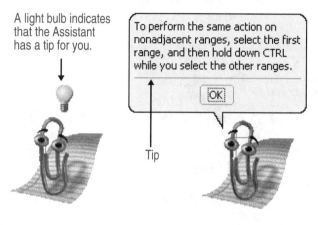

A light bulb indicates that the Assistant has a tip for you.

To perform the same action on nonadjacent ranges, select the first range, and then hold down CTRL while you select the other ranges.

OK

Tip

Other Help Features

- After reading the topic you selected from the Office Assistant's choices, you may wish to browse through Help further.
- The Help window contains three tabs: Contents, Answer Wizard, and Index.
- The *Contents* tab works like a table of contents.
  - Each topic in the table of contents appears with a small book icon.
  - Open the book to display its subtopics.
  - Close the book to hide its subtopics.

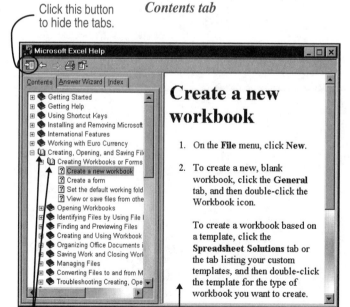

Click this button to hide the tabs.

Contents tab

Open a book to display its subtopics.

The text for the selected topic or subtopic appears here.

- The *Answer Wizard* tab is similar to the Office Assistant itself.
  - Type a question into the Answer Wizard's text box, click Search, and it displays a list of topics from which you can choose.

Answer Wizard tab

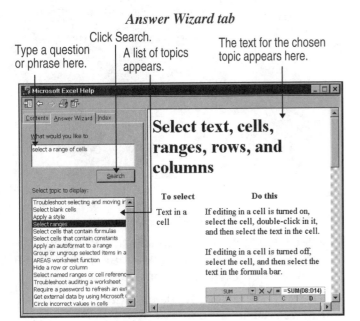

Type a question or phrase here.

Click Search. A list of topics appears.

The text for the chosen topic appears here.

- The *Index* tab allows you to look up all the topics that contain a keyword.
  - Type a keyword, click Search, and a list of topics appears.
  - A topic will appear in the Index list if its title or its text contains the keyword.

Index tab

Type a keyword here, or select one.

Click Search.

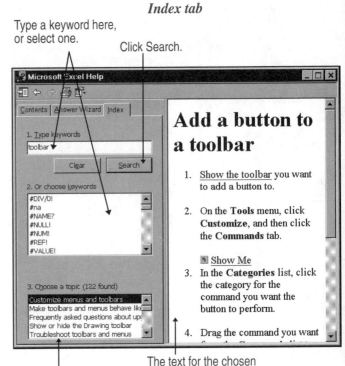

A list of topics appears.

The text for the chosen topic appears here.

- You can find out information about screen elements with the What's This? feature.
  - Press Shift+F1, point to an item on the screen, click, and a box appears that displays the item's name or its purpose.
  - To access the What's This? feature with the keyboard, open the Help menu and select What's This?
  - You can also use the What's This? feature to get help making selections within dialog boxes.

Help on the Internet

- If you have access to the **Internet**, you can connect to Microsoft on the **World Wide Web** (see Exercise 5 for more).
  - On the Microsoft Web site, you can get up-to-date information and support for Excel.
  - You can also download updates to Excel.

Procedures

Display Office Assistant *(F1)*

Click the **Microsoft Excel Help** button 🔲 on the Standard toolbar.

Hide Office Assistant

✓ *If you want to remove the Office Assistant from the screen, follow these steps.*

1. Right-click the Office Assistant.
2. Select **Hide** .... H

Redisplay Office Assistant Balloon

Click the Assistant to display its balloon.

Ask the Office Assistant a Question

1. Click the **Microsoft Excel Help** button 🔲 F1
2. Type a question or a few keywords in the balloon.
3. Click **Search** .... Enter
4. Click the topic you want.

   ✓ *If you don't see an appropriate topic, click **See more** to view additional topics. Click **See previous** to return to the previous list of topics.*

   ✓ *You can also type a new question or a few keywords into the balloon and start again.*

   ✓ *If you don't want to select a topic, press **Esc**.*

5. When you're done viewing the Help topic, click the Help window's **Close** button ❌.

   ✓ *The Help window may contain links to related Help topics. These links appear as blue underlined text. To use a link, click it.*

   ✓ *If you want to browse further through Help, click the **Show** button 🔲, if necessary, and follow the steps under "Use the Contents Tab," "Use the Answer Wizard," or "Use the Index."*

Change Office Assistant Options

1. Click the **Microsoft Excel Help** button 🔲 F1
2. Click **Options** .... Alt +O
3. Click the **Options** tab .. Alt +O
4. Select desired options.

   ✓ *If you want to turn the Office Assistant off, so that you can access Help directly when you click the Microsoft Excel Help button or press F1, then turn off the **Use the Office Assistant** option.*

5. Click **OK** .... Enter

Select a Different Office Assistant

1. Click the **Help** button 🔲 F1
2. Click **Options** .... Alt +O
3. Click the **Gallery** tab ... Alt +G
4. Click **Next** .... Alt +N

   OR

   Click **Back** .... Alt +B

   ✓ *Continue to click the **Next** or **Back** button until the Office Assistant you wish to use is displayed.*

5. Click **OK** .... Enter

   ✓ *If the Assistant you select is not already installed, you'll be prompted to insert the Office CD-ROM to install it.*

Use Contents Tab

1. Click the **Show** button 🔲 in the Help window.
2. Click the **Contents** tab............... Alt +C
3. Double-click a book to open it (display its topics).
4. Click a topic to display it.

Use Answer Wizard

1. Click the **Show** button 🔲 in the Help window.
2. Click the **Answer Wizard** tab .... Alt +A

3. Type a question or a keyword.
4. Click **Search** .... Alt +S
5. Click a topic to display it.

Use Index

1. Click the **Show** button 🔲 in the Help window.
2. Click the **Index** tab. ..... Alt +I
3. Type a keyword in Step 1 box.

   OR

   Click a keyword in Step 2 box.
4. Click **Search** .... Alt +S
5. Click a topic in the Step 3 box to display it.

Use What's This? Help *(Shift+F1)*

1. Click **Help** .... Alt +H
2. Click **What's This?**............. T

   ✓ *The mouse pointer changes to a question mark.*

3. Click the item you want to identify.

   ✓ *You may see the What's This button (a question mark) in a dialog box. If so, you can use it to find out more about a particular dialog box option.*

Get Help from Microsoft on the Internet

✓ *You must have a connection to the Internet to complete this task.*

1. Connect to the Internet.
2. In Excel, click **Help** ...... Alt +H
3. Click **Office on the Web** ..... W

   ✓ *Your Web browser will start, and display the Office Update page for Excel. Browse its contents to find additional help. You'll find a link to Assistance, where you should find help with a particular problem through the Support Online Knowledge Base and the FAQs (frequently asked questions). You'll also find links to downloads (updates and patches) to Excel.*

Exercise Directions

1. Start Excel.
2. Display the Office Assistant.
3. Display the Office Assistant dialog box and click the Reset my tips button.
4. Close the dialog box.
5. Type *April* in one cell.
6. Press Tab, and type *May* in the next cell.
7. Press Tab again and type *June* in the next cell.
8. Press Tab, and when a light bulb appears above the Office Assistant, click it.
9. Read the tip, and then click OK.
10. Display the Office Assistant's balloon.
11. Ask the Office Assistant how to save your workbook.
12. Select the topic *Save a workbook*.
13. Click the link *Save a new, unnamed workbook*.
14. Click the link *use long, descriptive file names*.

   ✓ Notice that as you move around Help, the Back and Forward buttons become available. Back returns you to a previously viewed Help page—you can click it as many times as you need. Forward returns you to the page you were on before you clicked Back.

15. Display the Help tabs.
16. Click the Contents tab.
17. Open the book *Formatting Worksheets*.
18. Open the book *Formatting Text and Cells*.
19. Click the topic *Change the size, font, color, or other text format*.
20. Click the link *Change the font or font size*.
21. Click the link *toolbar*.

   ✓ Click anywhere on the screen or press Esc to close the definition that appeared when you clicked the toolbar *link* in step 21.

22. Close the Help window.
23. Exit Excel.

On Your Own

1. Start Excel.
2. Use the Help system to find the answer to this question:

   How do I average numbers?

   ✓ You can use the Office Assistant, Contents tab, Answer Wizard, or Index to find the help you need.

   Write the name of the topic(s) in which you found help for this problem.

   What part(s) of Help did you use to find the answer?

3. Use the Help system to find the answer to this question:

   How do I print my worksheet on a single page?

   Write the name of the topic(s) in which you found help for this problem.

   What part(s) of Help did you use to find the answer?

4. Use the Help system to find the answer to this question:

   How do I color the background behind my data?

   Write the name of the topic(s) in which you found help for this problem.

   What part(s) of Help did you use to find the answer?

Exercise 4

◆ Change the Active Cell
◆ Explore the Worksheet with the Mouse or the Keyboard
◆ Use Go To ◆ Use the Name Box ◆ The Excel Keyboard Template

On the Job

You can enter data into the active cell only. To enter data into some cell other than the currently selected cell, you must change the location of the active cell. This is easy to do using either the mouse or the keyboard. You can also use the Go To command, the Name box, or shortcut keys which allow you to change the active cell even more quickly in some cases. Sometimes, in order to change the active cell (or to view particular data), you may wish to scroll through the worksheet. Scrolling simply changes the columns and rows that are displayed within the workbook window.

Your supervisor at the Peterson, Barney, and Smith law firm wants you to update case information in Excel. To get up to speed, you need to become more familiar with worksheets. In this exercise, you'll practice scrolling through a worksheet using various methods. You'll also practice changing the active cell.

Terms

active cell The cell that contains the cell pointer.

Name box The box located at the left end of the Formula bar. The Name box displays the location of the current (active) cell.

Formula bar The bar located above the worksheet frame. As you enter data into a cell, it simultaneously appears in the Formula bar.

cell reference The location of a cell in a worksheet, identified by the column letter and row number.

worksheet The work area for calculating data, made up of columns and rows separated by gridlines.

scroll To view locations on the worksheet without changing the active cell.

shortcut keys A combination of keys that, when pressed, activate a command. For example, if you press Ctrl+S (press and hold the Ctrl key and then press the S key), you activate the Save command. Using a shortcut key combination allows you to keep your hands on the keyboard while both typing data and activating commands.

Notes

Change the Active Cell

- A dark border appears around the **active cell**.

Active cell and Name box

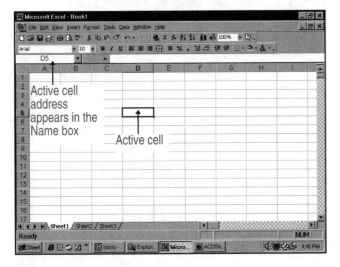

- The location of the active cell appears in the **Name box**, located on the left side of the **Formula bar**.

- The location of the active cell is identified by its column letter and row number, such as A1. This is known as the **cell reference** or address.

- To help you identify the column letter and row number of the active cell, they both appear highlighted (darkened) in the worksheet frame.

  ✓ In the figure, the active cell is D5. So the column letter, D, and the row number, 5, both appear highlighted.

- You can change the active cell using the mouse or the keyboard.

Explore the Worksheet with the Mouse or the Keyboard

- There are 256 columns and 65,536 rows in a **worksheet**, although only part of them are displayed at any one time.

- Since you can view only a small part of a worksheet, you **scroll** to view another location.

- Use the mouse or keyboard to scroll to different locations in a worksheet.

Use Go To

- Go To is a feature that allows you to tell Excel the exact address of the cell to which you want to go.

- Using Go To changes the location of the active cell.

Use the Name Box

- The Name box displays the location or address of the active cell.

- Like Go To, the Name box can be used to change the location of the active cell.

The Excel Keyboard Template

- If you prefer to use the keyboard to enter data into Excel and to activate commands, you can use **shortcut key** combinations.

- Not all commands have an equivalent shortcut key— only the most common commands.

- The following table contains many common shortcut keys.

  ✓ You'll find shortcut key combinations listed in the Procedures section throughout this book as part of the heading for a particular procedure.

Calculate
active worksheet............ `Shift`+`F9`

Calculate all open
workbooks...................... `F9`

Copy selection .... `Ctrl`+`C`

Create chart..................... `F11`

Cut selection
within a cell .... `Ctrl`+`X`

Display AutoComplete
list .... `Alt`+`↓`

Edit cell contents .... `F2`

Enter current date........... `Ctrl`+`;`

Enter current time... `Ctrl`+`Shift`+`;`

Extend selection .... `F8`

Find .... `Ctrl`+`F`

Format cells/object .... `Ctrl`+`1`

Go To..................................... `F5`

Help .... `F1`

Home cell (A1) .... `Ctrl`+`Home`

Next worksheet .... `Ctrl`+`Page Down`

Open a new
workbook.......................... `Ctrl`+`N`

Open a workbook .... `Ctrl`+`F12`

Paste .... `Ctrl`+`V`

Previous worksheet....... `Ctrl`+`Page Up`

Print.................................... `Ctrl`+`P`

Repeat last action .... `F4`

Replace .... `Ctrl`+`H`

Save .... `Ctrl`+`S`

Save As............................... `F12`

Select current
column .... `Ctrl`+`Space`

Select
entire worksheet .... `Ctrl`+`A`

Select current row .... `Shift`+`Space`

Spell check .... `F7`

Undo last action.............. `Ctrl`+`Z`

What's This? Help........... `Shift`+`F1`

Procedures

Change Active Cell Using Keyboard

One cell right .... `→`

One cell left............................... `←`

One cell down.............................. `↓`

One cell up .... `↑`

One screen up .... `Page Up`

One screen down .... `Page Down`

One screen right .... `Alt`+`Page Down`

One screen left .... `Alt`+`Page Up`

First cell in current row .... `Home`

First cell in worksheet .... `Ctrl`+`Home`

Intersecting cell of last column
and last row used in the
worksheet .... `Ctrl`+`End`

Change Active Cell Using Mouse

Click in the desired cell.

Change Active Cell Using Go To (CTRL+G)

1. Press **F5**............................. `F5`

   OR

   a. Click **Edit**............... `Alt`+`E`

   b. Click **Go To** .... `G`

      ✓ The **Go to** list box
        displays the last four
        addresses to which you
        went with Go To.

2. Type cell reference in
   Reference text box ..... `Alt`+`R`

3. Click **OK** .... `Enter`

   ✓ If you want to select a group of
     related cells using Go To, click
     the *Special* button in the Go To
     dialog box; then choose the
     type of cells you want to select
     and click OK.

Change Active Cell Using Name Box

1. Click in the Name box.
2. Type the cell reference.
3. Press **Enter** .... `Enter`

Scroll Using Mouse

✓ When you scroll with the mouse,
  the active cell doesn't change. To
  change the active cell with the
  mouse, you must click a cell within
  the worksheet.

✓ When you need to scroll through a
  large worksheet, drag the scroll
  box on the horizontal or vertical
  scroll bar. As you do, a ScreenTip
  appears, indicating the column or
  row to which you are scrolling.

To scroll one row up or down:
Click the up or down scroll arrow.

To scroll one column left or right:
Click the left or right scroll arrow.

To scroll one screen right or left:
Click the horizontal scroll bar to
the right or left of the scroll box.

To scroll one screen up or down:
Click the vertical scroll bar above
or below the scroll box.

To scroll to beginning rows:
Drag the vertical scroll box to the
top of the scroll bar.

To scroll to beginning columns:
Drag the horizontal scroll box to
the extreme left of the scroll bar.

To scroll to last row containing data:
Drag the vertical scroll box to the
bottom of the scroll bar.

Exercise Directions

1. Start Excel.

2. Move the cell pointer to cell B12 using the arrow keys.

   ✓ *Notice that the cell reference is displayed in the Name box.*

3. With the mouse, make cell E6 active.

4. Using the keyboard, perform the following tasks:

   a. Scroll so you can see cell FF44.

   b. Display cell A44.

   c. Scroll to cell Q73.

   d. Return to cell A1.

   e. Make cell M110 the active cell.

5. Type your first name in cell M110 and press Enter.

6. With the keyboard, return to cell A1.

7. With the mouse, perform the following tasks:

   a. Scroll so you can see cell H90.

   b. Scroll to cell B14.

   c. Scroll to cell L52.

   d. Scroll back to cell M110.

8. Exit Excel.

   ✓ *Do not save the workbook.*

On Your Own

1. Start Excel.

2. Using Go To, move the active cell to the following:
   - Q201
   - C96
   - HH302

3. Using the Name box, move the active cell to the following:
   - CQ102
   - P33
   - M937

4. Using Go To, move the active cell back to C96.

   ✓ *Note that your four previous Go To destinations are also displayed in the Go To box.*

5. Type the following in the indicated cells:

   ✓ *First move to the cell to make it active; then type what you want and press Enter.*

   - H33   Jack
   - CC46   jumps
   - L456   over
   - A3   the
   - Z201   candlestick

6. Zoom to 75%.

7. Using the mouse, change the active cell to the following:
   - A10
   - K21
   - R32

8. Zoom to 100%.

9. Repeat step 7 to change the active cell.

   ✓ *Notice that you need to scroll more, since less of the worksheet is displayed at any given time.*

10. Repeat step 7 with a custom percentage of your choice, such as 65%.

    ✓ *How low can you go in terms of zoom percentage, and still be comfortable reading your data?*

11. Move the active cell to A1.

12. Drag the scroll box on the vertical scroll bar and watch the ScreenTip change as it displays the row numbers.

13. Repeat step 12 with the horizontal scroll bar.

14. Exit Excel.

    ✓ *Do not save the workbook.*

Exercise 5

◆ Manage Multiple Workbooks ◆ Internet Basics
◆ Web Features in Excel 2000 ◆ Use Web Toolbars

On the Job

Sometimes, you may find it convenient to work on more than one workbook at a time. For example, you might want to create a report detailing your department's decreased costs by combining figures from two different Excel workbooks. Or you might have just downloaded some competitive information from the Internet, and you wish to add that data to an Excel customer database. When working with multiple files, you'll often want to arrange your workbooks on the screen for easy reference and quick access.

When you start a new job, you need to learn how to handle several tasks simultaneously. In this exercise, you'll practice opening and closing files and switching between open documents.

Terms

Places bar A navigation bar, located on the left-hand side of the Open and Save As dialog boxes, with buttons for files located in particular places such as the personal, Favorites, or Web folders.

workbook An Excel file. Each new workbook contains three new worksheets, although you can add or delete worksheets as needed.

tile To arrange windows side by side across the screen like floor tiles.

cascade To arrange windows so that they descend down the screen in a diagonal pattern, partially covering each other, like a deck of cards.

ISP Short for Internet Service Provider. You connect to an ISP and then, through its computer, to the Internet itself. ISPs typically provide the necessary software for logging onto their system as well as Web browser software for viewing the World Wide Web.

hyperlink Text or graphic that, when clicked, takes you to another Web page. When you move your pointer across a hyperlink, the pointer transforms into a hand 🖑 . Clicking a hyperlink can take you to another page within the current Web site or to another site altogether.

URL Short for Uniform Resource Locator. The URL identifies the location (the exact computer and directory) of a particular Web page or file.

Web browser A program specifically designed for viewing data on the Web. Some popular Web browsers include Microsoft Internet Explorer and Netscape Navigator.

HTML Short for Hypertext Markup Language. HTML makes it possible to combine text, graphics, sound, animations, hyperlinks, and other items on a single page, and to display that page properly within a Web browser.

intranet A company-wide Internet. Documents stored on such a network are viewed by employees using a Web browser.

FTP Short for File Transfer Protocol. An FTP site is a location on the Internet that specializes in file management (files being uploaded and downloaded to and from the site).

Notes

Manage Multiple Workbooks

- You can open multiple files in Excel, in order to view or change them.

  ✓ *The number of files you can open at one time is limited only by the resources of your computer. However, the more files you open, the more your computer has to manage, and the slower it may become.*

- You can open Excel with an existing file or with a new file. Once you start Excel, you can open as many additional files as you like.

- To open files, use the Open dialog box:

Open dialog box

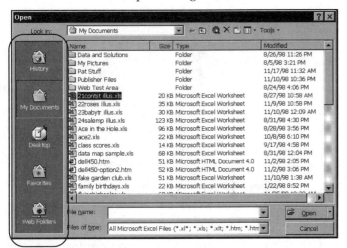

Places bar

- The Open dialog box contains buttons on the left-hand side in the **Places bar** that you can use to access files stored in any of the more common folders.

- When you open an Excel file (called a **workbook**), a button appears on the Windows taskbar. As you open more files, additional buttons appear.

- If you wish to view multiple sheets of a workbook, use the New Window command on the Window menu. Open a new window for each sheet you wish to view and click a different sheet tab in each window.

An open workbook

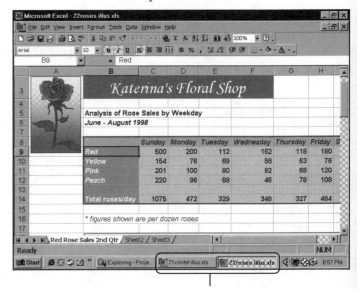

Each open workbook is represented by a button on the taskbar.

  ✓ *You can use the taskbar to switch from one open workbook to another.*

- You can arrange your open workbooks in a number of ways:

  • You can **tile** windows in rows going across your screen, like kitchen tiles.

Tiled windows

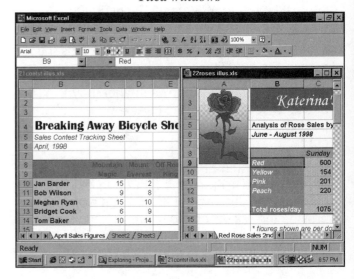

  • You can also arrange windows horizontally (in horizontal bars) or vertically (in vertical columns).

- In addition, you can **cascade** windows (arranged in a diagonal pattern, like a deck of cards).

Cascaded windows

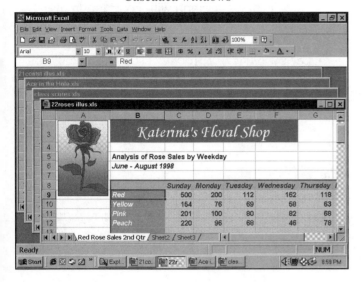

- In any arrangement, the active window appears with a different color title bar.

  ✓ *When you start typing, data is entered into the active window.*

Internet Basics

■ The Internet is a worldwide collection of interconnected computers and networks.

- These networks are located at schools, military bases, businesses, government facilities, and other such facilities.

- Through the Internet, you can exchange electronic mail (e-mail), files, and information with the other people connected to the Internet.

- Your company probably has a direct connection to the Internet. To use it, you simply log onto the company's network.

- If you don't have a direct connection, then you connect to the Internet through your modem.

  ✓ *Whether you have a direct connection or a modem, you're probably connected to the Internet through an Internet Service Provider (ISP).*

■ The World Wide Web (often just called "the Web") is a subset of the Internet, not the entire Internet itself.

- Information on the Web is graphical (a combination of text, graphics, animation, and sound).

- This is unlike the Internet itself, which is text-based.

- Documents on the Web are called Web pages.

- Web pages are interconnected through a network of **hyperlinks**. You click a link to display a different page. You can also display a Web page by typing its address, or **URL**.

- You view Web pages with a **Web browser** such as Microsoft Internet Explorer or Netscape Navigator.

Web Features in Excel 2000

■ You can use Excel to open and view **HTML** (Web) documents, just as you might view them in a Web browser.

- You can open documents you download from the Web.

- You can view documents stored on your company's **intranet** (local Internet).

- You can open HTML documents stored on **FTP** sites.

- You can also make changes to HTML documents, right in Excel.

■ You can save Excel workbooks as HTML files.

- An HTML file can be copied to your Web site and viewed by anyone who visits the site.

  ✓ *For example, you could post a sales worksheet or chart to your company's Web site or intranet.*

  ✓ *The process of publishing to the Web (or an intranet) is as easy as saving an ordinary file!*

  ✓ *If you like, you can make your worksheet or chart "editable" (changeable) by other users.*

- HTML files can be linked together.

  ✓ *This means that you can logically connect related documents through hyperlinks.*

- Excel provides many templates for you to use when creating Web pages—so it's easy to get a professional-looking result.

■ You can also use Excel to create an e-mail message that contains the current workbook.

Use Web Toolbars

■ Excel can display HTML files (Web documents), allowing you to use it as a Web browser of sorts.

■ To make it easier to browse the Web and view the documents you need, Excel includes a Web toolbar.

- The following is a description of the tools on the Web toolbar:
  - *Back, Forward* Move you back to previously viewed Web pages, and forward again.
  - *Stop Current Jump* Stops the process of displaying (loading) the current page.
  - *Refresh Current Page* Reloads the current page.
  - *Start Page* Displays the home page (the page that displays each time your Web browser starts).
  - *Search the Web* Displays the search page currently specified in your browser.
  - *Favorites* Displays a list of saved Web page addresses, or URLs.
  - *Go* Displays a menu with commands that allow you to open Web pages, search the Web, return to your start page, and more.
  - *Show Only Web Toolbar* Hides other toolbars so you have more room to display a Web page.
  - *Address* Allows you to enter the Web address or file path you want to go to, or click the down arrow to select a previous address from the list.

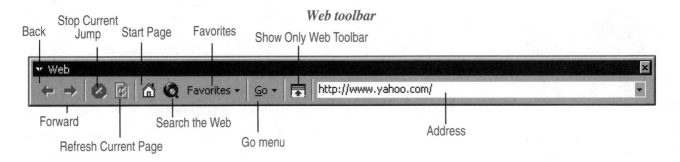

Web toolbar

Back • Stop Current Jump • Start Page • Favorites • Show Only Web Toolbar • Forward • Refresh Current Page • Search the Web • Go menu • Address

Procedures

Open a Document *(Ctrl+O)*

1. Click the **Open** button .... Alt + F , O
2. If the file isn't located in the current folder, perform one of the following steps:
   a. Open the **Look in** list............. Alt + I
   b. Select the correct drive and folder. .... ⬆⬇ , Enter

   OR
   - Click the appropriate button on the **Places bar**.
3. Click file you want to open ... ⬆⬇
   ✓ You can also type the name of the file in the **File name** box.
   ✓ To open multiple files at one time, press and hold the **Ctrl** key as you click each file.
4. Click **Open** .... Enter
   ✓ You can also open a file by double-clicking its file name.
   ✓ You can close a file by clicking its **Close** button X .

Switch Between Documents

- On the Windows taskbar, click the button of the document you wish to switch to.

OR

- To switch to another open Excel workbook, you can also:
  a. Click **Window**......... Alt + W
  b. Click the document you want to switch to .... ⬆⬇ , Enter

OR

- If the documents are arranged on the screen so that both are visible, simply click within the window of the document you wish to switch to.

Arranging Documents in the Excel Window

1. Click **Window** .... Alt + W
2. Click **Arrange** .... A
3. Click the option you want:
   a. **Tiled** .... T
   b. **Horizontal** .... O
   c. **Vertical** V
   d. **Cascade** C
   ✓ To arrange just the worksheets in the open workbook, open a window for each sheet, then select the option **Windows of active workbook**.
4. Click **OK** .... Enter
   ✓ You can also **Hide** and **Unhide** individual windows by selecting that option from **Window** menu.
   ✓ To display only a single workbook again, maximize the window you want by clicking the **Maximize** button ☐ .

Exercise Directions

1. Start Excel.

2. Open the file ⊘ 05_TESTSCORE.

3. Open ⊘ 05_FINALS.

4. Arrange the worksheets vertically.

5. Scroll through the 05_TESTSCORE file to view each test result.

   ✓ *Notice that the title bar of the active window is a different color.*

6. Switch back to 05_FINALS, and view the final grade for each student.

7. Arrange the windows horizontally.

8. Scroll through the final scores in the 05_FINALS file.

9. Review the results of the quiz in the 05_TESTSCORE file.

10. Maximize the 05_FINALS window.

11. If necessary, scroll down to view the final average scores.

12. Switch to the 05_TESTSCORE window.

13. Exit Excel.

On Your Own

1. Start Excel.
2. Open ⊚ **05_1998SALES**.
3. Open a second window for the workbook.
   - ✓ *Use the New Window command on the Window menu.*
4. Open ⊚ **05_CONTEST**.
5. Tile the open windows.
6. In the second window of **05_1998SALES**, change to the Charts tab.
7. Arrange just the worksheets in the **05_1998SALES** workbook in a horizontal fashion.
   - ✓ *First hide the window containing 05_CONTEST.xls.*
8. Arrange them again, but in a vertical fashion.
9. Arrange all open windows in a cascade fashion.
   - ✓ *First unhide the window containing 05_CONTEST.xls.*
10. Practice switching from window to window.
11. Arrange the windows in a vertical fashion.
12. Practice switching between windows.
13. Close the second window of the **05_1998SALES** workbook.
14. Resize the two remaining windows so that the **05_1998SALES** window takes up about $^2/_3$ of the window space.
15. Maximize the **05_CONTEST** window.
16. Close the **05_CONTEST** window.
17. Exit Excel.

Lesson 2

Key Worksheet Procedures

Exercise 6

- ◆ Start a Blank Workbook
- ◆ Enter Labels
- ◆ Make Corrections
- ◆ Save a Workbook
- ◆ Close a Workbook

Exercise 7

- ◆ Enter Numeric Labels and Values
- ◆ Enter Fractions and Mixed Numbers
- ◆ Change Data Alignment
- ◆ Center a Title (Merge and Center)
- ◆ Change Column Width
- ◆ Adjust Row Height
- ◆ Indent Text in Cells
- ◆ Add Comments to Cells

Exercise 8

- ◆ AutoComplete
- ◆ Pick From List
- ◆ AutoCorrect
- ◆ Undo and Redo
- ◆ Clear Cell Contents
- ◆ Check Spelling

Exercise 9

- ◆ Enter Line Breaks in a Cell Entry
- ◆ Enter Dates
- ◆ Format Dates

Exercise 10

- ◆ Open a Workbook
- ◆ Change Workbook Properties
- ◆ Save a Workbook with a Different Name
- ◆ Create a New Folder
- ◆ Create Backup Files
- ◆ Check for Potential Viruses
- ◆ Send a File

Exercise 11

- ◆ Critical Thinking

Exercise 6

Skills Covered:

◆ **Start a Blank Workbook** ◆ **Enter Labels** ◆ **Make Corrections**
◆ **Save a Workbook** ◆ **Close a Workbook**

On the Job

After planning the design of your worksheet, the first thing you'll usually do is enter a worksheet title (such as Sales for Quarter 2) and various labels (such as January, February, and so on). These labels form the backbone of the worksheet, enabling you to enter other data later on. As you enter data, you may need to make some simple corrections to it, to fix any typing errors. After entering this basic information, you'll want to save your worksheet to prevent the possible loss of any data.

You are the sales manager of a small network and systems consulting firm called NetConnect. You need to create a worksheet detailing your sales for the last three months, so you'll start by entering the column and row labels in this exercise. You'll enter the numeric data in a later exercise.

Terms

workbook An Excel file is called a workbook. By default, a workbook contains three worksheet tabs or pages.

template A predesigned or semi-completed document that you can use to create a new document, without having to start from scratch.

label A text entry in a cell.

defaults The standard settings Excel uses, such as column width or number of pages in a workbook.

Notes

Start a Blank Workbook

- Excel displays a blank **workbook** when you open the Excel application.

- After entering data into that workbook, you can start a new one if you like.

- When starting a new workbook, you can select a **template** upon which to base it, or you can start from scratch.

  ✓ *You will learn how to create a workbook by using a template in Exercise 31.*

Enter Labels

- The first character entered into a cell determines the status of a cell.

- If you enter an alphabetical character or a symbol (` ~! # % ^ & *( ) _ \ | { } ; : ' " < > ,?) as the first character in a cell, you are entering a **label**.

- A label is usually text data.

- The **default** width of each cell is 8.43 characters wide; however, a label longer than the cell width will display if the cell to the right is empty.

- You can type up to 32,767 characters in a cell entry.

32

■ As you type a label into a cell, it appears in the cell and the Formula bar.

Entry in cell and Formula bar

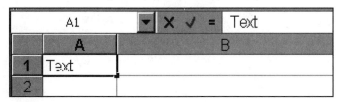

■ By default, when you enter a label in a cell, it is left-aligned.

Make Corrections

■ You can change data while you're typing it or after you enter it in a cell.

■ As you type the data, you can correct mistakes by using either the Backspace or Delete keys.

■ You can also cancel an entry prior to finalizing it.

■ After the text is entered, you can type over the data and replace it with something else, or you can edit the entry.

Save a Workbook

■ A saved workbook is referred to as a *file*.

■ A workbook can be saved on a hard drive or a removable disk for future use.

■ When saving a workbook, you must provide a name.

■ File names are limited to 218 characters for the name, drive, and path (folder).

■ Excel automatically adds a period and a file type *extension* (usually .xls) to the end of a file name when you save the file.

Close a Workbook

■ Save a workbook before you close it or you will lose the current data or updated entries that you made.

■ If you attempt to close a workbook or close Excel before saving, you will be prompted to save any changes.

■ If you have more than one file open in memory, Excel allows you to close and save all of the files before you exit the program.

■ It's a good idea to close workbooks you are no longer working on in order to free up your computer's resources.

Procedures

Open a Blank Workbook *(Ctrl+N)*

Click the **New** button 🗋.

OR

1. Click **File** .... `Alt`+`F`
2. Click **New** .... `N`
3. Double-click **Workbook**.
   OR
   a. Highlight **Workbook**.
   b. Click **OK** .... `Enter`

Enter Labels

1. Click cell for data entry .... `⟷`
2. Type label text.
3. Press **Enter** .... `Enter`
   OR

Press any arrow key to enter label and move to next cell.
OR

Click **Enter** button ✓ on Formula bar.

Edit Data While Typing

1. Type character(s) in cell.
2. Press `Backspace` to erase characters to the left of the cursor.
   OR
   Press `Del` to erase characters to the right of the cursor.

Replace Cell Contents

1. Click the cell with data to be replaced.
2. Type the new data.

Enable Cell Editing

1. Activate cell editing using one of the following methods:
   a. Click cell.
   b. Click in **Formula** bar.
   OR
   Press **F2** .... `F2`
   OR
   Double-click cell.
2. Make correction(s).
   ✓ *Position the cursor and use the Backspace or Delete key to erase characters and enter a correction.*
3. Press **Enter** .... `Enter`

Save Workbook *(Ctrl+S)*

Click the **Save** button 💾.

OR

1. Click **File** .... `Alt`+`F`
2. Click **Save** .... `S`
3. Type name in **File name** text box.
4. In the **Save in** list, select the folder in which you want to save the file .... `Alt`+`I`

   ✓ *You can click a button on the Places bar to change to that folder.*

5. Click the **Save** button .... `Enter`

Close Workbook and Save

1. Click **File** .... `Alt`+`F`
2. Click **Close** .... `C`
3. Click **Yes** to save changes .. `Y`

   OR

   Click **No** to cancel changes .... `N`

Exit Excel and Save Files

1. Click **File** .... `Alt`+`F`
2. Click **Exit** .... `X`
3. Click **Yes to All** to save all changes .... `A`

   OR

   Click **No** to cancel all changes .... `N`

Exercise Directions

1. Start Excel, if necessary.

2. Start a new blank workbook and save the file as **XL_06**.

3. Go to cell B2.

4. Begin typing *NetConnect Networking Specialists,* but do not finalize the entry.

5. Cancel the entry.

   ✓ *The **Cancel** button is located to the left of the Formula bar.*

6. Instead, enter *NetConnect Networking Specialists* in cell B3.

7. Type *Jon Baker* in cell B6 and press Enter.

8. Edit the entry so that it reads *John Barker*.

9. Change the Zoom to 135% so you can really see what you're doing.

10. Enter the rest of the labels as shown in Illustration A.

    ✓ *Make corrections as needed using the method you prefer.*

    ✓ *Notice that the names of the salespeople extend into column C. When data is entered into column C in an upcoming exercise, the names will be truncated. To fix that problem, you'll change the width of column B to fit the data.*

11. Save the file and exit Excel.

Illustration A

	A	B	C	D	E	F
1						
2						
3		NetConnect Networking Specialists				
4						
5			April	May	June	
6		John Barker				
7		Pat Smith				
8		Sally Cooper				
9		Jack Johnson				
10		Melanie McMann				
11						
12						
13						
14						
15						

On Your Own

1. Start Excel, if necessary.
2. Start a new blank workbook and save it as **OXL_06**.
3. Create a worksheet to track your daughter's cookie sales for her soccer team.

   ✓ *You'll enter sales data in a later exercise.*

   a. Enter a title for the worksheet.

   b. Enter column labels for each cookie type (such as chocolate chip, oatmeal, etc.)

   c. Enter row labels for each person in your office who has placed an order.

4. Save the file and exit Excel.

Exercise 7

◆ **Enter Numeric Labels and Values**

◆ **Enter Fractions and Mixed Numbers** ◆ **Change Data Alignment**

◆ **Center a Title (Merge and Center)** ◆ **Change Column Width**

◆ **Adjust Row Height** ◆ **Indent Text in Cells** ◆ **Add Comments to Cells**

On the Job

After entering your worksheet data, you'll want to make it look as presentable as possible before you print it. This usually entails adjusting the alignment of labels (for example, centering a title) and changing the width of columns so that your data is fully displayed. If you enter a lot of data into a cell, you may want to indent it to make it look more like regular paragraphs of text.

You are the owner of Carella's Hair Design. You want to use Excel to create a worksheet that lists the current prices your stylists charge for their services. After entering your data, you'll format the worksheet and add some comments to make the worksheet a little easier to use.

Terms

value A number entered in the worksheet.

numeric label A number entered in the worksheet as a label, not as a value.

label prefix An apostrophe (') used to indicate that a number should be used as a numeric label.

format To apply attributes to cell data to change the appearance of the worksheet.

standard column width The default number of characters that display in a column, based on the standard font.

point A way of measuring the height and width of a character. One point is equal to 1/72".

comment A text note attached to a worksheet cell.

Notes

Enter Numeric Labels and Values

- A cell contains a **value** when a number or one of the following symbols is typed as the first character in a cell: + - . = $

- If the number contains more than 11 characters, Excel displays it in scientific notation (such as 1.253E+11), with the following exceptions:
  - If you typed a dollar sign, fraction, or percent sign as part of the number, Excel widens the column to display the whole number.

- If you typed a decimal point as part of the number, Excel rounds the number visually to fit the column width. (Excel remembers the entire number, but displays only as much as will fit.)

- Excel adjusts column width automatically when you enter numbers, but not when calculating existing numbers. If the result of a calculation won't fit within the column width, Excel displays number signs (#) filling the cell.

- If a number is rounded, displayed in scientific notation, or replaced with number signs (#), widen the column or format the cell as necessary to display the number the way you want it.

- A **numeric label**, such as a Social Security number, is a number that will not be used in calculation.

  - If you type a combination of numbers and letters, Excel treats the entry as a numeric label automatically.

  - However, if the entry simply consists of numbers (such as a ZIP code) that you want Excel to treat as a label, you must precede the entry with an apostrophe (').

  - Although this **label prefix** (') is shown on the Formula bar, it's not displayed in the worksheet or printed.

Enter Fractions and Mixed Numbers

- If you type the value 1/3 into a cell, Excel thinks that it's a date (in this case, January 3rd).

- To enter a fraction, you must precede it with a zero (0), which tells Excel that the data is a number.

  ✓ *For example, to enter 1/3, type 0 1/3.*

- A fraction appears as a decimal value in the Formula bar. The fraction 1/3 appears as 0.333333333333333 in the Formula bar.

- The problem doesn't come up when you're trying to enter a mixed number (a number and a fraction, as in 4 1/2).

- To enter a mixed fraction, simply type it: Type 4, a space, then the fraction, 1/2.

  ✓ *For example, 4 1/2.*

- You can **format** existing data to look like fractions. Just use the Format Cells command, as explained in Exercise 13.

Change Data Alignment

- When you type a label in a cell, Excel automatically aligns it at the left side of the cell. Values are automatically right-aligned.

- To alter a worksheet's appearance, you can right-align or center column labels typed above numeric data.

Example of how data is aligned in cells

	A	B
1	**Text**	Test is aligned left.
2	**1200**	Values are aligned right.
3	**1998**	Numeric labels are aligned left.

- To change the alignment of a cell, use the alignment buttons on the Formatting toolbar or choose other alignment options through the Format Cells dialog box.

Format Cells dialog box

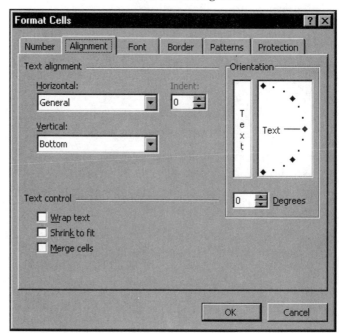

Center a Title (Merge and Center)

- To center a title over a worksheet area, you merge its cell with surrounding cells to form one large cell and then center the text.

- You can do this in one operation with the Merge and Center button on the Formatting toolbar.

Change Column Width

- By default, Excel uses a **standard column width**, which is the number of characters displayed in a cell when using the standard font.

- You can change (widen or narrow) the column widths so that text or values fit the longest line or have a better appearance.

- Changing column width changes the width of an entire column or a group of columns— not the width of a single cell.

- You can adjust a single column, or adjust multiple column widths at one time.

- You can adjust a column's width manually, or you can make it self-adjust to fit the longest cell of data.

- You can use the mouse to adjust the width of a column.
  - When you do so, the column width setting appears in a ScreenTip by the mouse pointer.

- You can also set a specific column width with the Column Width dialog box.

- You can also shrink text to fit in a cell or automatically adjust the **point** size to fit the column width.

Adjust Row Height

- You usually don't need to adjust row height, since Excel automatically adjusts row height to fit the font size of your data.
  - If you increase the size of data, then the row height is automatically made larger.
  - If you decrease the size of data, the row height is automatically made smaller.

- You can adjust the row height manually if you like.
  - For example, you might increase the row height of a title to make it stand out from the regular data.
  - After you specify a row height, Excel won't adjust the height of that row automatically.

- You can adjust a single row, or adjust multiple rows at one time.

Indent Text in Cells

- If you're entering a lot of text into a cell (a set of instructions for using the worksheet, for example), you can indent it just as you might indent regular text in a letter.

- Indented text is text in which all the lines of a paragraph are placed away from the left edge of a cell.

Add Comments to Cells

- You can attach a note to a cell to explain the significance of some data, or to provide instructions to a user.

- A user can tell that a **comment** is attached to a cell by the small red triangle that appears in the upper-right corner of the cell.

- When you rest the mouse pointer on a cell that contains a comment, the comment appears in a small box.
  - ✓ *You can make comments display permanently within the worksheet if you like.*

Comment displayed in a worksheet

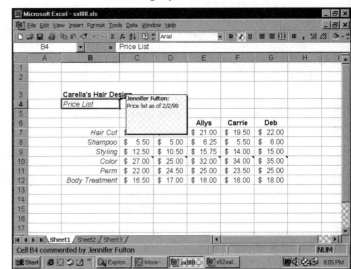

Procedures

Enter a Numeric Label

✓ *A number entered as a label is left-aligned and will not be calculated.*

✓ *You might use this format to enter Social Security numbers or ZIP codes.*

1. Click the cell in which you want to enter the label........
2. Press the apostrophe key ....
3. Type the number.
4. Press **Enter**...................... Enter

   ✓ *You can also press an arrow key to finalize the entry and move to the next cell.*

Enter a Number as a Value

✓ *A number entered as a value is right-aligned and can be calculated.*

1. Click the cell into which you want to enter the number...
2. Type the number.

   ✓ *Start the entry with a number from zero to nine or a decimal point. Enclose a negative number in parentheses () or precede it with a minus sign (-).*

3. Press **Enter**...................... Enter

   ✓ *You can also press an arrow key to finalize the entry and move to the next cell.*

   ✓ *If Excel displays scientific notation in the cell, the column needs to be widened.*

Enter a Number as a Fraction

1. Select the cell.
2. Press the **zero** key.............. 0
3. Press the **Spacebar**....... Space
4. Type a fraction.

   ✓ *Example: 0 1/5*

5. Press **Enter**...................... Enter

Enter Mixed Numbers

1. Select the cell.
2. Type a whole number.
3. Press the **Spacebar**....... Space
4. Type the fraction.

   ✓ *Example: 3 1/3*

5. Press **Enter**...................... Enter

Align Data Using Formatting Toolbar

1. Select cell(s)......................
2. Click **Align Left** button .
   OR

   Click **Center** button .
   OR

   Click **Align Right** button .

Merge and Center Data Across Several Columns

1. Select the cell with the label *and* the cells you want to center across.

   ✓ *To select the cells you need, click in the first cell and hold the mouse button down as you drag over the other cells in which you want to center the title.*

2. Click **Merge and Center** button .

Align Data Using Format Menu

1. Select cell(s) containing label(s) ....
2. Click **Format** .... Alt +O
3. Click **Cells** .... E
4. Click **Alignment** tab ... Ctrl +Tab
5. Click **Horizontal** .... Alt +H
6. Click **Left (Indent)**..... L , Enter
   OR

   Click **Center**..............C , Enter
   OR

   Click **Right** ....R , Enter
7. Click **OK** .... Enter

Change Column Width Using Menu

✓ *To adjust multiple columns at once, drag over the headings for the columns you wish to change.*

1. Select any cell in the column.
2. Click **Format** .... Alt +O
3. Click **Column** C
4. Click **Width**.......................... W

5. Type a number (0-255) in the **Column width** text box.

   ✓ *This number represents the number of characters to be displayed in a cell using the standard font.*

6. Click **OK** .... Enter

Change Column Width Using Mouse

✓ *To adjust multiple columns at once, drag over the headings for the columns you wish to change.*

1. Point to the right border of the column heading to be sized.

   ✓ *The pointer becomes ✛.*

2. Drag left or right to desired width.

   ✓ *Excel displays column width in a ScreenTip.*

Change Column Width Using Right Mouse Button

✓ *To adjust multiple columns at once, drag over the headings for the columns you wish to change.*

1. Right-click column heading.
2. Click **Column** Width .... C , C , Enter
3. Type a number (0-255).
4. Click **OK** .... Enter

Set Column Width to Fit Longest Entry

✓ *To adjust multiple columns at once, drag over the headings for the columns you wish to change.*

Double-click the right border of the column heading.
OR

1. Select cell with longest entry in the column.
2. Click **Format**.............. Alt +O
3. Click **Column** C
4. Click **AutoFit Selection** ...... A

Set Standard Column Width

✓ *This command adjusts all columns that have not been previously changed in a worksheet.*

1. Click **Format** .... `Alt`+`O`
2. Click **Column** .... `C`
3. Click **Standard Width** .... `S`
4. Type a new number (0-255) in the **Standard column width** text box.

   ✓ *This number represents the number of characters to be displayed in a cell using the standard font.*

5. Click **OK** .... `Enter`

Adjust Row Height Using the Menu

✓ *To adjust multiple rows at once, drag over the headings for the rows you wish to change.*

1. Select any cell(s) in the row(s) to size.
2. Click **Format** .... `Alt`+`O`
3. Click **Row** .... `R`
4. Click **Height** .... `E`
5. Type a number (0-409) in the **Row height** text box.

   ✓ *This number represents the height of the row in points.*

6. Click **OK** .... `Enter`

Change Row Height Using the Mouse

✓ *To adjust multiple rows at once, drag over the headings for the rows you wish to change.*

1. Point to the bottom border of the row heading.

   ✓ *The pointer becomes ⇕.*

2. Drag up or down.

   ✓ *Excel displays the row height in a ScreenTip.*

Set the Row Height to Fit the Tallest Entry

✓ *To adjust multiple rows at once, drag over the headings for the rows you wish to change.*

Double-click the bottom border of the row heading(s).

Increase Indent Using Formatting Toolbar

1. Select cell(s) with text to indent.
2. Click **Increase Indent** button.

Decrease Indent Using Formatting Toolbar

1. Select cell(s) with text to indent.
2. Click **Decrease Indent** button.

Indent Text Using Format Menu

1. Select cell(s) with text to indent.
2. Click **Format** .... `Alt`+`O`
3. Click **Cells** .... `E`
4. Click **Alignment** tab ... `Ctrl`+`Tab`
5. Click **Indent** .... `Alt`+`I`
6. Type the number (0-15).

   ✓ *Typing the number 1 increases the indent by one character; typing a zero removes the indent.*

7. Click **OK** .... `Enter`

Add Comments

1. Select cell to include a comment.
2. Click **Insert** .... `Alt`+`I`
3. Click **Comment** .... `M`
4. Type the text.

   ✓ *Note that handles appear around the box to resize or move it.*

5. Click outside comment box.

   ✓ *A red triangle displays in the upper-right corner of the commented cell. Place the mouse pointer anywhere in that cell to read the comment.*

Edit Comment

1. Right-click the cell with the comment.
2. Click **Edit Comment** .... `E`
3. Make your changes.
4. Click outside the cell.

Delete Comment

1. Right-click cell with comment.
2. Click **Delete Comment** .... `M`

Display Comments

1. Click **Tools** .... `Alt`+`T`
2. Click **Options** .... `O`
3. Click **View** tab .... `Ctrl`+`Tab`
4. Click **Comment & indicator** .... `Alt`+`M`
5. Click **OK** .... `Enter`

Exercise Directions

1. Start Excel, if necessary.

2. Start a new workbook and save it as **XL_07**.

3. In cell B3, enter the worksheet title: *Carella's Hair Design*.

   a. Adjust the row height to 24 points.

   b. Select cells B3:G3 by clicking in cell B3 and dragging to cell G3.

   c. Use the Merge and Center button to center the title.

4. Type *Price List* in cell B4.

5. In row 6, beginning in column C, type the column labels: *Susie*, *John*, *Allys*, *Carrie*, and *Deb*.

6. Center the labels.

7. In column B, beginning in row 7, type the row labels: *Hair Cut*, *Shampoo*, *Styling*, *Color*, *Perm*, and *Body Treatment*.

   a. Adjust the column width to fit the size of the row labels.

   b. Right-align the labels.

8. Enter the prices for each type of service, using the illustration as a guide.

   • Format the values with Currency Style.

   ✓ *Hint: Select the cells and click the Currency Style button* **$** *(You will learn more about formatting data in Exercise 13.)*

9. Add a comment to cell B4 that says: *Price list as of 4/2/99.*

10. Add a comment to each of the cells in row 10, to note which type of hair color each stylist uses:

    a. Susie: Golden color

    b. John: Valares color

    c. Allys: Golden color

    d. Carrie: Valares color

    e. Deb: Valares color

11. Save the file and exit Excel.

Illustration A

	A	B	C	D	E	F	G	H
1								
2								
3			Carella's Hair Design					
4		Price List						
5								
6			Susie	John	Allys	Carrie	Deb	
7		Hair Cut	$ 20.00	$ 17.50	$ 21.00	$ 19.50	$ 22.00	
8		Shampoo	$ 5.50	$ 5.00	$ 6.25	$ 5.50	$ 6.00	
9		Styling	$ 12.50	$ 10.50	$ 15.75	$ 14.00	$ 15.00	
10		Color	$ 27.00	$ 25.00	$ 32.00	$ 34.00	$ 35.00	
11		Perm	$ 22.00	$ 24.50	$ 25.00	$ 23.50	$ 25.00	
12		Body Treatment	$ 16.50	$ 17.00	$ 18.00	$ 18.00	$ 18.00	
13								
14								
15								

On Your Own

1. Start Excel, if necessary.

2. Start a new workbook and save it as **OXL_07**.

3. Create a worksheet to track the orders for new little league uniforms for the team you coach.

   a. Type a title for your report in cell B2.

   b. Experiment with the alignment of the title—you may even want to try merge and center.

4. Enter the following labels as column labels starting in column B:

   Name
   Address
   City
   State
   ZIP Code
   Uniform Size
   Cap Size
   Deposit

5. Play with the alignment of the column labels.

6. In the rows below each column heading, enter some fake data.

   a. Make sure you enter the ZIP codes as numeric labels.

   b. Enter uniform and cap sizes that use fractions.

   c. Adjust the widths of columns as needed.

7. Save the file and exit Excel.

Exercise 8

Skills Covered:

◆ **AutoComplete** ◆ **Pick From List** ◆ **AutoCorrect**
◆ **Undo and Redo** ◆ **Clear Cell Contents** ◆ **Check Spelling**

On the Job

Excel includes many features that help you increase the speed and accuracy with which you enter data into a worksheet. Using the AutoComplete and Pick From List features, you can quickly enter repetitive data. Meanwhile, AutoCorrect automatically corrects many common spelling errors you might make — and you can use the spelling checker to catch any others. If you accidentally make a change to the worksheet you don't like, you can undo it (or redo it) as needed. These features and others save time and energy.

You have been selected by your boss at Movie Time Video to prepare a worksheet listing the new video releases for the month of February, along with the categories of the videos.

Terms

AutoComplete A feature that completes an entry based on previous entries made in the column containing the active cell.

Pick From List A shortcut used to insert repeated information.

AutoCorrect A feature that automates the correction of frequently typed errors.

undo A command that reverses one or a series of editing actions.

redo A command that reverses an undo action.

spelling checker A tool that assists you in correcting typographical errors.

Notes

AutoComplete

■ When you need to repeat a label that was typed earlier in the same column, the **AutoComplete** feature allows you to enter the label automatically.

AutoComplete finishes a label entry

	A	B	C
1	Accounting		
2	Human Resources		
3	Accounting		

Pick From List

■ If several labels are entered in a column and the next items to be typed are repeated information, use the **Pick From List** command to enter them quickly.

List of labels for the next entry in a column

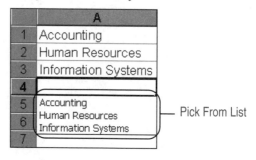

Pick From List

AutoCorrect

- If you type a word incorrectly and it's in the **AutoCorrect** list, Excel automatically changes the word as you type.
- You can even add words to the AutoCorrect list that you often type incorrectly.
- AutoCorrect makes other corrections as well:
  - It automatically capitalizes the first letter of a sentence and names of days of the week.
  - It changes incorrectly capitalized letters in the first two positions in a word.
  - It corrects accidental use of the Caps Lock key.

AutoCorrect dialog box

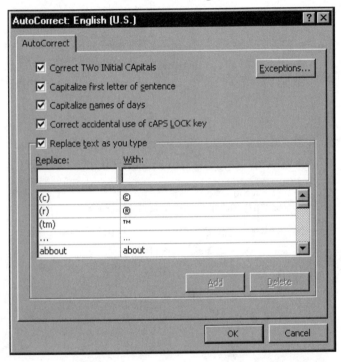

Undo and Redo

- Use the **undo** command to reverse any editing action.
- By repeating the undo command, you can reverse several previous editing actions.
- You can reverse the effects of the undo command with **redo**.
- The undo and redo commands list the editing actions that can be reversed, so you can select exactly how much you wish to undo/redo.

Clear Cell Contents

- You can press the Escape key or click the Cancel button on the Formula bar to clear a cell's contents before entering it into the cell.
- To erase the contents of a cell after you enter data, use the Clear Contents command.
  - ✓ *You can also use the Delete key to clear a cell's contents.*
- You can also clear just the format of a cell, without clearing its contents.
  - ✓ *You'll learn how to clear formats in Lesson 6.*

Check Spelling

- To check the spelling of text in a worksheet and obtain replacement word suggestions, use the **spelling checker** feature.

Procedures

AutoComplete

1. Type part of any label you've typed before in the same column.

    ✓ *Repetitive text is highlighted as you type a label.*

2. Press **Enter**......................... Enter

    ✓ *Just continue typing if you don't want to repeat label.*

    ✓ *If the AutoComplete entry is longer than the entry you're typing (for example, you want to type ten and AutoComplete displays tent), press Backspace or Delete to clear AutoComplete, then finish typing your entry.*

Pick From List

1. Right-click cell to display shortcut menu.
2. Click **Pick From List** .... K
3. Click desired text in list.

Add to AutoCorrect List

1. Click **Tools**.................. Alt + T
2. Click **AutoCorrect** .... A
3. Click **Replace** .... Alt + R
4. Type misspelled word.
5. Click **With** .... Alt + W
6. Type replacement characters.
7. Click **Add** .... Alt + A
8. Click **OK**.......................... Enter

Undo Last Action *(Ctrl+Z)*

Click **Undo** button .

OR

1. Click **Edit**.................... Alt + E
2. Click **Undo** *action name* .... U

Redo Last Reversed Action *(Ctrl+Y)*

Click **Redo** button .

OR

1. Click **Edit**.................... Alt + E
2. Click **Redo** *action name*..... R

Undo or Redo Several Actions

1. Click arrow on the **Undo** or **Redo** button ▼ arrow.
2. Drag to select actions to undo/redo; then click.

    ✓ *You can only undo/redo consecutive actions, beginning with the action at the top of the list.*

Cancel Entry into a Cell While Typing

Press **Escape** key................... Esc

OR

Click the **Cancel** button .

Clear Cell Contents

1. Click cell to clear.

    ✓ *You can select multiple cells and clear them in one step.*

2. Press **Delete** key. .... Del

OR

a. Click **Edit**............... Alt + E
b. Click **Clear** .... A
c. Click **Contents**.............. C

Check Spelling *(F7)*

1. Select a cell.

    ✓ *If you don't start the spelling check from the beginning of the worksheet, Excel completes the spelling check and then displays, "Do you want to continue checking at the beginning of the sheet?"*

    ✓ *To start checking at the beginning of the worksheet, press **Ctrl+Home** to move to cell A1.*

2. Click **Spelling** button .

OR

1. Click **Tools** .... Alt + T
2. Click **Spelling**..................... S
3. If Excel finds an error, select an option:

    a. **Ignore** the entry.
    b. **Ignore All** similar entries.
    c. **Change** the entry to the text shown in the **Change to** box.
    d. **Change All** similar entries to the text shown in the **Change to** box.
    e. **Add** the "error" to the dictionary.
    f. **Suggest** possible corrections for the error.
    g. Add the error and its correction to the **AutoCorrect** list.

4. Click .

Exercise Directions

1. Start Excel, if necessary.
2. Open a new workbook and save it as **XL_08**.
3. Create the worksheet as shown in Illustration A.
   a. Type the worksheet title and subtitle.
   b. Type the column labels and the data. Adjust the width of column B to show the contents of all cells.
      ✓ *When typing data in column C, use AutoComplete or Pick From List to enter repeated data.*
   c. Include the typing errors as shown.
4. Change cell C13 to read: *Historical.*
5. Change cell C14 to *Action/Adventure.*
6. Undo both changes.
7. Redo both changes.
8. Check spelling in your worksheet.
9. Save the file and exit Excel.

Illustration A

	A	B	C	D
1				
2		Movie Time Vidoe		
3				
4		New Releases for Febuary		
5				
6		Name	Catagory	
7		Actoin Bob	Action/Adventure	
8		Love Lorn	Romance	
9		Lots of Toys	Children	
10		The Big Ship	Action/Adventure	
11		I Saw You	Horror	
12		Robert and Mary	Romance	
13		Danielle's Holiday	Romance	
14		Blow 'Em Up Good	Children	
15		We Saw Them	Horror	
16		101 Spotted Dogs	Children	

On Your Own

1. Start Excel, if necessary.
2. Open a new workbook and save it as **OXL_08**.
3. Create a report of your expenses for the last month.
4. Type *Expenses for the Month of* as a title for the worksheet.
5. Type the column labels *Category* and *Amount*.
6. Enter your expense items in the Category column (you can make them up if you like). Suggested items are food, entertainment, rent, auto, clothes, etc.
   a. Do not enter the expense amounts — you'll learn how to do that in a later exercise. For now, enter only the month and expense category for each item.
   b. Leave two blank rows below the last category entry and type *Total* in the Category column.
7. Correct any errors that occur while typing.
8. Check spelling in your worksheet when you're through.
9. Save the file and exit Excel.

Exercise 9

Skills Covered:

◆ **Enter Line Breaks in a Cell Entry** ◆ **Enter Dates** ◆ **Format Dates**

On the Job

When entering labels, especially long ones, you may want to display them on more than one line. This enables you to make the column a bit smaller, which is useful if your data is not very wide. In addition, you may need to enter dates into a worksheet. For example, you could enter the current date each time you make a change to a worksheet. Or you may need to enter dates as part of your data, such as the date you sold some stock, or the time the second and third shifts begin. After entering a date, it's useful to format it to display exactly as you want.

You're a salesperson for a big pharmaceutical company, and you have to make a trip next week to a small town in Florida. This involves several flight changes, and you don't want to miss your meeting with an important client. So you've decided to enter the data into Excel to keep track of your travel schedule.

Terms

line break A code inserted into text that forces it to display on two different lines.

date format The way in which a date is entered or displayed in Excel.

Notes

Enter Line Breaks in a Cell Entry

- If you have long column labels, you can adjust the column width to fit them.
  - This doesn't always look pleasing, however, especially when the column label is much longer than the data in the column.
  - For example:

Unit Number	Total Annual Sales
2	$125,365.97

- One of the easiest ways to fix this problem is to enter the column label with **line breaks** to make several lines, like this:

Unit Number	Total Annual Sales
2	$125,365.97

- The height of the row adjusts automatically to accommodate the multiple-line label.

Enter Dates

- You can enter a date using one of these **date formats:**
  - mm/dd/yy, as in 1/14/99 or 01/14/99
  - dd-mmm-yy, as in 14-Jan-99
  - dd-mmm, as in 14-Jan
    - ✓ The current year is assumed.
  - mmm-yy, as in Jan-99
    - ✓ The first day of the month is assumed.
- If you attempt to enter a date in any other way, Excel simply changes it to one of these formats.

- After entering a date, you can change its display to suit your needs.
  - ✓ *For example, you can change the date 1/14/99 to display as January 14, 1999.*
    - Because dates in Excel are just numbers, you can add or subtract them as needed.
- To enter time, follow it with a or p to indicate AM or PM, like this:

  10:43 p
- You can enter a date and time in the same cell, like this:

  10/16/99 2:31 p

Format Dates

- You can change the way a date is displayed by formatting a cell or cells before or after entering the date.
- The standard formats you can use to display a date include the following:

5/6	6-Jan	10/16/99 2:45 PM
5/6/99	6-Jan-99	10/16/99 14:45
05/06/99	06-Jan-99	O
5/6/1999	6-Jan-1999	O-99
	Jan-99	
	January-99	
	January 6, 1999	

O represents October

- You can also customize the way you want the dates displayed.

Procedures

Enter Line Breaks in a Cell Entry

1. Type first line of label.
2. Press **Alt** + **Enter** ..... Alt + Enter
3. Type second line of label.
4. Repeat steps 2 and 3 as needed.
5. Press **Enter** .... Enter

Enter a Date

✓ *Because dates are numerical data, they're right–aligned and can be calculated.*

1. Click the cell in which you want to type the date.

   To enter current date:
   Press **Ctrl** + **;**
   (semicolon) .... Ctrl + ;

To enter a specific date:
Type date in a valid format.

✓ *You can use the following formats:*

m/d/yy	1/13/01
d-mmm	13-Jan
d-mmm-yy	13-Jan-01
mmm-yy	Jan-01

2. Press **Enter** .... Enter

Format Dates

1. Select cell(s) containing date(s) to format.
2. Click **Format** .... Alt + O
3. Click **Cells** .... E
4. Click **Number** tab ...... Ctrl + Tab
5. Select **Date** .... Alt + C, ↑↓
   in **Category** list.

6. Select desired format .... Alt + T, ↑↓
7. Click **OK** .... Enter

Customize Date Format

1. Select cell(s) containing date(s) to format.
2. Click **Format** .... Alt + O
3. Click **Cells** .... E
4. Click **Number** tab ...... Ctrl + Tab
5. Select **Custom** in **Category** list. .... Alt + C, ↑↓
6. In the **Type:** box, type the desired format.
   Example: *yyyy-mm-dd* or *yyyy/mmm dd*
7. Click **OK** .... Enter

Exercise Directions

1. Start Excel, if necessary.
2. Start a new workbook and save the file as **XL_09**.
3. Type the title *Flight Itinerary* in cell B2.
   - Merge and center the title over cells B2:H2.
4. Starting in cell B4, type the following column labels: *Airline, Flight Number, Date, From, To, Departure Time, Arrival Time*.
   a. Type the labels *Flight Number, Departure Time,* and *Arrival Time* on two lines.
   b. Center the column labels.
5. Type the flight data as listed below:

6. Adjust the column widths as needed to display the data.
7. Format the dates using the format *March 14, 1998*.
   ✓ *If you resized the Date column manually, the column isn't wide enough for the new format.*
8. Adjust the Date column's width again, if necessary.
9. Format the Departure Time and Arrival Time columns with the format *13:30*.
   ✓ *Notice that the times change to military format.*
10. Save the workbook and exit Excel.

Airline	Flight Number	Date	From	To	Departure Time	Arrival Time
SW Airlines	SW102	8/14/99	Sea City	Lake Town	6:48 a	8:02 a
SW Airlines	SW245	8/14/99	Lake Town	Orlando	10:47 a	12:32 p
Lil' Commuter	LC52	8/14/99	Orlando	Ocean City	2:43 p	3:55 p

On Your Own

1. Start Excel, if necessary.
2. Start a new workbook and save it as **OXL_09**.
3. Create a worksheet to track an imaginary family's schedule for today.
4. Type a title for the worksheet.
5. Enter today's date under the title.
6. Type the following column labels:
   ✓ *Enter the longer column labels on two lines.*

   Drop Off at School
   Pick Up at School
   Drop Off
   Pick Up
   Drop Off
   Pick Up

7. Enter at least four children's names as row labels.
8. Under each column, enter appropriate times for drop off and pick up for each child's activity.
   ✓ *For example, one child may have soccer, and another may have an after-school play date. Others may have multiple activities, such as football and Boy Scouts.*
9. Enter comments in the Pick Up cells to note the activity and its location.
   ✓ *For example, you might add a comment under Billy's second drop off time to indicate that this is for Boy Scouts, and that the location is Mr. Farmer's home.*
10. Format the worksheet as you like.
11. Adjust column widths as needed.
12. Save the workbook and exit Excel.

Exercise 10

◆ **Open a Workbook** ◆ **Change Workbook Properties**
◆ **Save a Workbook with a Different Name** ◆ **Create a New Folder**
◆ **Create Backup Files** ◆ **Check for Potential Viruses** ◆ **Send a File**

On the Job

After you save a file, you may need to make corrections to it or update it. Open the file from the disk drive where you saved it in order to change information. During the saving process, you may want to make an additional backup copy to protect yourself against accidental changes and viruses. You may also want to save the file in a new folder, which you can create from within the Save As dialog box. To make it easier for you to locate the saved file later on, you may want to change the workbook properties. Finally, when you're through with a workbook and have saved it, you can quickly send a copy of the workbook to your colleagues and friends for their comments.

As the sales manager of a small network and systems consulting firm called NetConnect, you created a worksheet to detail your sales for the last three months. However, your knowledge of Excel was rather limited at the time, so in this exercise you'll reopen that workbook and make additional changes to it. Then you'll send the finished workbook as an attachment in an e-mail message.

Terms

virus A computer program that can alter or damage other files when loaded into the computer's memory.

macro A small recorded program created in Excel's Visual Basic programming language to automate repetitive actions.

e-mail Short for electronic mail. E-mail is a message sent via modem or network cable to another computer.

Notes

Open a Workbook

- When you have saved and closed a workbook, you can open it with the same drive, folder, and file name you used during the save process.

- In the Open dialog box, click the Look in arrow to display a drop-down list with drives and folders.

- Click the Views button in the Open dialog box to preview a file, change the list to display file details, or display the properties of a file.

- You can quickly access a recently used file by clicking a file name from the list provided at the bottom of the File menu in Excel.

■ A newly-opened workbook becomes the active workbook and hides any other open workbooks.

Open dialog box

Click here for a drop-down list of drives and folders.   Views button

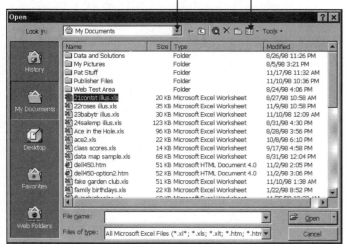

Change Workbook Properties

■ The workbook properties contain information that you can search for later, when trying to locate the file you wish to open.

■ By default, the workbook properties contain the author's name (in this case, your name) and your company name, both of which were entered when you installed Microsoft Excel.

■ In addition, you can add other information that might make it easier for you to locate the file later on, such as the workbook title and subject.

Workbook Properties dialog box

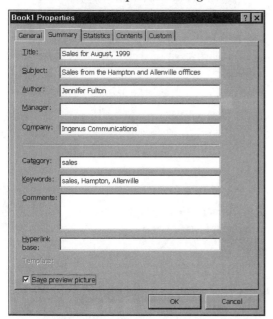

■ One of the options in the Workbook Properties dialog box is to save a preview picture of the worksheet.

• This option saves page one of the workbook so you can view it in the Open dialog box.

• Saving a preview will allow you to quickly identify a workbook, because you can see it before you open it.

• Saving a preview increases the size of your file on disk.

Save a Workbook with a Different Name

■ When you resave a previously saved file, the Save command overwrites the file, saving any new changes.

■ Use the Save As command to change the file name (to keep the previous and current versions of the file) or to change the drive and/or folder where the file is saved.

Save As dialog box

Click here to create backup files.

Create a New Folder

■ Whether you're saving a workbook for the first time, or simply saving it under a new name or in a new location, you can create a new folder in which to save it.

■ When you create a folder, you must give that folder a name.

✓ *The name can contain spaces and numbers.*

■ The new folder automatically appears in the Save As dialog box.

✓ *This makes it easy for you to save your file in the new folder.*

- You can create new folders on your own computer without any problems. However, you may not be able to create new folders on network drives unless you have specific permission to do so. See your network administrator for help.

Create Backup Files

- A backup is an extra copy of your workbook file.
- Backup files have a .BAK extension.
- You can tell Excel to create a backup of each file as you save it.

Save Options dialog box

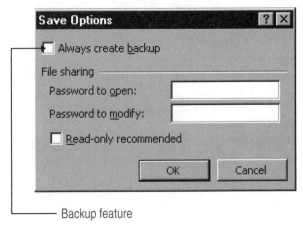

Backup feature

Check for Potential Viruses

- Excel can check your workbooks before you open them for the presence of potential macro viruses.
- Such a **virus**, hidden in a **macro**, could perform actions that might damage your workbook, corrupt your data, and disable your system.
- Excel can display a warning message to remind you of the possible dangers whenever you open a workbook that contains macros.
- When the warning message is displayed, you can choose to enable or disable the macros in the file.
- Disabling the macros will render them harmless, but it may prevent you from using the workbook.
- However, you should not enable macros in any workbook of whose origins you are not absolutely sure.

Security dialog box

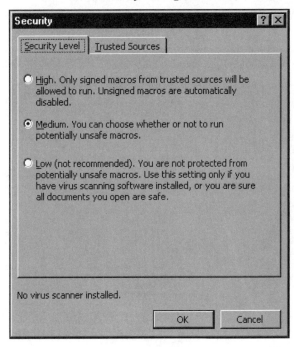

Send a File

- Worksheets and entire workbook files may be sent electronically via **e-mail**.
- You can perform this task if you're on a network or on the Internet and you have e-mail capability.

Send To menu

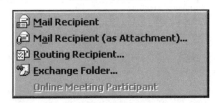

- There are many Send To options:
  - **Mail Recipient**—This option converts the current worksheet into text and sends it in the body of an e-mail message.
  - **Mail Recipient (as Attachment)** —This option sends the entire workbook file as an attachment to an e-mail message.
  - **Routing Recipient**—Routes the workbook as an e-mail attachment to a list of recipients.
  - **Exchange Folder**—Copies the workbook to a public folder on a Microsoft Exchange Server.
  - **On-line Meeting Recipient**—Shares the workbook with participants in an Outlook on-line meeting.

Procedures

Open a Workbook (Ctrl+O)

✓ *To view page one of a workbook you've saved with a preview, click the **Views** button in the Open dialog box and choose **Preview**. Then click the file you wish to view.*

Click **Open** button 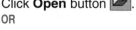.

OR

1. Click **File** .... `Alt`+`F`
2. Click **Open** .... `O`

   To select a different drive:

   a. Click **Look in** .... `Alt`+`I`
   b. Select desired
      drive .... `↕`, `Enter`

   To select a folder in specified drive:

   Double-click folder
   name .... `Tab`, `↕`, `Enter`

   ✓ *Press Tab to access the file list; then select desired file and press Enter.*

   To list files saved as a different type:

   a. Click **Files of type** ... `Alt`+`T`
   b. Click desired
      file type .... `↑` `↓`, `Enter`

      ✓ *Only files of specified type will appear in the file list. For example, to open a Lotus 1-2-3 file in Excel, select the Lotus 1-2-3 Files (*.wk?) option from drop-down list.*

   c. Double-click file to open in file list.

   OR

   a. Select **File name** .... `Alt`+`N`
   b. Type file name.
   c. Click **Open** button.... `Alt`+`O`

Change Workbook Properties

1. Click **File** .... `Alt`+`F`
2. Click **Properties** .... `I`
3. Enter whatever properties you wish:
   a. Enter the worksheet
      Title .... `Alt`+`T`
   b. Enter a **Subject** ...... `Alt`+`S`
   c. Enter your manager's
      name .... `Alt`+`M`

   d. Enter a **Category** for the
      worksheet data .... `Alt`+`E`
   e. Enter some **Keywords** you
      can search for later... `Alt`+`K`
   f. Enter any **Comments**
      about the file.......... `Alt`+`C`
   g. Enter the base file path or
      URL you want to use for any
      hyperlinks you might add to
      the workbook .... `Alt`+`H`
   h. Save a preview of
      your workbook for
      later display .... `Alt`+`V`

      ✓ *To view page one of a workbook you've saved with a preview, click the **Views** button in the Open dialog box and choose **Preview**. Then click the file you wish to view.*

4. Click **OK** .... `Enter`

Overwrite Previously Saved File (Ctrl+S)

Click **Save** button 🖫.

OR

1. Click **File** .... `Alt`+`F`
2. Click **Save** .... `S`

Save As New File

1. Click **File** .... `Alt`+`F`
2. Click **Save As**...................... `A`

   Select drive:

   a. Click **Save in**.......... `Alt`+`I`
   b. Select drive .... `↕`, `Enter`

   Select folder:

   Double-click folder name in the
   list box .... `Tab`, `↕`, `Enter`

   Create a new folder in which to save the file:

   a. Click **Create New Folder**
      button 📁.
   b. Type the name of the folder
      in the **Name** box in the New
      Folder dialog box........ `Enter`
   c. Click **OK** .... `Enter`

3. Click in **File name**
   text box........................ `Alt`+`N`

4. Type file name.
5. Click **OK** .... `Enter`

Create Backup Files When You Save

✓ *Sets Excel always to create a backup of previous version of this file when saving.*

1. Click **File**...................... `Alt`+`F`
2. Click **Save As** .... `A`
3. Click **Tools** button........ `Alt`+`L`
4. Click **General Options**........ `G`
5. Click **Always create**
   backup .... `Alt`+`B`
6. Click **OK** .... `Enter`
7. Click **Save** .... `Enter`
8. Click **Yes** to confirm that
   you want to replace
   existing file .... `Alt`+`Y`

Set Macro Virus Security

1. Click **Tools** .... `Alt`+`T`
2. Click **Macro** .... `M`
3. Click **Security**...................... `S`
4. Click **Security Level**.... `Alt`+`S`
5. Choose an option:
   • Click **Low** .... `Alt`+`L`
   • Click **Medium** .... `Alt`+`M`
   • Click **High**.............. `Alt`+`H`
6. Click **OK** .... `Enter`

Send a Workbook as an E-mail Attachment

1. Click **File**...................... `Alt`+`F`
2. Click **Send To** .... `D`
3. Click **Mail Recipient (as**
   Attachment)........................ `A`
4. Address the e-mail message.
5. Click **Send** .... `Alt`+`S`

Send a Worksheet as Text in an E-mail Message

1. Click the **E-mail** button 📧.
2. Click **Send the current sheet**
   as the message body.
3. Address the e-mail message.
4. Click **Send This Sheet**.

Exercise Directions

1. Start Excel, if necessary.
2. Open ⊙ **10_NETWORK**.
3. Save the file as **XL_10**.
4. Enable the check for viruses option at the high security level.
5. Widen column B so that it displays the names of the salespeople completely.
6. Center the headings in cells C5, D5, and E5.
7. Enter the following sales data:

	April	May	June
John Barker	33250	29458	55678
Pat Smith	12998	21754	11590
Sally Cooper	34780	45958	125650
Jack Johnson	54875	33560	25885
Melanie McMann	34780	42100	29758

8. Format the sales data using Currency format, zero decimal places.
   - ✓ Hint: Select the cells and click the Currency Style button **$** . Then click the Decrease Decimal button **.00→.0** until no decimals show. (You'll learn more about formatting data in Exercise 13).

9. Add the following workbook properties:
   a. Change the author's name to your name.
   b. Change the title to Qtr 2 Sales.
   c. Change the company name to NetConnect Networking Specialists.
   d. Change the category to Sales.
   e. Change the keywords to sales, quarter 2.
   f. Save a preview of the file.
10. Save the file again and create a backup file as well.
11. Send the workbook as an attachment to an e-mail message.
    - ✓ If you do not have e-mail capability, skip this step.
    a. For this test, you may wish to send the workbook to yourself.
    b. After receiving the e-mail message, open it and look at your workbook.
12. Close the file.
13. Open the file again, previewing it before you open it.
14. Close the file and exit Excel.

On Your Own

1. Start Excel, if necessary.
2. Open the file ⊙ **10_COOKIES**.
3. Save the file as **OXL_10**.
4. Adjust the width of column E to accommodate the Chocolate Chip heading.
5. Change the alignment of the column headings to suit your preference.
6. Enter the number of boxes of cookies that each person ordered, making up the numbers. Leave some cells blank.
7. Format the data as you like.
8. Send the workbook to some classmates, asking them if they would like to help out and buy some cookies.
9. Save the workbook and exit Excel.

Exercise 11

◆ Critical Thinking

You're the accounting manager of NetConnect, a networking company located in Atlanta. Looking to curb the costs involved in sending four technical specialists to an upcoming networking conference in Chicago, you'll use your knowledge of Excel and your connection to the Internet to scout out the best prices on airfare, hotel accommodations, and car rental.

Exercise Directions

1. Start Excel, if necessary.

2. Start a new workbook and save the file as **XL_11**.

3. Type the titles, column, and row labels for the worksheet shown in Illustration A.

   a. Enter the current date in cell B7.

   b. Format this date with the format *March 14, 1998*.

   c. Format the dates in cells D4 and D5 with the format *14-Mar-98*.

   d. Center the column headings.

   e. Right-align cell A7.

4. Use the Internet to look up the costs for various roundtrip flights from Atlanta to Chicago.

   ✓ *Use Yahoo (or a Web site of your choice).*

   To use the DDC Internet simulation:

   a. Click **Go**.

   b. Click **Open**.

   c. In the Address line, type the following: C:/Simulation/Ex11/Yahoo!.htm

   ✓ *If you've copied the Internet simulation files to your hard drive or your CD-ROM drive is not C:, substitute the correct drive letter for C.*

   d. Click **OK**.

   e. Click the *Travel* link near the top of the page.

   ✓ *The Yahoo! Travel page displays on your screen.*

   f. Click the *Air* link near the top of the page.

5. Enter your travel schedule into the Round trip Flight Search form.

   a. The convention takes place October 12th through the 14th.

   b. The convention begins at noon on the 12th, and ends at 2:30 pm on the 14th.

   ✓ *If you're using the Internet simulation, enter:*

   • *Leaving from:* Atlanta

   • *Going to:* Chicago

   • *Departing:* October 12, Morning

   • *Returning:* October 14, Evening

   • Click Show me available Flights

6. Enter the information you find into the worksheet for at least three flights.

   a. Use the comment feature to make a note of which Chicago airport is being used.

   b. Right-align the row labels.

   ✓ *A sample worksheet with data is shown in Illustration B.*

7. Format the Cost per Ticket column as you like.

8. Save the file and exit Excel.

   ✓ *Make a note of the arrival and departure times of the least expensive flight; you'll use this information in the On Your Own exercise.*

Illustration A

	A	B	C	D	E	F	G	H	I	J	K
1		Ticket Prices									
2		From Atlanta to Chicago									
3											
4		For NetWorld Convention		10/12/99	12:00 PM						
5				10/14/99	2:30 PM						
6											
7	As of:		2/3/99								
8											
9		Airline	Flight Number	Cost per Ticket	Depart Atlanta	Arrive Chicago	No. of Stops	Flight Number	Depart Chicago	Arrive Atlanta	No. of Stops

Illustration B

	A	B	C	D	E	F	G	H	I	J	K
4		For NetWorld Convention		12-Oct-99	12:00 PM						
5				14-Oct-99	2:30 PM						
6											
7	As of:		February 3, 1999								
8											
9			Airline	Flight Number	Cost per Ticket	Depart Atlanta	Arrive Chicago	No. of Stops	Flight Number	Depart Chicago	Arrive Atlanta	No. of Stops
10			United	1139	$ 163.80	6:30 AM	7:21 AM	0	1690	5:00 PM	7:49 PM	0
11			AirTran	820	$ 163.80	8:15 AM	8:59 AM	0	825	4:30 PM	7:13 PM	0
12			American	1347	$ 168.77	7:07 AM	7:55 AM	0	1788	4:14 PM	7:12 PM	0
13			Delta	1410	$ 168.77	10:15 AM	11:12 AM	0	1649	5:40 PM	8:46 PM	0
14			Proair	211	$ 172.27	6:00 AM	8:20 AM	0	210	6:10 PM	10:42 PM	0
15			Delta	1454	$ 190.67	6:15 AM	7:07 AM	0	681	4:10 PM	6:59 PM	0

On Your Own

1. Start Excel, if needed.
2. Start a new workbook and save it as **OXL_11**.
3. Create a worksheet similar to **XL_11**, except this time you'll be comparing the cost of rental cars and hotels.

   a. Enter the actual arrival and departure times somewhere in the worksheet.

   b. Using these times, look up the costs for a rental car and a hotel, using the Internet.

   c. Select an economy car.

   d. Select a hotel near the airport.

   e. Base your needs on two rooms, double occupancy.

4. Enter your findings into the worksheet.

   ✓ Enter rental car prices for at least three rental agencies.

   ✓ List at least three hotel options as well.

5. Format the worksheet however you like.

6. Save the file and exit Excel.

Lesson 3

Use Formulas and Formatting

Exercise 12

- ◆ Use Formulas
- ◆ Mathematical Operators
- ◆ Natural Language Formulas

Exercise 13

- ◆ Format Data with Formatting Toolbar
- ◆ Fonts and Font Size
- ◆ Add Bold, Italic, and Underline
- ◆ Currency, Percent, Comma, and Accounting Formats
- ◆ Increase or Decrease Decimals
- ◆ Format Numbers with the Format Cells Dialog Box
- ◆ Create Custom Number Formats

Exercise 14

- ◆ Use Ranges
- ◆ Name Ranges

Exercise 15

- ◆ Copy Data
- ◆ Copy Using AutoFill
- ◆ Copy Part of a Cell's Contents
- ◆ Copy a Formula (Absolute, Relative, and Mixed Reference)

Exercise 16

- ◆ Create a Series
- ◆ AutoSum

Exercise 17

- ◆ Use Functions
- ◆ Formula Bar and Palette
- ◆ Paste Function
- ◆ Noncontiguous Ranges in a Function
- ◆ AutoCalculate

Exercise 18

- ◆ Critical Thinking

Exercise 12

◆ **Use Formulas** ◆ **Mathematical Operators**
◆ **Natural Language Formulas**

On the Job

One of the benefits of Excel is its capacity to create formulas within a worksheet to perform calculations. When you make a change to a cell that's referenced in a formula, Excel performs the recalculation and the result is updated automatically to reflect the change. If you create a lot of formulas, you'll appreciate Excel's ability to understand natural language (plain English) and to interpret what you're trying to calculate — without forcing you to create Excel formulas on your own.

In an earlier exercise, you created a sales worksheet for the company you work for, NetConnect. You sent the workbook in an e-mail message to a colleague. Your colleague suggests adding totals so you can compare the sales records for each person. You think that's a pretty good idea, but you've decided to add some additional calculations as well.

Terms

formula An instruction Excel uses to calculate a result.

Formula bar The toolbar you use to enter and edit cell data. When you type a formula into a cell, the formula appears in the Formula bar, but the result appears in the cell itself. When you enter a complex formula, the Formula bar expands to help guide you.

mathematical operators Symbols used in mathematical operations: + for addition, – for subtraction, * for multiplication, / for division, and ^ for exponentiation.

cell reference The column letter and row number that identify a cell's location in the worksheet.

function A predefined formula that performs calculations by using specific values, or arguments, in a particular order.

order of precedence The order in which Excel performs the calculations specified in a formula.

natural language formula A formula that refers to column or row labels instead of a cell reference or range.

Notes

Use Formulas

- A **formula** is a worksheet instruction that performs a calculation.

- Enter a formula in the cell where the answer should display.

- The formula displays in the cell and in the **Formula bar** as you type.

- After you enter a formula into the cell, the answer displays in the cell, while the formula appears in the Formula bar.

- When creating formulas, you use **mathematical operators**, values, and **cell references**.

  ✓ *A formula can also contain Excel's predefined calculations (**functions**), which are covered in Exercise 17.*

- Type the equal sign (=) at the beginning of a formula. For example, the formula =B2+B4+B6 adds the values in these cell locations.

  ✓ *If you enter the formula (+B2+B4+B6), using the plus sign as the first character, Excel automatically inserts the equal sign.*

- When you make a change to a value in a cell that's referenced in a formula, the result in the formula cell automatically changes.

Mathematical Operators

- The following are standard mathematical operators used in formulas:

  - **+ Addition**
  - **– Subtraction**
  - *** Multiplication**
  - **/ Division**
  - **^ Exponentiation**

- The **order of precedence** is important to remember when creating formulas.

  - Operations enclosed in parentheses are performed first.

    ✓ *Parenthetical operations are performed from innermost to outermost and left to right; for example, in the formula =((6+2)*(4+9))/3, Excel first adds 6+2 and 4+9, then multiplies those totals and divides the result by 3.*

  - Exponential calculations have the next priority.

- Multiplication and division operations are then calculated before the addition and subtraction operations.

- Mathematical operations are performed from left to right in the order of their appearance.

- In the formula =(D1+E1)/F1, the D1+E1 in parentheses will be calculated first.

- When typing a percentage as a numeric factor in a formula, you can enter it with the percent symbol or as a decimal.

- Excel automatically provides assistance in correcting common mistakes in a formula—for example, omitting a parenthesis.

Natural Language Formulas

- Excel allows you to create **natural language formulas** that refer to column and row labels in place of the cell reference or range.

- For example, =SUM(Jan) totals the range of cells in the Jan column that are located above the formula.

  ✓ *=SUM() is a function—a preprogrammed calculation that computes the total of the values in the given range of cells. Here, it's totaling all the cells under the label Jan.*

  ✓ *You'll learn more about functions in Exercise 17.*

Column labels in natural language formulas

	A	B	C	D
1	Jan	Feb	Mar	
2	1500	2500	1650	
3	600	1000	800	
4	3000	1200	900	
5	=SUM(Jan)	=SUM(Feb)	=SUM(Mar)	
6				

  ✓ *Excel prompts you for the range of cells if the worksheet contains more than one label with that name.*

- Excel does not normally recognize labels in formulas, so if you want to create natural language formulas, you'll have to turn that option on for each workbook. Choose Options on the Tools menu. On the Calculation tab in the Options dialog box, select the Accept labels in formulas box under Workbook options.

- Following are some additional examples of natural language formulas, written for the sample worksheet shown here:

Sample natural language worksheet

	A	B	C	D	E	F
1						
2						
3						
4			Qtr 1	Qtr 2	Qtr 3	Qtr 4
5		East	$ 105,479	$ 115,485	$ 129,879	$ 119,986
6		West	$ 124,573	$ 132,654	$ 125,645	$ 135,248
7		North	$ 156,687	$ 150,487	$ 135,426	$ 154,879
8		South	$ 154,877	$ 145,887	$ 140,326	$ 141,987

=Qtr 1 East+Qtr 2 East

✓ *This formula computes the total of cells C5 and D5.*

✓ *Notice that in creating the natural language argument, you must enter the column label first, then the row label, just as you would with a regular cell address.*

=Sum(Qtr 1)

✓ *This formula computes the total of cells C5, C6, C7, and C8.*

=Average(North)

✓ *This formula computes the average of cells C7, D7, E7, and F7.*

Procedures

Enter Formula Using Mathematical Operators

1. Click cell where answer should display .... ⬚
2. Press the **equal (=)** key ...... ⬚
3. Type formula.
   ✓ *Example: =(C2+C10)/2*
   OR

Instead of typing cell references in a formula:

a. Type necessary operator or opening parenthesis.
b. Click cell(s) you want to reference in formula.
   ✓ *A marquee surrounds the cell reference and the address appears in the formula.*
c. Type next mathematical operator or parenthesis.
d. Repeat steps a-c until formula is complete.
e. Press **Enter** ....

Create Natural Language Formula

1. Click cell .... ⬚
   where answer will display.
2. Press the **equal (=)** key .... ⬚
3. Type a column or row label.
4. Type a mathematical operator.
5. Type another label or a value.
6. Press **Enter** .... Enter

Exercise Directions

1. Start Excel, if necessary.
2. Open ⊚ **12_NETWORK**.
3. Save the workbook as **XL_12**.
4. In cell F5, type the label *Total Sales for Qtr 2*.
   - Enter the label on two lines.
     - ✓ *You may have to widen the column to get the label to appear on just two lines.*
5. In cell F6, type the following formula:

   =C6+D6+E6
   - ✓ *Type cell references or names in lowercase. Excel automatically converts the case for you.*
6. In cells F7, F8, F9, and F10, enter similar formulas to compute the Qtr 2 totals:
   - ✓ *You can click the cells you want to use in the formulas, instead of typing their cell addresses.*
   a. The formula for cell F7 is as follows:
      =C7+D7+E7
   b. The formula for cell F8 is as follows:
      =C8+D8+E8
   c. The formula for cell F9 is as follows:
      =C9+D9+E9

   d. For cell F10, try entering a natural language formula:
      =April Melanie McMann+May Melanie McMann+June Melanie McMann
      - ✓ *You must activate this option on the Calculation tab of the Options dialog box.*
7. In cell B12, type the label *Average Sales*.
8. Enter formulas to compute the average sales per month:
   a. In cell C12, type =(C6+C7+C8+C9+C10)/5
   b. In cell D12, type =(D6+D7+D8+D9+D10)/5
   c. In cell E12, type =(E6+E7+E8+E9+E10)/5
   d. Format these cells using Currency format with no decimal places.
      - ✓ *Hint: Select the cells and click the Currency Style button* **$** . *Then click the Decrease Decimal button* **.00→.0** *until no decimals show. (You will learn more about formatting data in Exercise 13.)*
9. Save the workbook and exit Excel.

On Your Own

1. Start Excel, if necessary.
2. Open the file ⊚ **12_COOKIES**.
3. Save the file as **OXL_12**.
4. Add formulas to compute the total cookies ordered by each person.
5. Compute the total cost of each order as well — the cookies sell for $3 a box.
6. Add formulas to compute the total number of each type of cookie ordered.
   - ✓ *Use natural language formulas if you like.*
7. Widen any columns as necessary.
8. Close the file and exit Excel, saving all changes.

Exercise 13

Skills Covered:

◆ **Format Data with Formatting Toolbar** ◆ **Fonts and Font Size**
◆ **Add Bold, Italic, and Underline** ◆ **Currency, Percent, Comma, and Accounting Formats** ◆ **Increase or Decrease Decimals**
◆ **Format Numbers with the Format Cells Dialog Box**
◆ **Create Custom Number Formats**

On the Job

When you need to change the appearance of worksheet data to make it more attractive and readable, you can format it. You can change the font (typeface) and size of data and add bold, italics, or underline, along with other attributes. When formatting numbers, you can select from a wide range of formats to achieve the exact look you want, adding dollar signs or other currency symbols and commas and controlling the number of decimal places.

As the night manager of the Movie Time Video store, you've been asked to modify a worksheet that lists the February order for new videos, and the videos that will be returned with the order. You'll compute the cost of the new videos, and deduct the refund you expect for the videos you're returning.

Terms

font The typeface or design of the text.

font size The measurement of the typeface in points ($^1/_{72}$ of an inch).

Currency format A style that displays numbers with dollar signs ($) immediately preceding the number and includes a thousands separator (,).

Percent format A style that displays decimal numbers as percentages.

Comma format A style that displays numbers with a thousands separator (,).

Accounting format A style that vertically aligns cell entries with dollar signs ($), thousands separators (,), and decimal points.

Notes

Formatting toolbar

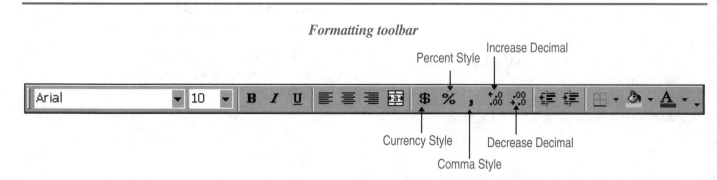

Format Data with Formatting Toolbar

■ Format data by selecting it and clicking the appropriate button on the Formatting toolbar or by choosing options from the Format Cells dialog box.

   ✓ *The simplest way to apply most formats is with the Formatting toolbar.*

   ✓ *In this exercise, you'll learn how to use the Formatting toolbar to apply the most common formats. See Lesson 6 for information on using the Format Cells dialog box to change fonts and sizes, apply attributes, change alignment, and so on.*

Fonts and Font Size

■ A **font** is a set of characters with a specific design and name.

■ **Font size** is measured in points. One point is equal to $1/72$ of an inch.

   ✓ *You can change the font and size of both numbers and text.*

■ Windows TrueType fonts are scalable, which means a single TrueType font can be set to various sizes.

   ✓ *This makes TrueType fonts more accurate when displayed on a monitor. If you select a TrueType font, what you see on the screen is what you will get when you print out your workbook.*

■ When you change the size of a font, Excel automatically adjusts the row height but doesn't adjust the column width.

■ You can change the standard (default) font and font size using the General tab settings in the Options dialog box.

Add Bold, Italic, and Underline

■ You can add bold, italic, and underline formats with the buttons on the Formatting toolbar.

   ✓ *You can apply bold, italic, or underline to both numbers and text.*

■ The underline format applied with the Formatting toolbar is a single underline. Additional underline styles are available through the Format Cells dialog box.

■ You can apply multiple formats such as bold italic, or italic underline.

■ When a format is applied to a cell, that formatting button appears pressed or pushed in.

   ✓ *When a format is removed from a cell, the button "pops up," and no longer appears pressed.*

Currency, Percent, Comma, and Accounting Formats

■ Because they're the most common number formats, Currency, Percent, and Comma formats are available on the Formatting toolbar.

   ● **Currency format** displays numbers with currency symbols: dollar signs, commas, and decimals.

   ● To change decimals into percentages, use **Percent format**.

   ● If you want to make large numbers easier to read, use the **Comma format** to include a comma with a set number of decimal places.

   ● **Accounting format** displays numbers with currency symbols and aligns decimal points and dollar signs in a column.

   ✓ *The Currency Style button on the Formatting toolbar actually applies the Accounting format. If you really want to apply the Currency format, use the Format Cells dialog box.*

■ By default, the Currency and Comma formats are applied with two decimal places.

■ The Percent format initially uses no decimal places.

Increase or Decrease Decimals

■ When you use the Formatting toolbar to apply a number format, Excel displays the number with two decimal places.

   ✓ *Percent format displays numbers with zero decimal places.*

■ You can use the Increase Decimal or Decrease Decimal button on the Formatting toolbar to increase or decrease the number of decimal places displayed.

■ Keep in mind that even if you display zero decimal places, the actual number is the one Excel uses in any formulas referring to the cell. As a result, your formulas may appear to display incorrect data.

Format Numbers with the Format Cells Dialog Box

■ The Format Cells dialog box includes many number formats you can choose from — however, the most common formats, Currency (Accounting), Percent, and Comma, are more quickly applied using the Formatting toolbar.

- When choosing a number format, you can also select how you want negative numbers displayed. Options include preceding the number with a minus sign (the default setting), displaying the number in red, displaying the number in parentheses, and displaying the number in red and in parentheses.

Number tab of the Format Cells dialog box

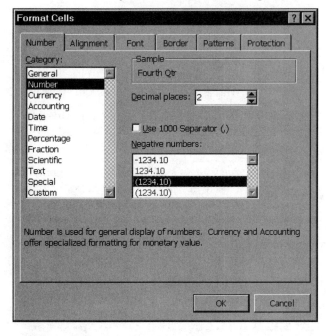

Create Custom Number Formats

- When a number format doesn't fit your needs, you can create a custom number format.
  - ✓ *Typically, you use a custom number format to preformat a column or row, prior to data entry. The custom format speeds the data entry process.*

- You create a custom number format by typing a series of special codes.
  - ✓ *To speed the process, select an existing format and customize it.*

- You can specify format codes for positive numbers, negative numbers, zeros, and text.
  - If you wish to specify all four formats, you must type the codes in the order listed above.
  - If you specify only two formats, you must type a code for positive numbers and zeros first, and a code for negative numbers second.
  - If you specify only one format, all numbers in the row or column will use that format.
  - To separate the formats, use a semicolon, as in the following custom number format: $#,##0.00;[red]($#,##0.00);"ZERO";[blue]

- This format displays positive numbers as 0,000.00, negative numbers in red and parentheses, a zero as the word ZERO, and text in blue.

- Standard colors you can use by typing the name in brackets include: red, black, blue, white, green, yellow, cyan, and magenta.

- The following table shows examples of codes you can use in creating a format:

#	Digit placeholder
0	Zero placeholder
?	Digit placeholder
@	Text placeholder
.	Decimal point (period)
%	Percent
,	Thousands separator (comma)
$	Dollar sign
-	Negative sign
+	Plus sign
( )	Parentheses
:	Colon
_	Underscore (skips one character width)
[color]	Type the name of one of the eight colors mentioned above.

- Examples of formats you can create:

To display	Use this code
5.56 as 5.5600	#.0000
5641 as $5,641	$#,##0
5641 as $5,641 and -5641 as ($5,641) in red	$#,##0;[red]($#,##0)
5641 as $5,641.00 and -5641 as ($5,641.00) in red	$#,###0.00;[red]($#,##0.00)

- You can also format numbers based on specified conditions. For example, you could format a column of numbers so that all numbers greater than or equal to 100 appear in blue and all numbers less than 100 appear in red. The format for this example is: [blue][>=100];[red][<100]

- Custom number formats are saved with the worksheet.
  - To use a number format you've created in another worksheet, copy the format from a cell in the worksheet to a cell in the other worksheet manually. (You will learn more about copying in Exercise 15.)

Procedures

Change Font Using Font Box

1. Select cells (or characters in cells) you want to format.
2. Click **Font** box arrow button `Arial ▼`.
3. Click font .... `↑↓` , `Enter`

Change Font Size Using Font Size Box

1. Select cells or characters you want to format.
2. Click **Font Size** box arrow button `10 ▼`.
3. Click point size .... `↑↓` , `Enter`

OR

1. Select cells or characters you want to format.
2. Click **Font Size** box `10 ▼`.
3. Type desired number.
4. Press **Enter** .... `Enter`

Apply Bold, Italic, or Underline

1. Select data or cells to be formatted.
2. Click one or more of the following Formatting toolbar buttons:
   - **Bold** .... `B`
   - **Italic** .... `I`
   - **Underline** .... `U`

Format Numbers Using the Formatting Toolbar

1. Select cell(s) to format.
2. Click one of the following Formatting toolbar buttons:
   - **Currency Style** .... `$`
   - **Percent Style** .... `%`
   - **Comma Style** .... `,`
3. To increase or decrease decimal places, click a button:
   - **Increase Decimal** .... `+.0 .00`

- **Decrease Decimal** .... `.00 +.0`

✓ *You can click the Increase Decimal or Decrease Decimal buttons as many times as needed to display the exact number of decimal places you want.*

✓ *In the next four procedures, you can also open the Format Cells dialog box by right-clicking a cell and selecting* **Format Cells** *from the shortcut menu.*

Apply Percent Format with the Format Cells Dialog Box

1. Select cell(s) to format.
2. Click **Format** .... `Alt`+`O`
3. Click **Cells** .... `E`
4. Select **Number** tab ..... `Ctrl`+`Tab`
5. In the **Category** list box, click **Percentage** .... `Alt`+`C` , `↑↓`
6. Click **Decimal places** .. `Alt`+`D`
7. Set number of places.
8. Click **OK** .... `Enter`

Apply Comma Format with the Format Cells Dialog Box

1. Select cells(s) to format.
2. Click **Format** .... `Alt`+`O`
3. Click **Cells** .... `E`
4. Select **Number** tab ..... `Ctrl`+`Tab`
5. In the **Category** list box, click **Number** .... `Alt`+`C` , `↑↓`
6. Click **Decimal places** .. `Alt`+`D`
7. Set number of places.
8. Click **Use 1000 Separator (,)** .... `Alt`+`U`
9. Click **OK** .... `Enter`

Apply Currency Format with the Format Cells Dialog Box

1. Select cells(s) to format.
2. Click **Format** .... `Alt`+`O`

3. Click **Cells** .... `E`
4. Select **Number** tab ..... `Ctrl`+`Tab`
5. In the **Category** list box, click **Currency** .... `Alt`+`C` , `↑↓`
   OR
   Click **Accounting**.
6. Click **Decimal places**... `Alt`+`D`
7. Set number of places.
   ✓ *You can choose a symbol other than the U.S. dollar sign and specify how negative numbers display in the cell.*
8. Click **OK** .... `Enter`

Create Custom Number Format

1. Select cell(s) to format.
2. Click **Format** .... `Alt`+`O`
3. Click **Cells** .... `E`
4. Select **Number** tab ..... `Ctrl`+`Tab`
5. In the **Category** list box, click **Custom** ...... `Alt`+`C` , `↑↓`
6. Type the format you want to use in the **Type** box..... `Alt`+`T`
   ✓ *It's usually easier to select a format from those listed in the* **Type** *box and then customize it.*
7. Click **OK** .... `Enter`

Format Negative Values

1. Select cell(s) to be formatted.
2. Click **Format** .... `Alt`+`O`
3. Click **Cells** .... `E`
4. On Number tab, select **Category** and click **Number** .... `Alt`+`C` , `↑↓`
5. Select style in **Negative numbers** list .... `Alt`+`N` , `↑↓`
6. Click **OK** .... `Enter`

Exercise Directions

1. Start Excel, if necessary.
2. Open ☉ **13_VIDEO**.
3. Save the file as **XL_13**.
4. In cell B2, type the title *Movie Time Video*.
   a. Format the title with a decorative font of your choice.
   b. Make the title 24 point bold.
5. In cell B4, type *Movie Order for February*.
   a. Format the cell as 14 point bold.
   b. Italicize the label.
6. Select the column headings in the upper table.
   ✓ *Hint: Click in cell B5 and drag to cell F5. (You will learn more about selecting multiple cells in the next exercise).*
   a. Add bold formatting.
   b. Center all titles except the label *Movie Title*.
      ✓ *Select cells C5 through F5 and click the Center button to align the titles.*
7. In cell B20, type *Returns for February*.
   a. Format the cell as 14 point bold.
   b. Italicize the label.
8. Add bold formatting to the column headings in the lower table and center all titles except the label *Movie Title*.

9. In cell F17, create a formula to compute the sum of the values in the *Total Cost* column.
   ✓ *To avoid typing the formula =F6+F7+F8 plus the other cells through F16, click each cell rather than entering its address.*
10. In cell F25, create a formula to compute the sum of the values in the Total Value column.
11. In cell F27, type the formula *=F17-F25* to compute the Total Due.
12. Format the cells in the *Cost per Copy* column (E6:E16) with Currency format, two decimal places.
13. Apply Currency format, two decimal places to all other cells that contain dollar values, including the totals.
14. To highlight the most popular videos, create a custom number format that will display all orders of 20 or more copies in red and all copies less than 20 in blue:
    a. Select the cells D6:D16. In the Format Cells dialog box, create this custom format: [red][>=20]General;[blue][<20]General
    b. Check the accuracy of the formatting in the Number of Copies column.
       ✓ *The number of copies of the Queen Elizabeth video, for example, should be in red.*
15. Save the workbook and exit Excel.

On Your Own

1. Start Excel, if necessary.
2. Open the file named **OXL_08** that you created in the On Your Own section of Exercise 8.
3. Save the file as **OXL_13**.
4. Enter your expense amounts for the past month.
5. Select the cells that contain the expense amounts and apply a numeric format you like.
   ✓ *Use the Format Cells dialog box to apply your numeric format.*

6. Add formatting of your choice to the column labels and title you entered earlier.
   ✓ *Use the Formatting toolbar to apply different fonts, font sizes, and other attributes.*
7. Create a formula to compute your total expenses for the month.
8. Adjust column widths as needed.
9. Save the workbook and exit Excel.

Exercise 14

Skills Covered:

◆ Use Ranges ◆ Name Ranges

On the Job

To format a group of similar cells in the worksheet (a range), select them, then apply the formatting you want. You can also give names to ranges to make the formulas in your worksheet easy to read and formatting and printing easier to accomplish.

You've been asked by the regional sales manager of Taber Video to complete a sales report you've been working on in time for the monthly sales meeting.

Terms

range A block of cells in an Excel workbook.

contiguous cells An adjacent block of cells in a worksheet.

noncontiguous cells A block of cells that aren't adjacent to each other.

range name An identification assigned to a cell or group of cells.

Name box The box located at the left end of the Formula bar.

Notes

Use Ranges

- A **range** is an area of a worksheet or workbook made up of one or many cells.

- When you select cells A1, A2, and A3, for example, the range is indicated as A1:A3.

- The range A1:B5 may be defined as a block of cells that includes all the cells in columns A through B in rows one through five.

- A range of cells can be **contiguous** (all cells are adjacent to each other) or **noncontiguous** (not all cells are adjacent to each other).

Selected range of contiguous cells

	A	B	C	D
1	5000	5000	5000	
2	3000	3000	3000	
3				

Selected range of noncontiguous cells

	A	B	C	D
1	5000	5000	5000	
2	3000	3000	3000	
3				

- There are many reasons why you might want to select a range of cells:
  - To format a group of cells so they look alike.
  - To use the range in a function (a predefined calculation).
  - To name the range.
  - To define a group of cells to use with some Excel feature, such as sorting.
  - To enter the same formula into a group of contiguous cells.

- When you need to enter cell addresses or ranges in a dialog box that has a Collapse Dialog button, you can click the Collapse Dialog button on the right side of the text box to display the worksheet temporarily so you can select the range. (Such dialog boxes appear when you add certain formulas, or when you set up a page for printing, for example.)

Text box with a Collapse Dialog button

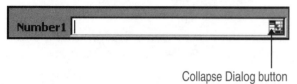

Collapse Dialog button

Name Ranges

- A **range name** is a descriptive name assigned to a cell or range of cells for identification.

- Range names can be referenced across worksheets or workbooks.

- A range name can use up to 255 characters, although short, descriptive names are easier to read and remember.

- Some rules for naming ranges include:
  - Spaces aren't allowed. Use the underscore character to simulate a space.
  - You can't use range names that could be interpreted as a cell address or a number, such as Q2. (Use Qtr2 instead of Q2, for example.)

- A range name can include letters, numbers, underscores (_), backslashes (\), periods (.) and question marks (?).

- You can't begin a range name with a number.

- After selecting a range, use the Name, Define command from the Insert menu or use the **Name box** [B2 ▼] to assign the range name.

Define Name dialog box

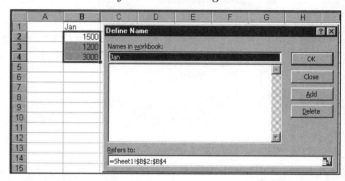

- To select any of the ranges you have named, click the drop-down arrow in the Name box and click the desired range.

- If you wish to show a list of the named ranges somewhere on your worksheet for quick reference, use the Name, Paste command from the Insert menu. This command inserts the list of named ranges with their corresponding cell references into the cells of your choice in the worksheet.

- You can use a range name in a formula. For example, =SUM(April_Sales) totals all the cells in the named range April_Sales.

Procedures

Use Keyboard to Select Range of Cells

✓ *When you select a range of cells, the active cell within the selection is white and all other cells are highlighted in color.*

Select range of adjacent cells:

1. Press **arrow keys** .... [↕↔] to move to first cell of range.

2. Press **Shift** + **arrow keys** to select the cells....... [Shift] + [↕↔]

Select entire column containing active cell:

Press **Ctrl + Spacebar** ..... [Ctrl] + [Space]

Select entire row containing active cell:

Press **Shift + Spacebar** .... [Shift] + [Space]

Select adjacent rows:

1. Press arrow keys .... [↕↔] to move to a cell in the first row to select.

2. Press and hold down **Shift** and .... [Shift] , then press the **Spacebar**...................... [Space] , to select first row.

3. While still pressing **Shift**, press **up** or **down arrow key** ...... [↑/↓] to select additional adjacent rows.

Select worksheet from the upper-left cell to lower-right cell:

1. Press **arrow keys** .... 🔼 to move to first cell in selection.
2. Press and hold down **Ctrl**, press and hold down **Shift**, and then press and release **End** ...... Ctrl + Shift + End
3. Release **Ctrl** and **Shift** keys.

Use Mouse to Select Range of Cells

Select range of adjacent cells:

Click and drag across cells.

Select entire row:

Click row heading.

Select entire column:

Click column heading.

Select adjacent rows:

Click and drag across row headings.

Select adjacent columns:

Click and drag across column headings.

Select range of noncontiguous cells:

1. Click and drag across first selection of cells.
2. Press and hold down **Ctrl** key while making additional selections.

Select noncontiguous rows:

1. Click first row heading.
2. Press and hold down **Ctrl** key and click additional row headings.

Select noncontiguous columns:

1. Click first column heading.
2. Press and hold down **Ctrl** key and click additional column headings.

Entering a Similar Formula into a Range of Cells

1. Select the range you want to use.
2. Press the **equal** key .... =
3. Type the formula you want into the first cell in the range.
4. Press **Ctrl + Enter** ... Ctrl + Enter

Select a Range Using Collapse Dialog Button

1. Click **Collapse Dialog** button 🔲 at right end of text box.
   - ✔ The dialog box collapses to provide a better view of the worksheet.
2. Select desired cell(s).
3. Press **Enter** .... Enter
   OR
   Click **Collapse Dialog** button 🔲.
   - ✔ The dialog box returns to normal size and the text box displays the cell reference(s).

Name a Range with the Insert Menu

1. Select range.
2. Click **Insert** .... Alt + I
3. Click **Name** .... N
4. Click **Define** .... D
   - ✔ Note that selected range appears in **Refers to** text box and any contiguous column or row heading appears in **Names in workbook** text box.
5. If necessary, type a name in **Names in workbook** text box .... Alt + W
6. Click **OK** .... Enter

Name a Range with Name Box

1. Select range.
2. Click in Name box.
3. Type range name.
4. Press **Enter** .... Enter

Modify a Named Range

1. Click **Insert** .... Alt + I
2. Click **Name** .... N
3. Click **Define** .... D
   To change name:
   a. Click name in list ... Tab, 🔼
   b. Double-click **Names in workbook** text box... Alt + W
   c. Type a new name for range.
   d. Click **Add** button .... Alt + A

   e. Click old name in list .... Tab, 🔼
   f. Click **Delete** button .. Alt + D
   To change name reference:
   a. Click name in list .... Tab, 🔼
   b. Drag through reference in **Refers to** text box ... Alt + R
   c. Use **Collapse Dialog** button to collapse the dialog box; then select new range(s).
      OR
      Type new range(s).
4. Click **OK** .... Enter

Select Named Range

Using Name box:

1. Click drop-down arrow in Name box.
2. Click desired named range.

Using Go To:

1. Press **F5** F5
2. Type name in **Reference** text box .... Alt + R
   OR
   Click the name in the Go to list .... Alt + G, 🔼
3. Click **OK** .... Enter

Insert List of Named Ranges into a Worksheet

1. Click in upper-left cell of range to receive list.
2. Click **Insert** .... Alt + I
3. Click **Name** .... N
4. Click **Paste** .... P
5. Click **Paste List** button .. Alt + L
   - ✔ The list includes names with their corresponding sheet name and cell references.
6. Press an **arrow key** to deselect the list .... 🔼

Exercise Directions

1. Start Excel, if necessary.

2. Open 💿 14_SALES.

3. Save the file as XL_14.

4. Format cell A2 in the font of your choice, with a size of 16 point bold.

5. Select cells A4, A5, and A18. Format in 12 point bold.

6. Select the range B8:G8. Center the column labels and make them bold.

   ✓ You can do both while the range is selected.

7. Select the following cells by pressing the Ctrl key and clicking each cell: A10:A13, A15, A20:A23, and A25. Format them as bold.

   ✓ You can drag through cells that are contiguous.

   ✓ You may need to scroll down to see all the labels.

8. Using the Name, Define command on the Insert menu, name the range B10:B13 *Qtr1*.

9. Using the Name box, name the range C10:C13 *Qtr2*.

10. Name the corresponding ranges in the third and fourth quarter columns *Qtr3* and *Qtr4*, respectively. Use the naming method of your choice.

11. Select cell A28. Use the Name, Paste command in the Insert menu to display the range names in the worksheet.

12. Select the range F10:F13. Click the Edit Formula button (with the = sign) on the Formula bar and type *SUM(*.

    a. When you type the first parenthesis, a dialog box will open.

    b. Click the first Collapse Dialog button and drag through the cells B10:E10. Notice that the cell references appear in the text box as you select the cells.

       ✓ You could also type the cell references in the text box, but selecting the cells with the mouse is usually easier.

    c. Click the Collapse Dialog button to return to the larger dialog box.

    d. Press the Ctrl key and click OK.

       ✓ If you click OK without pressing the Ctrl key, the formula will appear only in the first cell.

13. Select the range G10:G13 and repeat step 12, this time typing =AVERAGE instead of =SUM.

    ✓ Use the same range of cells in the dialog box, and remember to press Ctrl when clicking OK.

14. Select cell B15 and click the Edit Formula button on the Formula bar. Type *SUM(* and type *Qtr1* in the Number 1 text box when it opens. Click OK.

15. Repeat step 14 to get the totals for the second, third, and fourth quarters, using the appropriate range names.

16. In cell F15, use any formula you wish to calculate the totals.

17. Select all the cells that contain values and, using the Format Cells dialog box, format the cells as Currency, with negative values in red with no parentheses.

18. In cell B25, enter a formula to calculate the combined profits of the stores.

19. Save the workbook and exit Excel.

On Your Own

1. Start Excel, if necessary.

2. Open a new workbook and save it as **OXL_14**.

3. Type the information given in the table below into the worksheet.

Division	1998	1999
North	53412	58455
South	23100	19254
East	45378	48622
West	61823	68566

4. Create a column to calculate the increase or decrease in sales.

5. Create a row to calculate the total sales for both years. Create range names to use in your formulas.

6. Create a row to calculate the average sales each year. Use the range names in the formulas. Remember that range names cannot start with a number.

7. Format sales figures with Comma Style, no decimals.

8. Format negative numbers in red.

9. Format column and row labels to distinguish them from the data cells.

10. Display the range names and their cell references in the worksheet.

11. Close the file and exit Excel, saving all changes.

Exercise 15

Skills Covered:

◆ **Copy Data** ◆ **Copy Using AutoFill** ◆ **Copy Part of a Cell's Contents**
◆ **Copy a Formula (Absolute, Relative, and Mixed Reference)**

On the Job

Excel provides many shortcuts to save you time as you enter data and write formulas in your worksheets. For example, you can use the copy and paste features to reuse data and formulas in the same worksheet, in another worksheet, or in another workbook. The AutoFill handle bypasses the copy and paste features and allows you to fill adjacent cells with similar data.

As the owner of a new bakery called The Harvest Time Bread Company, you figure it's about time that you used your knowledge of Excel to analyze your sales. In this exercise, you'll create a worksheet to track your sales volume for one week, and to compute the percentage of the total sales that each item represents.

Terms

AutoFill A method to copy data from a cell or range of cells to an adjacent cell or range of cells by dragging the fill handle.

fill handle The small square located in the lower-right corner of the active cell.

relative reference An address in a formula that changes when the formula is copied to a new location.

absolute reference An address in a formula that doesn't change when the formula is copied to a new location.

mixed reference An address in a formula that includes both relative and absolute components. When the formula is copied to a new location, the relative components adjust; the absolute components don't.

Notes

Copy Data

■ Worksheet data (labels, values, and formulas) can be copied to another cell, a range of cells, another worksheet, another workbook, or even another program.

■ To copy a range of data to a new location, use the Copy and Paste buttons on the Standard toolbar or the Copy and Paste commands from the Edit menu.

✓ *You can also use drag-and-drop editing to copy cells to another location. See more on this in Exercise 24.*

Copy Using AutoFill

■ You can copy data to adjacent cells quickly with Excel's **AutoFill** feature. Simply drag the **fill handle** (located in the lower-right corner of the cell) across or down the cells to fill.

■ When you point to the fill handle, the mouse pointer changes to a crosshair. As you drag the fill handle, a shaded border surrounds the cells to fill. When you release the mouse, the data is copied to the new location and the contents of the source cell display in the Formula bar.

- To copy several cells at once to adjacent cells, select the source cells and then drag the fill handle across the cells to fill.

- AutoFill results vary depending on the type of data you're copying — values, formulas, or labels. The following examples show some typical results when using AutoFill:

  - If you use AutoFill to copy an ordinary label such as *Midwest*, the word *Midwest* is copied to the cells you select.

Using the fill handle

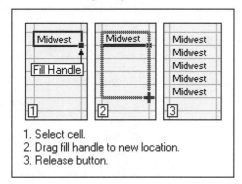

1. Select cell.
2. Drag fill handle to new location.
3. Release button.

  - However, if you use AutoFill to copy certain labels such as Monday or Jan, then you'll create a series: *Monday, Tuesday, Wednesday,* and so on, or *Jan, Feb, Mar,* and so on.

  - If you use AutoFill to copy a number, you'll copy just the value, such as *123.50.*

  - You can also use AutoFill to create a series of numbers, such as *1, 2, 3,* and so on.

    ✓ *You'll learn the specifics of creating a series in the next exercise.*

Copy Part of a Cell's Contents

- You can copy part of a cell's contents instead of the entire cell.

- The process is similar to copying text in a word processing document. You select what you want, and use the Copy and Paste commands to copy it to another location.

- To select part of a cell, you enable cell editing first, as if you were going to change part of the cell's contents.

Copy a Formula (Absolute, Relative, and Mixed Reference)

- When you copy a formula to a new location, the cell addresses referenced in the formula are automatically adjusted based on the new location.

- For example, suppose you type the following formula in cell C13:
    =C10+C11

    If you then copy the formula to cell D13, it's changed to the following formula:
    =D10+D11

  - The formula was adjusted by one column, because you copied the formula to a cell one column over.

  - If you copied the formula to cell C23 instead, it would be changed to this formula:
    =C20+C21

  - The formula was adjusted by 10 rows, because it was copied to a cell 10 rows down from the original cell.

- A cell address that adjusts when you copy a formula is called a **relative reference**.

- If you don't want an address to adjust when the formula is copied, enter it as an **absolute reference**.

  - Absolute references are preceded by dollar signs, like this:
    =$C$10+C11

    ✓ *To add the dollar signs quickly, type the cell address and then press F4.*

  - If this formula is copied from cell C13 to cell C23 (as before), it becomes the following formula:
    =$C$10+C21

  - The same formula, if copied to cell D13, becomes this formula:
    =$C$10+D11

- You can also use **mixed references**.

  - Mixed references are preceded by a dollar sign in front of the part you don't want to change, like this:
    =$C10+C11

  - If this formula is copied from cell C13 to cell C23 (as before), it becomes this formula:
    =$C20+C21

  - The same formula, if copied to cell D13, becomes this formula:
    =$C10+D11

Procedures

Copy Data Using the Edit Menu *(Ctrl+C)*

1. Select cell(s) to copy.
2. Click **Edit**..................... `Alt`+`E`
3. Click **Copy** .... `C`

   OR

   Click **Copy** button 🗐 on Standard toolbar.

   ✓ *A moving line (marquee) surrounds selected cell(s).*

Paste Data Using the Edit Menu *(Ctrl+V)*

1. Select cell(s) to receive data.

   ✓ *Click upper-left cell of destination range or select entire range of cells to receive data on current worksheet, another worksheet, or another workbook.*

2. Click **Edit**..................... `Alt`+`E`
3. Click **Paste** .... `P`

   OR

   Click **Paste** button 🗐 on the Standard toolbar.

   ✓ *Press Escape key to remove marquee that surrounds selected cell(s).*

Copy Data Using AutoFill

1. Select cell(s) to copy.
2. Point to fill handle.

   ✓ *The mouse shape changes to a crosshair.*

3. Drag fill handle across or down to adjacent cells to fill them.

Copy or Move Part of a Cell's Contents

1. Double-click the cell that contains the data to move or copy.

   ✓ *This step enables cell editing.*

2. In the cell, select the characters to move or copy.
3. To move the selection, click the **Cut** button ✂ on the Standard toolbar.

OR

1. To copy the selection, click the **Copy** button 🗐 on the Standard toolbar.
2. Double-click the cell to receive the data.
3. In the cell, click where data is to be placed.
4. Click the **Paste** button 🗐 on the Standard toolbar.
5. Press **Enter** .... `Enter`

Exercise Directions

1. Start Excel, if necessary.

2. Open 💿 **15_BREAD**.

3. Save the file as **XL_15**.

4. Add formatting to the worksheet:

   a. Add italics to cell C5.

   b. Change the range C7:G7 to bold, Berlin Sans FB Demi font (or another sans serif font), 10 points.

   c. Change the range D18:D20 to bold, Berlin Sans FB Demi font (or another sans serif font), 10 points as well.

   d. Adjust the column widths as needed.

5. Enter the following sales data:

Description	No. Sold	Sale Price
Honey Wheat Rolls	1025	.52
Butter White Rolls	983	.49
Seven Grain Rolls	1254	.53
Butter White Bread	456	2.20
Honey Nut Bread	698	2.45
Honey Wheat Bread	752	2.30
Seven Grain Bread	563	2.30
Italian Bread	384	1.75
Basil and Tomato Foccacia	238	3.25

6. In the range F8:F16, enter formulas that compute the total sales for each item:

   a. In cell F8, type the formula *=D8*E8*.

   b. Using the fill handle, copy the formula to the range F9:F16.

7. Type this formula in cell F18:
   =F8+F9+F10+F11+F12+F13+F13+F15+F16

8. Type *–123.56* in cell F19.

9. Type this formula in cell F20:
   =F18+F19

10. Format the sales data:

    a. Select the range E8:E16.

    b. Using the Format Cells dialog box, apply Currency format, two decimal places, no symbol, and negative numbers in red with parentheses.

    c. Select the range F8:F16.

    d. Using the Format Cells dialog box again, apply Currency format, two decimal places, with $ symbol, and negative numbers in red with parentheses.

    e. Select the range F18:F20.

    f. Using the Format Cells dialog box again, apply Currency format, two decimal places, with $ symbol, and negative numbers in red with parentheses.

11. Add the percentage of sales formulas:

    a. In cell G8, type this formula:
       =F8/$F$18

    b. Using the fill handle, copy the formula to the range G9:G16.

    c. Format the range G8:G16 with Percent format, no decimal places.

12. Save the workbook and exit Excel.

On Your Own

1. Start Excel, if necessary.

2. Open the workbook 💿 **15_FURNITURE**.

3. Save the file as **OXL_15**.

4. Format the column labels in the range C8:H8 and the label *Totals* in cell C14 however you like.

5. In the range F9:F12, enter formulas to compute the percentage of the gross sales that the discounts represent.

   ✓ *Keep in mind that the discount amount is shown as a negative. To display a positive number as a result, you'll need to use a negative address (such as –E9) in each formula.*

6. In the range G9:G12, enter formulas to compute the net sales, which is the gross sales minus any discounts or coupons.

   ✓ *Again, keep in mind that the discount amount is already negative.*

7. In the cells D14, E14, and G14, enter formulas to compute the total for each column.

8. In cell F14, compute the percentage as you did in step 5.

9. In the range H9:H12, enter formulas to compute the percentage of the total net sales that each store's net sales represents.

10. Format the values however you like.

11. Save the workbook and exit Excel.

Exercise 16

Skills Covered:

◆ Create a Series ◆ AutoSum

On the Job

Create a series of labels and values in a worksheet, using Excel's AutoFill feature to save data-entry time and reduce errors. You can also save time with Excel's AutoSum feature, which lets you add a range of cells without creating a formula.

You're the employment manager of KinderBaby Day Care, and you need to calculate the number of care givers you'll need on staff for the first part of the upcoming school year. To do that, you'll create a worksheet that details enrollments by month for each of your care areas, and use that to estimate the number of care givers needed.

Terms

series A list of sequential numbers, dates, times, or text.

AutoSum A toolbar button that automatically generates a formula that computes a sum of the nearest range of cells.

Notes

Create a Series

■ When you need to enter sequential values (numbers, dates, times) in a range of cells, use the Fill, Series command from the Edit menu.

Series dialog box

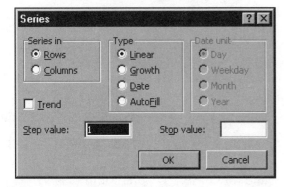

■ To enter a **series** based on the active cell, drag the fill handle (the small square in the lower-right corner of the active cell) over the range of cells to fill.

Drag the fill handle of the active cell to create a series

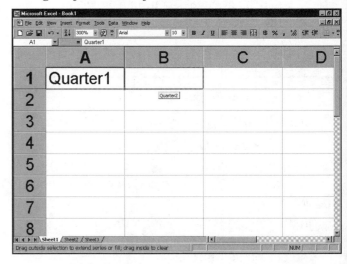

✓ The series displays in the cells after you release the mouse button.

- To create an incremental series (for example, 1, 3, 5, 7) enter the data for the first and second cells of the series, select the two cells, and then drag the fill handle for the selection over the range of cells to fill.

AutoSum

- The **AutoSum** feature quickly creates a formula that totals the nearest range of cells.

- When you click the AutoSum button ▣ Σ, Excel surrounds the range it thinks you want to total with a dotted line (marquee).

- You can accept this suggestion, or you can change it by dragging over the cells you want to total instead.

5.55
7.23
6.18
4.66
6.57
8.65
=SUM(C9:C15)

Procedures

Create Series Using the Edit Menu

1. Enter first series of data in cell.
2. Select range of cell(s) including series data and cells to fill.
3. Click **Edit** .... `Alt`+`E`
4. Click **Fill** .... `I`
5. Click **Series** .... `S`

   ✓ In the Series dialog box, you specify how the series displays, the type of series, and the step and stop values.

   Set direction of series:
   Click **Rows** ....`Alt`+`R`
   OR
   Click **Columns**.............`Alt`+`C`

   Change step value:
   Type value in **Step value** text box ....`Alt`+`S`

   ✓ The step value specifies the value increments for linear, growth, and AutoFill series.

   Enter stop value:
   Type value in **Stop value** text box ....`Alt`+`O`

   ✓ The stop value ends the series at a specific number.

   Select series type:
   Click **Linear** ....`Alt`+`L`

   ✓ If **Trend** isn't selected, adding the specified step value to each cell value in turn creates a linear series.

OR
Click **Growth**..............`Alt`+`G`

   ✓ If **Trend** isn't selected, multiplying the specified step value by each cell value in turn creates a growth series.

OR
Click **Date** ....`Alt`+`D`

Select date unit:
- **Day**......................`Alt`+`A`
- **Weekday**...............`Alt`+`W`
- **Month** ....`Alt`+`M`
- **Year** ....`Alt`+`Y`

OR
Click **AutoFill**..............`Alt`+`F`

   ✓ Creates series from data cells in selection.

6. Click **OK** ....`Enter`

Create AutoFill Series of Dates and Times Using Mouse

1. Enter data in active cell.
2. Select cell containing data.
3. Point to fill handle so that the mouse pointer looks like a crosshair: ✛.
4. Drag fill handle to adjacent cells in range to fill.

   ✓ Drag the fill handle down or to the right to create a series that displays in the cells after you release the mouse button.

Create Single-Value Series Using Mouse

   ✓ When you use this method, Excel will increment each cell in the series by 1.

1. Enter number in active cell.
2. Select cell containing number.
3. Point to fill handle to display the crosshair pointer: ✛.
4. Press **Ctrl** and drag fill handle to adjacent cells in range to fill.

   ✓ Drag the fill handle down or to the right to create a series of numbers that displays in the cells after you release the mouse button.

Create Multiple-Value Series Using Mouse

1. Enter first and second values in adjacent cells.

   ✓ The value can be numbers, dates, or times.

2. Select cells containing series data.

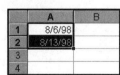

3. Point to fill handle.
4. Drag fill handle to last cell in range to fill.

   ✓ Drag the fill handle down or to the right to create a series of numbers or dates based on the selection.

Use AutoSum

1. Click the cell in which you want the result of the AutoSum formula to appear.

   ✓ *This cell must be located close to the cells you want to total, or AutoSum will suggest the wrong cells to total.*

2. Click **AutoSum** button Σ on Standard toolbar.

   OR

   Press **Alt + equal** .... Alt + =

   ✓ *Excel inserts =SUM( ) function in the Formula bar, and a marquee may surround cells to be totaled.*

3. If necessary, drag over the cells you want to sum.

4. Press **Enter** .... Enter

Exercise Directions

1. Start Excel, if necessary.

2. Open 💿 **16_KINDER**.

3. Save the file as **XL_16**.

4. In cell C8, type *August*.

   a. Use the fill handle to fill in the months September, October, November, and December in the range D8:G8.

      ✓ *Notice that Excel displays a ScreenTip as you drag, showing the planned entry for each cell in the series.*

   b. Make these column labels bold.

   c. Adjust the column widths as needed.

5. Add other formatting:

   a. Change cell C4 to a script font, 24 point bold.

   b. Add italics to cell C5.

   c. Select the range B9:B15 and make it italic, right-aligned.

6. Enter the enrollment data shown in the table below.

7. In cell B17, type *Total Enrollments* and make it bold. If Excel copies the italics from the entries above, remove the italics by clicking the Italic button on the Formatting toolbar.

   a. Using AutoSum, enter a formula into cell C17 that computes the total enrollment for August.

      ✓ *Excel will automatically select the range C9:C16, but you only want C9:C15. Hold down the Shift key as you click cell C15 to end the range there, or simply drag through the range C9:C15 when the marquee appears.*

   b. Using the fill handle, copy that formula to the range D17:G17.

8. In cell B18, type *Approx. No. of Care Givers Needed,* and apply bold, right-aligned formatting. (If necessary, remove italics.)

   a. Enter a formula into cell C18 that computes the number of care givers needed for August. Base your estimate on an average of 5 children per care giver.

   b. After entering the formula into cell C18, copy it to the range D18:G18.

   c. While the row is still selected, decrease the decimals so none are displayed.

9. Save the workbook again and exit Excel.

	August	September	October	November	December
Infant Care I	21	15	18	23	21
Infant Care II (crawlers)	16	20	18	20	17
Infant Care III (walkers)	23	25	24	23	18
Toddler Playland Ages 2-3	32	30	28	30	27
Preschool, Age 4	18	17	17	19	20
Preschool, Age 5	22	15	16	16	18
Kindergarten Prep (5½ and above)	15	12	12	14	15

On Your Own

1. Start Excel, if necessary.

2. Open a new workbook.

3. Save the file as **OXL_16**.

4. As a salesperson for a cleaning solutions company, Klean Kan, you travel a lot. You need to create a worksheet to track your deductible expenses for the week of March 15th through the 19th.

   a. Enter the dates as column labels at the top of the worksheet.

   b. Enter row labels for the various categories of expenses: mileage, gas, hotel, long distance, lunch, dinner, and so on.

5. Enter your actual expenses per day. (Make up these numbers.)

6. Create totals for each day and each expense category.

7. Create a grand total for expenses.

   a. Adjust the amounts included in the worksheet data, including only amounts that apply to the rules in steps 7b-7e.

   b. Your mileage is reimbursable at 33½ cents a mile.

   c. Lunches are reimbursable up to $5.00.

   d. You can only have dinner reimbursed (up to $25.00) if you stay overnight on business.

   e. Hotel and long distance charges are also reimbursable for overnight stays.

8. Save the workbook and exit Excel.

Exercise 17

Skills Covered:

◆ **Use Functions** ◆ **Formula Bar and Palette** ◆ **Paste Function**
◆ **Noncontiguous Ranges in a Function** ◆ **AutoCalculate**

On the Job

Use an Excel function to help you write a formula to perform specific calculations in your worksheets. Excel's Paste Function feature provides a list of available functions with a wizard to assist you in "filling in the blanks" to complete a formula.

As a portfolio manager at Investco Group, you've decided to perform an analysis of the trading volume of some of your stocks. Using the trading data for today, you'll create a worksheet to help you analyze the number of trades and the trade volume for each of your hottest technology stocks.

Terms

function A predefined formula that depends on specific values to perform a special calculation.

function name The name given to one of Excel's predefined formulas.

argument Part of a formula that contains the specific values necessary to perform the function.

nest To insert a function into another function.

noncontiguous ranges Two or more ranges that aren't located next to each other, but are separated by at least one column or one row.

AutoCalculate A feature that temporarily performs the following calculations on a range of cells without writing a formula: Average, Count, Count Nums, Max, Min, or Sum.

Notes

Use Functions

- Excel provides built-in formulas called **functions** to perform special calculations.
- A function contains these elements in the following order:
  - The equal symbol (=) starts the function.
  - The **function name** is entered in uppercase or lowercase letters.
  - An opening parenthesis separates the **arguments** from the function name.
  - The arguments (if any — some functions don't require arguments) identify the data required to perform the function.

- A closing parenthesis ends the argument. Example: =SUM(A1:A40)
  - ✓ *This SUM function adds the values listed in the argument, which is the range of cells A1 through A40.*

- Functions are divided into categories based on their purpose; for example, Math & Trig, Statistical, Financial, and so on.

Following are some common functions and their descriptions:
  - =SUM() adds the values in a range of cells.
    - ✓ *Click the AutoSum button* Σ *on the Standard toolbar to display the SUM function quickly.*

- =AVERAGE() returns the arithmetic mean of the values in a range of cells.

- =COUNT() counts the cells containing numbers in a range of cells (blank cells or text entries are ignored).

- =MAX() finds the highest value in a range of cells.

- =MIN() finds the lowest value in a range of cells.

- =ROUND() adjusts a value to display a specific number of digits.

  ✓ *For example, if you wanted to round the value in cell G9 to one decimal place, you would use the formula =ROUND(G9,1). Thus, a value of 78.3544 would become 78.4. The rounding is for display purposes only. Excel will still use the value 78.3544 when performing calculations.*

- =CEILING() rounds a number up to the nearest multiple you choose.

  ✓ *For example, if you want to round prices up to the nearest nickel, you would use a formula like =CEILING(G9,0.05)*

- =NOW() returns the current date and time.

- =DATE() converts a date into a date value that can then be used in calculations.

- =PMT() calculates either the future value of an investment (given a set interest rate, a time period for the investment, and the investment amount) or the periodic payment on a loan (given the interest rate, number of payments in the loan, and the loan amount).

- =FV() calculates the future value of an investment (given the interest rate, number of payments, and the payment amount).

■ A function can be inserted into a formula.

■ When a function is used as an argument for other functions, it's called a **nested** function.

Formula Bar and Palette

■ To enter a function and display a list of functions, click the Edit Formula button on the Formula bar; then choose from a list of functions from the drop-down menu.

■ When you use the Edit Formula button, the Formula Palette appears with information about the function and the result of the formula.

Click the Edit Formula button on the Formula bar to use the Formula Palette

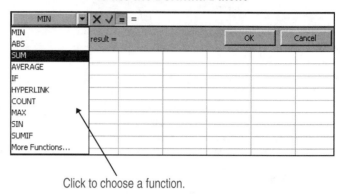

Click to choose a function.

Paste Function

■ To display functions by category and enter the arguments in the Formula Palette, click the Paste Function button f_* on the Standard toolbar.

■ When you use the Formula Palette, Excel automatically enters the equal sign (=) in the formula.

Noncontiguous Ranges in a Function

■ You can use **noncontiguous ranges** as arguments in a function.

  ✓ *You can also use individual cell addresses as arguments.*

■ When specifying noncontiguous ranges or single cell addresses in a function, separate them with commas, like this: =SUM(E4,C2:C10,G10)

AutoCalculate

■ When you want to quickly calculate the Average, Count, Count Nums, Max, Min, or Sum function for a cell or range of cells in your worksheet, use **AutoCalculate**.

■ With AutoCalculate, you don't need to type a formula to see the result.

■ Using the mouse, drag across the range of cells to display the AutoCalculate result on the status bar (the default calculation is SUM).

■ To change the calculation, right-click anywhere on the status bar and select from the list of functions.

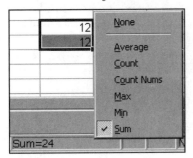

AutoCalculate function list

	12	None
	12	
		Average
		Count
		Count Nums
		Max
		Min
		✓ Sum
Sum=24		

■ If AutoCalculate is set to None, the AutoCalculate area of the status bar stays blank even when cells with numeric entries are selected. To turn on AutoCalculate, right-click anywhere on the status bar and select the function you want from the pop-up list.

Procedures

Use Formula Bar and Palette

1. Click cell in which you want the formula to display ....
2. Click **Edit Formula** button `=` on the Formula bar.
3. Type formula.
   OR
   a. Select function from drop-down list.
   b. Click in the argument text box.
   c. Delete data and type new data, if necessary.

   You can enter any or all of the following:
   - Numeric value
   - Cell reference
   - Range of cells
   - Range name
   - Function

   ✓ *When entering a cell reference or range address, you can use the Collapse Dialog button to hide the dialog box temporarily so you can select the address or range from the worksheet.*

   d. Repeat steps b and c to complete arguments.
4. Click **OK** .... `Enter`

Use Paste Function

1. Click cell .... `⬍`
   where answer will display.
   If editing a formula:
   a. Double-click cell to edit formula.

b. Click in formula .... `→` `←`
   where function will be inserted.
2. Click **Paste Function** button `fx`.
   OR
   a. Click **Insert** .... `Alt` + `I`
   b. Click **Function** .... `F`
3. Select category from **Function category** list ..... `Alt` + `C`, `↑` `↓`
4. Select function from **Function name** list .... `Alt` + `N`, `↑` `↓`
5. Click **OK** .... `Enter`

   ✓ *The Formula Palette defines the function, describes the required arguments, and displays the result of the suggested argument(s). Click the Office Assistant button in the lower-left corner of the palette for additional assistance.*

6. Click in the argument text box .... `Tab`
7. Type data.
   You can enter any or all of the following:
   - Numeric value
   - Cell reference
   - Range of cells
   - Range name
   - Function

   ✓ *To enter a cell reference or range of cells from the worksheet, click the Collapse Dialog button located to the right of the argument text box, select the cell(s), and then click the Collapse Dialog button again to expand the palette.*

8. Repeat steps 6 and 7 to complete arguments.
9. Click **OK** .... `Enter`

Edit a Formula

1. Click formula cell .... `⬍`
   a. Click in Formula bar in location to edit.
   b. Type correction.
   OR
   a. Click **Edit Formula** button on the Formula bar `=`.
   b. Click in argument text box.
   c. Type correction.
2. Click **OK** .... `Enter`

Enter a Function into a Formula

1. Click formula cell .... `⬍`
   where answer will display.
2. Press **equal** key .... `=`
3. Type name of function.
4. Type opening parenthesis .... `(`
5. Type arguments(s).
6. Type closing parenthesis ..... `)`
7. Press **Enter** .... `Enter`

Use AutoCalculate

1. Select cells .... `Shift` + `⬍`
   you want to calculate.
2. View result of calculation on status bar.
3. If necessary, right-click anywhere in the status bar.
4. Click desired function in list .... `↑` `↓`, `Enter`

Exercise Directions

1. Start Excel, if necessary.

2. Open ⊚ **17_STOCK**.

3. Save the file as **XL_17**.

4. In cell C4, use the NOW() function to display the current date.

5. Format the worksheet:

   a. Format the column labels in row 6 with Arial Narrow font, 12 points, bold, centered.

   b. Format the column labels in row 7 with Arial font, 8 points, bold, centered.

   c. Format the column labels in row 8 with Arial font, 8 points, bold, italic, centered.

   d. Format the range B9:B16 with Arial font, 10 points, italic, right-aligned.

   e. Format the range B18:B22 with Arial font, 10 points, bold, right-aligned.

   f. Format the range C9:G16 with Accounting format (Currency Style), zero decimal places.

   g. Repeat step f with the range C19:G22.

   h. Widen columns as needed.

6. In cell C18, use the Paste Function button to enter the COUNT function.

   ✓ COUNT() is a statistical function.

   a. In the Formula Palette, type the range C9:C16 in the Value1 text box.

   b. There is no Value2 in this instance, so leave that text box blank.

7. In cell C19, use the function list to enter the AVERAGE function.

   a. Begin by clicking the Edit Formula button.

   b. Then select the function you want from the function list.

   c. Enter the required values (C9:C16).

8. In cell C20, use the AutoSum button to enter the SUM function.

   ✓ Verify that you have totaled the correct range, C9:C16.

9. In cell C21, use the Paste Function button to enter the MIN function.

   ✓ Instead of typing the range into the Number1 text box, use the Collapse Dialog button to select the range C9:C16 from the worksheet.

10. Enter the MAX function in cell C22, using C9:C16 as the argument.

11. Use AutoCalculate to check your results in the formula cells.

12. Copy the formulas across to columns D through G.

13. Save the file and exit Excel.

On Your Own

1. Start Excel, if necessary.

2. Open 🖸 **17_FURNITURE**.

3. Save the file as **OXL_17**.

4. Delete the formulas previously written to total the monthly gross sales, discounts and coupons, and net sales.

5. Replace these formulas with new ones created using the SUM function.

6. In rows 15, 16, and 17, create formulas that compute the AVERAGE, MAX, and MIN of the gross monthly sales, monthly discounts and coupons, and monthly net sales.

7. Use the AutoCalculate function to check your formula results.

8. In cell C6, type today's date.

   ✓ *Don't use the NOW() function; just type the actual date. Or use the shortcut and press Ctrl+;.*

9. In cell E5, type *Taxes due*.

   ✓ *Apply bold formatting to cell E5.*

10. In cell E6, use the DATE function to display a date that's one month from now.

    a. To solve this problem, you'll need to use some other date functions as well: YEAR(), which extracts the year from any given date, MONTH(), which extracts the month, and DAY, which extracts the day.

       ✓ *You can't just add 30 to the date in cell C6 because, depending on the month, that may not be right. What's best is a calculation that adds one month to the date, not 30 or 31 days.*

       ✓ *To add one month, you have to dissect the date into its various parts—year, month, and day—add a month, and then put the date back together again.*

    b. Your calculation will look something like this: =DATE(YEAR(C6),MONTH(C6)+1,DAY(C6))

       ✓ *The DATE function puts the pieces back together—the year, month (current month plus one), and day—to create the new date.*

11. Save the workbook and exit Excel.

Exercise 18

◆ Critical Thinking

Your boss at Java Jungle Wholesale wants a worksheet that compares the prices of Java Jungle coffees to those of its competitors. The prices for Java Jungle coffees don't have to be the lowest on the market, but they should be lower than the average price of the main competition by about 5%. Your job is to set the new prices and round them up to the nearest nickel.

Exercise Directions

1. Start Excel, if necessary.

2. Open ⊙ **18_JAVA**.

3. Save the file as **XL_18**.

4. In cell H9, type *Average Price* on two lines. Use bold format, centered.

5. In cell H10, create a formula to compute the average price of the competitors' coffees, and then copy the formula to the appropriate rows.

6. In cell D10, create a formula to decrease the average price in cell H10 by 5% and round that price up to the nearest nickel.

   a. Use this nested formula:
      =CEILING(H10*.95,0.05).

      ✓ *The 0.05 in the formula rounds up to the nearest nickel. If you wanted to round up to the nearest dime or quarter, you would use 0.1 or 0.25, respectively.*

   b. Copy the formula to the appropriate rows.

7. Format all the prices using Accounting format, two decimal places.

8. Widen all columns containing prices to 10.00.

9. In cell D9, insert a comment describing how you arrived at the new prices.

10. Save the workbook and exit Excel.

Lesson 4

Print a Worksheet

Exercise 19

- ◆ Preview a Worksheet
- ◆ Quickly Print a Worksheet

Exercise 20

- ◆ Set the Print Area
- ◆ Print Options
- ◆ Page Setup

Exercise 21

- ◆ Page Breaks
- ◆ Page Break Preview
- ◆ Headers and Footers

Exercise 22

- ◆ Print Titles

Exercise 23

- ◆ Critical Thinking

Exercise 19

Skills Covered:

◆ **Preview a Worksheet** ◆ **Quickly Print a Worksheet**

On the Job

After you've entered data into a worksheet, you may need to print it out in order to share it with a colleague or your boss. Of course, you want your work to look professional when printed, so you'll want to preview the result before printing and making any necessary adjustments.

You're the accounting manager of The Harvest Time Bread Company. It's payroll time again, and you're the one in charge of getting invoices out. In this exercise, you'll create two invoices for the Java Jungle Café, then preview and print them.

Terms

Print Preview The command used to display a worksheet and see how it will look when it's printed.

portrait orientation In this mode, your worksheet is printed across the narrowest width of the page. On an 8½" by 11" sheet of paper, the worksheet would be printed across the 8½" width.

landscape orientation In this mode, your worksheet is printed across the widest width of the page. On an 8½" by 11" sheet of paper, the worksheet would be printed across the 11" width.

Notes

Preview a Worksheet

- Prior to printing a worksheet, it's usually a good idea to preview it.

- The preview displays your worksheet as it will look when printed.

Print Preview window

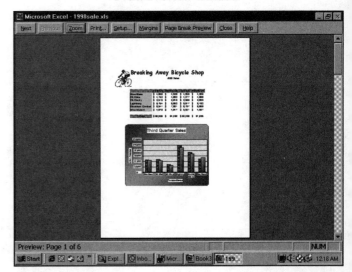

- Previewing a worksheet gives you the opportunity to correct any errors or make any necessary adjustments prior to printing the worksheet.

- To view worksheet output before you print, use the **Print Preview** command.

- You can access the Print Preview command through the File menu, through a button in the Print dialog box, or through a button on the Standard toolbar.

- Within the Print Preview window, an entire page of the worksheet is displayed. However, you can zoom in on any area of the worksheet you wish to view in greater detail.

- You can also access the Page Setup dialog box and set print options from within the Print Preview window.

Quickly Print a Worksheet

- To print a worksheet quickly, use the Print button 🖨.

  ✓ *When you print a worksheet this way, Excel will print only the current worksheet or the selected range. If you want to print the entire workbook, you'll need to use the Print dialog box, as discussed in the next exercise.*

- Excel's default page size for a printed worksheet is letter size (8½" x 11").

  - By default, Excel prints your worksheet in **portrait orientation**.

- To print the output across the page rather than down the page, select **landscape orientation** on the Page tab of the Page Setup dialog box, as discussed in the next exercise.

- The default page margins are set to .75" for the left and right margins and 1.0" for the top and bottom margins.

  ✓ *Again, if you wish to make changes to the margins, you will need to do so from the Page Setup dialog box, as discussed in the next exercise.*

Print dialog box

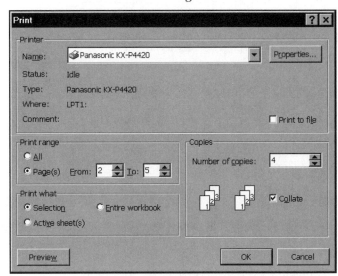

Procedures

Quickly Print Worksheet
(Ctrl+P)

- Click the **Print** button 🖨 on the Standard toolbar.

  ✓ *When you click the Print button on the Standard toolbar, the active worksheet is sent directly to the printer without displaying the Print dialog box.*

Preview and Then Print a Worksheet

1. Click **Print Preview** button 🔍.
2. To zoom in on an area of the worksheet, click it.
3. To zoom back out, click the worksheet again.

4. To close the Print Preview window without printing, click the **Close** button .... Ⓒ

5. To print the worksheet, click the **Print** button .... Ⓣ

   a. Make adjustments as needed to the Print settings.

   b. Click **OK**.

Exercise Directions

1. Start Excel, if necessary.
2. Open ⊘ **19_BREAD**.
3. Save the file as **XL_19**.
4. Enter the quantity sold:

Description	Qty
Honey Wheat Rolls	320
Butter White Bread	125
Honey Wheat Bread	220
Seven Grain Bread	175
Honey Nut Bread	100
Basil and Tomato Foccacia	75

5. Create formulas to compute the total sale for each item:
   a. Type the formula in cell F8.
   b. Using the fill handle, copy the formula to the range F9:F13.
   c. Format the range F8:F13 with Currency format, two decimal places.
      ✓ *Be careful not to apply Accounting format using the Currency Style button on the Formatting toolbar.*

6. Using AutoSum, create a formula in cell F15 that computes the pre-tax total.
7. In cell F16, enter a formula to compute the sales tax at 5%.
8. In cell F17, enter a formula to compute the grand total, which is the total plus the tax.

9. Format the range F15:F17 with Currency format, two decimal places.
10. Copy the range C7:F17 to the range C59:F69.
11. Edit cell C57 to say *Week of May 11th, 1999*.
12. Enter the quantity sold:

Description	Qty
Honey Wheat Rolls	355
Butter White Bread	136
Honey Wheat Bread	245
Seven Grain Bread	179
Honey Nut Bread	139
Basil and Tomato Foccacia	124

13. Preview the worksheet.
    a. Zoom in on the grand total for May 4th.
    b. Zoom back out.
    c. Press Page Down to move to page 2.
    d. Zoom in on the grand total for May 11th.
    e. Zoom back out.
14. Print the worksheet:
    a. Close the Print Preview window.
    b. Click the Print button.
       ✓ *You can also print from the Print Preview window by clicking the Print button, and then clicking OK.*
15. Save the workbook and exit Excel.

On Your Own

1. Start Excel, if necessary.
2. Open ⊘ **19_HARVEST**.
3. Save the file as **OXL_19**.
4. Preview the worksheet.
   a. Notice that the title is too long to fit on a printed page.
   b. Scroll down to view the second page in the preview.

5. Alter the title as necessary, without changing the text, so that the worksheet will print on one page. Try each of the following methods, previewing the page after each change:
   a. Reduce the font size.
   b. Change font and font size.
   c. Place the title on two lines, beginning in cell C3.
   d. Choose the most appealing of the above changes and print one copy.
6. Save the workbook and exit Excel.

Exercise 20

Skills Covered:

◆ Set the Print Area ◆ Print Options ◆ Page Setup

On the Job

Change the page setup of your worksheet and use the available print options to control the printed output. For example, if you need to fit the worksheet on one page, you can choose to change the margins, change the print orientation, change the paper size, and change the scaling.

As the accounts payable manager for Magnolia Steel Bearings & Fittings, you're pretty proud of the budget worksheet you've just created, which details the company's projected sales and cash collections for the upcoming fiscal year. The only problem remaining is to make the worksheet look as good on paper as it does on the screen.

Terms

print area The area selected to print. If you don't select an area of the worksheet, Excel prints the entire contents of the sheet.

print options Selections that control what, where, how, and how many copies to print.

Page Setup A dialog box that includes options to control the appearance of printed output.

Notes

Set the Print Area

- Normally, when you print a worksheet, Excel prints its entire contents.
  - If the worksheet contains data and a chart, then both are normally printed.
- If you want to print a selected area of the worksheet, you can set the **print area**.
  - The print area is the area that has been selected to print.
  - If you don't set a print area, Excel prints the entire worksheet.
  - You can select a print area and later reset it to something else, or simply clear the print area (allowing Excel to once again print the entire worksheet).

- Normally, once you set a print area, you'll only be able to print that area of the worksheet — until you remove or change the print area settings. However, you can select and print a range without changing the print area setting.
- When you set a print area, a dotted line appears in the worksheet, defining the print area.
- When you set a print area, the range *Print_Area* will be set and included in the Name box, just as if you had selected and named the range. Open the Name box at any time and select Print_Area to view the current print area.

Print Options

- Access the Print dialog box from the File menu by selecting Print. (You can also access the Print dialog box from the Print Preview window.) Choose from a number of **print options**.

Print dialog box

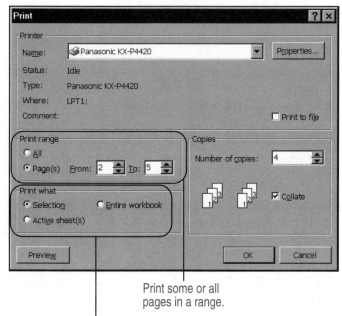

Print some or all pages in a range.

Print part or all of a worksheet or workbook.

✓ *When you use the Print button on the Standard toolbar, you bypass the Print dialog box and print the current worksheet or selection, using the default settings.*

Page Setup

- Access the **Page Setup** dialog box with the Page Setup command on the File menu to control printed output. (You can also access the Page Setup dialog box from the Print Preview window.)

- The following page tabs display in the Page Setup dialog box: Page, Margins, Header/Footer, and Sheet.

Page Tab

Page tab of the Page Setup dialog box

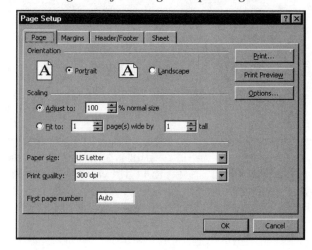

Orientation
- Print in Portrait (vertical) or Landscape (horizontal) orientation.

Scaling
- Reduce or enlarge information with the Adjust to % normal size option. Use the Fit to page(s) option to compress worksheet data to fill a specific number of pages.

Paper size
- Change the paper size when printing on a paper size other than 8½" x 11".

Print quality
- Reduce the print quality to print draft output.

First page number
- Change the starting page number for the current worksheet.

Margins Tab

Margins tab of the Page Setup dialog box

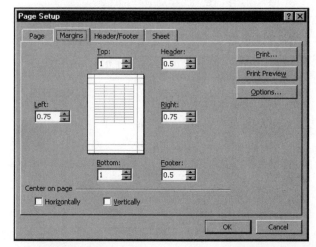

Margins

- Increase or decrease the top, bottom, left, or right margins to control the amount of data printed on a line.
- Specify the distance of the header from the top margin and the footer from the bottom margin.
- Print the worksheet centered horizontally or vertically on the page.

Header/Footer Tab

✓ *The Header/Footer tab is discussed in greater detail in the next exercise.*

Header

- Specify text to print at the top of every page.

Footer

- Specify text to print at the bottom of every page.

Sheet Tab

Sheet tab of the Page Setup dialog box

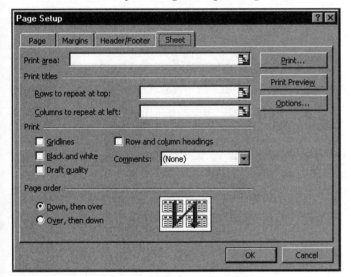

Print area

- Use this option to define a range of cells to print. You can click the Collapse Dialog button and use the mouse to select the range to be printed, or you can type the range.
- If you wish to print named ranges, just type in the range name(s).

  ✓ *To select multiple ranges, hold down the Ctrl key as you click the ranges, or type the range addresses or names in the text box, adding a comma (,) between ranges.*

Print titles

- Specify row labels to print at the top of every page or column labels to print on the left of every page.

Print

- Select options to print gridlines, black and white, draft quality, row and column headings (the column letters and row numbers from the worksheet frame), and comments.

Page order

- Specify whether the worksheet pages should be printed down and then across to the right, or across to the right and then down.

Procedures

Select Print Options *(Ctrl + P)*

1. Click **File** .... Alt + F
2. Click **Print** .... P
3. Select options you want.
4. Click **OK** .... Enter

Print Selection

✓ *Use this option to print a selected area of the worksheet without resetting the print area.*

1. Select range.
2. Click **File** .... Alt + F
3. Click **Print** .... P
4. Click **Selection** .... Alt + N
5. Click **OK** .... Enter

Set Print Area

1. Select the range you want to set as the print area.

   ✓ *If you select noncontiguous ranges, they'll print on separate pages.*

2. Click **File** .... Alt + F
3. Click **Print Area** .... T
4. Click **Set Print Area** .... S

Clear Print Area Settings

1. Click **File** .... `Alt`+`F`
2. Click **Print Area** .... `T`
3. Click **Clear Print Area** .... `C`

View Current Print Area

1. Click arrow button in **Name** box.
2. Click **Print_Area**.

Print Named Range

✓ *This option is useful when you want to print a specific area of the worksheet.*

1. Click **File** .... `Alt`+`F`
2. Click **Page Setup** .... `U`
3. Click **Sheet** tab .... `Ctrl`+`Tab`
4. Click **Print area** .... `Alt`+`A` text box.
5. Type name of range.
6. Click **Print** button .... `Alt`+`P`

   ✓ *Choose print options as required.*

7. Click **OK** .... `Enter`

Access Page Setup Dialog Box

1. Click **File** .... `Alt`+`F`
2. Click **Page Setup** .... `U`
3. Select tabs and options.
4. Click **OK** .... `Enter`

Preview Before Printing

1. Click **File** .... `Alt`+`F`
2. Click **Print Preview** .... `V`

   OR

   Click **Print Preview** button `🔍`.

Preview Selection Before Printing

1. Select range.
2. Click **File** .... `Alt`+`F`
3. Click **Print** .... `P`
4. Click **Selection** .... `Alt`+`N`
5. Click **Preview** button ... `Alt`+`W`

Exercise Directions

1. Start Excel, if necessary.
2. Open ⊙ **20_MAGNOLIA**.
3. Save the file as **XL_20**.
4. Select the range A3:F16.
5. Set the range as the print area.
6. Access the Print Preview window.

   ✓ *Print Preview shows how the printed page would appear if you were to print it now.*

7. Access the Page Setup dialog box.

   ✓ *You can do that from within the Print Preview window by clicking the Setup button.*

8. Change the page orientation to landscape.
9. Center the data horizontally.
10. Return to the Print Preview window.
11. Display the Print dialog box.
12. Set the number of copies to 2.
13. Print the selection.
14. Close the file and exit Excel, saving all changes.

On Your Own

1. Start Excel, if necessary.
2. Open ⊙ **20_COOKIES**.
3. Save the file as **OXL_20**.
4. Add formatting as desired to the worksheet title, column labels, row labels, and values.
5. Adjust column widths as needed.
6. Set up the page to print in landscape mode.
7. Adjust the scale so that the text is as large as possible, printed on one page.
8. Print one copy of the report.
9. Close the file and exit Excel, saving all changes.

Exercise 21

Skills Covered:

◆ Page Breaks ◆ Page Break Preview ◆ Headers and Footers

On the Job

If you're not satisfied with the default page layout settings in Excel, you can change them. For example, automatic page breaks are set if a worksheet doesn't fit on one page, but you can set your own page breaks before printing. If you need to print only part of a worksheet, you can change the print area temporarily. In addition, to enhance the appearance of a worksheet, you can add headers and footers to the top and/or bottom of each page.

Your boss has asked you to make some changes in the Magnolia Steel worksheet and print the worksheet again, this time with a custom header.

Terms

page break Dashed lines that specify where a page will end in printed output.

scaling Reducing or enlarging information to fit on a specified number of pages.

Normal view The default worksheet view for performing most Excel tasks.

Page Break Preview A view that allows you to move and delete page breaks and resize the print area.

print area The specified range of cells to be printed.

header Repeated information that appears in the top margin of a page.

footer Repeated information that appears in the bottom margin of a page.

Notes

Page Breaks

- When worksheet data won't fit on one page, Excel inserts automatic **page breaks** based on the paper size, margins, and **scaling** options.

- Automatic page breaks appear as dashed lines on the worksheet.

- You can choose whether to display automatic page breaks with the Options dialog box.

Select options from the View tab

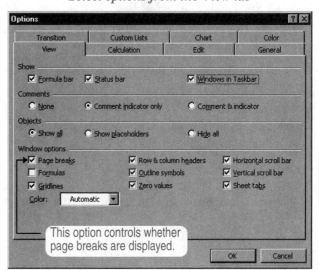

This option controls whether page breaks are displayed.

- If you prefer, you can override automatic page breaks and set manual page breaks before printing.
- Manual page breaks display on the worksheet as bold, solid lines in Page Break Preview.

Page Break Preview

- Switch between **Normal view** and **Page Break Preview** from the View menu.
  - ✓ *You can also access Page Break Preview from within the Print Preview window.*
- In Page Break Preview, when you drag a dashed line to move a page break it changes to a solid line.
- When you adjust page breaks, Excel automatically scales the worksheet data to fit the page(s).
- In Page Break Preview, drag a dashed line off the worksheet to remove a page break and reset the page breaks.
- You can also edit worksheet data and resize the **print area** from Page Break Preview.

Headers and Footers

- When you want to repeat the same information at the top of each page, create a **header**.
- When you want to repeat the same information at the bottom of each page, create a **footer**.

- In Excel, you can choose to add built-in headers and footers or create customized ones.
- Custom header and footer text is separated into three sections: left (text is left-aligned), center (text is centered), and right (text is right-aligned).
- In a custom header or footer, you can enter text or insert codes that display current date, current time, page number, file name, and/or sheet name.
- The font, font style, and font size of header and footer text can be changed.

Header/Footer tab of the Page Setup dialog box

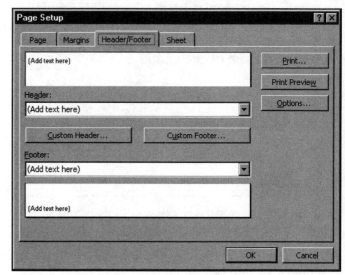

Procedures

Page Break Preview

1. Click **View** .... Alt + V
2. Click **Page Break Preview** .. P

OR

1. Click **Print Preview** button.
2. Click **Page Break Preview** button V

   - ✓ *When you're already in Page Break Preview, the Normal View button appears instead of the Page Break Preview button on the Print Preview toolbar.*
   - ✓ *If the Welcome to Page Break Preview dialog box displays, click OK.*

Return to Normal View

1. Click **View** .... Alt + V
2. Click **Normal** .... N

OR

1. Click **Print Preview** button.
2. Click **Normal View** V

Set Manual Page Breaks

- ✓ *The following procedures are done in Page Break Preview.*
- ✓ *Automatic page breaks following the manual page break will adjust automatically.*

To adjust an automatic page break:

1. Drag the break to where you want it to occur.
2. Release the mouse button.

To insert horizontal page break:

1. Click the heading for the row where new page should begin.
2. Click **Insert** .... Alt + I
3. Click **Page Break** .... B

   - ✓ *You don't have to select the entire row if you click the first cell in the row. If any other cell is selected, inserting a page break will create both a horizontal and a vertical page break.*

To insert vertical page break:

1. Click the heading for the column where the new page should begin.
2. Click **I**nsert .... `Alt`+`I`
3. Click **Page Break**................. `B`

✓ *You don't have to select the entire column if you click the first cell in the column. If any other cell is selected, inserting a page break will create both a horizontal and a vertical page break.*

To insert both horizontal and vertical page breaks:

1. Click cell where new page should begin.
2. Click **I**nsert .... `Alt`+`I`
3. Click **Page B**reak................. `B`

Remove Manual Page Breaks

To remove horizontal page break:

1. Click cell in row below manual page break.
2. Click **I**nsert .... `Alt`+`I`
3. Click **Remove Page Break** .... `B`

To remove vertical page break:

1. Click cell in column to right of manual page break.
2. Click **I**nsert .... `Alt`+`I`
3. Click **Remove Page B**reak... `B`

To remove all manual page breaks:

1. Click **Select All** button in the upper-left corner of worksheet frame.
2. Click **I**nsert .... `Alt`+`I`
3. Click **Reset A**ll **Page Breaks** .... `A`

To move a page break:

- Drag dashed or solid line to the new location.

   ✓ *An automatic page break dashed line changes to a solid line.*

To remove all page breaks:

1. Right-click any cell in worksheet.

   ✓ *Shortcut menu appears.*

2. Click **Reset A**ll **Page Breaks**.

   ✓ *Automatic page breaks are restored.*

To adjust print area:

- Drag dark outline (border of print area) to resize the print area.

To restore print area:

1. Right-click any cell in worksheet.

   ✓ *Shortcut menu appears.*

2. Click **Reset Print Area**......... `R`

Create Header or Footer

1. Click **F**ile .... `Alt`+`F`
2. Click **Page Set**up .... `U`
3. Click **Header/Footer** tab .... `Ctrl`+`Tab`

   To select built-in header or footer:

   a. Click **He**ader drop-down arrow .... `Alt`+`A`
      OR
      Click **F**ooter drop-down arrow .... `Alt`+`F`

   b. Click desired header or footer type in list .... `↑↓`, `Enter`

To create custom header or footer:

a. Click **C**ustom Header ..... `Alt`+`C`
   OR
   Click **Cu**stom Footer ...... `Alt`+`U`

b. Click appropriate section:

   - **Left section** ...... `Alt`+`L`
   - **Center section** . `Alt`+`C`
   - **Right section** ... `Alt`+`R`

c. Type text to appear in header or footer.
   OR
   Click appropriate button to insert a code:

   - **Page Number** `#`.
   - **Total Pages** `⊡`.
   - **Date** `⊡`.
   - **Time** `⊙`.
   - **File Name** `⊡`.
   - **Sheet Name** `⊡`.

To change font of header or footer text:

a. Select header or footer text.
b. Click **Font** button `A`.
c. Choose from available font, font style, and font size options.

4. Click **OK** .... `Enter`

Exercise Directions

1. Start Excel, if necessary.
2. Open ⊚ 21_MAGNOLIA.
3. Save the file as **XL_21**.
4. Select the range A1:F16.
5. Set the print area to the currently selected range.

   ✓ Restricting the print area prevents any extraneous data from being printed.

6. Access Page Break Preview.
7. Set a page break so that Page 1 encompasses only the first two rows (rows 1 and 2).

   ✓ If you can't see what you're doing in Page Break Preview, zoom the window to a higher magnification.

8. Select cell A5 and insert a new page break.

   ✓ The page break appears as a solid line above cell A5.

9. Drag the page break down to include row 9.

10. Access the Print Preview window.

    ✓ The status bar should indicate that there are three pages in this worksheet.

    ✓ You can page through the worksheet if you like.

11. Access the Page Setup dialog box.
12. Change the print orientation to landscape.
13. Center the contents to be printed both horizontally and vertically.
14. Create a custom header containing the current date in the left section and the text *Magnolia Steel Budget Sheet* in the center section.
15. Start the print process from the Print Preview window.
16. Close the file and exit Excel, saving all changes.

On Your Own

1. Start Excel, if necessary.
2. Open ⊚ 21_VIDEO.
3. Save the file as **OXL_21**.
4. Set the print area to exclude the first three rows.
5. Create a page break between the Movie Order for February section and the Returns for February section.
6. Create a custom header:
   a. On the left, insert your name.
   b. In the center, type the words, *Movie Time Video* and *February Order* (on two lines)
   c. On the right, type the word *Page* followed by a space and then the page number.
   d. Format everything in the header as bold, 10 points.

7. Create a custom footer:
   a. In the center, insert the current date and time (type a space between the date and time codes).
   b. Format it as bold, 10 points.

8. Make any additional changes you want, such as centering the data on the page, changing its scale, and so on.
9. Print two copies of the worksheet.
10. Close the file and exit Excel, saving all changes.

Exercise 22

Skills Covered:

◆ Print Titles

On the Job

Use the print titles feature when workbook data is too wide or too long to fit on one page. For example, your worksheet may contain more columns than will fit on one page and you might like to repeat the titles (the row labels) on the second page. If your worksheet has too many rows for a single page, you can repeat the column labels as well.

You're the new payroll clerk for KinderBaby Day Care. You've been doing the payroll on paper for a few weeks now, and you're pretty tired of it. So you've created a payroll worksheet to help you compute the totals and prepare the checks. After entering the data for this week, you'll prepare the worksheet for printing, then print off a nice copy for your files.

Terms

row titles Repeated column labels (the rows the column labels are in) at the top of page 2 and subsequent pages when worksheet data is too long for one page.

column titles Repeated row labels (the columns the row labels are in) on the left side of page 2 and subsequent pages when worksheet data is too wide for one page.

Notes

Print Titles

- When the printed output of a worksheet is too long to fit on one page, you may want the **row titles** (column labels and worksheet title) to be repeated at the top of each page.

Set for row titles to be repeated

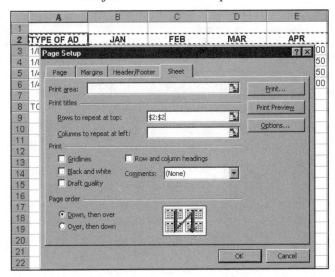

- When the printed output of a worksheet is too wide to fit on one page, you may want the **column titles** (row labels) to be repeated on the left side of each page.

Set for column titles to be repeated

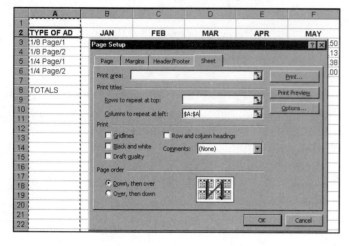

- You set row or column titles with the Print titles options in the Page Setup dialog box.
  - ✓ *The Print titles options are unavailable if you access Page Setup from the Print Preview window.*

- Titles repeat starting on the second page of the printed output.

Procedures

Set Print Titles

1. Click **File** .... Alt + F

2. Click **Page Setup** .... U

3. Select **Sheet** tab .... Ctrl + Tab

   To select rows to repeat at top:
   - ✓ *The rows must be contiguous.*

   a. Click in **Rows to repeat at top** text box .... Alt + R

   b. Type row reference(s).
      - ✓ *Example: $2:$2*

   OR

   a. Click **Collapse Dialog** button 🔳.

   b. Select row(s) in the worksheet.
      - ✓ *A marquee surrounds selection.*

   c. Click **Expand Dialog** button 🔳.
      - ✓ *Row selection appears in text box.*

   To select columns to repeat at left:
   - ✓ *The columns must be contiguous.*

   d. Click in **Columns to repeat at left** text box .... Alt + C

   e. Type column reference(s).
      - ✓ *Example: $A:$A*

   OR

   a. Click **Collapse Dialog** button 🔳.

   b. Select column(s) in the worksheet.
      - ✓ *A marquee surrounds selection.*

   c. Click **Expand Dialog** button 🔳.
      - ✓ *Column selection appears in text box.*

4. Click **OK** to return to worksheet .... Enter

   OR

   Click the **Print** button and then click **OK** to print worksheet .... Ctrl + P , Enter

Exercise Directions

1. Start Excel, if necessary.

2. Open the file ⊙ **22_PAYROLL**.

3. Save the workbook as **XL_22**.

4. Create totals for the payroll:

   a. In cell A28, type *Totals*.

   b. Make the cell bold and right-aligned.

   c. In cell B28, use the AutoSum button to create a formula that totals the range B9:B26.

   d. Copy this formula to the other cells in row 28, except cell H28.

      ✓ *An easy way to do this procedure is to copy the formula to the whole row and then delete the contents of cell H28.*

   e. Format the range I28:P28 with Accounting format, two decimal places.

5. Prepare the worksheet to be printed:

   a. Change to landscape orientation.

   b. Copy cells B4 and B5 to cells I4 and I5 so the worksheet title will print on both pages.

      ✓ *You copy the worksheet titles rather than repeating them with the Page Setup dialog box so that the KinderBaby graphic will repeat on every page.*

   c. Set a manual page break to fall between columns H and I, if necessary.

6. Print both pages of the worksheet.

7. Close the file and exit Excel, saving all changes.

On Your Own

1. Start Excel, if necessary.

2. Open the file ⊙ **22_SOCCER**.

3. Save this worksheet as **OXL_22**.

4. Enter additional members of your son's soccer team.

   a. Follow the examples as shown in the worksheet.

   b. Enter at least five additional members.

5. Preview the worksheet.

6. Make any changes you want before printing. Here are some suggestions:

   a. Set up the worksheet to print on two pages in portrait orientation.

   b. Print the uniform number and member name on each page of the worksheet to make it easier to read.

   c. Add a custom header and/or footer.

   d. Adjust the page breaks so that all phone numbers and emergency information are together on page 2.

   e. For printing purposes only, copy the title in cell C5 to cell F5 so it will also appear on the second printed page. Delete the second title after printing.

7. Print the worksheet.

8. Save the workbook and exit Excel.

Exercise 23

◆ **Critical Thinking**

You're the training manager at CompuTrain, a computer training company. Your boss has been looking into the idea of expanding the business by adding a couple of new training facilities. Your job is to summarize the projections and provide printed worksheets for your boss to study.

Exercise Directions

1. Start Excel, if necessary.
2. Open the workbook ⊙ **23_COMPUTRAIN**.
3. Save the file as **XL_23A**.
4. In cell D17, enter a formula to compute the total projected expenses for January. Copy the formula to the rest of the columns.
5. In row 8, right-align the column labels.
6. Select the range D9:O17 and format it as Accounting with the $ symbol and no decimal places.
7. Set up the worksheet for printing with the following criteria:
   a. Print the worksheet in portrait orientation on two pages with six months of data on each page.
   b. Make the first three columns appear on each page as print titles.
   c. Create a header with your name and page numbers.
8. Print one copy of the worksheet.
9. Save the file.
10. Now save the file as **XL_23B**.

11. Rearrange the worksheet to print on just one page with a summary of the totals:
    a. Copy the range C9:C17 and paste it in cells C22 and C35.
    b. Cut the range J8:O17 and paste it in cell D21.
    c. In cell D35, create a formula to calculate the total cost projection for the year for Extra Trainer Salaries. Copy the formula to the remaining items on the list.
    d. Change the text in cell C43 to *Grand Total* in bold, and add a formula in cell D43 to compute the grand total.
    e. Check the accuracy of the grand total formula by selecting the ranges D9:I15 and D22:I28 and viewing the sum with AutoCalculate.
    f. Type *12-Month Totals* in bold and 12 points, right-aligned in cell D34.
    g. Format cells D35:D43 to match similar cells in the tables above.
12. Adjust margins, page breaks, etc., as needed to print on one page.
    ✓ *If the data still looks compressed when you view it in Print Preview, open the Page Setup dialog box and use the Fit to option on the Page tab to fit the worksheet to one page wide by one page tall.*
13. Print one copy of the worksheet.
14. Save the workbook and exit Excel.

Lesson 5

Exercise 24

- ◆ Insert and Delete Selected Cells
- ◆ Insert and Delete Columns and Rows
- ◆ Move Data (Cut/Paste)
- ◆ Drag-and-Drop Editing
- ◆ Copy or Move Data with the Office Clipboard

Exercise 25

- ◆ Copy and Paste Special
- ◆ Transpose Data

Exercise 26

- ◆ Move Between Worksheets
- ◆ Rearrange Worksheets
- ◆ Name a Worksheet
- ◆ Add and Delete Worksheets
- ◆ Copy a Worksheet
- ◆ Group Sheets

Exercise 27

- ◆ Copy and Paste Special (Combine Data)

Exercise 28

- ◆ Freeze Titles
- ◆ Split Panes
- ◆ Scroll Tips
- ◆ Move Between Workbooks
- ◆ Arrange Workbooks
- ◆ Save the Workspace
- ◆ New (or Duplicate) Workbook Window

Exercise 29

- ◆ 3-D Formulas

Exercise 30

- ◆ Drag-and-Drop Editing Between Workbooks
- ◆ Find and Replace

Exercise 31

- ◆ Use Templates (Spreadsheet Solutions)

Exercise 32

- ◆ Create Original Templates

Exercise 33

- ◆ Critical Thinking

103

Exercise 24

Skills Covered:

◆ **Insert and Delete Selected Cells**

◆ **Insert and Delete Columns and Rows** ◆ **Move Data (Cut/Paste)**

◆ **Drag-and-Drop Editing** ◆ **Copy or Move Data with the Office Clipboard**

On the Job

After you create a worksheet, you may want to rearrange data or add information. For example, you may need to insert additional rows in a section of your worksheet because new employees have joined a department. With Excel's editing features, you can easily edit and rearrange rows and columns in the worksheet.

You're the payroll manager at Magnolia Steel Bearings & Fittings, and you've set up a worksheet so you can compute the payroll checks. You still need to make a few changes, however, because you forgot to include data you need, such as each employee's department number and rate. After making the final changes and calculating this week's payroll, you want to set up next week's payroll worksheet.

Terms

Cut The command used to remove data from a cell or range of cells and place it on the Clipboard.

Paste The command used to place data from the Clipboard into the worksheet.

drag-and-drop feature A method used to move or copy a range of cells by dragging the border of a selection from one location in a worksheet and dropping it in another location.

Copy The command used to place data from a cell or range of cells on the Clipboard, in order to repeat it in another location.

Undo The command used to reverse one or a series of editing actions.

Clipboard A storage location in the computer's memory that temporarily holds cut or copied data so that it can be pasted in another location. There are two Clipboards — the Windows Clipboard, which is used to copy or move data between or within Windows programs, and the Office Clipboard, which is used to copy or move multiple pieces of data between or within Office programs.

Notes

Insert and Delete Selected Cells

- You can insert or delete a selected group of cells within your worksheet data.

  ✓ *You might do this if you've entered some data into the wrong columns or rows accidentally, and you simply want to shift it over.*

- When you insert cells, surrounding cells are shifted either down or to the right in order to make room.

- Likewise, if you delete a selected group of cells, the surrounding cells are shifted up or to the left to fill the gap.

Insert and Delete Columns and Rows

■ You can insert or delete columns or rows when necessary to change the arrangement of the data on the worksheet.

✓ Although Excel uses the terms insert and delete for these operations, you can't actually insert or delete cells, columns, or rows. Every worksheet has 256 columns, 65,536 rows, 16,777,216 cells. If you insert a blank row above existing rows of data, for example, the existing data moves down one row. You're not actually adding to the number of rows in the worksheet.

■ Existing columns and rows shift their position to accommodate a newly inserted column or row.

✓ When the SUM function is used to total a range of cells in the rows directly above the formula, it will incorporate any rows inserted between the formula cell and the range specified in the argument. This adjustment is also made when columns are added in a similar situation.

■ When you delete a column or row, existing columns and rows shift their position to close the gap.

■ Before you insert or delete columns or rows, you should save the original workbook in case you have problems and need to retrieve it.

Move Data (Cut/Paste)

■ Use the **Cut** and **Paste** commands from the Edit menu or the Cut and Paste buttons on the Standard toolbar to move data.

✓ The data's format is moved with the data.

✓ You can also use drag-and-drop editing to move data. See the next section for help.

■ When data already exists in the new location, Excel gives you the option to overwrite it.

Drag-and-Drop Editing

■ The **drag-and-drop feature** allows you to use the mouse to drag selected cells to a new location and drop them.

✓ You can use drag-and-drop editing to *copy* or to move cells.

✓ The drag-and-drop feature works best when you can see both the location you're copying/moving data from (the source), and the location you're copying/moving data to (the target or destination).

✓ You can use drag-and-drop editing to copy/move data from one worksheet to the next. See Exercise 30 for more information.

✓ An outline of the selection appears as you drag it to its new location on the worksheet.

Example of drag-and-drop editing

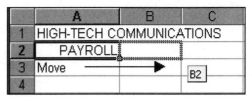

■ When data already exists in the new location, Excel gives you the option to overwrite it.

✓ Insert, delete, move, and copy operations can affect formulas, so check the formulas after you have made changes to be sure that the formulas are still correct.

■ When a drag-and-drop action doesn't move data correctly, use the **Undo** feature.

■ The Undo and Redo buttons are located on the Standard toolbar.

Copy or Move Data with the Office Clipboard

■ When you cut (or copy) data, it's temporarily stored on the **Clipboard**.

■ Actually, the data is stored on two Clipboards — the Windows Clipboard and the Office Clipboard.

Office Clipboard

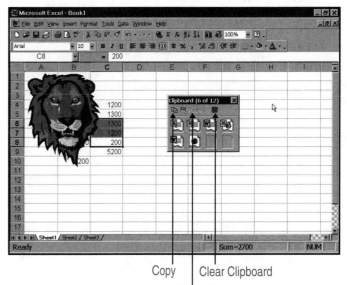

Copy   Clear Clipboard

Paste All

- The Windows Clipboard stores the last item you cut or copy.
- The Office Clipboard stores the last item as well as previously cut or copied items (up to a total of 12) so you can cut or copy multiple items with ease.
  - ✓ Data is stored on the Windows Clipboard until you copy or cut something else, which then replaces it.
- ✓ Data is not replaced on the Office Clipboard until you cut or copy the thirteenth item.
- You can paste any item you want from the Office Clipboard — multiple times, if you like.
- You can clear the Office Clipboard of all items.
  - ✓ The Windows Clipboard is cleared as well.

Procedures

Insert Cells

1. Select the range where you want to insert new cells.
2. Click **Insert**.................. `Alt`+`I`
3. Click **Cells**........................ `E`
4. Click **Shift cells right**.......................... `Alt`+`I`
   OR
   Click **Shift cells down**......................... `Alt`+`D`
5. Click `OK` .... `Enter`

Remove Cells

1. Select the range you want to remove.
2. Click **Edit**..................... `Alt`+`E`
3. Click **Delete**....................... `D`
4. Click **Shift cells left**.... `Alt`+`L`
   OR
   Click **Shift cells up**..... `Alt`+`U`
5. Click `OK` .... `Enter`

Insert Columns/Rows with the Insert Menu

1. Select as many adjacent columns or rows as number you need to insert.
   - ✓ Drag across column letters or row numbers to select entire columns or rows.
2. Click **Insert**.................. `Alt`+`I`
3. Click **Columns**.................... `C`
   OR
   Click **Rows** .... `R`

- ✓ New columns are inserted to left of selected column(s). New rows are inserted above selected row(s).

Insert Columns/Rows with Mouse

1. Select as many adjacent columns or rows as the number you need to insert.
   - ✓ Drag across column letters or row numbers to select entire columns or rows.
2. Right-click selection.
3. Click **Insert**.......................... `I`

Delete Columns/Rows with the Edit Menu

1. Select column(s) or row(s) to be removed.
2. Click **Edit**..................... `Alt`+`E`
3. Click **Delete**........................ `D`

Delete Columns/Rows with Mouse

1. Select column(s) or row(s) to be removed.
2. Right-click selection.
3. Click **Delete**........................ `D`

Cut and Paste *(Ctrl+X, Ctrl+V)*

1. Select cell or range of cells to move.
2. Click **Edit**..................... `Alt`+`E`
3. Click **Cut**............................. `T`
   - ✓ A marquee surrounds selection.
4. Select target cell or range.

- ✓ You only need to select the upper-left cell of destination range. You can also move data to another worksheet or another workbook.

To move selection to destination cells and *overwrite* existing data:

a. Click **Edit** .... `Alt`+`E`
b. Click **Paste** .... `P`

To move selection and *insert* it between existing cells:

a. Click **Insert** .... `Alt`+`I`
b. Click **Cut Cells** .... `E`
c. Click **Shift cells right**....................... `Alt`+`R`
   OR
   Click **Shift cells down** .... `Alt`+`D`
d. Click **OK** .... `Enter`

Move Selection with Drag-and-Drop Editing

1. Select cell or range of cells you want to move.
2. Move mouse pointer to border of selection.
   - ✓ The pointer shape becomes 🔍.

To move selection to destination cells and *overwrite* existing data:

a. Drag selection outline to new location.
b. Release mouse button.
c. Click **OK** .... `Enter`

To move selection to destination cells and *insert* it between existing data:

a. Press **Shift** while dragging selection outline to column or row gridline .... `Shift`

   ✓ *If you drag outline to a column gridline, existing data shifts right. If you drag outline to a row gridline, existing data shifts down.*

b. Release mouse button, and then Shift key.

Copy Selection with Drag-and-Drop Editing

1. Select cell or range of cells to copy.
2. Move mouse pointer to border of selection.

   ✓ *The pointer shape becomes* ⬉.

To copy selection to destination cells and *overwrite* existing data:

a. Press **Ctrl** while dragging selection outline to the destination .... `Ctrl`

b. Release Ctrl key, and then mouse button.

To copy selection to destination cells and *insert* it between existing data:

c. Press **Ctrl+Shift** and drag selection outline to column or row gridline........ `Ctrl`+`Shift`

   ✓ *If you drag the outline to a column gridline, existing cells shift right. If you drag outline to a row gridline, existing cells shift down.*

d. Release mouse button, and then Ctrl and Shift keys.

Display the Office Clipboard

1. Click **View** .... `Alt`+`V`
2. Click **Toolbars** .... `T`
3. Click **Clipboard** .... `↓`, `Enter`

   ✓ *The Clipboard will appear automatically if you copy or cut two items in the same program without pasting, OR copy or cut the same item twice.*

Use the Office Clipboard

- To copy a selected item, click the **Copy** button 📋.
- To paste an item from the Clipboard, click its icon 📋.

   ✓ *To identify the particular item you want, rest the mouse pointer on any icon. A ScreenTip appears, displaying a short summary of that item's contents.*

- To paste all the items from the Clipboard, click the **Paste All** button `Paste All`.

   ✓ *This button is not available in Excel if the Clipboard contains a graphic item. You need to paste individual items instead.*

- To clear the Clipboard, click the **Clear Clipboard** button 🗙.

Exercise Directions

1. Start Excel, if necessary.
2. Open 💿 **24_PAYROLL**.
3. Save the file as **XL_24**.
4. Insert two new columns between columns A and B.
5. Using the drag-and-drop feature, move the Dept data (previously D8:D18) to the new column B (B8:B18).
6. In cell C8, type the label *EE ID #*.
7. Enter the following employee ID numbers in column C:

Name	EE ID #
James Fulton	54193
Kindley Wilson	12934
Michael Ryan	43197
Maria Diaz	53149
Carol Hawkins	78664
Relia Marcus	33964
Bob Canton	79341
Lee Chang	49781
Vic Swain	63978
Walter Brown	56791

8. In column F (which is vacant, since you moved the Dept. data), type the label *Rate* in cell F8, and enter each employee's rate:

Name	Rate
James Fulton	17.35
Kindley Wilson	15.64
Michael Ryan	14.98
Maria Diaz	15.62
Carol Hawkins	17.75
Relia Marcus	14.23
Bob Canton	15.62
Lee Chang	14.78

9. You accidentally typed some information wrong:

  a. Insert cells in the range F13:F14.

  b. Shift the selected cells down.

  c. Type the correct information:

Name	Rate
Carol Hawkins	14.35
Relia Marcus	16.55
Bob Canton	17.75
Lee Chang	14.23
Vic Swain	15.62
Walter Brown	14.78

10. Adjust the widths of columns to fit the titles and data, if necessary.

11. In row 8, right-align all column headings except the first one.

12. Format the range F9:F18 with Currency format, $ symbol, two decimal places.

13. In cell G9, enter a formula to compute the gross pay:

  a. Multiply the rate times the number of regular hours.

  b. Then multiply the rate times 1.5 times the number of overtime hours.

  c. Add these two figures to compute the gross pay.

14. Copy this formula to the range G10:G18.

15. In cell O9, enter a formula to compute the net pay. Copy this formula to O10:O18.

  ✓ Net pay is the gross pay minus all taxes and other deductions.

16. Format the range G9:O18 with Currency format, $ symbol, two decimal places.

17. Using the drag-and-drop feature, move the title and subtitle from cells D4:D5 to B4:B5.

18. Set up the worksheet for next week:

  a. Click the graphic, then click the Copy button to copy it to the Clipboard.

  b. Using the Copy button, copy the range B4:B5 as well.

  c. Click in cell B25, and paste the Magnolia Steel Bearings & Fittings title and subtitle.

  ✓ Change the date in cell B26 to read March 14-20.

  d. Click in cell A21, and paste the graphic from the Office Clipboard.

  e. Clear the Office Clipboard and remove it from the screen by clicking its Close button.

  f. Using the drag-and-drop feature, copy the range A8:O18 to the range A28:O38.

  ✓ You may find this easier to do if you change the zoom level so you can see more of the worksheet.

  g. Delete the contents of the range D29:E38.

19. Select the range for the first set of payroll data (A1:O18) and print it.

  a. Change to landscape orientation.

  b. Adjust the scale so that it prints on one page.

20. Save the workbook and exit Excel.

On Your Own

1. Start Excel, if necessary.
2. Open ✪ **24_ORDER**.
3. Save the file as **OXL_24**.
4. Insert two columns between B and C.
5. Enter the labels *Cartons Ordered* and *Price per Carton* in cells C7 and D7.

   ✓ *Use two-line column labels.*

   a. Add bold formatting to C7:D7 and center the labels.

   b. Adjust the column widths.
6. Use the drag-and-drop feature to move the worksheet titles (B2:B4) to column A.

7. Type your name in cell C5.

   a. Remove the formatting from that cell.

   b. Insert two rows above row 5.
8. In the table, enter some sales data and create formulas to compute the total sale per product.
9. Create a grand total as well.
10. Format the data as you wish.
11. Preview and print the worksheet.
12. Close the file and exit Excel, saving all changes.

Exercise 25

◆ **Copy and Paste Special** ◆ **Transpose Data**

On the Job

You can control how to paste data after you copy it to the Clipboard. For example, you may want to copy cells that contain formulas to the Clipboard but only paste the results. Use the time-saving Copy and Paste Special commands for this type of editing.

You're the manager of a local video rental store called Movie Time Video. You've constructed a worksheet that tracks the rental amounts of your newest videos, and now you'd like to analyze the data. You want to transpose the column and row labels in the recap area to make it easier to read, so you'll use the Paste Special command to create the recap area.

Terms

Paste Special An editing feature used to control how data is inserted from the Clipboard into the current file.

paste options The attributes of the data that can be pasted.

Skip blanks An option that avoids replacing values in the paste area with blank cells from the copy area.

Transpose An option that pastes a column of data to a row or a row of data to a column in the current file.

Notes

Copy and Paste Special

■ The **Paste Special** feature gives you control over how to insert data into a file from the Clipboard.

■ From the Edit menu, open the Paste Special dialog box for the following options:

- **Paste options** specify the attributes of the selection to be pasted.

    - *All* pastes the contents and the formatting of the copied cells.
    - *Formulas* pastes only the formulas as shown in the Formula bar.
    - *Values* pastes only the values as shown in the cells.
        - ✓ Select *Values* if the range to be copied contains formulas that reference cells outside the copy area.

- *Formats* pastes only the formats of the copied cells.
- *Comments* pastes only the comments attached to the copied cells.
- *Validation* pastes data validation rules for the copied cells. You will learn more about validation in Lesson 10.
- *All except borders* pastes the contents and formatting of the copied cells, except for borders.
- *Column widths* pastes the column widths of the selected cells.

- **Operation** options specify the mathematical operation to be used when data from the copy area is to be combined with data in the paste area.

- **Skip blanks** skips blanks in the copy area so they don't overwrite data in the paste area.

- **Transpose** pastes a column of data in the copy area to a row or a row of data in the copy area to a column.

Paste Special dialog box

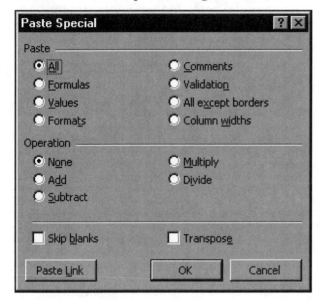

Transpose Data

■ You can copy data in a column and then paste it into a row, or copy data in a row and then paste it into a column.

■ Use the Values option and the Transpose option to transpose the results of selected formulas rather than the actual formulas.

✓ *You can't transpose actual formulas using the Paste Special command because the cell references would be invalid for the new formula location.*

The row labels are transposed and pasted into the column

	A	B	C	D	E	F
1						
2		1st Qtr.	2nd Qtr.	3rd Qtr.	4th Qtr.	
3						
4		▼				
5		1st Qtr.				
6		2nd Qtr.				
7		3rd Qtr.				
8		4th Qtr.				
9						

Procedures

Paste Special

1. Select range to copy.
2. a. Click **Edit** .... Alt+E
   b. Click **Copy** C
   OR
   a. Right-click within selection.
   b. Click **Copy** C
3. Click upper-left corner of the target range.
4. a. Click **Edit** .... Alt+E
   b. Click **Paste Special** .... S
   OR
   a. Right-click destination cell.
   b. Click **Paste Special** .... S

5. Select desired options from Paste Special dialog box.
6. Click **OK** .... Enter

Transpose Data

1. Select range to copy.
2. a. Click **Edit** .... Alt+E
   b. Click **Copy** C
   OR
   a. Right-click within selection.
   b. Click **Copy** C
3. Click upper-left corner of the target range.

4. a. Click **Edit** .... Alt+E
   b. Click **Paste Special** .... S
   OR
   a. Right-click destination cell.
   b. Click **Paste Special** .... S
5. Click **Transpose** check box .... E

   To paste transposed data as values, not as formulas:
   Click **Values** option V
6. Click **OK** .... Enter
7. Press **Escape** to clear marquee from cells .... Esc

Exercise Directions

1. Start Excel, if necessary.
2. Open 💿 **25_MOVIE**.
3. Save the file as **XL_25**.
4. Add totals:
   a. In cell C17, type a formula that computes the total copies rented of the movie *Queen Elizabeth*.
   b. Copy this formula to the range D17:M17.
5. Select the range B10:M11.
6. Press Ctrl and select the range B17:M17 as well.

7. Using the Copy and the Paste Special commands, paste the *values only* of the selected ranges as follows:
   a. Transpose the ranges.
   b. Paste the transposed range to C22:E33.
      ✓ *Just select cell C22.*
   c. Edit cell E22 so that it reads just *Total Rented*.
   d. Adjust column widths as needed.
8. In cell B20, type *Recap*.
   a. Apply Impact (or another sans serif font), 20 points.
   b. Apply bold formatting to the column labels in cells C22:E22.
9. Preview and print the worksheet.
   • Change to landscape orientation.
10. Save the workbook and exit Excel.

On Your Own

1. Start Excel, if necessary.
2. Open 💿 **25_RUGS**.
3. Save the file as **OXL_25**.
4. Add formulas to calculate the totals in row 13.
5. This report would look better if the expense items were listed in rows instead of columns. To rearrange the layout of the expense table, start by copying the range B7:H13.
6. Using the Paste Special command, transpose the values in the range to cell B18.
   ✓ *Notice that the number formatting has changed. You have transposed values, but not copied the formatting.*
7. Format the value cells with Currency style, two decimal places.

8. Cut the range B18:H24 and paste it into cell B7.
9. Enter some fictitious numbers into the blank cells in the table.
   ✓ *Notice that the totals don't change. You have transposed values, but not the formulas.*
10. Enter formulas to recalculate the totals.
11. Enter a formula to calculate a grand total of expenses for the week.
12. Format the worksheet however you like.
13. Preview and print the worksheet.
14. Save the workbook and exit Excel.

Exercise 26

Skills Covered:

◆ **Move Between Worksheets** ◆ **Rearrange Worksheets**
◆ **Name a Worksheet** ◆ **Add and Delete Worksheets**
◆ **Copy a Worksheet** ◆ **Group Sheets**

On the Job

Use workbook sheets to organize your reports. Perhaps each worksheet can represent one month's data. After organizing a workbook into individual sheets representing one month, for example, you can group multiple sheets and work on them simultaneously. When you're ready to print the worksheet, you can instruct Excel to fit the worksheet on a specific number of printed pages.

You're the owner of a small coffee shop called Java Jungle Café. You've recently started an on-line coffee business, and you're anxious to see the results of the last two month's sales. In this exercise, you'll copy a worksheet you've designed to track sales, and enter the latest sales data.

Terms

sheet tabs Labels that appear at the bottom of the workbook window and display the names of the worksheets.

tab split box A control that appears between the sheet tabs and horizontal scroll bar to control the number of sheet tabs displayed.

tab scrolling buttons Buttons that appear next to the sheet tabs and scroll hidden sheet tabs into view.

copy a sheet To copy the entire worksheet, including the arrangement of the data.

group Two or more selected worksheets.

active sheet tab The selected sheet name that appears in bold.

Notes

Tab scrolling buttons   Sheet tabs   Tab split box

Move Between Worksheets

- The default workbook window contains three sheets named Sheet1 through Sheet3.
- A **sheet tab** displays the name of each sheet.

- Point to the **tab split box**. Drag the mouse right or left to increase or decrease the number of displayed sheet tabs, respectively.
  - ✓ This will also increase or decrease the size of the horizontal scroll bar.

- When you need to bring hidden sheet tabs into view, use the **tab scrolling buttons**.

Rearrange Worksheets

- When a workbook is first created, it contains three worksheets, in order: Sheet1, Sheet2, and Sheet3.

- You can change the arrangement of these sheets when needed.

  ✓ *For example, you might want to move a worksheet containing inventory data behind the sheet that contains sales data.*

Name a Worksheet

- Initially, sheets are given generic names. If you place data on more than one sheet, giving the sheet a specific name will help you identify the type of data it contains.

- To change a worksheet's name, you change the name that appears on the worksheet's tab.

- You can use numbers, letters, special characters such as !, @, and $, and even spaces in the worksheet name.

Add and Delete Worksheets

- Right-clicking a sheet tab displays a shortcut menu with available actions.

- You can use two of the commands on this shortcut menu to add and delete worksheets in a workbook.

- A new worksheet is inserted in front of the current worksheet.

  ✓ *The new worksheet's tab is inserted to the left of the current tab, and Excel activates the new worksheet automatically.*

  ✓ *You can rearrange worksheets as needed.*

- New worksheets are always named Sheet*x*, where *x* is the next available sheet number. Excel doesn't reuse sheet numbers even if you delete the sheets to which they apply.

  ✓ *The worksheet name can be changed easily to something more specific.*

- If you delete a worksheet, all the data it contains is removed as well.

Copy a Worksheet

- When you need to copy the data in a worksheet, including the data arrangement (such as column widths), use the Move or Copy Sheet command on the Edit menu.

- When you **copy a sheet**, Excel renames the sheet tab with a new number in parentheses. For example:

  Sheet1 (2)

  ✓ *You can change the worksheet name to something more specific.*

Group Sheets

- To work on several worksheets simultaneously, select multiple worksheets and create a **group**.

  - To select contiguous worksheets, click the first sheet, hold down Shift, and click the last sheet in the group.

    ✓ *Hint: To select a worksheet, click its sheet tab.*

  - To select noncontiguous sheets, click the first sheet and then hold down Ctrl while clicking additional sheets to select them.

  - Grouped sheet tabs appear white when selected, and the name of the **active sheet tab** appears in bold.

- When you select a group, any editing, new entries, and formatting you make to the top sheet are simultaneously made to the entire group.

  ✓ *Remember to deselect the group when you no longer want to make changes to all the sheets in the group.*

- When worksheets are grouped, the [Group] indicator appears in the workbook window's title bar. If the workbook window is maximized, the [Group] indicator appears in the program window's title bar.

Procedures

Change the Number of Sheet Tabs Displayed

1. Point to tab split box.
   - ✓ Mouse pointer changes shape to split pointer ✛╟╢.
2. Click and drag split pointer left or right.

Scroll through Sheets

- Click tab scrolling button in direction you want to scroll ◁◀▶▷.
  - ✓ The first and last scrolling buttons, left to right, take you to the first or last worksheet in the workbook. The middle scrolling buttons move one sheet in the direction of the arrow.

Rename Sheet

1. Double-click sheet tab.
   OR
   a. Right-click sheet tab.
   b. Select **R**ename.............. R
2. Type new name.
3. Press **Enter**.................... Enter

Select One Sheet

1. If necessary, click the tab scrolling buttons to view hidden sheet tabs.
2. Click sheet tab to select it.

Select All Sheets

1. Right-click any sheet tab.
2. Click **S**elect All Sheets................. S , Enter

Move One Sheet Within Workbook

1. If necessary, click tab scrolling buttons to view hidden sheet tabs.
2. Click and drag sheet tab to new position.
   - ✓ Mouse pointer shape changes to . A black triangle indicates where sheet will be inserted.

Move Multiple Sheets Within Workbook

1. If necessary, click tab scrolling buttons to view hidden sheet tabs.
2. Select sheet tabs. (Press **Ctrl** as you select each new tab.)
3. Click and drag selected sheet tabs to new position.
   - ✓ Mouse pointer shape changes to . A black triangle indicates where sheets will be inserted.

Copy Sheets in Workbook with Mouse

To copy one sheet:

Hold down **Ctrl** and drag appropriate sheet tab to copy it to desired location.

- ✓ The mouse pointer changes to 🗎. A black triangle indicates where sheet will be inserted.

To copy multiple sheets:

1. Select sheets you want to copy.
   To select group of contiguous sheet tabs:
   Click first sheet tab, hold down **Shift**, and click last sheet tab.
   To select group of noncontiguous sheet tabs:
   Click first sheet tab, hold down **Ctrl**, and click additional sheet tabs.
2. Hold down **Ctrl** and drag the selected sheet tabs to copy them to desired location.
   - ✓ The mouse pointer changes to . A black triangle indicates where sheets will be inserted.

Deselect Grouped Sheets

1. Right-click any sheet tab in group.
2. Click **U**ngroup Sheets........ U
   OR
   Click any sheet tab not in group.

Delete One Sheet

1. Right-click sheet tab.
2. Click **D**elete .... D
3. Click **OK** .... Enter

Delete Multiple Sheets

1. Select sheet tabs.
2. Right-click any sheet tab in group.
3. Click **D**elete .... D
4. Click **OK** .... Enter

Insert One Sheet

1. Right-click sheet tab.
   - ✓ The new sheet will be inserted before that sheet.
2. Click **I**nsert I
3. Click **General** tab in the Insert dialog box .... Ctrl + Tab
4. Click the **Worksheet** icon .... → ←
5. Click **OK** .... Enter

Insert Multiple Sheets

1. Select number of sheet tabs that matches the number of sheets to be inserted.
2. Right-click any sheet tab in the group.
   - ✓ The new sheets will be inserted before that sheet.
3. Click **I**nsert I
4. Click **General** tab in the Insert dialog box .... Ctrl + Tab
5. Click the **Worksheet** icon .... → ←
6. Click **OK** .... Enter

Copy Sheets in Workbook with the Edit Menu

1. Select sheet(s) you want to copy.
2. Click **E**dit .... Alt + E
3. Click **M**ove or Copy Sheet........................ M

4. Select desired location in the **Before sheet** list .... `Alt`+`B`, `↑` `↓`

5. Click **Create a copy** option .... `Alt`+`C`

6. Click **OK** .... `Enter`

Group Contiguous Sheets

1. If necessary, click tab scrolling buttons to view hidden sheet tabs.

2. Click first sheet tab in group.

3. Hold down **Shift** and click last sheet tab in group.

   ✓ *The [Group] indicator appears in the title bar.*

Group Noncontiguous Sheets

1. If necessary, click tab scrolling buttons to view hidden sheet tabs.

2. Click first sheet tab in group.

3. Hold down **Ctrl** and click each additional sheet tab to be included in group.

   ✓ *The [Group] indicator appears in the title bar.*

Exercise Directions

1. Start Excel, if necessary.

2. Open 💿 **26_COFFEE**.

3. Save the file as **XL_26**.

4. Copy Sheet1, and place the copy before Sheet2.

5. On Sheet1 (2) change cell C8 to read *On-Line Sales -October*.

6. Enter these sales amounts:

	Pds. Sold
Java Columbian	234
Java Mocha Blend	218
Java Hazelnut	75
Java Kona Blend	143
Java Costa Rican	201
Java Kenyan	87
Java Amaretto	48
Java Jamaican	121
Java Breakfast Blend	256
Java Ethiopian	87
Java Expresso	121
Java Guatemala	63
Java Sumatra	75

7. Rename Sheet1 *Sept Sales*.

8. Rename Sheet1(2) *Oct Sales*.

9. Rename Chart1 *Sept Chart*.

10. Move the Sept Chart sheet to follow the Oct Sales sheet, and delete Sheet2 and Sheet3.

11. Select both the Sept Sales and Oct Sales worksheets, and make the following formatting changes to the grouped sheets:

    a. Make the column labels bold and centered.

    b. Make the row labels bold, italic, and right-aligned.

    c. Apply Accounting format (two decimal places) to the ranges C12:C24 and E12:E24.

12. Ungroup the sheets and check that the formatting changes have been made to both sheets.

13. Save the workbook and exit Excel.

On Your Own

1. Start Excel, if necessary.

2. Open 🖸 **26_BONUS**.

3. Save the file as **OXL_26**.

4. On the March worksheet, copy the ranges C8:C12 and G8:G12.

    a. Use Paste Special to paste the selection as values in cell C19.

    b. Repeat this process for the April and May worksheets.

5. Select the March, April, and May worksheets.

    a. Add the label *Bonus* in cell E19.

    b. Create formulas that calculate a bonus at 3% of net sales.

    c. Add a column called *Bonus per Person* in cell F19.

    d. Create formulas that calculate the bonus amount per person.

      ✓ Bonuses are shared equally among all employees at the store.

      ✓ Alabama Ave. store has 12 employees; Market Square has 15, Green Dale Court has 17, and County Line Road has 11.

6. Format the selected worksheets:

    a. Format the value cells D20:F23 with Currency Style.

    b. Add a title, *Bonuses*, to cell C17.

    c. Format the title and column labels as you like.

    d. Check all three worksheets to make sure the formatting is the same.

7. Copy the May worksheet and create a June worksheet.

    • Make up some sales data in the June worksheet.

8. Close the file and exit Excel, saving all changes.

Exercise 27

Skills Covered:

◆ Copy and Paste Special (Combine Data)

On the Job

With the Paste Special command, you can copy data and combine it with values in the paste area. You might want to do this to combine sales totals for several months, for example. With the Paste Special command, you can even paste the values from your formulas and combine them with data in the paste area.

You've been asked to prepare a summary worksheet for the June sales of The Harvest Time Bread Company. You have to decide what you want to include in the summary, and then combine the data from each week's worksheet.

Terms

Paste Special An editing feature used to control how data is inserted from the Clipboard into the current file.

source The area that contains the data to be copied.

destination The area that receives the copied data.

Operation options Mathematical functions that can be applied to copied data.

Notes

Combine Data

- With the **Paste Special** command, you can control how **source** data you copy to the Clipboard is pasted into a **destination** worksheet or other workbook.

- If you select any of the **Operation options** in the Paste Special dialog box, you'll combine data from the copy area with the data in the paste area.

Paste Special dialog box

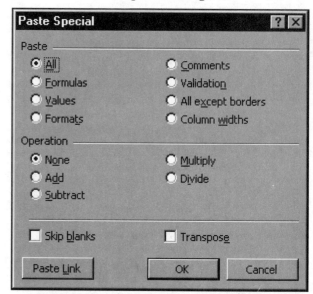

■ In order to use this function appropriately, it's very important that the two areas be set up in a similar fashion.

■ You can perform these operations:
  - Add the copied data to the data in the paste area.
  - Subtract the copied data from the data in the paste area.
  - Multiply the copied data by the data in the paste area.
  - Divide the data in the paste area by the copied data.

■ When pasting formulas, you'll need to select the Values option in order to combine the result of a copied formula with data in the paste area.

Procedures

Combine Data

1. Select range to copy.
2. a. Click **Edit** .... `Alt`+`E`
   b. Click **Copy** .... `C`
   OR
   a. Right-click within selection.
   b. Click **Copy** .... `C`
3. Click upper-left corner of the target range.
4. a. Click **Edit** .... `Alt`+`E`
   b. Click **Paste Special** .... `S`
   OR
   a. Right-click destination cell.
   b. Click **Paste Special** .... `S`
5. Select an option from the Operation area:
   a. **Add** .... `D`
   b. **Subtract** .... `S`
   c. **Multiply** .... `M`
   d. **Divide** .... `I`

To combine the results of formulas, paste them as values:
  - Click **Values** option .... `V`
6. Click **OK** .... `Enter`
7. Press **Escape** to clear marquee from cells .... `Esc`

Exercise Directions

1. Start Excel, if necessary.
2. Open 💿 27_BREAD.
3. Save the file as **XL_27**.
4. Copy the range A1:E16 from the June 7th worksheet, and paste it at cell A1 of the Summary worksheet.
5. On the Summary worksheet, select the range E7:E16.
   a. Cut the range.
   b. Insert the cut range between C7:C16 and D7:D16.
6. Copy the range F7:F16 from the June 7th worksheet to the same cells on the Summary worksheet.
   - Use Paste Special to paste only the values.
7. Select the two ranges D8:D16 and F8:F16 on the June 14th worksheet.
   a. Copy the selected ranges.
   b. Use Paste Special to paste only the values, and add those values to the ones already in the Summary worksheet.
   c. Paste the values at cell E8 of the Summary worksheet.
8. Select the two ranges D8:D16 and F8:F16 on the June 21st worksheet.
   a. Copy the selected ranges.

b. Use Paste Special to paste only the values, and add those values to the ones already in the Summary worksheet.
   c. Paste the values at cell E8 of the Summary worksheet.
9. Select the two ranges D8:D16 and F8:F16 on the June 28th worksheet.
   a. Copy the selected ranges.
   b. Use Paste Special to paste only the values, and add those values to the ones already in the Summary worksheet.
   c. Paste the values at cell E8 of the Summary worksheet.
10. On the Summary worksheet, change cell C5 to read *June Sales Summary*.
11. Right-align the labels in row 7 except for the first one.
12. In cell E18, type *June Total Sales*.
    a. Apply bold and right-aligned formatting.
    b. Create a formula to compute the total in cell F18.
13. Format the data in the Total Sales column with Currency Style, two decimal places.
14. Adjust columns widths as necessary.
15. Save the workbook and exit Excel.

On Your Own

1. Start Excel, if necessary.
2. Open 💿 27_EXPENSES.
3. Save the file as **OXL_27**.
4. In cell F5, type *Recap*.
5. Using the Copy and Paste Special commands, combine the data for each month into the Recap column. Use the Values and Add options.

6. In cell F14, create a formula totaling the column.
7. Verify the accuracy of your combining of the data by selecting the range B6:D11 and comparing the AutoCalculate total with your total.
8. Save the workbook and exit Excel.

Exercise 28

◆ **Freeze Titles** ◆ **Split Panes** ◆ **Scroll Tips**
◆ **Move Between Workbooks** ◆ **Arrange Workbooks**
◆ **Save the Workspace** ◆ **New (or Duplicate) Workbook Window**

On the Job

When working with a large worksheet, you can freeze titles to keep them in view and split the worksheet window into two or four panes. If you need to see more than one worksheet in the same workbook, you can create a duplicate workbook window. If you're working with more than one workbook, you can quickly switch from one file to the other when needed. In addition, you can arrange the workbooks on the screen so you can see them all at once. You can even save this arrangement in a workspace that can be used to quickly reopen and rearrange the same workbooks on the screen when needed.

You're the accounting manager for Movie Time Video. You've been working on a new worksheet that lists the monthly sales for each of your video stores. You want to add the October sales figures you've just received; to do that, you'll need to open a few files and arrange them on the screen.

Terms

freeze A method to keep titles in view when scrolling through a worksheet.

panes Worksheet sections that allow you to see different parts of the worksheet at the same time.

arrange Display open windows in a preset pattern.

Tiled An option to display open windows in small rectangles.

Horizontal An option to display open windows in rows.

Vertical An option to display open windows in columns.

Cascade An option to display open windows stacked with only the title bars visible.

workspace A file that allows you to save specific information about a group of open workbooks, including locations, screen positions, and window sizes.

duplicate workbook window An exact copy of the active window.

Notes

Freeze Titles

■ When you need to keep titles in view at the top or left edge of the worksheet as you scroll through it, you can **freeze** them in place.

■ Position the insertion point in the column to the right or the row below the data to be frozen and choose the Window, Freeze Panes command.

■ To remove the freeze, use the Unfreeze Panes command on the Window menu.

Column A titles remain in view as you scroll the worksheet horizontally

	A	D	E
1			
2	TYPE OF AD	MAR	
3	1/8 Page/1	$ 1,800.00	
4	1/8 Page/2	$ 1,650.00	
5	1/4 Page/1	$ 2,550.00	
6	1/4 Page/2	$ 3,200.00	
7			
8	Totals	$ 9,200.00	
9			
10			

Split Panes

- When you need to view different parts of a large worksheet at the same time, split the worksheet horizontally or vertically into **panes**.

  - When you position the cell pointer in a cell in row 1 and use the Split command, the vertically split panes scroll together when scrolling up and down and independently when scrolling left or right.

  - When you position the cell pointer in a cell in column A and use the Split command, the horizontally split panes scroll together when scrolling left or right and independently when scrolling up and down.

  - When you position the cell pointer somewhere in the middle of the worksheet and use the Split command, two of the four panes scroll together, depending on which of the four scroll bars you use.

Window split into four panes

	A	B	C	D	E
1					
2	TYPE OF AD	JAN	FEB	MAR	APR
3	1/8 Page/1	$ 1,500.00	$ 1,200.00	$ 1,800.00	$ 1,890.00
4	1/8 Page/2	$ 1,875.00	$ 1,550.00	$ 1,650.00	$ 1,732.50
5	1/4 Page/1	$ 2,500.00	$ 2,400.00	$ 2,550.00	$ 2,677.50
6	1/4 Page/2	$ 3,250.00	$ 3,000.00	$ 3,200.00	$ 3,360.00
7					
8	Totals	$ 9,125.00	$ 8,150.00	$ 9,200.00	$ 9,660.00
9					
10					
11			Total Sales	Percentage of Total Sales	
12		JAN	$ 9,125.00	6.9%	
13		FEB	$ 8,150.00	6.1%	
14		MAR	$ 9,200.00	6.9%	
15		APR	$ 9,660.00	7.3%	
16		MAY	$ 10,143.00	7.6%	
17		JUN	$ 10,650.15	8.0%	

- With the mouse, drag the horizontal or vertical split box to split the window into panes.

- To cancel the split, use the Remove Split command on the Window menu or simply drag the split bar to a parallel edge of the pane.

Scroll Tips

- If you scroll through a worksheet by dragging the scroll box, a ScreenTip will appear next to the mouse pointer displaying the approximate row or column number.

- These scroll tips make it easy for you to scroll quickly through a large worksheet and find the exact location you need.

Move Between Workbooks

- When you open a workbook, a button for that workbook appears on the Windows taskbar. As you open more workbooks, additional buttons appear.

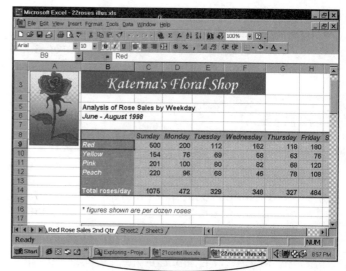

Each open file is represented by a button on the taskbar.

- You can use the taskbar to switch from one open document to another.

  - ✓ A button appears on the taskbar for each open Office document, so you can use this method to switch between programs as well.

- You can also use the Window menu to change from workbook to workbook.

  - ✓ Workbooks are listed by name at the bottom of the Window menu.

Window menu displays the list of open files

Arrange Workbooks

■ When you want to see two or more open workbooks on the screen at the same time, use the **Arrange** command on the Window menu.

■ The Arrange Windows dialog box provides four arrangement options.

Arrange Windows dialog box

• *Tiled* arranges windows in small rectangles to fill the screen.

Tiled windows

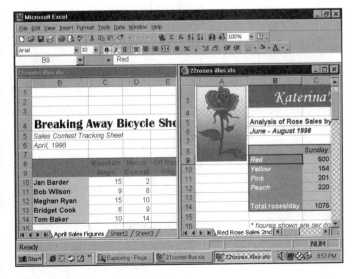

• *Horizontal* arranges windows in rows.

• *Vertical* arranges windows in columns.

• *Cascade* stacks windows with only the title bar of each in view.

Cascaded windows

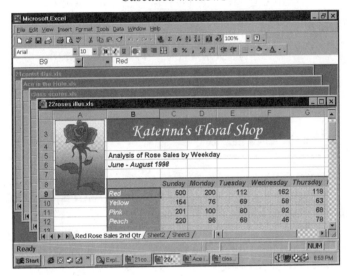

• To display just a single file again, maximize it by clicking the Maximize button ▣.

   ✓ *You can close a file by clicking its Close button* ☒.

• In any arrangement, the active window appears with a different color of title bar.

   ✓ *When you start typing, data is entered into the active window. To move from one visible window to another, click the window you wish to make active.*

Save the Workspace

■ After arranging workbooks on the screen, you can save the arrangement permanently as a **workspace**.

■ The approximate screen location, size, and arrangement of open workbook windows are saved in the workspace file.

   ✓ *Data is not saved in the workspace file; therefore, you must save each open workbook independently.*

■ After you create a workspace file and then open it, the workbooks associated with the file are automatically opened and arranged on the screen as before in one quick step.

New (or Duplicate) Workbook Window

- To view more than one worksheet in the active workbook at the same time, use the New Window command on the Window menu to open a **duplicate workbook window**.
  - Use the Arrange command on the Window menu to view the duplicate windows on the screen at the same time.
  - In each window, click the sheet tab of the sheet you want to view.

- The number of duplicate windows that can be opened is determined by the amount of system memory.
- You can add or edit data in the original or the duplicate window.
- If you close a duplicate window, the workbook itself remains open.

- When you create a duplicate window, Excel displays the workbook name in the title bar as usual, followed by a colon and a number (*worksheet title:1* and *worksheet title:2*, for example).

Procedures

Freeze Titles

1. Select the row below horizontal titles to freeze.
   OR
   Select column to the right of vertical titles to freeze.
   OR
   Select cell located in row below horizontal titles and column to right of vertical titles to freeze both titles.
2. Click **Window** .... Alt + W
3. Click **Freeze Panes** .... F
   - ✓ Use this feature if window is not split into panes.

Unfreeze Titles

1. Click **Window** .... Alt + W
2. Click **Unfreeze Panes**......... F

Split Worksheet into Panes with the Window Menu

- ✓ This feature provides simultaneous pane scrolling.

1. Select row below desired horizontal split.
   OR
   Select column to right of desired vertical split.
   OR
   Select a cell located below and to right of desired horizontal and vertical split.
2. Click **Window** .... Alt + W
3. Click **Split**............................ S

Split Worksheet into Panes with Split Boxes

- ✓ This feature provides simultaneous pane scrolling.

1. Point to horizontal split box on scroll bar ▶ .
   OR
   Point to vertical split box on scroll bar ▲ .
2. The mouse displays this pointer: ↔ .
   Drag the split box right or left along horizontal scroll bar until split is positioned.
   OR
   The mouse displays this pointer: ↕ . Drag the split box up or down along vertical scroll bar until split is positioned.

Remove Split

Double-click split bar.
OR
1. Click **Window**............. Alt + W
2. Click **Remove Split**............ S
   OR
   Drag the split bar to a parallel edge of the window.

Adjust Panes

1. Point to horizontal split box ▶ or vertical split box ▲ on scroll bar.
2. Drag the split box along scroll bar until split is positioned.

OR
Drag split bar to desired position.

Move Between Panes

Click in desired pane.
OR
Press **F6** key............................ F6
until active cell is positioned in desired pane.

Freeze Panes in Split Window

- ✓ This procedure is used to lock top or left pane when scrolling.

1. Click **Window** .... Alt + W
2. Click **Freeze Panes**............ F

Unfreeze Panes in Split Window

1. Click **Window** .... Alt + W
2. Click **Unfreeze Panes** .... F

View Scroll Tips

1. Click horizontal scroll bar or vertical scroll bar.
2. Drag scroll box to left or right on horizontal scroll bar or up and down on vertical scroll bar.
   - ✓ Note the scroll tip that appears.

Move Between Workbooks

- On the Windows taskbar, click the button of the workbook to which you wish to switch.
OR
1. Click **Window** .... Alt + W
2. Click workbook name in list at bottom of menu....... , Enter

✓ If the workbook you wish to switch to is at least partially visible, just click within its window to switch to it.

✓ If the window has been minimized in the Excel program window, double-click its title bar to restore the window.

Arrange Workbooks

1. Click **Window** .... Alt + W
2. Click **Arrange** .... A
3. Select from four options:
   - **Tiled** .... T
   - **Horizontal** .... O
   - **Vertical** V
   - **Cascade** C
4. Click **OK** .... Enter

Open Duplicate Workbook Window

1. Open workbook to duplicate.
2. Click **Window** .... Alt + W
3. Click **New Window** .... N

   ✓ To arrange just the worksheets in the open workbook, select Windows in active workbook in the Arrange Windows dialog box.

Close Duplicate Workbook Window

1. Select duplicate workbook .... Ctrl + Tab
2. Click Close button ▣.
   OR

Double-click workbook window's Control menu box.

Save a Workspace

1. Click **File** .... Alt + F
2. Click **Save Workspace** .... W
3. Type name in **Filename** text box.
4. In the **Save in** list, select the folder in which you want to save the file.

   ✓ Make sure that Workspace (*.xlw) is selected in **the Save as type** text box.

5. Click the **Save** button ...... Enter

Exercise Directions

1. Start Excel, if necessary.
2. Open ◈ **28_SALES**.
3. Save the file as **XL_28**.
4. Click in cell B13.
5. Select the Freeze Panes option on the Window menu.
6. Scroll down to the Norez Street store, and change the January sales total to $11,028.

   ✓ Notice how the row labels scroll with you, but the column labels remain stationary.

7. Scroll right and change the June total to $10,568.

   ✓ Notice how the column labels scroll with you, but the row labels remain stationary.

8. Unfreeze the panes.
9. Click in cell B13, and select the Split option from the Window menu.
10. Scroll to the right and enter these totals for October:

Nahalo Ave.	10987
El Mercado Market	11455
Lasalle Ave.	18457
Oak Street	19630
Main Street	11858
Peachtree Street	27841
La Bella Shopping Center	11234
Duez Ave.	10645
Mihalo Drive	21975

(Note: Meridan Street 21566)

Bluebird Hill	11625
Kanoga Lake Drive	20774
Siesta Market	19663
Grange Ave.	11414
Flemming Ave.	18796

11. To enter the total for Norez Street, open the file ◈ **28_NOREZ**.
12. Arrange the two workbooks in a tiled fashion.
   a. Scroll **28_NOREZ** so you can see the total for October sales.
   b. Type that total into the **XL_28** worksheet.
13. Save the arrangement as a workspace called **XL_28Oct**.
14. Close all workbooks.
15. Open the workspace.

   ✓ Notice that the two workbooks are opened and displayed as before, minus the split window.

16. Maximize the **XL_28** workbook.
17. Create a duplicate window.
18. Arrange just these two windows in a vertical fashion.
19. In the duplicate window, change to Sheet2 by clicking its tab.
   a. View the chart in the duplicate window.
   b. View the corresponding totals in the original window.
20. Save the workbooks and exit Excel.

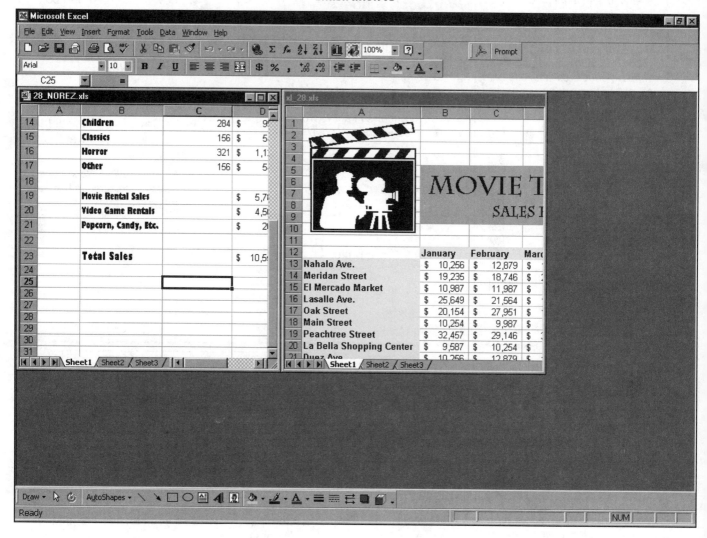

On Your Own

1. Start Excel, If necessary.

2. Open ⊙ **28_NETSPICE**.

3. Save the workbook as **OXL_28A**.

4. Add data to cells D20:E23 to represent the number of hits that two pages on your Web site have received in the last four days. (Make up these numbers.)

   a. Keep the chart in view as you add the data with the split or freeze panes method.

   b. The fictitious data you add should be in the range of the previous numbers.

5. Open ⊙ **28_WORLDSPICE**.

6. Save the workbook as **OXL_28B**.

7. You are also tracking your competitor's Web site, so add the data that you have obtained. The fictitious data you add should be in the range of the previous numbers.

8. Arrange the two workbooks in the Excel window so that you can compare the charts.

9. Save changes to both workbooks and save them as a workspace named **OXL_28SPACE**.

10. Exit Excel.

Exercise 29

Skills Covered:

◆ 3-D Formulas

On the Job

Write a 3-D formula to reference values across worksheets. For example, you may want to total or average data from several worksheets into a summary worksheet. When you want to create multiple similar worksheets, copy the sheet instead of copying and pasting the data in order to retain arrangements, such as column widths, on the new sheet. This will make it easier when summarizing data with 3-D formulas.

Your boss has asked you to create a summary of bread sales for The Harvest Time Bread Company. You're anxious to use your knowledge of 3-D formulas to create a summary worksheet.

Terms

3-D formula A formula that references values across worksheets.

3-D reference A reference to a value from any other sheet(s) used in a formula.

Notes

3-D Formulas

- Create a **3-D formula** when you want to summarize data from two or more worksheets into a summary worksheet.

- A 3-D formula contains references to values in other sheets in a workbook, called **3-D references**.

  - In a 3-D reference, exclamation points separate a sheet name from a cell reference:

    Sheet1!A1

  - Double or single quotation marks surround a sheet name that contains a space:

    "January 1998"!A1

- Colons (:) appear between sheet names to indicate a range of worksheets:

  Sheet1:Sheet3!A1:A3

- You can combine a 3-D reference with a function.

  ✓ For example, the 3-D formula
  =SUM(Sheet1:Sheet4!B4:G9)
  uses a function.

- As you create or edit a 3-D formula, you can select the cells of a 3-D reference in the worksheets or type them into the formula.

A 3-D formula to total the three cells in the worksheets below: =SUM(Sheet1:Sheet3!A2)

Procedures

Create 3-D Formula

To type 3-D reference in formula:

1. Type or edit formula.
2. Position insertion point in formula where cell reference should be typed.
3. Type sheet name.
   - ✓ *Remember to type single or double quotation marks surrounding any sheet name that contains a space.*

To type 3-D reference for range of worksheets in formula:

a. Type **colon** (:) ....
b. Type last sheet name in range.
4. Type **exclamation point** (!)..

5. Type cell reference or range.
   - ✓ *Examples:*
     Sheet2:Sheet6!C4:C10
     'Quarter1'!C4:C10.
6. Press **Enter** .... `Enter`

To insert 3-D reference in formula:

1. Type or edit formula.
2. Position insertion point in formula where cell reference should be entered.
3. Click sheet tab containing cell(s) to reference.

   To enter 3-D reference for a range of worksheets:
   - Press **Shift** and click the last sheet tab in the range to reference.

   - ✓ *The name of the sheet(s) appears in the Formula bar.*
4. Select cell(s) to reference.
   - ✓ *The complete 3-D reference appears in the Formula bar when you select the cell(s).*
5. Type or insert remainder of formula.
6. Press **Enter** .... `Enter`
   - ✓ *The formula is complete and Excel returns to the starting worksheet.*
   - ✓ *3-D references in a formula don't have to consist of ranges of contiguous cells in multiple worksheets. A formula like the following is also valid:*
     =Sheet2!B2/Sheet4!X11+ Sheet1AB19.

Exercise Directions

1. Start Excel, if necessary.
2. Open 💿 **29_BREADSUM**.
3. Save the file as **XL_29**.
4. Copy the June 28th worksheet and place the copy after that sheet.
   a. Rename the worksheet *Summary*.
   b. In cell C5, type *June Sales Summary*.
   c. Delete the range D8:G20 and delete columns D, E, and G.
   d. In cell D8, create a 3-D formula to compute the total June sales for Honey Wheat Rolls.
      - ✓ *Try creating the formula by clicking the sheet tabs and then the appropriate cell references. The first part of your formula should look something like:*
        ='June 7th'!F8 +
   e. Copy the formula to the rest of the column.
   f. In cell D18, create a formula to compute the grand total. Add an appropriate row title for this entry. Format and align the title as you wish.

5. To check your work, create a 3-D formula in cell D20 adding the *Total Sales for the week* figures from each worksheet.
   - ✓ *This time, try creating the formula by typing in the appropriate sheet and cell references.*
6. If the totals don't match, troubleshoot the formulas until they do match.
7. Save the workbook and exit Excel.

On Your Own

1. Start Excel, if necessary.

2. Open ⊚ **29_MINIMART**.

3. Save the file as **OXL_29**.

4. Create a sheet named *Summary* and place it before Sheet1.

5. Create a duplicate workbook and arrange the two workbook windows so you can see both Summary and Sheet1 at the same time.

6. From the raw data on Sheet1, use 3-D formulas to create a summary on the Summary sheet that includes the following:

   a. A table that shows each store's total sales by quarter.

   b. Annual sales by store.

   c. Total quarterly sales for all stores.

   d. Grand total for all stores.

   e. Use the MAX and MIN functions to identify the stores with the highest and lowest quarterly sales. List the store names with the values.

7. Create and format a title for the summary sheet.

8. Format labels and values to make the worksheet easily understandable.

9. Save the workbook and exit Excel.

Exercise 30

Skills Covered:

◆ **Drag-and-Drop Editing Between Workbooks** ◆ **Find and Replace**

On the Job

Rather than create a new workbook from scratch, you may wish to copy elements from an existing work-book. With the new workbook and the existing workbook arranged on the screen, you can perform this task easily using drag and drop. With drag and drop, you can copy or move items between workbooks. With Find and Replace, you can update information in a worksheet quickly and easily.

As a manager at CompuTrain, a computer training company, you've been put in charge of the budget. After compiling an estimate for next year, you discovered that there are plans in the works to add one, or possibly two, new training rooms. So you'll use drag and drop to copy the projected costs for the new rooms into your budget worksheet.

Terms

drag and drop Use the mouse to copy or move information from one location to another in a worksheet, across worksheets, or across workbooks.

Find A command that helps you locate specific data in a worksheet.

Replace A command that works with Find to replace specific data with something else.

Notes

Drag-and-Drop Editing Between Workbooks

■ If you arrange open workbooks on the screen, you can **drag and drop** to copy or move data across workbooks.

✓ You should only use drag and drop when you can see both the original data and its intended location.

✓ If you can't use drag and drop in a particular situation, you can use the Copy/Cut/Paste buttons instead.

■ To copy data, press the Ctrl key while dragging the border of the selected range from the source to the destination.

■ To move data, drag the border of the selected range from the source to the destination.

Find and Replace

■ With **Find**, you can locate text or numbers in a worksheet.

✓ You might do this to locate an area of the worksheet you need to change or view. For example, you could search for a particular employee, or a particular sales office.

■ Using **Replace**, you can replace what you find with something else.

✓ You could use this technique to quickly replace outdated information in a worksheet.

■ You can confirm each replacement, or simply replace all occurrences without confirmation.

✓ Don't use Replace All without verifying each instance unless you're absolutely sure that you won't accidentally replace the wrong data. Using Replace All to change Jan to Feb throughout a worksheet, for example, can easily change Janice Smith to Febice Smith and Tom Jansen to Tom Febsen.

Procedures

Use Drag-and-Drop Editing Between Workbooks

- Select range.
  To copy data:
  a. Press **Ctrl** while dragging border of selected range to new location in current worksheet, another worksheet, or another workbook.
  b. Release mouse, then **Ctrl** key.
  To move data:
  Drag border of selected range to new location in current worksheet, another worksheet, or another workbook.

Find (Ctrl+F)

1. Select any cell to search entire worksheet.
   OR
   Select cells to search.
   OR
   Select sheet(s) to search.
2. Click **Edit** .... `Alt`+`E`
3. Click **Find**............................ `F`
4. Click in **Find what** text box .... `Alt`+`N`
5. Type character(s) to find.

   ✓ You can use wildcard characters (* and ?) to represent any character (?) or group of characters (*) in a search. To find data containing a question mark (?) or asterisk (*), you must type a tilde (~) before the character (~? or ~*).

   To set a search direction:
   a. Click **Search** .... `Alt`+`S`
   b. Click desired search direction .... `↓`|`↑`, `Enter`

To make search case sensitive:
- Select **Match case** .... `Alt`+`C`

To find cells that match exactly:
- Select **Find entire cells only** .... `Alt`+`O`

6. Click **Find Next** .... `Alt`+`F`

   ✓ Excel selects first cell meeting the search criteria.

7. Perform one of the following:
   To find next match:
   - Click **Find Next** ...... `Alt`+`F`
   OR
   To close the dialog box and discontinue the search:
   - Click **Close** .... `Esc`

Replace (Ctrl+H)

✓ Replaces text in one or more worksheets with specified text.

1. Select any cell to search entire worksheet.
   OR
   Select cells to search.
   OR
   Select sheet(s) to search.
2. Click **Edit**..................... `Alt`+`E`
3. Click **Replace**..................... `E`
4. Click in **Find what** text box........................ `Alt`+`N`
5. Type character(s) to find.

   ✓ You can use wildcard characters (* and ?) to represent any character (?) or group of characters (*) in a search. To find data containing a question mark (?) or asterisk (*), you must type a tilde (~) before the character (~? or ~*).

6. Click in the **Replace with** text box.............. `Alt`+`E`
7. Type the character(s) you want to use as a replacement.
   To set a search direction:
   a. Click **Search**........... `Alt`+`S`
   b. Click desired search direction.......... `↓`|`↑`, `Enter`

   To make search case sensitive:
   - Select **Match case** .... `Alt`+`C`

   To find cells that match exactly:
   - Select **Find entire cells only** .... `Alt`+`O`

8. Click **Find Next** .... `Alt`+`F`

   ✓ Excel selects first cell meeting the search criteria.

9. Perform one of the following:
   To globally replace matching cells:
   - Click **Replace All** ... `Alt`+`A`
   OR
   To replace active cell and find the next match:
   - Click **Replace**......... `Alt`+`R`
   OR
   To retain contents of active cell and find next match:
   - Click **Find Next** ...... `Alt`+`F`
   OR
   To close the dialog box and discontinue the search:
   - Click **Close**.................... `Esc`

Exercise Directions

1. Start Excel, if necessary.
2. Open 💿 **30_BUDGET**.
3. Save the workbook as **XL_30**.
4. Open 💿 **30_TRAINING**.
5. Arrange both workbooks on the screen in a tiled or horizontal fashion.
6. Using drag and drop, copy the range A9:O20 from the Training Room D worksheet of the 30_TRAINING workbook to the range A23:O34 in Sheet1 of XL_30.
7. Using drag and drop, copy the range A9:O20 from the Training Room E worksheet of the 30_TRAINING workbook to the range A37:O48 in Sheet1 of XL_30.
8. Close the 30_TRAINING workbook and maximize the XL_30 workbook.
9. In cell D51, type *Budget Recap*.
   - Format the cell as bold, 12 points.
10. Using drag and drop, copy the range D39:O39 to D53:O53.

11. In cell C54, type *Original Totals*.
    a. In cell C55, type *Costs Including D.*
    b. In cell C56, type *Costs Including D & E.*
    c. Apply italic, right-aligned formatting to the range C54:C56.
12. In the range D54:O56 create formulas that display the original totals from row 20.
    ✓ *For example, you could type =D20 in cell D54.*
    a. In the range D55:O55 create formulas that compute the sum of the original totals plus the projected costs for Training Room D.
    b. In the range D56:O56 create formulas that compute the sum of the original totals plus the projected costs for Training Room D, and for Training Room E.
13. Search for *Internet* in the worksheet and replace it with *Internet/Network*. For instances where the cell already says *Internet/Network*, don't make any changes.
14. Save the workbook and exit Excel.

On Your Own

1. Start Excel, if necessary.
2. Open a new workbook.
3. Save the file as **OXL_30**.
4. Open 💿 **30_PAYROLL**.
5. Save this file as **OXL_30A**.
6. Arrange the two workbook windows and use drag and drop to copy data into the new workbook:
   a. Copy the logo and company name into the new workbook.
   b. Adjust the column widths to accommodate the logo.
   c. Copy the range B9:D17 into the new workbook.
7. Maximize the **OXL_30** workbook.

8. Compute a raise for each employee at 4.5%.
   a. Katerina and Maria get a 5.3% raise.
   b. Compute the amount of the raise per hour and the new rate.
   c. Format the columns however you like.
9. Use Find and Replace to locate some errors in the worksheet:
   a. Find employee ID 23419 and change the ID to 23421.
   b. Find employee ID 42311 and change the ID to 42312.
   c. Perform this task in both workbooks.
10. Save both workbooks and exit Excel.

Exercise 31

◆ Use Templates (Spreadsheet Solutions)

On the Job

If you want to create a new workbook, you don't always need to start completely from scratch. Excel provides a number of templates that you can use as a basis for your new worksheet. These templates provide a semi-completed worksheet that you can quickly customize to fit your needs.

You're an account manager with Investco Group, an investment company. In this exercise, you'll use an Excel template to create an expense report for a recent business trip to Chicago and several client dinners.

Terms

template A worksheet designed for a specific purpose, complete with formatting, formulas, text, and row and column labels that you can customize.

Spreadsheet Solutions This tab in the New dialog box provides a set of templates that you can use to create new workbooks.

Notes

Use Templates (Spreadsheet Solutions)

- Excel includes many customized **templates** that you can use when creating a new workbook.

- In a template, much of the work is already done for you, including most of the formatting, formulas, and layout design.

- When using a template, all you need to do is customize it as needed, and add your own data.

  - If you customize a template, you can resave it as a new template file so that you can use the already customized template as a starting point the next time.

  - You can create your own template from any Excel workbook.

    ✓ You'll learn how to create your own templates in the next exercise.

- Initially, only a few templates are available on the **Spreadsheet Solutions** tab in the New dialog box.

Spreadsheet Solutions tab

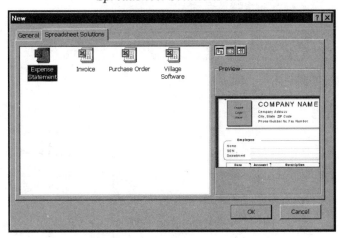

✓ You can add more templates by downloading them from the Internet.

- *Expense Statement* Use this template to create a statement of business expenses.

- *Invoice* Use this template to create an invoice.

- *Purchase Order* Use this template to create a purchase order for new equipment or office supplies.

- *Village Software* Use this icon to open a template from which you can link to the Village Software Web site, where you can order additional customizable templates. (You also can use the template form to place an order.)

  ✓ *Village Software is the creator of the Spreadsheet Solutions templates in Excel 2000.*

- Each template contains a separate worksheet into which you enter your custom information, such as company name, address, logo, etc.

- In addition, each template displays a special toolbar that you can use when customizing and completing the new workbook.

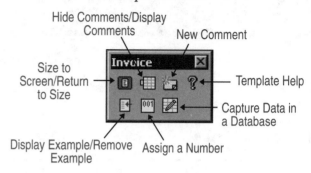

Template toolbar

Hide Comments/Display Comments
New Comment
Size to Screen/Return to Size
Template Help
Capture Data in a Database
Display Example/Remove Example
Assign a Number

- If you have enabled virus protection in Excel, a warning will display when you open a template from the Spreadsheet Solutions tab.

  ✓ *Since these templates contain macros that you need to use in order to customize the templates, you'll have to enable the macros to load each template with all its features.*

Procedures

Use a Built-in Excel Template

1. Click **File** .... Alt + F
2. Click **New** .... N
3. Click the **Spreadsheet Solutions** tab .... Ctrl + Tab
4. Double-click the desired template.

   ✓ *Some of these templates may not yet be installed — in which case, you'll need to insert the Office CD-ROM when prompted.*

Exercise Directions

1. Start Excel, if necessary.

2. Start a new workbook using the Expense Statement template.

   ✓ *Be sure to enable macros.*

3. Save the workbook as **XL_31**.

   ✓ *When prompted, continue without updating.*

   ✓ *Normally, if this were not a classroom simulation, you might want to update the employee information into the central database.*

4. Change to the Customize Your Statement worksheet.

   Enter the company name information:
   Company Name: Investco Group
   Address: 2178 Bouillon Drive, Springville, Iowa 69810.
   Phone #: (441) 798-2120
   Fax #: (441) 798-1467

6. Enter a travel reimbursement rate of $0.28 a mile.

7. Click the Lock/Save Sheet button.

   ✓ *Choose the **Lock but don't save** option.*

8. Change to the Expense Statement sheet and enter your personal data:

   Name: Bob Cooper
   SSN: 441-90-0012
   Department: International Investments
   Emp #: 497852
   Position: Account Manager
   Manager: David Cook
   From: 3/22/99
   To: 3/28/99

9. Enter expense data as shown in Illustration B.

10. Print a copy of the expense statement.

11. Save the workbook and exit Excel.

    ✓ *Excel creates a database file for your expense report template. When you close the expense report, Excel will prompt you to save changes even if you don't update the database. Continue without updating the database.*

Illustration A: Customize your statement

CUSTOMIZE YOUR EXPENSE STATEMENT

Hover your Pointer
HERE for a Useful Tip!

Type Company Information Here...

Company Name	Investco Group	Phone Number	(441) 798-2120
Address	2178 Bouillon Drive	Fax Number	(441) 798-1467
City	Springville		
State	Iowa		
ZIP Code	69810		

Specify Default Expense Statement Information Here...

Travel Reimbursement $0.28
(per mile/km)

☐ Expenses categorized as 'Entertain'
or 'Other' are non-reimbursable.

☐ Share expense statement numbers
on network.

Counter Location [   ]

☑ Enable Select Employee function.

Common Database c:\program files\microsoft office\office\library

Template Wizard Database c:\program files\microsoft office\office\library\expdb.xls

Formatted Information

Investco Group
2178 Bouillon Drive
Springville, Iowa 69810
(441) 798-2120 fax (441) 798-1467

Illustration B: Expense Statement

Investco Group

2178 Bouillon Drive
Springville, Iowa 69810
(441) 798-2120 fax (441) 798-1467

EXPENSE STATEMENT

Statement No. 1

Employee	
Name	Bob Cooper
SSN	441-90-0012
Department	International Investments

Emp #	497852
Position	Account Manager
Manager	David Cook

Pay Period
From 3/22/99
To 3/28/99

Date	Account	Description	Accom	Transport	Fuel	Meals	Phone	Entertain	Other	TOTAL
3/22/99	814567	Stockholders meeting	$234.50	$185.98		$48.73	$34.98	$34.18	$325.00	$863.37
3/23/99	814567					$42.21		$48.97		$91.18
3/24/99	814567					$32.71	$17.22	$8.93	$21.95	$80.81
3/26/99	73114	Account review				$21.65				$45.09
3/26/99	61487	New account				$73.61		$23.44	$87.97	$161.58
			$234.50	$185.98		$218.91	$52.20	$115.52	$434.92	$1,242.03

Sub Total $1,242.03
Subtract Advances
TOTAL $1,242.03

⦿ Reimbursement
◯ Payment Needed

Note
Current mileage reimbursement rate is $.28

Approved By

Office Use Only

Insert Fine Print Here

On Your Own

1. Start Excel, if necessary.

2. Create a new workbook with the Purchase Order template.

   ✓ *Be sure to enable macros.*

3. Save the workbook as **OXL_31**.

4. Create a purchase order for your new office: Include a desk, chair, computer, printer, telephone, file cabinet, and bookcase.

   a. You work for a Wall Street investment firm called LoRisk Investments.

   b. You're ordering your office equipment from a company called Nu Tek Office Equipment.

   c. The company's account number is 456-890-182. Click the Account No. option button and type the account number in the blank space next to the button.

   d. Make up any other information as needed.

5. Print a copy of the purchase order.

6. Save the workbook and exit Excel.

   ✓ *Continue without updating the database.*

Exercise 32

Skills Covered:

◆ Create Original Templates

On the Job

After spending a lot of time designing and formatting a worksheet, adding formulas, and customizing the page setup, you may find it a relief to know that you can save your work in a reusable format — called a *template*. With a template, you can create as many similar workbooks as you like, with only a minimum of effort.

As the owner of The Elegant Table woodworking shop, you need to keep track of daily sales and maintain a list of customers with their addresses for follow-up promotion. Because you'll be using a new sheet each day, you decide to design a template that contains all the necessary formulas.

Terms

template A worksheet designed for a specific purpose, complete with formatting, formulas, text, and row and column labels that you can customize.

Notes

Create Original Templates

- If you create workbooks with a lot of similar elements — a company name and logo, similar column and row labels, and so on, create one workbook and save it as a **template**.

- With a template, you can quickly create new documents that contain the same elements.

- By default, templates are saved in the C:\Windows\Application Data\Microsoft\Templates folder, although you can save them in a subfolder if you like.

  - If you create a subfolder off the Templates folder, that subfolder will appear as its own tab in the New dialog box.

New dialog box with a custom subfolder for templates

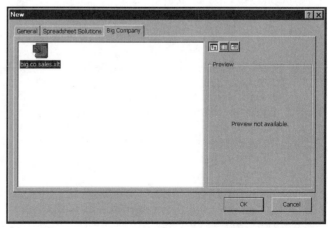

  - When saving a template, you can save it as read-only to prevent any accidental changes.

    ✓ *Template files have .XLT file name extensions.*

Procedures

Create a Template Workbook

1. Click **File** .... Alt + F
2. Click **Save As** .... A
3. Click **Save as type** ...... Alt + T
4. Select **Template**
   file type .... ⬆⬇ , Enter

   ✓ *The Templates folder is displayed. If you want to create a subfolder of your own, click the **Create New Folder** button ▣ in the Save As dialog box, type a folder name, and click **OK**.*

5. Select the file name in
   File name text box ...... Alt + N
6. Type new file name.
7. Click **Save** .... Enter

Save File as a Template with Read-Only Recommendation

1. Click **File** .... Alt + F
2. Click **Save As** .... A
3. Click **Save as type** ...... Alt + T
4. Select **Template**
   file type .... ⬆⬇ , Enter

5. Select the file name in
   File name text box .... Alt + N
6. Type new file name.
7. Click the **Tools** button.. Alt + L
8. Click **General Options** .... G
9. Click **Read-only**
   recommended .... Alt + R
10. Click **OK** .... Enter
11. Click **Save** .... Alt + S

Exercise Directions

1. Start Excel, if necessary.
2. Open 💿 **32_TABLE**.
3. Save the workbook as a template file called **XL_32.xlt**.
4. In cell C4, type *Sales for,* and in cell D4 enter today's date in the format of your choice.
5. In cell H8, enter a formula to compute the total sale for a given order.

   ✓ *Hint: You'll need to multiply the number of units that will be entered in the cells of row 8 by the price for that unit, and then add the products.*

   ✓ *The references to the cells that contain the costs of the tables should be absolute references so that you can change the price of a table without changing formulas.*

   ✓ *Your formula should look something like this: =$C$7*C8+$D$7*D8+ and so on.*

6. Copy the formula to the rest of column H, through row 27. Format the column with Currency style, two decimal places.
7. Copy cells A7:B27 to the same cells on Sheet2. Copy cell C4 to the same cell on Sheet2.

8. Copy the logo and the title to the same cells on Sheet2.
9. In cell D4 on Sheet2, enter the formula *=Sheet1!D4.* This will automatically display any new date entered on Sheet1.
10. In cell B8 on Sheet2, enter a formula that has this cell duplicate an entry in the same cell on Sheet1. Copy the formula to the rest of column B, through row 27.

    ✓ *The number 0 should appear in all the cells. The 0's can be eliminated by using an IF function, which you'll learn about in Lesson 8.*

11. In cells C7:G7 on Sheet2, enter these headings: *Street, City, State, Zip Code, Total.*
12. In cell G8 on Sheet2, enter a formula that duplicates the value in cell H8 on Sheet1. Copy the formula to the rest of column 6, through row 27.
13. On both sheets, enter a formula to calculate the grand total of the day's sales. Format to match the other dollar values.
14. Bold and center the column labels on both sheets. Adjust column widths on both pages to accommodate the data that will be entered.

15. Rename Sheet1 *Daily Sales* and rename Sheet2 *Customer Info.*

16. When you switch back and forth between worksheets, the columns with similar data will probably seem to jump sidewise because the columns widths are not the same. To fix this problem follow these steps:

    a. Create a new window.

    b. Arrange the window horizontally with a different sheet in each window.

    c. Adjust the first two columns so they're the same width and adjust the Totals columns so they're in the same location on the two sheets.

17. Save the template and close it.

18. Reopen the **XL_32.xlt** template and save it as **XL_32.xls**.

19. Enter some data on the Daily Sales sheet to see whether the formulas work properly and the data is automatically entered on the Customer Info sheet.

20. Save the workbook and exit Excel.

On Your Own

1. Start Excel, if necessary.

2. Create a template for tracking a day's worth of sales at Country Crazy Antiques.

   • Save the template as **OXL_32.xlt**.

3. You need to keep track of the salesperson who took the order, the items sold, and the dollar amount of the sale.

   ✓ *Typical items include dressers, tables, chairs, bed frames, mirrors, and accessories.*

   • You might also want to keep track of how the item was purchased (check, credit card, or cash), the inventory number for the item, a description, and the customer's name and phone number.

4. Create totals for the day's sales.

5. Format the template however you like.

6. Save the template and close it.

7. Create a new workbook based on the template, and enter today's sales.

   • Save the workbook as **OXL_32A.xls**.

8. Print the workbook.

9. Close the workbook and exit Excel.

Exercise 33

As the inventory clerk for CompuTrain, it's your responsibility to keep an eye on the amount of office and training supplies and order replacements, when needed, in a timely fashion.

Exercise Directions

1. Start Excel, if necessary.

2. Open the workbook ☻ **33_SUPPLIES**.

3. Save the file as **XL_33**.

4. Format the worksheet:

    a. Apply Arial Black, 14 points formatting to cell B9.

    b. Apply bold and the custom date format mmmm/yy to cell B10.

    c. Apply Arial, bold, 9 points formatting to the column labels.

    d. Apply Arial, italic, 10 points, right-aligned formatting to the row labels.

    e. Adjust column widths as needed.

5. Insert three rows above row 16.

6. Add these items in cells B16:E18:

    a. Highlighter-Blue, 17, 10, 20

    b. Highlighter-Yellow, 21, 10, 20

    c. Laser Printer Paper, 7, 10, 24

7. Insert a new column between columns B and C.

    a. Type the column label *Inventory Number* in cell C12 (use two lines).

    b. Format the label with Arial, bold, 9 points.

    c. Use the fill feature to enter the inventory numbers, beginning with number 21978, 21979, and so on.

    d. If Excel makes the inventory numbers italic, remove the italics.

8. In cells G13:G40, enter the reorder amount for each item, if applicable (make up numbers, subject to the following rules).

    a. Order an item only if the Beginning Inventory amount is less than the Time to Order amount.

    b. When ordering, use the amount shown in the Amount to Use When Reordering column.

    c. Type the amount you're ordering (don't enter zeroes) in column G.

9. In cells H13:H40, enter formulas that compute the ending inventory amount, including any additional items ordered.

10. Copy the Sheet1 worksheet, placing the copy just before Sheet2.

    a. Rename Sheet1 *July Inventory*.

    b. Rename Sheet1 (2) *August Inventory*.

    c. Change the date in cell B10 of the August Inventory sheet to August/99.

    d. Use Paste Special to copy the values only from H13:H40 on the July sheet to D13:D40 on the August sheet.

    e. Delete cells G13:G40 on the August Inventory sheet.

11. Move Sheet2 between the July Inventory sheet and the August Inventory sheet.

    a. Rename Sheet2 *July Order*.

    b. Copy the range B9:H40 on the July Inventory sheet to the range B4:H35 on the July Order sheet.

    c. Use Paste Special to paste the column widths and formats to the same range.

    d. Change cell B4 to *Office Supply Order*.

    e. Delete columns D, E, F, and H.

    f. Delete any rows containing items that aren't being ordered.

12. Save the workbook and exit Excel.

Lesson 6

Modify the Appearance of a Worksheet

Exercise 34

- ◆ Use the Font Tab
- ◆ Rotate Text
- ◆ Wrap Text
- ◆ Merge Cells

Exercise 35

- ◆ Change Cell Colors and Patterns
- ◆ Change Cell Borders
- ◆ Hide Worksheet Gridlines
- ◆ Format Worksheet Background
- ◆ Copy Formats with Format Painter
- ◆ Clear Cell Formats
- ◆ Create Styles

Exercise 36

- ◆ The Drawing Toolbar
- ◆ Insert AutoShapes
- ◆ Draw Objects
- ◆ Format Objects

Exercise 37

- ◆ Insert WordArt

Exercise 38

- ◆ Insert and Size Clip Art
- ◆ Download Clip Art from the Internet

Exercise 39

- ◆ Use AutoFormat to Format Ranges

Exercise 40

- ◆ Add and Format a Text Box
- ◆ Add Callouts
- ◆ Add Shadows

Exercise 41

- ◆ Critical Thinking

Exercise 34

Skills Covered:

◆ **Use the Font Tab** ◆ **Rotate Text** ◆ **Wrap Text** ◆ **Merge Cells**

On the Job

You can do some formatting with the tools on the Formatting toolbar, but if you have a lot of changes, such as changing the font, size, and color of text, it's a lot easier to use the Format Cells dialog box. Using the Format Cells dialog box offers another advantage as well — it provides quick access to other formatting options, such as changing alignment, adding borders and patterns, and adjusting number formats.

You're a lawyer at the law firm Peterson, Barney, and Smith. Every week, you must prepare a worksheet detailing your cases for review by a senior partner. You've entered the data for this week, but you want to jazz up the worksheet with some snazzy formatting.

Terms

font A set of characters that share the same design. By default, Excel uses Arial font for any data you enter, but you can easily change the font when necessary.

point The size of text is measured in points. A point is equal to $\frac{1}{72}$ inch. By default, Excel uses 10 point text. To make text larger, choose a higher number of points. To make text smaller, choose a lower number.

alignment Text can be aligned against the left or right margins of a cell, or centered. Text can also be aligned vertically in a cell, along the top or bottom margins, or centered vertically.

Notes

Use the Font Tab

- To apply multiple formats to data, use the Format Cells dialog box.

  ✓ *You can also format data with the appropriate toolbar buttons, as explained in Exercise 13.*

- One change you can make using the Font tab of the Format Cells dialog box is selecting a different font.

- A **font** is a set of characters that share a similar design.

✓ *When selecting a font, choose TrueType fonts (marked by a TT symbol) whenever possible. TrueType fonts are displayed on the screen in approximately the same manner in which they will appear when printed, which is not always true of other font types.*

- The font size is the height of the characters, measured in **points**.

  ✓ *A point is $\frac{1}{72}$ inch.*

  ✓ *When the size of a font is changed, Excel automatically adjusts the row height but doesn't adjust the column width.*

- The current font name (usually Arial) is displayed in the Font box, and the current font size is displayed in the Font Size box.

    ✓ *You can change the default font that Excel uses. Just select the General tab in the Options dialog box. You can then select the standard font and font size you want.*

- When you use the Format Cells dialog box to change the font and size of data, you can apply additional formats as well, such as bold, italic, or underline. You can also select a font color and other special formatting.

Font tab in the Format Cells dialog box

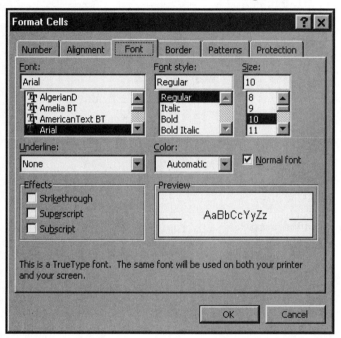

Rotate Text

- You can align text horizontally using the Formatting toolbar, as discussed in Exercise 7.

- With the **Alignment** tab in the Format Cells dialog box, you can align text vertically (at the top, bottom, or center of the cell), and rotate it as well.

- When you enter a positive number in the Degrees box, text is rotated from horizontal to read from lower left to upper right in the cell.

- When you enter a negative number in the Degrees box, text is rotated from horizontal to read from upper left to lower right in the cell.

Alignment tab in the Format Cells dialog box

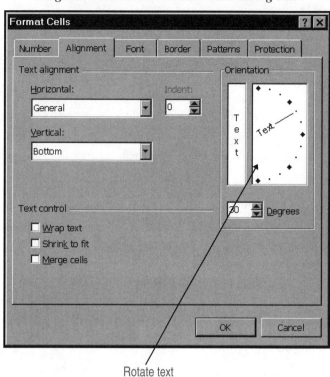

Rotate text

Wrap Text

- On the Alignment tab, the Wrap text option allows you to enter more text within one cell.

    ✓ *When you don't use the Wrap text option, and you enter a long label or other text, it will overflow into the next cell, if that cell is empty. If that cell contains data, the text is cut off until you widen the column to display it.*

- You can use the Wrap text option when you need to enter long column labels or notes, for example.

- When text is wrapped, it's displayed on multiple lines so that it fits between the cell's left and right margins.

    ✓ *Row height is not adjusted when you wrap text, so you may need to adjust it manually.*

Merge Cells

- To combine a range of cells into one cell, select the Merge cells option on the Alignment tab of the Format Cells dialog box.

- If the cells you want to merge contain data, only the data in the upper-left cell in the range will be retained. Any data in the other cells of the merged range will be cleared.

- You can use the Merge cells option with the Wrap text option, if desired.

Procedures

Change Data Using Format Tab *(Ctrl+1)*

1. Select cell(s) or characters in a cell to format.
2. Click **Format** .... `Alt`+`O`
3. Click **Cells** .... `E`
4. Select **Font** tab .... `Ctrl`+`Tab`

   To set font:

   a. Click **Font** .... `Alt`+`F`

   b. Select desired font .... `↑↓`

   To set font style:

   a. Click **Font style** ..... `Alt`+`O`

   b. Select desired style .... `↑↓`

   To set font size:

   a. Click **Size** .... `Alt`+`S`

   b. Select desired font size .... `↑↓`

   To set underline:

   a. Click **Underline** ...... `Alt`+`U`

   b. Select desired style .... `↑↓`

   To set a color:

   a. Click **Color** .... `Alt`+`C`

   b. Select the desired color .... `↑↓`

To select a special effect:

- Click **Strikethrough** .... `Alt`+`K`
- Click **Superscript** ... `Alt`+`E`
- Click **Subscript** ...... `Alt`+`B`
5. Click **OK** .... `Enter`

Rotate Text *(Ctrl+1)*

1. Select cell(s) to format.
2. Click **Format** .... `Alt`+`O`
3. Click **Cells** .... `E`
4. Select **Alignment** tab ... `Ctrl`+`Tab`
5. Select **Degrees** .... `Alt`+`D`
6. Enter degrees of rotation.

   OR

   Use the mouse to move the pointer to the rotation setting.

   OR

   To display text so that it reads vertically in the cell, click the box to the left of the Orientation dial (with the word *Text* displayed vertically).
7. Click **OK** .... `Enter`

Wrap Text *(Ctrl+1)*

1. Select cell(s) to format.
2. Click **Format** .... `Alt`+`O`
3. Click **Cells** .... `E`
4. Select **Alignment** tab ... `Ctrl`+`Tab`
5. Select **Wrap text** .... `Alt`+`W`
6. Click **OK** .... `Enter`

   OR

   Type the label and press **Alt+Enter** at the point(s) at which you wish to wrap the text.

Merge Cells

1. Select cells to format.
2. Click **Format** .... `Alt`+`O`
3. Click **Cells** .... `E`
4. Select **Alignment** tab .... `Ctrl`+`Tab`
5. Select **Merge cells** ...... `Alt`+`M`
6. Click **OK** .... `Enter`

   ✓ *If the selected range contains data, Excel will warn you that only the data in the upper-left cell in the range will be retained.*

Exercise Directions

1. Start Excel, if necessary.

2. Open ⊚ **34_CASES**.

3. Save the file as **XL_34**.

4. Using the Format Cells dialog box, change the text in cell D6 to the font of your choice, using regular style, 24 points, double underlined.

5. Again using the Format Cells dialog box, change the text in cell B8 to Arial Rounded MT Bold, 12 points.

6. Use the Formatting toolbar to change the text in cell B9 to 10 points.

7. Select cells B11:H11.

8. Using the Format Cells dialog box, change the text in the selected cells to Arial Rounded MT Bold, 10 points.

9. Using the Alignment tab, continue to format the selected cells, changing their orientation to 30 degrees.

10. Select cells H12:J12.

11. Using the Format Cells dialog box, change the selected cells to Arial Narrow, regular style, 8 points.

12. Using the Alignment tab, continue to format the selected cells, selecting the Wrap text and Merge cells options.

13. Repeat steps 10 and 11, selecting cells H13:J13, then cells H14:J14, and finally, cells H15:J15.

14. Adjust the height of row 15 so the text in cells H15:J15 is displayed.

    ✓ *Row height is adjusted in a manner similar to column width (Exercise 7). Drag the bottom edge of row 15 downward until the text is revealed.*

15. Save the workbook and exit Excel.

On Your Own

1. Start Excel, if necessary.

2. Start a new worksheet and save it as **OXL_34**.

3. Type *Pete's Pets* at the top of the worksheet.

4. Create columns for each day of the week (the store is closed on Mondays, but open Saturday and Sunday). Add a *Totals* column.

5. Create rows labeled Birds, Dogs, Cats, Fish, and Other.

6. Type in some fake sales data, depicting the number of items sold each day.

    ✓ *For example, you might have sold 10 dogs on Tuesday.*

7. Format the title, column, and row labels however you like, using the Format Cells dialog box.

    ✓ *Make sure you try various fonts, font sizes, and effects.*

    ✓ *Be sure to also try various alignment styles including rotated text and merged cells.*

8. Print your worksheet.

9. Save the file and exit Excel.

Exercise 35

Skills Covered:

◆ **Change Cell Colors and Patterns** ◆ **Change Cell Borders**
◆ **Hide Worksheet Gridlines** ◆ **Format Worksheet Background**
◆ **Copy Formats with Format Painter** ◆ **Clear Cell Formats**
◆ **Create Styles**

On the Job

Each worksheet tells a story — of lost profits, increased costs, or skyrocketing sales. To help your worksheet tell its "story," you can add shading to highlight important information, and borders to help organize information in a complex worksheet. After applying appropriate formats to a group of cells, use the Format Painter to quickly copy your selections throughout the worksheet. If you create a lot of worksheets, you can save your selections as a style, so you can quickly apply those saved formats to new worksheets as well.

You're the manager of Pine Tree Apartments, a very popular apartment complex located on the north side of Bigtown, Texas. In fact, the complex is so popular that you have a pretty long waiting list. With so many people anxious to rent from you, you've decided to create a worksheet that lists apartments that will become available soon. You've entered the raw data, but now you want to format the worksheet before you print it.

Terms

pattern A cell can be filled with a plain color and/or a pattern. A pattern is laid on top of the cell in your choice of layouts, such as a vertical stripe or a thin crosshatch. You can also select a pattern of dots, which has the effect of muting the fill color so that it's less intense.

reverse type Normal type is typically black on a light background; reverse type is white text on a black or dark background.

border An outline applied to the sides of a cell.

gridlines A light gray outline that surrounds each cell on the screen. Gridlines don't normally print; they're there to help you enter your data into the cells of the worksheet.

Format Painter A button on the Standard toolbar that allows you to copy formatting from a selected object or cell and apply it to another object or cell.

style A set of formats that are saved together with a special name. You can apply the formats to other cells by simply applying the style you saved.

Notes

Change Cell Colors and Patterns

■ Cells in a worksheet can be filled with a background color and/or **pattern**.

✓ *Even if you're using a black-and-white printer, you can still achieve an interesting look by applying a fill color to the cells. Depending on the color you choose, the cell may appear light, medium, or dark gray when printed.*

✓ *A fill color without a pattern can be applied by using the Fill Color button on the Formatting toolbar. For the greatest variety, use the Format Cells dialog box to apply color.*

■ When changing the fill color of a cell, you may also wish to change the font color of the data inside.

✓ *Font color can be set with the Font tab in the Format Cells dialog box. It's more efficient, however, to use the Font Color button on the Formatting toolbar.*

■ It's possible to display and print data in white against a black (or dark colored) background. This is sometimes called **reverse type**.

Change Cell Borders

■ To outline or separate data, you can include a variety of line styles that **border** the edge (top, bottom, left, or right) of a cell or range of cells.

✓ *Borders can be set with the Border tab in the Format Cells dialog box or by using the Borders button on the Formatting toolbar.*

Border tab in the Format Cells dialog box

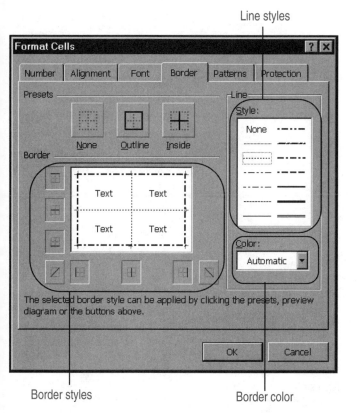

Line styles

Border styles

Border color

■ The Border tab contains many preset border styles from which you can choose, or you can set a border exactly where you want.

✓ *You can vary the border line style and color as well.*

Hide Worksheet Gridlines

■ Although cell **gridlines** appear on the screen, they don't print unless you select the Gridlines option on the Sheet tab in the Page Setup dialog box.

● If you don't want to view the gridlines on the screen, you don't have to.

● To turn off gridlines, open the Tools menu, select Options, and click the View tab. Then select the Gridlines option to turn it on or off.

■ To print the gridlines, you can apply borders to individual cells, or you can turn on an option to print the gridlines.

● Open the File menu, select Page Setup, and click the Sheet tab. Then select the Gridlines option to turn it on or off.

Format Worksheet Background

■ You can add a graphic to the background of the worksheet, behind the data.

■ For the best effect, be sure to use a graphic that's very light in color, so that your data can still be read.

■ A worksheet background, while visible on the screen, doesn't print.

■ The background isn't included when you create a Web page from the sheet, unless you create the Web page from the whole workbook.

Copy Formats with Format Painter

■ Once you make several formatting selections for a cell or group of cells, you may wish to duplicate those settings elsewhere in the worksheet.

■ The **Format Painter** button ▨ on the Standard toolbar allows you to copy all the formats from one cell to another in two steps.

■ You can "paint" formats from a cell onto as many other cells as you like.

■ The Format Painter copies all formats, including font, font size, cell background, and borders.

Clear Cell Formats

- You can clear all formats from a cell or range with the Clear, Formats command on the Edit menu.
- When you delete cell contents, cell formats aren't removed.
- You can clear a cell of its formats without removing its contents.
  - If you clear a cell of both data and formats, you also remove any attached comments.
  - If you delete the contents of a cell but not the formats, when you later type something else in the cell, it takes on the former format of the cell.
- When you clear a cell's formats, the data is then displayed in General format.
  - In General format, text is displayed left-aligned, and numbers are displayed right-aligned in the cell.

Create Styles

- Another method of reusing formats is to create and name a **style** that can be used when needed.
- For example, you can create a label style and use it to format the column labels on all your worksheets.

Procedures

Change Cell Color Using the Formatting Toolbar

1. Select cell(s) to format.
2. Apply the color you want.
   - Click the **Fill Color** button 🖌️ to apply the displayed color.

   OR

   a. Click arrow on the **Fill Color** button 🖌️.
      - ✓ *Excel displays a color palette.*

   b. Click desired color on palette.
      - ✓ *To apply colors to several cells or ranges during the same session, drag color palette off the toolbar to keep the color palette open.*

Set Color or Pattern Using the Format Cells Dialog Box
(Ctrl+1)

1. Select cell(s) to format.
2. Click **Format**.............. Alt + O
3. Click **Cells** .... E
4. Click **Patterns** tab ...... Ctrl + Tab

   To select a fill color for cells:
   - Click desired color .... Alt + C, ↕ in **Color** palette.

   To select a pattern for cells:
   a. Click **Pattern** .... Alt + P
   b. Select a pattern .. ↕, Enter
   c. Click **Pattern** again .... Alt + P
   d. Select a pattern color, if desired............. ↕, Enter
5. Click **OK** .... Enter

Change Borders Using the Formatting Toolbar

1. Select cell(s) to format.
2. To select the border you want:
   - Click the **Borders** button ▦ to apply the displayed border.

   OR

   a. Click arrow on the **Borders** button ▦.
      - ✓ *Excel displays a border palette.*

   b. Click desired border on palette........... ↕, Enter
      - ✓ *To apply borders to several cells or ranges during the same session, drag border palette off the toolbar to keep the border palette open.*

Change Borders with the Format Cells Dialog Box *(Ctrl+1)*

1. Select cell(s) to format.
2. Click **Format** .... Alt +O
3. Click **Cells** .... E
4. Click **Border** tab .... Ctrl + Tab
5. Select a **Style** ..... Alt + S , ⬆⬇
6. Select a
   Color .... Alt + C , ⬄ , Enter
7. Select a border setting:
   - **None** .... Alt + N
   - **Outline** .... Alt + O
   - **Inside** .... Alt + I

   ✓ *You can create a custom border by clicking one of the other preset designs, or by clicking inside the preview box at the point(s) where you would like to add a border line.*

8. Click **OK** .... Enter

Remove All Borders from Cells

1. Select cell(s).
2. Press **Ctrl+**
   Shift+- (minus).... Ctrl + Shift + -

Format Sheet Background

1. Click **Format** .... Alt +O
2. Click **Sheet** .... H
3. Click **Background** .... B
4. Select the file you want to use as a background.

   ✓ *The graphic will be tiled to fill the worksheet.*

5. Click **Insert** .... Enter

Copy Formats Using Format Painter

- Select cell(s) containing formats to copy.

   To copy formats only once:

   a. Click **Format Painter** button 🖌 on Standard toolbar.
   b. Select cell or range where you want to apply the formats.

   OR

   To copy formats to several ranges:

   a. Double-click **Format Painter** button 🖌 on Standard toolbar.
   b. Select destination cells.
   c. Repeat step b for as many cells as desired.
   d. Click **Format Painter** button 🖌 to end copying.

Create a Style by Example

1. Select cell containing desired formats.
2. Click **Format** .... Alt +O
3. Click **Style** .... S
4. Type a name in the **Style name** text box.

   ✓ *You can remove certain elements (such as the font) from the style by deselecting them.*

5. Click **OK** .... Enter

Apply a Style

1. Select cell or range(s) to be formatted.
2. Click **Format** .... Alt +O
3. Click **Style** .... S
4. Select desired
   Style name .... ⬆⬇ , Enter
5. Click **OK** .... Enter

Clear Cell Formats

1. Select cell or range(s) to be cleared.
2. Click **Edit** .... Alt + E
3. Click **Clear** .... A
4. Click **Formats** .... F

Clear Cell Borders

1. Select cell or range(s) to be cleared.
2. Press **Ctrl+Shift+-** (minus) ....
   .... Ctrl + Shift + -

Exercise Directions

1. Start Excel, if necessary.

2. Open 💿 **35_APARTMENT**.

3. Save the file as **XL_35**.

4. Select the cells C5:H5, and format them using the Format Cells dialog box with Times New Roman font, 20 points, White.

5. With the cells still selected, change the horizontal alignment to Center. Select the Merge cells option as well.

6. With the cells still selected, select a Sea Green for the fill color.

7. Select cell B9 and use the Formatting toolbar to add italics.

8. Select cell B11.

9. Change to Arial Black font, 8 points, Light Yellow, using the Format Cells dialog box.

10. Use the Format Painter to copy the format of cell B11 to cells C11:I11.

11. On the Patterns tab in the Format Cells dialog box, select Sea Green for the range B11:I11.

12. Select cells F11 and G11, and change their alignment to 45 degrees.

13. Select cells B11:I19, and add a Yellow border in your choice of style.

    ✓ Select the color first and then add the border.

14. You don't need to include the rental amount in your report.

    a. Delete the contents of the range I11:I19.

    b. The formats still remain. Remove them as well.

    c. If the Yellow border on the right side of the report got lost in the process, replace it.

15. Select the label, *Pine Tree Apartments*.

16. Using your selection, create a style called Title with the Format, Style command.

    ✓ Accept all elements of the style — Number, Alignment, Font, and so on.

17. Select cell B11 and create a second style called Column Labels.

    ✓ Don't accept the Border element of the style.

18. Using your new styles, format the title and column labels on the February Available worksheet.

    ✓ You'll need to merge the title cells manually by selecting C5:H5 and clicking the Merge and Center button on the Formatting toolbar.

    ✓ In addition, you'll need to apply 45° orientation to cells F11 and G11, using the Alignment tab in the Format Cells dialog box.

19. Apply italics to cell B9, and add a Yellow border to cells B11:H16, to make the February Available worksheet look the same as the January Available worksheet.

20. Print the worksheet.

21. Save the workbook and exit Excel.

On Your Own

1. Start Excel, if necessary.

2. Open **OXL_34**, the file you created in Exercise 34, or open ⊚ **35_PETS**.

3. Save the file as **OXL_35**.

4. Using the Format, Sheet, Background command, add a background graphic to the worksheet.

   ✓ Use the file ⊚ *BW_DOG.BMP* as your background.

5. Add a different fill color to the background of your worksheet title (Pete's Pets).

6. Add the same fill color to the column and row labels.

7. Add a border anywhere you like.

   ✓ For example, you might add a border around the title, or around the data area, or both.

   ✓ If you added totals for each category to your worksheet, you could place a different border around the totals area.

8. Preview the worksheet.

   ✓ Notice that the worksheet background isn't displayed. It won't print; it's for on-screen viewing only.

   ✓ Notice also that the gridlines aren't visible in Print Preview. They don't normally print, even if they're displayed on the screen.

9. Turn off the gridlines with the Options dialog box.

10. Preview the worksheet again.

    ✓ Notice that the gridlines still aren't displayed.

11. Print the worksheet.

    ✓ Remember that gridlines are not normally printed. If you want gridlines to print, use the File, Page Setup command (Sheet tab).

12. Save the workbook and exit Excel.

Exercise 36

On the Job

After putting all that hard work into designing and entering data for a worksheet, of course you want it to look its best. In previous lessons, you've learned how to add formatting, color, and borders to a worksheet to enhance its appeal. But to make your worksheet stand out from all the rest, you may need to do something "unexpected," such as adding your own art. You can quickly insert predesigned AutoShapes or draw your own designs with the tools on the Drawing toolbar.

You're the office manager of a small OB/GYN office. Doctor Child has asked you to compile a list of the upcoming deliveries — based on either expected due dates or scheduled cesareans. You've put the raw data together, but since you're new, you'd like to impress the good doctor with your knowledge of Excel. So you're going to dress up the worksheet with some simple AutoShapes and drawings.

Terms

object A distinct entity that can be inserted, deleted, moved, resized, formatted, and otherwise manipulated separately from the document itself.

AutoShape A predesigned object (such as a banner or star) that can be drawn with a single dragging motion.

handles When an object is selected, small handles black boxes appear around its perimeter. You can resize an object by dragging these handles.

adjustment handle A yellow diamond-shaped handle that appears with some objects. You can drag this handle to manipulate the shape of the object.

order The position of an object with respect to other objects that are layered or in a stack.

stack Objects can be layered on top of one another, partially obscuring the objects underneath. Use the Order command on the Draw button to change the position of a selected object within the stack.

group Objects can be grouped together so they can act as a single object. Grouping makes it easier to move or resize a drawing that consists of several objects.

format The process of adding color, patterns, and/or borders to an object.

Notes

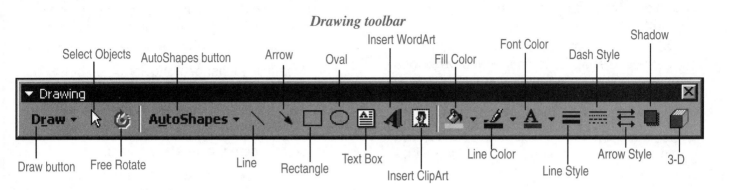

Drawing toolbar

The Drawing Toolbar

■ The Drawing toolbar has all the tools you need to add drawn **objects** to the worksheet.

■ From the toolbar, you can select **AutoShapes** or click buttons to insert WordArt or clip art.

■ The Drawing toolbar provides tools for drawing lines, arrows, circles, rectangles, and text boxes (for adding text).

■ The Draw button provides a menu that you can use to group, order, align, rotate, and edit an object:

- *Group, Ungroup, and Regroup* After selecting several objects (such as a square and a circle), you can group them together so they can be moved as one. You can later ungroup and then regroup the same objects.

- *Order* With this command, you can place an object "underneath" or "on top of" another object.

- *Snap* Quickly align an object to a grid or to another object.

- *Nudge* Move an object by very small increments.

- *Align or Distribute* Align two or more objects to an imaginary line.

- *Rotate or Flip* Rotate an object (move around its center) or flip an object (flip horizontally or vertically).

- *Reroute Connectors* Changes the path of the AutoShape connector line connecting two objects, such as an oval and a rectangle.

  ✓ *The rest of the commands on the Draw menu are used on AutoShapes only.*

Insert AutoShapes

■ With the AutoShapes button on the Drawing toolbar, you can create many shapes.

■ The AutoShapes button works with a simple menu system that makes it easy for you to select the shape you want to insert.

■ To insert an object, simply select the shape you want, then drag in a cell to create it — no drawing needed!

AutoShapes

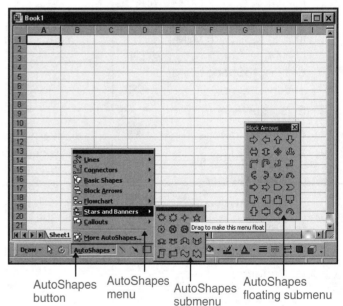

AutoShapes button — AutoShapes menu — AutoShapes submenu — AutoShapes floating submenu

■ An AutoShape can also be resized, moved, and copied, like any other object (such as clip art).

■ To resize an object, drag one of the selection **handles**.

■ To manipulate the shape of an object, drag the **adjustment handle** if one is available with that particular object.

- To add text to an AutoShape, click the shape and type the text.
- Add AutoShape arrows, starbursts, and banners to highlight important information in your worksheet.
- You can move shapes so that they partially cover other shapes. To change the **order** of objects that are layered (in a **stack**), use the Draw, Order command to control which object is brought forward or sent back.
- Use the Draw, Group command to **group** two or more objects together so they act as one object.

Draw Objects

- You can draw objects such as lines, arrows, rectangles, and text boxes by selecting the appropriate tool on the Drawing toolbar and dragging in the worksheet.
- Treat drawn objects the same as AutoShapes when sizing, formatting, etc.

Format Objects

- With the tools at the right side of the Drawing toolbar, you can **format** shapes and objects you've drawn by adding fill color and patterns, changing border size and color, rotating, etc.
  - *Fill Color* Fill the selected object(s) with color.
  - *Line Color* Change the color of the border surrounding the selected object.
  - *Font Color* Change the color of selected text.
  - *Line Style* Change the thickness of the border surrounding the selected object.
  - *Dash Style* Change the style of the dashed or solid border surrounding the object.
  - *Arrow Style* Change the style of the selected arrow object or change a line to an arrow.
  - *Shadow* Add a drop shadow to an object, a cell, or a range of cells.
- *3-D* Make an object appear three-dimensional.

Procedures

Insert an AutoShape

1. If necessary, click the **Drawing** button 🔲 on the Standard toolbar to show the Drawing toolbar.
2. Click **AutoShapes** button .... Alt + U
3. Select submenu:
   a. **Lines**............................. L
   b. **Connectors**................. N
   c. **Basic Shapes**............... B
   d. **Block Arrows**............... A
   e. **Flowchart**..................... F
   f. **Stars and Banners** .... S
   g. **Callouts**........................ C
   h. **More AutoShapes** .... M

   ✓ Selecting *More AutoShapes* displays the More AutoShapes window, which contains many shapes you might want to insert, such as banners, bubbles, and line art.

4. Click the desired shape......

5. Click in the worksheet or chart where you want to draw the shape.
6. Drag downward and to the right, creating the shape.

Draw Object

1. If necessary, click the **Drawing** button 🔲 on the Standard toolbar to show the Drawing toolbar.
2. Click desired drawing tool on Drawing toolbar.
3. Click the worksheet or chart where you want to draw the shape.
4. Drag downward and to the right, creating the shape.

   ✓ Use the **Shift**, **Alt**, and **Ctrl** keys to affect the objects as you draw. For example, hold down **Shift** while drawing a rectangle to draw a perfect square. If you press **Alt**, the object is sized to fit the cells in which it's drawn. Press **Ctrl** and the object is sized vertically, horizontally, or diagonally from the center.

5. If you draw a text box, a blinking insertion point indicates that you can type text.

   ✓ You can use the tools on the Formatting toolbar or Format menu to change the style of the text.

Format Object

1. Select object.
2. Right-click and select **Format AutoShape**............. O

   OR

   a. Click **Format**.......... Alt + O
   b. Click **AutoShape**............ O

3. Use the Colors and Lines, Size, Protection, Properties, and Web tabs to format the AutoShape.

   ✓ You can quickly format an AutoShape with the buttons on the Formatting and Drawing toolbars, such as Fill Color, Line Color (which colors the outer border), Line Style, Arrow Style, Shadow, and 3-D.

4. Click **OK**..........................

Resize Object

1. Click object to select it.
2. Position mouse pointer over a handle.
3. Click handle and drag outward to make the shape larger, or inward to make it smaller.
   a. To resize the object proportionally, press **Shift** and drag a corner handle.
   b. To resize the object in one direction, drag the handle in that direction.
   c. To resize the object from the center outward, press **Ctrl** and drag a handle.
   d. To resize the object proportionally from the center outward, press **Ctrl+Shift** and drag a corner handle.
   e. If a yellow diamond-shaped adjustment handle appears with the object, you can drag it to manipulate the shape of the object.
4. Release mouse button.

Move Object

1. Click object to select it.
2. Position mouse pointer over shape.
3. Click and hold mouse button as you drag object.
4. Release mouse button.

Change Order of Stacked Objects

1. Select object you wish to bring forward or send backward.
2. Click **Draw** button........ Alt+R
3. Click **Order**......................... R
4. Choose from:
   a. **Bring to Front**.............. T
   b. **Send to Back**............... K
   c. **Bring Forward**............. F
   d. **Send Backward**........... B

   ✓ Hint: The **Bring Forward** and **Send Backward** buttons move the object one place at a time in the stack. You may have to select these buttons repeatedly to move the object to the correct position.

Group Objects

✓ Grouped objects can be resized, formatted, copied, deleted, and moved as one object.

1. Hold down **Shift** and select the objects you want to group.

   ✓ You can also use the **Select Objects** tool on the **Drawing toolbar** to select multiple objects by dragging an outline around them.

2. Click **Draw** button........ Alt+R
3. Click **Group**........................ G

Ungroup Objects and Regroup Objects

1. Select grouped objects.
2. Click **Draw** button........ Alt+R
3. Click **Ungroup**.................... U
4. Leave ungrouped if you wish, or make adjustments and then:
   a. Click **Draw** button... Alt+R
   b. Click **Regroup**................ O

Exercise Directions

1. Start Excel, if necessary.
2. Open ◉ **36_BABIES**.
3. Save the file as **XL_36**.
4. Select the ranges C6:J6 and B10:J11. Apply Brown fill color and White font color.

   ✓ Hint: When you point to a color on any of the color palettes, Excel displays a ScreenTip with the color's name.

5. Select the three ranges C7:J7, B12:B15, and J12:J15. Apply Tan fill color.
6. Select cells C12:I15. Apply Light Yellow fill color.
7. Add an outside border to the ranges C6:J7 and B10:J15.

8. Add an Up Arrow Callout pointing to cell F15.

   ✓ It's located on the Block Arrows menu, second to the last row, third button.

9. Add the text *Covered by Dr. Smithe* to the callout.

   ✓ Just click on the shape and type the text.

10. Add a 1½ point border to the shape.

    ✓ Click the shape and select the border style from the Line Style button.

11. Fill the shape with Tan color. Drag the yellow adjustment handles to manipulate the shape of the callout arrow to your satisfaction. Align the callout so that the arrow is centered in the Wed column.

    ✓ If you have trouble selecting the shape so you can add color, click near the top of the arrow.

12. In cell E2, type the text *The Big Day:* and format the text as 12 points, bold.

13. Add a 5-point star AutoShape just to the right of the text.

    ✓ *It's the last button in the first row of the Stars and Banners submenu.*

14. Move and size the star as necessary.

15. While the star is still selected, click in the Formula bar and type an equal (=) sign. Click in cell I14 and press Enter.

    ✓ *This is a cool way to place text in an AutoShape that comes from a cell in the worksheet.*

16. With the star still selected, choose Arial Rounded MT Bold font, 14 points, centered using the Formatting toolbar.

17. Draw an arrow from the star to cell I14.

18. Print the worksheet.

19. Save the workbook and exit Excel.

On Your Own

1. Start Excel, if necessary.

2. Open ⊚ **36_ANTIQUE**.

3. Save the file as **OXL_36**.

4. Select the range A7:G10, and format it however you like.

5. Create your choice of banner using AutoShapes, and place it under the title, Country Crazy Antiques.

   ✓ *You can try out various banner styles easily by selecting the original banner shape, clicking Draw, selecting Change AutoShape, and selecting a new shape to try.*

6. Add the following text to the banner: *Inventory as of: 1/10/99.*

   ✓ *You can select the text and format it as well, using the buttons on the Formatting toolbar.*

7. Format the banner however you like, perhaps by adding a fill color and a thicker border.

8. Using AutoShapes or your own drawings, create a logo for Country Crazy Antiques:

   a. In the area below the table, create at least five objects such as squares, rectangles, ovals, or other shapes of your choice.

   b. Color and format them as you like.

   c. Move the objects so they overlap.

   d. Change the order of the objects and continue moving them until you get the effect you want for the logo.

   e. Group the objects.

   f. Ungroup the objects, make some changes, and then regroup them.

   g. Move the finished logo to the area at the left of the *Country Crazy Antiques* title.

   h. Resize the logo, if necessary, to best fit the area.

9. Save the workbook and exit Excel.

Exercise 37

◆ Insert WordArt

On the Job

WordArt allows you to bend, stretch, and rotate text to create dynamic effects. With a simple piece of WordArt, you can add an element of surprise to an otherwise boring worksheet full of numbers. WordArt gives your worksheets a professional touch, enabling you to create a lasting impression with something that takes only minutes to create.

You're the office assistant for a group of doctors, and it's your job to create a worksheet each week that lists which doctor is in the office or on call for each day. You've been doing this for awhile now, and no one seems to notice the schedule worksheet anymore, so you've decided to jazz it up with some WordArt and professional formatting.

Terms

WordArt An Office tool that allows you to twist, bend, and stretch text to create interesting effects.

Notes

Insert WordArt

- With **WordArt**, you can bend, stretch, or twist small bits of text, such as a word or two.
- The WordArt Gallery provides the basic effects from which you can choose.

WordArt Gallery

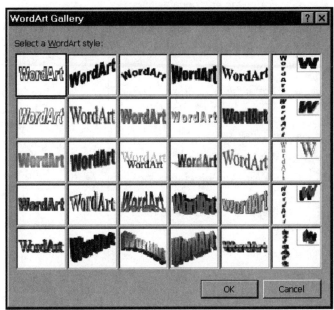

- After selecting an effect, you enter the text you want WordArt to use.

  ✓ *For best results, keep the text short, such as two or three short words at most.*

- After a WordArt object is created, you can format it with the buttons on the WordArt toolbar.

WordArt toolbar

Change the WordArt text

Rotate the object

Adjust the spacing between characters

Format the WordArt object

Flip text vertically

Insert WordArt

Select a different effect

Change the shape

Make all letters the same height

Change the alignment

- A WordArt object can be moved, resized, copied, and deleted, just like any other object.

- You can manipulate the shape of a WordArt object by dragging the yellow diamond-shaped adjustment handle.

- Because WordArt is an object, many of the procedures you learned with AutoShapes work with WordArt as well, such as order, grouping, etc. For example, you could place a WordArt object in a bordered rectangle you created with AutoShapes, group them together, and resize and move them as one object.

Procedures

Insert WordArt Object

1. Click **Insert WordArt** button ▣ on the Drawing toolbar.
2. Select a style .... ▣
3. Click **OK** .... Enter
4. Select **Font** .... Alt + F , ▣

   ✓ *You can add bold or italics by clicking the appropriate button.*

5. Select **Size** .... Alt + S , ↑
6. Type desired text.
7. Click **OK** .... Enter

   ✓ *Format the WordArt as needed, using the WordArt toolbar that appears automatically.*

Resize WordArt Object

1. Click WordArt object to select it.
2. Position mouse pointer over a handle.

3. Click handle and drag outward to make the object larger, or inward to make it smaller.

   a. To resize the object proportionally, press **Shift** and drag a corner handle.

   b. To resize the object in one direction, drag the handle in that direction.

   c. To resize the object from the center outward, press **Ctrl** and drag a handle.

   d. To resize the object proportionally from the center outward, press **Ctrl+Shift** and drag a corner handle.

   e. If a yellow diamond-shaped adjustment handle appears with the object, you can drag it to manipulate the shape of the object.

4. Release mouse button.

Format WordArt

1. Right-click the WordArt object and select **Format WordArt** .... ▣

   OR

   a. Click the WordArt object to select it.

   b. Click **Format** .... Alt + O

   c. Click **WordArt** .... O

2. Use the Colors and Lines, Size, Protection, Properties, and Web tabs to format WordArt.

3. Click **OK** .... Enter

Move WordArt Object

1. Click WordArt object to select it.
2. Position mouse pointer over object.
3. Click and hold mouse button as you drag object.
4. Release mouse button.

Exercise Directions

1. Start Excel, if necessary.
2. Open ◎**37_SCHEDULE**.
3. Save the file as **XL_37**.
4. Select cells C4:I4.
5. Merge and center the title.
   a. Fill the cell with Lavender color.
   b. Change to white text.
   c. Add a thick border around the cell.
5. Click the Insert WordArt button on the Drawing toolbar.
6. Select the second style from the left in the fourth row and click OK.
7. Type the text *WPA* into the box.
   a. Select Times New Roman font.
   b. Select 40 points.
8. Move the new logo to the open area (cells A1:B5) to the left of the worksheet title.
9. With the WordArt logo selected, click the Format WordArt button on the WordArt toolbar.
10. On the Colors and Lines tab, click the Color list and select Fill Effects.
11. Change Color 2 to Aqua and then click OK twice to implement this change.
12. Drag the yellow adjustment button as necessary to obtain the most desirable effect for the logo.
13. Print your worksheet.
14. Save the workbook and exit Excel.

On Your Own

1. Start Excel, if necessary.
2. Open ◎**37_CATER**.
3. Save the file as **OXL_37**.
4. Format the table in the worksheet however you like, adding fonts, changing point size, and adding colors and borders.
5. Replace the title, *Kat's Catering*, with WordArt of the same title.
6. Try different styles of WordArt for the title and experiment with the adjustment handle.
7. Experiment with different fill colors to match the formatting you set for the table.
8. Create a rectangle to house the WordArt title.
   a. Format the rectangle with colors and a border to go with the title design.
   b. Place the title in the rectangle and size one or the other to fit.
   c. Group them together and move them to the location you prefer.
8. Add a background to the sheet using the ◎**parch_gray.jpg** image or ◎**parchment.gif** image.
9. Hide the gridlines (use the View tab in the Options dialog box).
10. Save the workbook and exit Excel.

Exercise 38

Skills Covered:

◆ **Insert and Size Clip Art** ◆ **Download Clip Art from the Internet**

On the Job

Images bombard us every day — on billboards, in magazines, on television — like it or not, we're an image-conscious society. If you don't want your worksheet to get lost in the shuffle of daily data overload, you should add a graphic or two to draw your audience's interest. Clip art also lends a more professional air to your worksheet, helping it to carry a stronger message.

You're the sales manager for a local computer store. The owner is unhappy because sales are down from last month, and he wants you to get the message out to your sales team — sell, sell, sell! You've decided that, although the numbers tell a pretty sad story, a graphic or two might help you emphasize exactly what's wrong.

Terms

clip art Images that you can insert into any Office program, including Excel.

Clip Gallery The collection of clip art images included with Microsoft Office.

public domain image An image that isn't copyrighted. Before using any image in a worksheet, you should make sure that it's not protected by copyright law. You may need to obtain permission to use an image before inserting it into a worksheet — this is especially true of images you download from the Internet.

Notes

Insert and Size Clip Art

- You can insert **clip art** and other graphics into your worksheet to enhance its appearance.

- Office provides a variety of graphics in the **Clip Gallery**, or you can insert your own graphics.

  ✓ *You can also download clip art from the Internet to use in your worksheets.*

- The images in the Clip Gallery are organized into categories. Select the category you want, and then insert the desired image.

  ✓ *You can also search the gallery for an appropriate image by typing a few words to describe the image you want — for example, words that describe a concept, such as "goal" or "frustration."*

Clip Gallery

Type search words here   Appropriate images appear

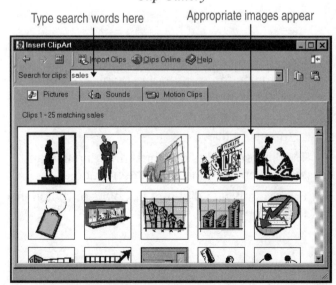

■ The Clip Gallery also contains a few animated images for use in worksheets that will eventually be saved as Web pages.

   ✓ *After inserting an animated image, you must use the File, Web Page Preview command to view it in motion in your Web browser.*

■ After inserting a graphic, you can move and resize it as needed.

■ You can also adjust the brightness and contrast of most graphics by using the Picture toolbar.

Picture toolbar

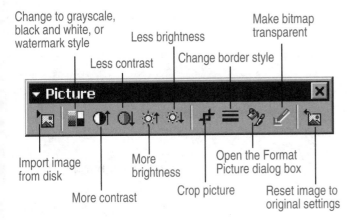

Change to grayscale, black and white, or watermark style

Less brightness

Less contrast

Make bitmap transparent

Change border style

Import image from disk

More brightness

Open the Format Picture dialog box

Crop picture

Reset image to original settings

More contrast

Download Clip Art from the Internet

■ The Clip Gallery provides a connection to the Microsoft Web site, from which you can easily download additional images from the Internet.

   ✓ *You'll need an Internet connection and a Web browser to complete this task.*

■ Images you select from the site are added to the Clip Gallery.

■ You can download **public domain images** such as clip art, pictures, animated graphics, and sound files from Microsoft's Web site.

Procedures

Insert Clip Art Object

1. Select cell where object will be inserted.
2. Click **Insert** .... `Alt`+`I`
3. Click **Picture** .... `P`
4. Click **Clip Art** .... `C`
5. Select category .. `Tab`, `Tab`, `↕`, `Enter`

   ✓ *You can also type a few keywords that describe the image you want in the **Search for clips** text box and press **Enter**.*

6. Click clip art image.. `↕`, `Enter`

   ✓ *You can click **Keep looking** at the bottom of the page to display additional clips in this category.*

7. Click the **Insert clip** button........................ `Enter`

   ✓ *You can also click **Preview clip** (to preview the clip), **Add clip to Favorites or other category** (to copy the clip to some other category), or **Find similar clips** (to locate more clips like this one).*

Size Clip Art Object

1. Click object.

   ✓ *Handles (small black squares) appear around object's perimeter.*

2. Point to handle.

   ✓ *Use a corner handle to resize the object proportionally.*

3. Drag handle outward to make object larger, or inward to make it smaller.

Move Clip Art Object

1. Click object.

   ✓ *Handles (small black squares) appear around object's perimeter.*

2. Drag object to its new location.
3. Release mouse button.

   ✓ *Object appears at the new location.*

Import Clip Art into the Clip Gallery

1. In the Clip Gallery, click **Import Clips** .... `Alt`+`I`
2. Select drive and folder for clip art.
3. Select clip art file.
4. Click **Import** .... `Alt`+`P`
5. Type description for the clip art image, if desired.
6. Click **Categories** tab .... `Ctrl`+`Tab`
7. Click categories to which you want to copy the clip............. `↓`, `Space`
8. Click **Keywords** tab.... `Ctrl`+`Tab`
9. Click **New Keyword** ....

10. Type keyword(s) that describe the clip.

   ✓ Separate keywords with commas.

11. Click **OK**..........................⌜Enter⌟

Download Clips from the Internet

1. In the Clip Gallery, click **Clips Online**. ......

   ✓ If you see a message reminding you that you must have an Internet connection, click **OK**.

   ✓ You may also see a Web page asking you to register your software. If so, click **Accept** to continue.

2. At the top of the Web page, click the option you want: Clip Art, Pictures, Sounds, or Motion.

3. Click the category you want, such as **Office**.

4. Click the **Download This Clip Now!** button under the clip to add it to the Gallery.

   ✓ Click the clip itself to preview it first.

   ✓ Click the check box under the clip to add it to the Selection Basket. After selecting all the clips you want, click **Selection Basket** to view and download the basket's contents.

Exercise Directions

1. Start Excel, if necessary.
2. Open ⊙ **38_COMPUTER**.
3. Save the file as **XL_38**.
4. Insert a clip art image of a computer on the January Sales worksheet. Do a search for *computer* in the Insert ClipArt dialog box and select an image you like.
5. Resize the image to fit in the area to the left of the title (A1:B5).
6. Move the clip art object, if necessary.
7. Copy the image to the same area on the February Sales worksheet. Move the image, if necessary.
8. Click the Sales Trend tab to switch to that worksheet.
9. Insert an appropriate clip art image. Search for *sales down* and select an image you like.
10. Resize and reposition the image as needed.
11. Save the workbook and exit Excel.

On Your Own

1. Create a sales worksheet for Country Crazy Antiques.
2. Save the file as **OXL_38**.
3. List sales (in dollars) for beds, dressers, dining tables, end tables, china cabinets, and chairs sold within the month.

   ✓ Break sales down for the last three months.

   ✓ You might create a row for each type of furniture and a column for each month, or vice versa.

4. Format the worksheet however you like.
5. Insert a piece of clip art as a logo.

   ✓ Move and resize the object as needed.

6. Since you're printing in black and white, change the image to grayscale.

   ✓ Use the Image Control button on the Picture toolbar.

7. Add a box around the image.

   ✓ Use the Line Style button on the Picture toolbar.

8. Open the Clip Gallery again.
9. Import an image into the gallery.

   ✓ If you have a connection to the Internet, try downloading an image from Microsoft. If not, import the image ⊙ **QUILT.BMP** from the DDC CD-ROM.

10. Print the worksheet.
11. Save the workbook and exit Excel.

Exercise 39

◆ Use AutoFormat to Format Ranges

On the Job

Sometimes you want to format a table with colors, borders, and font attributes, but don't want to spend much time doing it. You can use AutoFormat to do the job quickly and professionally. Choose from over a dozen predesigned formats, which you can use as is or make minor changes to suit your fancy.

You're the accounting manager for Corporate Computer Solutions, and the sales people are standing outside your door because it's payday and they want their commissions! While your assistant cuts the checks, you're going to take a few minutes to put the finishing touches on your glorious masterpiece.

Terms

AutoFormat A feature that quickly formats a range of cells with predesigned styles.

Notes

Use AutoFormat to Format Ranges

- To format a range quickly, use AutoFormat.
- With AutoFormat, you can apply number style, fonts, alignment, colors, borders, and so on in a few quick steps.
- In the AutoFormat dialog box, you select the style you like, and then apply all of its formats in one motion.
  - ✓ *You can also select individual formats to apply, instead of the entire AutoFormat style.*
- Once the format is applied, you can modify it any way you like, or remove it.

Select a format design from the AutoFormat dialog box

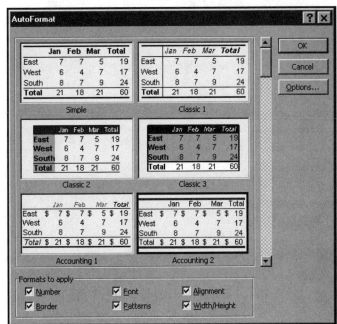

Procedures

Apply AutoFormat

1. Select range of data to be formatted.
2. Click **Format** .... `Alt`+`O`
3. Click **AutoFormat** .... `A`
4. Select desired format .... `↕`
   a. If desired,
      click **Options** .... `O`

b. Select any options you wish to turn off (not apply).
5. Click **OK** .... `Enter`

Remove AutoFormat

✔ *This procedure also removes formatting you have applied manually.*

1. Select formatted range.

2. Click **Format** .... `Alt`+`O`
3. Click **AutoFormat** .... `A`
4. Scroll to the bottom of the AutoFormat choices and select **None** .... `↕`
5. Click **OK** .... `Enter`

Exercise Directions

1. Start Excel, if necessary.
2. Open ⊙ **39_COMMISSION**.
3. Save the file as **XL_39**.
4. Apply the Classic 2 AutoFormat to the range B6:I13.
5. Fill the three *Comm.* columns from row 7 down with Light Yellow color.
6. Add ovals around the best commissions in each category (cells D11, F7, and H11):
   a. Click the Oval button on the Drawing toolbar.
   b. Drag to create a small oval that's large enough to surround the data in one of the cells.
      ✔ *You can test the size by dragging the oval over a cell and then bringing it back to a clear area before releasing the mouse button.*
   c. With the oval selected, click the Fill Color button and select No Fill.
      ✔ *If the fill is removed from a drawn object, you can see the contents of the cell(s) under the object. When you position the drawn object over a cell containing data, the underlying data is visible through the object.*
   d. Click the Line Color button and select Red.
   e. Click the Line Style button and select 1½ pt.
   f. Make three copies of the oval anywhere in an open space of the worksheet.
   g. Drag the first oval into place over the commission figure in cell D11.
   h. Drag the second oval into place over the commission figure in cell F7.
   i. Drag the third oval over the commission figure in cell H11.

7. Resize the last oval so it's slightly larger than the rest; you'll use this oval to highlight the total commission figure:
   a. Format it with a 3 pt Square Dot line.
   b. Move the oval into place over the number in cell I13.
8. Use the Drawing toolbar to create a rectangle below the table.
   a. Add the text *Significant increase over last month*.
      ✔ *Hint: Right-click on the rectangle and select the Add Text command.*
   b. Resize the rectangle so that it just fits the text.
   c. Format the rectangle with Light Yellow fill color and a Violet border 1½ points in size.
   d. Draw an arrow connecting the rectangle to cell E13.
   e. Format the arrow with Violet color and 1½ pt size.
9. Add an AutoShape behind the rectangle:
   a. Select Explosion 1 from Stars and Banners.
   b. Click the Fill Color button and select Orange.
   c. Drag one of the green rotate handles.
   d. Click the Draw button and select Order, Send to Back to place the starburst behind the rectangle.
10. Move the individual objects around as you like. Group them and resize the group, if necessary.
11. Delete the title *CCS* and replace it with a WordArt title with colors that complement the rest of the worksheet.
12. Save the workbook and exit Excel.

On Your Own

1. Start Excel, if necessary.

2. Open ☉ **39_TOYS**.

3. Save the file as **OXL_39**.

4. Replace the title with a WordArt title and use AutoFormat to format the table. Modify the color formats of both so that they complement each other.

5. Using various tools on the Drawing toolbar, draw attention to the unexpectedly high sales of the Rockem, Sockem, BarKnee toy — last year's favorite.

   ✓ *You might add an arrow, shape, and/or a star, and even highlight a cell with a special border and color.*

6. The Silly Toy Company can't afford to have a professional artist design a logo for them, so they want you to do it. Use the Drawing toolbar to design whatever you like.

   ✓ *Some ideas: a box with the letters STC on it, a present, a jack-in-the-box, a top, a yo-yo, or any other toy.*

7. Print the worksheet.

8. Save the workbook and exit Excel.

Exercise 40

◆ **Add and Format a Text Box** ◆ **Add Callouts** ◆ **Add Shadows**

On the Job

If you need to place text in some spot within the worksheet that doesn't correspond to a specific cell, you can "float" the text over the cells by creating a text box. A text box can be placed anywhere in the worksheet, regardless of the cell gridlines. You might use a text box to draw attention to some particularly important data in the worksheet. If you don't like the look of a plain text box, you can add a callout instead—text that's placed within a balloon, in a manner similar to that in a comic strip. Add shadows to these objects to really make them stand out.

You're the accounts receivable clerk for Dr. Benjamin Child & Associates, and you've just prepared the AR report for this month. Since Dr. Child doesn't usually spend a lot of time going over the report, you've decided to add a text box and a callout to call attention to some special issues.

Terms

text box A small rectangle that "floats" over the cells in a worksheet, into which you can add text. A text box can be placed anywhere you want.

callout Text that's placed in a special AutoShape balloon. A callout, like a text box, "floats" over the cells in a worksheet— so you can position a callout wherever you like.

Notes

Add and Format a Text Box

- A **text box** is an independent object that contains text.
  - A text box can be resized, moved, copied, deleted, formatted, and manipulated independently of the data in the worksheet.
  - The text in the text box can be formatted in the same way in which you format worksheet text.
  - You can use a text box to point out important information within a worksheet, or to add a comment that's displayed all the time.
    - ✓ *By default, a comment like the ones you learned how to add in Exercise 7 isn't visible until the mouse pointer rests on the cell that contains it.*

- A text box is created with tools on the Drawing toolbar.
  - When you create a text box, you drag with the mouse pointer to create the exact size you need.
  - You then type text into this box.
- A text box's border can be formatted in a variety of styles. You can even make it disappear.
- In addition, you can fill the text box with a color or pattern, as you might fill a cell.
- You can also add a shadow behind the box.
- The border of a selected drawing object changes to indicate whether you're editing the object itself (dotted border) or the text in the object (hatched border). To move, resize, copy, or delete the object, the border must be dotted.

Text box with hatched border

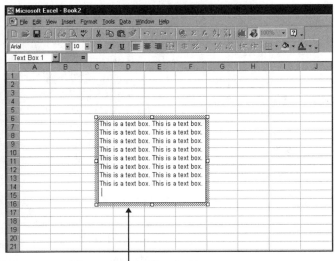

When editing text in a text box,
the border appears hatched.

Text box with dotted border

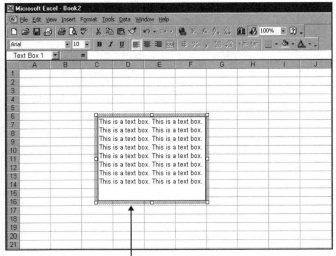

When editing a drawing object,
the border appears dotted.

Add Callouts

- A **callout** is a type of AutoShape.

- A callout is basically a text box, shaped into something more interesting, such as a cartoon balloon.

- You can use a callout like a text box, to draw attention to important information, or to add a comment to a worksheet.

AutoShapes menu

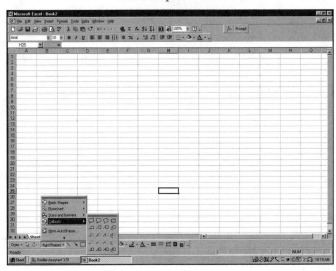

Add Shadows

- Adding a shadow to an object gives it a 3-D effect that makes it stand out.

- You can add shadows to most objects, including WordArt, AutoShapes, and objects you draw, such as text boxes.

- You can also add shadows to cells or ranges.

- Select the style of shadow you want from the Shadow menu.

- Adjust the color and the dimensions of the shadow with the Shadow Settings on the Shadow menu.

Shadow Menus

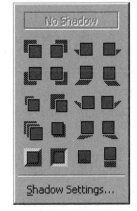

Procedures

Create a Text Box

1. Click **Text Box** button 🔳 on Drawing toolbar.

   ✓ *Pointer becomes a* ⊥.

2. Position ⊥ where corner of box will be.

   To create a text box:
   Drag box outline until desired size is obtained.

   To create a square text box:
   Press **Shift** and drag box outline until desired size is obtained.

   To create a text box that aligns to gridlines:
   Press **Alt** and drag box outline until desired size is obtained.

3. Type text as desired:
   Click outside text box to return to normal operations.

Format Text in Text Box

1. Click the text box to select it.
2. Select text to be formatted.
3. Click **Format** .... 🄾
4. Click **Text Box** .... 🄾
5. Format the text with the option in the dialog box.
6. Click **OK** .... Enter

Format Text Box Object

1. Click text box object to select it.
2. Click the desired formatting tool on Drawing toolbar:

   ✓ *Click the arrow on the Fill Color, Line Color, or Font Color button to make a selection. If you click the button itself, you'll apply the selection shown on the button.*

   a. **Fill Color**
   b. **Line Color**
   c. **Font Color**
   d. **Line Style**
   e. **Dash Style**
   f. **Shadow**
   g. **3-D**

3. Select the option you want to apply to the selected object.

Create a Callout

1. Click **AutoShapes** button on Drawing toolbar .... Alt + U
2. Click **Callouts** C
3. Click the callout shape you want .... ↕↕, Enter

   ✓ *The pointer becomes* +.

4. Position + over the cell where the callout should point.
5. Drag the callout outline until desired size is obtained.
6. Type the text for the callout.
7. Drag adjustment handle (yellow diamond), if necessary, to adjust the callout balloon.

Add a Shadow

1. Select object.
2. Click **Shadow** button 🔳 on Drawing toolbar.
3. Click shadow style .... ↕↕, Enter

Modify a Shadow

1. Select the object with the shadow.
2. Click **Shadow** button 🔳 on Drawing toolbar.
3. Select **Shadow Settings** ... 🅂
4. Use the buttons on the Shadow Settings toolbar to change the shadow as desired:

   a. Turn shadow on/off.
   b. Nudge shadow in direction of arrows.
   c. Change the color of the shadow.

Exercise Directions

1. Start Excel, if necessary.

2. Open ⊙ **40_ACCTS_REC**.

3. Save the workbook as **XL_40**.

4. Add a text box to the logo:

   a. Draw a small text box.

   b. Type *13 years of quality care!*

   c. Apply Arial Narrow font, 8 points to the text, and center it.

   d. Resize the text box so that it just fits the text.

   e. Move the text box so that it rests at the bottom of the clip art image.

5. Format the text box:

   a. Add a 4½ pt border to the text box (use the style with the darker outer edge).

   b. Apply Shadow Style 14.

6. Add a callout to the worksheet:

   a. Use the Rectangular Callout style.

   b. Anchor the callout to cell G11.

      ✓ *If necessary, drag the adjustment handle (the yellow diamond that appears at the balloon's origin point) to cell G11.*

   c. Type *MM Health has been late on a lot of payments this month.*

   d. Apply Arial Narrow, 8 points, bold to the text.

   e. Resize the balloon as needed.

7. Format the callout balloon:

   a. Apply the Tan fill color.

   b. Change the border to 1 pt.

   c. Apply Shadow Style 14.

8. Apply an AutoFormat of your choice to the range C10:I16.

9. Format all dollar amounts as Accounting with two decimal places.

   ✓ *Adjust column widths, if necessary.*

10. Preview and print the worksheet.

11. Save the workbook and exit Excel.

On Your Own

1. Start Excel, if necessary.

2. Open ⊙ **40_TABER**.

3. Save the workbook as **OXL_40**.

4. Add a callout to explain the net loss at the Crown Point store. Make up a reason.

5. Delete the title *Taber Video* and replace it with a WordArt title of the same name.

6. Create a text box and type the text from A4:A5; then clear those cells.

7. Position the title and the text box as you like above the table.

8. Format the text box to complement the title.

9. Save the workbook and exit Excel.

Exercise 41

◆ **Critical Thinking**

You're the training manager at CompuTrain, and you've just created a worksheet that lists each of your trainers, along with the classes they're qualified to teach. But before you show your hard work to anyone, you want to dress it up.

Exercise Directions

1. Start Excel, if necessary.
2. Open ✪ **41_TRAIN**.
3. Save the file as ✪ **XL_41**.
4. Format the worksheet:
   a. Change the color of cells C8:J8 to Turquoise.
   b. Change the color of cells B9:B16 to Aqua.
   c. Add these colors to cells containing this text:
      - *Train:* Tan
      - *Train with Observer:* Light Green
      - *Co-Train:* Light Yellow
      - *Observe:* Light Turquoise
      ✓ *Just leave the cells that contain N/A blank.*
      ✓ *Remember to fill in the matching cells in the "key", located below the worksheet data.*
      ✓ *To color the cells quickly, color one cell, then double-click the Format Painter button and color the matching cells. Click the Format Painter button again to turn it off.*
   d. Select cells C9:J16.
   e. Add cell borders with the All Borders button. (Click the arrow on the Borders button and then click the All Borders button).
5. Select cells C20:D23.
   a. Add cell borders with the All Borders button. (Just click the Borders button to apply this format again.)
   b. Add a heavier border around the whole range. (Use the Format Cells dialog box.)
6. Format cell C3 to use a decorative font of your choice, 24 points, bold or not bold as you prefer.
7. Add italics to cell C4.
8. Select cells C3 to I3, and use the Merge and Center button to center the title.
9. Fill the title with Aqua.
10. Center the tagline in cell C4 under the title. Fill the tagline with turquoise. Then add a shadow:
    a. Select cells C3:C4.
    b. Apply a shadow of your choice.
11. Insert a piece of computer-related clip art (your choice) into the blank area in cells A1:B6. Size the graphic to fit.
12. Using the Picture toolbar, change the graphic to grayscale, and add a 3 pt border. Add a light fill color (your choice) using the Drawing toolbar.
    ✓ *You may not be able to add a border or fill color to some graphics.*
13. Replace the text in cell C19 with WordArt:
    a. Click the Insert WordArt button.
    b. Select a style you like.
    c. Type *Key*. Change to 24-point text. You can change the font if you want.
    d. Move the WordArt object to the left of the key.
    e. Format the WordArt object however you like: Change the color, the size, and so on.
    f. Add ✪ **parchment.gif** as a background to the sheet.
    g. Remove gridlines from view on the worksheet.
14. Save and close the workbook.
15. Exit Excel.

Lesson 7

Integrate Excel with Other Applications and the Internet

Exercise 42

◆ **Object Linking and Embedding (OLE)** ◆ **Link Workbooks** ◆ **Link Files**
◆ **Edit a Linked File** ◆ **Embed a File** ◆ **Integrate Office Documents**

On the Job

When you need to use Excel data within a Word document and keep the source data updated, you can create a link between the two files. However, if you choose not to update the source data, you can embed the file instead. You can also link data between Excel workbooks, if necessary.

You're a chef at The Harvest Time Bread Company, and you're tired of being caught under inventory. So you've created a worksheet that tracks daily sales amounts for each of your items, and you want to link it to your inventory worksheet so you can maintain a more accurate daily inventory.

Terms

OLE Object Linking and Embedding enables many Windows applications to share data.

link A link in the destination document references a location in the source document.

source The document that contains the data being referenced.

destination The document that references the data in the source.

external references References to cells in other documents.

embed The method of inserting an object in a file with no link to the source.

Notes

Object Linking and Embedding (OLE)

■ Microsoft provides the Object Linking and Embedding (**OLE**) feature to link or embed objects between Windows applications.

Link Workbooks

■ When you need to consolidate information from one or more workbooks into a summary workbook, create a **link**.

■ The **source** workbook provides the data.

■ The **destination** workbook contains the link(s) to the **external references** in the source workbook(s).

■ The default setting for linking is to update workbook links automatically.

- If you change data in the source workbook, the linked data is automatically updated in the destination workbook.

- This update happens immediately if the destination workbook is already open; if not, the update occurs when the workbook is opened at a later time.

■ You can link workbooks in one of three ways:

- Copy data from the source workbook and paste it into the destination workbook using the Paste Special, Paste Link command to create an external reference that links the workbooks.

- Type the external reference as a formula using the following format:

  drive:\path\[file.xls]sheetname!reference

Example:

=c:\excel\mydocuments\[report.xls]\sheet1!H5

✓ *You can omit the path if the source and destination files are saved in the same directory (folder).*

- While editing or creating a formula in the destination workbook, you can include an external reference by selecting a cell or range in the source workbook.

■ When a cell in an external reference includes a formula, only the formula result displays in the destination workbook.

■ If possible, save linked workbooks in the same directory (folder). You should save source workbook(s) first, and then save the destination workbook(s).

The source workbook contains the data being referenced in the destination workbook

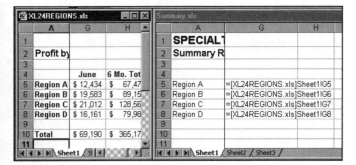

Link Files

■ Use linking to communicate between files in different applications. For example, you can insert an Excel worksheet (source file) into a Word document (destination file).

■ As when you link workbooks, when you create a link between files from different applications the data in the destination file changes if you update the source file.

  ✓ *An Excel link updates when source data is changed and the destination file is open, or when you later open the destination file.*

■ To link files, use the Copy command to copy data to the Clipboard; then use a Paste Special command. From the Paste Special dialog box:

- Identify the object or type of file to link.

- Select the Paste Link option.

Paste Special dialog box

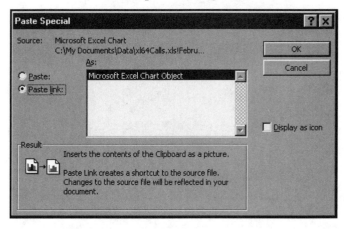

Edit a Linked File

■ When you double-click a linked file within another application, the source application and the file open for you to make changes.

■ Changes that you make to the source file within another application will automatically update the linked file.

■ When you directly change the source file and then open the destination file containing the link(s), the updated file will display.

■ The linking feature saves disk space because the file is stored in the source location with the link as a shortcut to that location.

Embed a File

■ When you **embed** a file, you can edit the data in that file within the source application without changing the source file. For example:

- You can embed an Excel worksheet in a Word document.

- Double-click the embedded Excel worksheet within the Word application to make edits using Excel without changing the source worksheet.

■ To embed a file, use the Insert, Object command, Create from File option; or use the Edit, Copy and Edit, Paste Special commands (without the Paste Link option).

Object dialog box

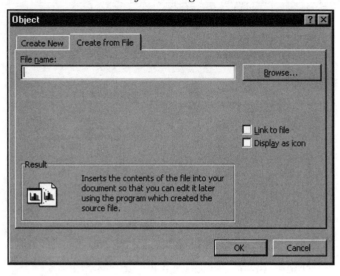

- Embedding a file uses more disk space because the embedded file is part of the destination file.

Integrate Office Documents

- Embed a new worksheet in a Word document by clicking the Insert Microsoft Excel Worksheet button located on the Standard toolbar in Word.
- You can also embed a new file using the Insert, Object, Create New, Microsoft Excel Worksheet command.
- When you create a new Excel workbook within a Word document, you have all of Excel's capabilities within the document.

Procedures

Link Workbooks Using Paste Link

1. Open source and destination workbooks.
2. Arrange workbooks on the screen.
3. Select cells to reference in source workbook.
4. Click **Edit**..................... Alt +E
5. Click **Copy** C
6. Select cells in destination workbook to receive cell references.
7. Click **Edit**..................... Alt +E
8. Click **Paste Special** .... S
9. Click **Paste Link** L

Link Data Between Applications

1. Open appropriate applications and files.
2. Select data to be copied from source file.
3. Click **Edit**..................... Alt +E
4. Click **Copy** C
5. Switch to destination file.
6. Position insertion point.
7. Click **Edit**..................... Alt +E
8. Click **Paste Special** .... S

9. Click in the **As** list to choose format............. ↑ ↓
10. Click **Paste link** .... Alt +L
11. Click **OK** .... Enter

Edit Link

1. Open appropriate application and destination file.
2. Double-click linked file.
   ✓ The source application and file open so that you can make changes to the source.
3. Make changes to source file.
4. Switch to destination file.
   ✓ Destination file is updated.

Embed Object: Create from File

1. Open appropriate application and destination file.
2. Click **Insert** .... Alt +I
3. Click **Object** .... O
4. Click **Create from File** tab .... Alt +F
5. Click **Browse**.............. Alt +B
6. Click **Look in** .... Alt +I
7. Type or select drive letter containing file to insert............... ↑ ↓ , Enter

8. Double-click directory (folder) in Directories list containing file to insert.
9. Click file name in list box .... ↑ ↓
10. Click **Insert** .... Alt +S
   ✓ This procedure can be used to link the file by selecting the Link to file check box in the Object dialog box.
11. Click **OK**.......................... Enter

Embed Object: Create New

1. Open appropriate application and destination file.
2. Click **Insert** .... Alt +I
3. Click **Object**...................... O
4. Click **Create New** tab .... Alt +C
5. Select object type in the Object type list............ Alt +O , ↑ ↓
6. Click **OK** to create new object .... Enter
   ✓ Selected application opens.
7. Type desired information.
8. Click outside of object to embed the object and return to original application.

Embed Data by Using Paste Special

1. Open appropriate applications and files.
2. Select data to be copied from source file.
3. Click **Edit** .... `Alt`+`E`
4. Click **Copy** .... `C`
5. Switch to destination file.
6. Position insertion point in document.
7. Click **Edit** .... `Alt`+`E`
8. Click **Paste Special** .... `S`
9. Select type from **As** list .... `Alt`+`A`, `↑`|`↓`
10. Click **OK** .... `Enter`

Edit Embedded Object

1. Open appropriate application and destination file.
2. Double-click embedded file.
   - ✓ *The source application and file open so that you can make changes to the file.*
3. Make changes to embedded file.
4. Click outside of embedded object to close source application.

Exercise Directions

1. Start Excel, if necessary.
2. Open 🔘 **42_INVENTORY**.
3. Save the file as **XL_42A**.
4. Open 🔘 **42_WKLYSALES**.
5. Save the file as **XL_42B**.
6. Arrange the workbooks on the screen in a tiled fashion.
7. Copy the range B8:B16 in the **XL_42B** workbook.
8. Link the data to the range C8:C16 in the **XL_42A** workbook.
9. Repeat steps 6 and 7 to link each day's sales in **XL_42B** to the proper column in the **XL_42A** workbook.
10. Select the range B8:T16 in the **XL_42A** workbook, and format it with Number format, zero decimal places.
11. Print Sheet1 in the **XL_42A** workbook.
12. Switch back to the **XL_42B** workbook and make the following changes:
    - ✓ *Hint: So you can see what you're doing in XL_42B, position the cell pointer in cell B8 and freeze the window before making these changes. If you want to see the result in XL_42A, arrange the window to show appropriate columns before making the changes.*
    a. Change the number of honey wheat rolls sold on Friday to 245, and on Saturday to 302.
    b. Change the number of butter white bread loaves sold on Wednesday to 58.
    c. Change the amount of foccacia sold on Tuesday to 34, and on Friday to 63.
13. Print the **XL_42A** worksheet again and compare the two printouts.
    - ✓ *Notice how the changes you made were reflected in the XL_42A worksheet immediately.*
14. Save both workbooks and exit Excel.

On Your Own

1. Start Excel and Word, if necessary.
2. In Word, create a memo to Brian Hagley at Magnolia Steel Bearings & Fittings.
   - The topic of the memo is an overdue invoice.
3. Save the document as **OXL_42.doc**.
4. Type an introduction that explains that the invoice is overdue by two weeks.
5. In Excel, open **OXL_24**, created in an earlier exercise.
6. Copy the invoice data from **OXL_24** and embed it in the memo.
7. In the Word document, change the invoice data to reflect a 10% additional charge for late payment.
8. Write an ending paragraph explaining about the extra charge, and telling Brian that he can avoid additional charges by paying the total due within five days.
9. Save **OXL_42.doc** and exit Word.
10. Close the **OXL_24** workbook and exit Excel.
    - ✓ *Notice that the changes you made in Word didn't affect the workbook.*

Exercise 43

◆ **Integrate an Excel Worksheet and a Word Document**
◆ **Financial Data on the Internet**

On the Job

You can create a report in Excel and copy it to a Word file to enhance information in a letter, memo, proposal, or other word processing document.

You're the senior investment manager for Investco Group, and one of your new clients has asked you to look into some stock investments for him. You'll use your knowledge of the Internet, Excel, and Word to prepare a memo that details the stocks' current values and prior histories.

Terms

source file The file that contains the data to be copied.

destination file The file that receives the copied data.

drag and drop A method used to move or copy a range of cells by dragging the border of a selection from one location and dropping it in another.

Internet The Internet is a world wide network of computers located in businesses, research foundations, institutions, schools, and/or homes that allow users to share and search for information.

Notes

Integrate an Excel Worksheet and a Word Document

- Microsoft Office is an integrated software package, which means data can be shared or combined among the applications.
  - ✓ *If you don't have both Excel and Word software, skip the integration part of this exercise.*
- The **source file** sends the data and the **destination file** receives it.
  - • For example, an Excel worksheet (the source file) can provide support material for a Word document (the destination file).
- If you want to copy data from the source to the destination file, you can use the Copy and Paste commands or **drag and drop**.

- The Copy command places the data from the source file onto the Clipboard. The data can then be pasted into the destination file.
- With both the source and destination files open and displayed on the screen, you can use drag and drop to bypass the Clipboard and directly copy the data.
- After you copy the data to the destination file, you can edit it. However, when you use the Paste command, there's no connection to the original data, which you must edit separately.
  - ✓ *You can create a link between the source file data and the destination file so that changes made to the source file are automatically updated in the destination file, and vice versa. See the previous exercise for more information on linking.*

Financial Data on the Internet

- You can access a vast array of financial information on the **Internet**.

- Major financial publications have Web sites to provide business news, market data, and specific company data.

- At some sites, market prices reflect the day's actual prices, as they're updated several times each hour.

- If you need a market quote, you must search for the stock using the ticker symbol.

Procedures

Copy and Paste Data Between Applications

1. Open applications and appropriate source and data files.
2. In the source file, select data to be copied.
3. Click **Copy** button 📋.
   OR
   a. Click **Edit** .... Alt + E
   b. Click **Copy** C
4. Switch to destination file.
5. Position insertion point in the desired location.
6. Click **Paste** button 📋.
   OR
   a. Click **Edit** .... Alt + E
   b. Click **Paste** .... P

Copy Data Between Applications with Drag and Drop

1. Open applications and display source and destination files.
   ✓ *Display the area in the source file that contains the data to copy and the area in the destination file to receive the data.*
2. In the source file, select data to be copied.
3. Move pointer to selection to display arrow.
4. Hold down **Ctrl** while dragging selected data to its position in destination file.
   ✓ *The + symbol attached to arrow indicates that selected data is being copied, not moved.*
   ✓ *After dragging the data to its new location, release the mouse and then the Ctrl key to copy to the destination.*

Display Web Toolbar

1. Click **View** .... Alt + V
2. Click **Toolbars** .... T
3. Select **Web** .... ↓, Enter
   OR
   a. Right-click any displayed toolbar.
   b. Click **Web**.

Exercise Directions

1. Start Excel and Word, if necessary.

2. In Word, open ⊙ **43_STOCK.doc**.

3. Save the file as **XL_43.doc**.

4. Open the file ⊙ **43_STOCK.xls**.

5. Save the file as **XL_43.xls**.

6. Display the Web toolbar.

7. Use the Internet or use the DDC CD-ROM simulation to complete the worksheet by finding the current market price, 52 week high/low, earnings per share, and price-to-earnings ratio.

   ✓ *Use the Yahoo search engine, or one of your own preference.*

   To open the Internet simulation:

   - Click **Go**.
   - Click **Open**.
   - In the Address line, type the following: C:/Simulation/Ex43/Yahool!.htm

   ✓ *If you've copied the Internet simulation files to your hard drive or your CD-ROM drive is not C:, substitute the correct drive letter for C.*

   - Click **OK**.

   a. Click the Stock Quotes link.

   b. Type in the symbol MSFT.

c. Click Get Quotes to get current information about the stock.

d. Click the Detailed link for more information.

e. Click Home to return to the Stock Quotes page.

f. Repeat steps b-e for DELL, CPQ, YHOO, and AMZN.

g. Type the information into the appropriate cells in the worksheet.

   ✓ *Use Illustration A as an example.*

h. Exit your browser and disconnect from the service provider, or exit the DDC Internet simulation.

   ✓ *Exit the Internet simulation by clicking the Close button* ☒ .

8. Select the range B7:I14.

9. Click the Copy button.

10. Switch to Word and click just under the opening paragraph.

11. Click the Paste button.

   ✓ *Your Word document should look something like Illustration B.*

12. Save the Word document and exit Word.

13. Save the Excel workbook and exit Excel.

Illustration A

Investco Group
Stock Analysis

Stock Analysis

Company Name	Symbol	Exchange	Current	52 Week Hi	52 Week Lo	Earn/Share	P/E
Microsoft Corporation	MSFT	Nasdaq	175 15/16	175 15/16	76 7/16	2.35	68.35
Dell Computer Corporation	DELL	Nasdaq	102 1/8	110	26 3/4	0.93	104.30
Compaq Computer Corporation	CPQ	NYSE	45	51 1/4	22 15/16	(1.71)	N/A
Yahoo! Inc.	YHOO	Nasdaq	159	222 1/2	15 3/16	0.11	1,294.32
Amazon.com	AMZN	Nasdaq	121 3/4	221 1/4	21 5/8	(1.87)	N/A

INTEROFFICE MEMORANDUM

TO: BOB THORTON

FROM: JENNIFER FULTON

SUBJECT: THOSE STOCKS YOU WERE INTERESTED IN

DATE: 9/1/99

CC:

Bob, after our conversation yesterday, I took a moment to look up those stocks you said you were interested in. I'm not sure that all of them will make the kind of addition to your portfolio that you really need. However, some do indeed look interesting, as you can see here:

Stock Analysis

Company Name	Symbol	Exchange	Current	52 Week		Earn/Share	P/E
Microsoft Corporation	MSFT	Nasdaq	175 15/16	76 7/16	175 15/16	2.35	68.35
Dell Computer Corporation	DELL	Nasdaq	102 1/8	26 3/4	110	0.93	104.30
Compaq Computer Corporation	CPQ	NYSE	45	22 15/16	51 1/4	(1.71)	N/A
Yahoo! Inc.	YHOO	Nasdaq	159	15 3/16	222 1/2	0.11	1,294.32
Amazon.com	AMZN	Nasdaq	121 3/4	221 1/4	21 5/8	(1.78)	N/A

After reviewing their current price and history, give me a call and we can look into investing in the ones you like.

Jennifer Fulton

Senior Investment Manager
Investco Group

On Your Own

1. Start Excel, if necessary.

2. Open a new workbook and save it as **OXL_43**.

3. Create a new worksheet that tracks ten different mutual funds of interest to you.

4. Track information that will help you evaluate the fund, such as 1-year, 5-year, and 10-year performance return percentages, net asset value, profit-to-earnings ratio, and so on.

5. Create a memo in Word that reports your conclusions.

   - Save the file as **OXL_43.doc**.

6. Copy the worksheet data into the memo.

7. Save both files and exit Word and Excel.

Exercise 44

◆ **Save a Worksheet as a Web Page** ◆ **Web Page Preview**
◆ **Create an Interactive Worksheet** ◆ **View a Web Page**

On the Job

Save a worksheet in HTML format to publish it on the World Wide Web or company intranet. You can choose to publish an entire workbook, but viewers won't be able to make changes to it. If you publish just a worksheet, you can choose whether you want to allow changes.

You're an employee at the Java Jungle Café, and because you accidentally let it slip one day that you know all about Excel, the boss has asked you to help him publish a Web page. You need to create a worksheet that lists the prices for coffee by the pound, and then publish it on the company's new Web site.

Terms

HTML Hypertext Markup Language, used to publish information on the World Wide Web.

Web page Information published on the World Wide Web, which can include text, graphics, and links to other pages.

interactive worksheet An online Excel worksheet that can be manipulated by other Office 2000 users.

PivotTable A reporting feature that allows you to summarize data and change the layout of the data for further analysis.

Web browser Software that enables you to view electronic documents.

Notes

Save a Worksheet as a Web Page

- Excel worksheet data can be saved in **HTML** (Hypertext Markup Language) format for publication as a **Web page**.

- The Save as Web Page command on the File menu helps you convert a worksheet to a Web page.

  ✓ *You can convert an entire workbook into a series of Web pages, if you want.*

- Before Excel publishes the page, it displays a dialog box to confirm the item to publish, viewing options, and publishing options.

- You can use the Save as Web Page command on the File menu to republish a selected worksheet if you need to make changes or save it to a new location.

Web Page Preview

■ With the Web Page Preview command, you can preview a workbook as it will look in HTML without actually converting it.

• You can't preview a single worksheet — preview an entire workbook.

• Excel provides tabs at the bottom of the preview window that you can use to move from worksheet to worksheet, just as you might within the Excel window.

Create an Interactive Worksheet

■ You can publish an Excel worksheet and allow other Office 2000 users to manipulate the data.

✓ You can only create an interactive worksheet if you publish a worksheet — not an entire workbook.

■ Create an **interactive worksheet** by selecting the Add interactivity option in the Save As dialog box.

■ You can choose from two types of viewing options from the Publish as Web Page dialog box: interactivity with spreadsheet functionality or **PivotTable** functionality (an advanced Excel reporting feature).

Publish as Web Page dialog box

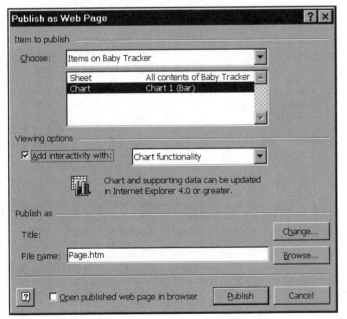

View a Web Page

■ To view a Web page, you must use a **Web browser**, such as Internet Explorer.

✓ Although you can view an HTML page in Excel, you won't see the page as others will when they view it in a Web browser. For example, you won't see animated GIFs.

■ Use the Web browser's Open command on the File menu to choose the appropriate folder and open the file.

■ When the interactive worksheet is viewed in the Web browser, a toolbar appears at the top of the worksheet, providing the same commands you have within Excel for changing and formatting data.

Changing worksheets in a Web browser

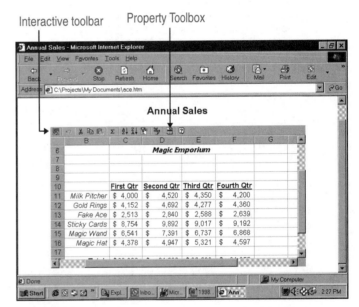

■ The toolbar also displays a Property Toolbox, with which you can change the properties of a cell (its formatting and such).

■ To change data in an interactive worksheet, simply double-click the cell and make your change — just as if you were in Excel.

Procedures

Preview a Workbook as a Web Page

1. Click **File** .... `Alt`+`F`
2. Click **Web Page Preview** .... `B`
3. When you're through, click the **Close** button on your Web browser.

Publish a Workbook, Worksheet, or Range as a Web Page

1. Select the cell(s) you want to publish.

   ✓ When publishing the entire workbook or the current worksheet, you don't need to select any cells.

2. Click **File** .... `Alt`+`F`
3. Click **Save as Web Page** .... `G`

   ✓ You can save either the range you selected in the worksheet, or the entire workbook.

4. Click **Selection** .... `Alt`+`E`

   OR

   Click **Entire Workbook** .... `Alt`+`W`

5. Click **File name** text box .... `Alt`+`N`
6. Type file name for the Web page.

   To change the title for the Web page:

   a. Click **Change Title** .... `Alt`+`C`
   b. Type new title.
   c. Click **OK** .... `Enter`

   ✓ The title of the Web page appears in the browser's title bar when someone is viewing the Web page.

7. Click **Publish** .... `Alt`+`P`

   ✓ The Publish as Web Page dialog box displays publishing options.

8. Click **Open published web page in browser** .... `Alt`+`O`

9. Click **Publish** .... `P`

   ✓ The Web page is complete and automatically displays in the browser. It will be published as a static page without interactive functionality.

Publish an Interactive Worksheet

1. Create and save report in Excel.
2. Select range of cells to publish.

   ✓ If you don't select a range of cells, you can choose to publish the current worksheet.

3. Click **File** .... `Alt`+`F`
4. Click **Save as Web Page** .... `G`
5. Click **Selection** .... `Alt`+`E`
6. Click **Add interactivity** .... `Alt`+`A`
7. Click **Publish** .... `Alt`+`P`

   ✓ The Publish as Web Page dialog box displays publishing options.

   To select item to publish:

   • Click an item in the **Choose** list .... `Alt`+`C`, `↕`, `Enter`

   To publish a range:

   a. Click **Range of cells** option in the **Choose** list .... `Alt`+`C`, `↕`, `Enter`
   b. Type range of cells in text box.

   OR

   a. Click **Collapse Dialog** button `⬚`.
   b. Select cells on worksheet.

      ✓ A marquee surrounds cells.

   c. Click **Expand Dialog** button `⬚`.

      OR

      Click **Items on Sheet**(n).

To select viewing options:

a. Click **Add interactivity with** ..... `Alt`+`A`
b. Click arrow button ... `Tab`, `↓`
c. Click **Spreadsheet functionality** ..... `↕`, `Enter`

   OR

   Click **PivotTable functionality** ..... `↕`, `Enter`

To change the Web page title:

a. Click **Change** .... `Alt`+`H`
b. Type title.
c. Click **OK** .... `Enter`

To change file name:

a. Click **File name** text box .... `Alt`+`N`
b. Type path and file name.

   ✓ You can save the file to a temporary location on your hard drive until you are ready to publish it at your assigned Web address.

To open published Web page in browser:

• Click **Open published Web page in browser** .... `Alt`+`O`

   ✓ You can open the file in the browser at another time.

8. Click **Publish** .... `Alt`+`P`
9. View the file in the browser.
10. Click **File** .... `Alt`+`F`
11. Click **Close** .... `C`

Open a Web Page File in a Web Browser

1. Click **Start** .... `Ctrl`+`Esc`
2. Select **Programs** .... `P`
3. Click **Internet Explorer** ..... `↓`, `Enter`
4. Click **File** .... `Alt`+`F`
5. Click **Open** .... `O`
6. Click **Browse** button .... `Alt`+`R`

To select a different drive:

a. Click **Look in** .... [Alt]+[I]

b. Select
desired drive ...... [↑↓], [Enter]

**To select a folder in
the specified drive:**

- Double-click
folder name .... [↹], [Enter]

7. Double-click file
to open in file list ..... [↹], [Enter]

8. Confirm file path and name.

9. Click **OK** .... [Enter]

10. View the file.

11. Click **File** .... [Alt]+[F]

12. Click **Close** .... [C]

Republish a Web Report

1. Open Excel file.

2. Select range to publish.

3. Click **File** .... [Alt]+[F]

4. Click **Save as Web Page** .... [G]

5. Click **Republish** .... [Alt]+[E]

6. Click
Add interactivity .... [Alt]+[A]

7. Click **Publish** .... [Alt]+[P]

8. In the **Choose** list,
click **Previously published**
items .... [Alt]+[C], [↑↓], [Enter]

   ✓ Previously published range
   appears in list.

9. Make any necessary changes
in the options.

   ✓ Follow steps outlined in Publish
   an Interactive Worksheet
   procedure section.

10. Click **Publish** .... [Alt]+[P]

11. View the Web page in the
browser.

12. Click **File** .... [Alt]+[F]

13. Click **Close** .... [C]

Exercise Directions

1. Start Excel, if necessary.

2. Open 💿 **44_COFFEE**.

3. Save the file as **XL_44**.

4. Enter the prices for coffee:

	1/2 lb.	1 lb.	2 lbs.
Java Colombian	5.75	10.50	20.00
Java Mocha Blend	6.25	11.00	21.25
Java Hazelnut	5.75	10.50	20.00
Java Costa Rican	5.80	10.75	21.00
Java Ethiopian	5.75	10.50	20.00
Java Expresso	4.5	8.75	15.75

5. Enter the prices for coffee flavorings:

	1 oz.	3 oz.
Mint Madness	3.25	9.25
Almond Angel	3.25	9.25
Chocolate Lover	3.40	9.85

6. Format the prices as 11 points with Accounting
format, two decimal places.

   ✓ You can use the Currency Style formatting button, if
   you like.

7. Save the workbook and print one copy.

8. Preview the workbook as a Web page before
you attempt to publish it.

   ✓ When a workbook contains only one worksheet of
   data, you'll see only one worksheet in the preview.

9. Publish the worksheet as a noninteractive Web
page:

   a. Change the title to *Coffee by the Pound* in the
   Publish as Web Page dialog box.

   b. Use the file name POUND.htm.

   c. Choose to open the published Web page in a
   browser.

10. Your manager has just told you that the price
for Java Colombian has gone up:

   a. Switch back to the worksheet and make your
   changes.

   b. Change the price for 1/2 lb. to $6.25.

   c. Change the price for 1 lb. to $11.00.

   d. Change the price for 2 lbs. to $21.25.

11. Republish the worksheet.

12. Switch back to the Web browser. If necessary,
click Refresh to reload the Web page.

13. Exit the Web browser.

14. Save the workbook and exit Excel.

Java Jungle Café

	1/2 lb.	1 lb.	2 lbs.
Java Colombian	$ 6.25	$ 11.00	$ 21.25
Java Mocha Blend	$ 6.25	$ 11.00	$ 21.25
Java Hazelnut	$ 5.75	$ 10.50	$ 20.00
Java Costa Rican	$ 5.80	$ 10.75	$ 21.00
Java Ethiopian	$ 5.75	$ 10.50	$ 20.00
Java Expresso	$ 4.50	$ 8.75	$ 15.75

	1 oz.	3 oz.
Java Flavors: Mint Madness	$ 3.25	$ 9.25
Java Flavors: Almond Angel	$ 3.25	$ 9.25
Java Flavors: Chocolate Lover	$ 3.40	$ 9.85

Illustration B

Coffee by the Pound

Java Jungle Café

	1/2 lb.	1 lb.	2 lbs.
Java Colombian	$ 6.25	$ 11.00	$ 21.25
Java Mocha Blend	$ 6.25	$ 11.00	$ 21.25
Java Hazelnut	$ 5.75	$ 10.50	$ 20.00
Java Costa Rican	$ 5.80	$ 10.75	$ 21.00
Java Ethiopian	$ 5.75	$ 10.50	$ 20.00
Java Expresso	$ 4.50	$ 8.75	$ 15.75

	1 oz.	3 oz.
Java Flavors: Mint Madness	$ 3.25	$ 9.25
Java Flavors: Almond Angel	$ 3.25	$ 9.25
Java Flavors: Chocolate Lover	$ 3.40	$ 9.85

On Your Own

1. Start Excel, if necessary.

2. Open the **OXL_43** file created in Exercise 43.

3. Save the file as **OXL_44**.

4. Publish the worksheet as an interactive Web page.

5. If you have a connection to the Internet, go online and update the information on the mutual funds you selected.

6. Save the workbook and exit Excel.

Exercise 45

Skills Covered:

◆ **Import Text Files** ◆ **Import Data from Other Applications**
◆ **Import a Table from an HTML File** ◆ **Use the Clipboard to Import Data**
◆ **Export Data to Other Applications**

On the Job

If you have data that was created in another program, such as Lotus 1-2-3, you can import that data into Excel. Even if the program's files aren't directly supported by Excel, you can save the data in text format and import it that way instead. You can also import data from HTML files taken from the Internet. Finally, when necessary, you can export your data to other applications.

You're in charge of putting together some information for your boss at the Little Kids Toy Shoppe. He wants to start making decisions on what to order for the upcoming Christmas season, and that means analyzing information from a variety of sources. He wants you to put together a workbook that contains the latest sales figures from Bob (who uses Lotus 1-2-3), a list of children who have recently signed up for a special birthday discount (for a targeted marketing campaign), and the latest prices from the Little Ones Web site, which carries some of the hottest toys selling right now.

Terms

text file A file that contains only data and no formatting. Text files are also known as ASCII (pronounced *ASKee*) files and have a .txt file extension.

import Bring data into Excel from some outside source, such as Lotus 1-2-3.

delimiter Typically a comma, tab, or space, which separates one piece of data from another.

field A single cell's worth of data within a text file.

round trip The path that data takes from the Internet/intranet to Excel, then back again to the Internet/intranet. Round tripping can also involve taking data from Excel, publishing it to the Internet/intranet, and then downloading it back into Excel.

export Convert data from Excel into a format supported by other applications.

Notes

Import Text Files

- A **text file** can be **imported** into Excel, saving you the time and trouble of reentering the data.
  - The data in a text file is typically separated by commas, tabs, or spaces.
  - These separators (**delimiters**) allow Excel to convert data into columns.

- Each line of data in the file is placed on a different row in Excel.

- If Excel has problems deciding how the **fields** of data should be separated within the file, it displays the Text Import Wizard.
  - The Text Import Wizard is a series of dialog boxes that help you guide Excel through the process of importing the file correctly.

Import Data from Other Applications

- Excel supports the native formats of many popular applications.
  - If the file you wish to import is in one of these formats, you don't need to do anything special — just open it.
- Excel supports the following formats for importing:
  - ✓ *If the format you need isn't listed, open the file in its native program, and save the file in a format that Excel does support, such as text.*
  - Lotus 1-2-3 (release 1.x, 2.x, 3.x, and 4.x)
  - Quattro Pro for DOS
  - Quattro Pro for Windows (versions 5.0, 6.0 and 7.0)
  - Microsoft Works 2.0
  - Microsoft Works for DOS
  - dBASE II, III, and IV
  - Symbolic Link Format (SYLK)
  - HTML
  - Data Interchange Format (DIF)
  - Text files in PRN, TEXT, CXV, and other formats
- After importing the data into Excel, you'll need to use the Save As command to save it in Excel format.
  - ✓ *If you click Save, the file is saved in its native format.*

Import a Table from an HTML File

- Although Excel can open any HTML file (Web page), if you want to use the HTML data in an Excel worksheet, you'll have the most success if that data is in an HTML table.
- To import just the table, you use the Web Query Wizard.
  - A Web query is used to pull data from a specific Web page.
  - You can pull data from a table or a preformatted section (a section of the Web page in which data has been laid out in columns without using the HTML table format).
  - You can import the formatting with the table.

- Excel comes with several predesigned Web queries you can use to import common data from the Web, such as stock quotes.
- Since Excel can save data in HTML format and publish it on the Internet, you can **round trip** data by taking it from the Internet/intranet, making changes as needed, and republishing it on the Internet or intranet.

Use the Clipboard to Import Data

- Another way to import data into Excel is to use the Clipboard.
- The Clipboard enables you to copy or move data from one Windows application to another.
- To use this method, you simply open the file that contains the data you wish to import, select the data, then copy and paste that data into an Excel worksheet.

Export Data to Other Applications

- Excel can save (**export**) data in a variety of formats for use in other programs.
  - ✓ *You might do this, for example, if you need to share data with a colleague who doesn't use Excel, or who uses an older version.*
- When you save data in another format, you may lose some formatting.
  - ✓ *This will always happen if you convert the data to text format.*
- In addition to the file formats listed in the previous section, Excel can save data in these formats:
  - Excel version 4.0
  - Excel version 3.0
  - Excel version 2.0
- If data is saved in Excel version 4.0, 3.0, or 2.0 format, only the active worksheet will be saved — not the entire workbook.
  - Likewise, if you save data in Lotus 1-2-3 format, release 1.x, 2.x, or 3.x, only the current worksheet is saved.
  - If you save data in Quattro Pro or dBASE format, only the current worksheet is saved.
    - ✓ *Excel saves data only in Quattro Pro for DOS format, not Quattro Pro for Windows.*

Procedures

Import a Text File

1. Click **Data** .... `Alt`+`D`
2. Click **Get External Data** ...... `D`
3. Click **Import Text File** .... `T`
4. Select the text file.
5. Click **Import** .... `Alt`+`M`
   - ✓ *The Text Import Wizard dialog box opens.*
6. Choose the file type:
   - **Delimited** .... `Alt`+`D`

   OR
   - **Fixed width** .... `Alt`+`W`
7. Choose the row at which to begin importing in the **Start import at row** box ...... `Alt`+`R`
8. Choose operating system used to create file from the **File origin** list .... `Alt`+`O`
9. Click **Next>** .... `Enter`
10. Select how fields are separated:

    If you're importing a delimited file:
    - ✓ *To select a delimiter:*
    - **Tab** .... `Alt`+`T`
    - **Space** .... `Alt`+`S`
    - **Semicolon** .... `Alt`+`M`
    - **Comma** .... `Alt`+`C`
    - **Other** .... `Alt`+`O`
      (Enter the delimiter for other.)
      - ✓ *To skip empty columns:*
    - **Treat consecutive delimiters as one** .. `Alt`+`R`

    If you're importing a fixed-width file:
    - ✓ *To set column breaks:*
    - Click ruler at the desired position (follow the instructions in the dialog box).
11. Click **Next>** .... `Enter`
12. Select the formats to apply:

a. Click column in the Data preview section.
b. Select column data format:
   - **General** .... `Alt`+`G`
   - **Text** .... `Alt`+`T`
   - **Date** .... `Alt`+`D`

   OR

   Do not import column (skip) .... `Alt`+`I`
13. Repeat step 12 for each column.
14. Click **Finish** .... `Alt`+`F`
15. Specify where you want to put the imported data:

    a. **Existing worksheet** .... `Alt`+`E`
       - ✓ *Specify the upper-left cell.*
    b. **New worksheet** ..... `Alt`+`N`
16. Click **OK** .... `Enter`

Import Data from Other Applications *(Ctrl+O)*

1. Click **Open** button 🗁.

   OR

   a. Click **File** .... `Alt`+`F`
   b. Click **Open** .... `O`
2. Select the file type you want to import from the **Files of type** list .... `Alt`+`T`, `↑` `↓`, `Enter`
3. Select the file.
4. Click **Open** .... `Alt`+`O`

Import a Table from an HTML File

1. Click **Data** .... `Alt`+`D`
2. Click **Get External Data** ...... `D`
3. Click **New Web Query** .... `W`
4. Enter the address of the Web page whose table you wish to import.
   - ✓ *You can also click **Browse Web** and use your Web browser to locate the page. Once you find it, switch back to the dialog box without closing the Web browser.*

5. Select the part of the Web page that contains the data you want to import:
   - **The entire page** ..... `Alt`+`P`

   OR
   - **Only the tables** ...... `Alt`+`T`

   OR
   - **One or more specific tables on the page** .... `Alt`+`O`
6. Choose the amount of formatting you wish to retain, if any:
   - **None** .... `Alt`+`N`

   OR
   - **Rich text formatting only** ..... `Alt`+`R`

   OR
   - **Full HTML formatting** .... `Alt`+`F`
7. Click **OK** .... `Enter`
   - ✓ *You can click **Save Query** and save the query information in a reusable file that you can use to import this same table from this Web page at a later date.*

Export Data to Other Applications

1. Click **File** .... `Alt`+`F`
2. Click **Save As** .... `A`
3. Select drive:
   a. Click **Save in** .... `Alt`+`I`
   b. Select drive .... `↕`, `Enter`
4. Select folder in drive:
5. Double-click folder name in list .... `Tab`, `↕`, `Enter`
6. Select file type to which you wish to export in the **Save as type** list box .... `Alt`+`T`, `↑` `↓`, `Enter`
7. Click in **File name** text box .... `Alt`+`N`
8. Type file name.
9. Click **OK** .... `Enter`

Exercise Directions

1. Start Excel, if necessary.

2. Open ⊘ **45_BESTSELLERS.wk4**, a Lotus 1-2-3 file.

   ✓ *Change the* Files of type setting *in the Open dialog box to* Lotus 1-2-3 Files *in order to find the file.*

3. Save the workbook in Microsoft Excel Workbook format as **XL_45**.

   ✓ *Change the* Save as type *setting to* Microsoft Excel Workbook (*.xls) *to save the workbook properly.*

4. Rename Sheet1 *Hot Sellers*.

5. Change to Sheet2 and import the text file ⊘ **45_BIRTHDAY.txt**.

   a. It's a delimited file, so make that selection on the first page of the Text Import Wizard.

   b. Set Start import at row to 1.

   c. Choose tabs as the delimiter.

   d. Use General format for each column of data except for the second column, where you should apply MDY Date format.

   ✓ *In step 3 of 3 of the Wizard, scroll down in the Data preview area until you can select the second column of data. Then select the* Date: MDY *option.*

   e. Import the data beginning in cell A1 of Sheet2.

   f. Rename Sheet2 *Kid's Birthday DB*.

6. Apply formatting to the Kid's Birthday DB worksheet.

   a. Apply Red fill, Arial 20 points, and Yellow text color to cells A1:C1.

   b. Apply Light Orange fill, Arial 12 points, bold, and Light Yellow text color to cells A2:C2 and A4:B4.

   c. Apply Red fill, Arial 10 points, bold, and Yellow text color to cells A6:E6.

7. Type the following column labels in cells A6:E6:

Child's Name	Birthday	Address	City	Zip Code

   • Adjust the width of columns to fit the headings and data.

8. In Sheet3, import an HTML table.

   a. Import the table from the HTML file ⊘ **45_LITTLEONES.html**, located on the DDC CD-ROM.

   ✓ *The path you need to enter in step 1 will look something like this:*
   file://D:/Learning Excel/45_LITTLEONES.html

   b. You need to import table number 3 from the HTML file, so select the option *One or more specific tables on the page* in step 2, and type *3* in the text box.

   c. In step 3, select Full HTML formatting.

   d. Import the data into cell A5 of Sheet3.

   e. In cell A2, type *Little Ones Price List*. Apply Arial 20 points, with Red fill and Yellow text color to A2:B2.

   f. In cell A3, type *As of 6/10/99*, and apply Arial 12 points, bold, with Light Orange fill and Light Yellow text color to A3:B3.

   g. Rename Sheet3 *Little Ones Prices*.

9. Change the prices for some of the items shown in the Little Ones Price List.

   a. Select the range A1:C20 and publish it as a Web page.

   b. Change the title to *Price List Update*.

   c. Save the file as **XL_45UPDATE.htm**.

10. View the file in the browser and then close the browser.

11. Save the workbook and exit Excel.

Illustration A

Little Kids Toy Shoppe
Birthday Database

Updated: February 12, 1999

Child's Name	Birthday	Address	City	Zip Code
John Marsh	12-Oct-94	567 Hillsdale Road	Cantersville	45678
Billy Marsh	3-Aug-97	567 Hillsdale Road	Cantersville	45678
Sue Cooper	21-Jun-89	4102 56th Street	Cantersville	45681
Sade Jones	4-Apr-87	4141 45th Street	Cantersville	45681
Chin Li	22-Jan-93	2145 Blandon Ave.	Glenwood	45721
Su Li	25-Oct-94	2145 Blandon Ave.	Glenwood	45721
Carter Jackson	3-Mar-97	5124 River Glen	Glenwood	45722
Shiree Jackson	21-Apr-95	5124 River Glen	Glenwood	45722
Tony Jackson	12-Sep-98	5124 River Glen	Glenwood	45722
Nicole Gamble	13-Jun-98	4123 44th Street	Cantersville	45681
Antonio Melez	28-Oct-97	212 Hillsdale Road	Cantersville	45678
Maria Melsz	15-Jan-90	212 Hillsdale Road	Cantersville	45678
Marcus Harris	10-Apr-91	3412 River Creek Dr.	Cantersville	45678
Terisha Harris	3-Jul-92	3412 River Creek Dr.	Cantersville	45678
Vanessa Combs	12-Mar-92	2156 Blandon Ave.	Glenwood	45721
Cheriece Martin	24-Sep-93	584 Hillsdale Road	Cantersville	45678
Tony Martin	15-Mar-90	584 Hillsdale Road	Cantersville	45678

Little Ones Price List
As of 6/10/99

Furball 32.95
Here it is — the one and only electronic furry thing.

Teddy the Bear 21.25
What could be more endearing than a talking bear?

Big Blue 24.25
From the best-selling children's book series, here is Big Blue. Predicted to be this season's hottest seller! Taking orders now.

Blue Town 79.95
The perfect accessory for your Big Blue.

Old Town Girls — Bessie 112.45
From the Old Town Girls collection. Bessie comes with two outfits, shoes, school books, hat, and her little dog, Bonnie.

Old Town Girls — Victoria 112.45
From the Old Town Girls collection. Victoria comes with two outfits, and accessories, including a chiffon pink dress for her coming out party.

Tickle Me, I'm Elmer! 19.75
This little bear is just irresistible.

Furball Collector's Case 19.25
For the true furball.

On Your Own

1. Start Excel and Word, if necessary.

2. In Word, create a text document to import into Excel.

   a. Create a list with at least four columns and five rows.

   b. Some examples for the column headings: *Name, Address, City, State, Zip Code,* or *Movie, Subject, Female Lead, Male Lead, Star Rating* or *Name, Position, Years with Company, Salary.*

   c. In each line, follow each entry with a comma.

   d. Add a comma to the last entry in a line before you press Enter.

   e. Purposefully leave some entries blank, but follow each blank with a comma.

   f. Save the file as **OXL_45.txt** and close Word.

     ✓ In the *Save as type* box, select *Text Only (*.txt)*.

3. In Excel, import the text file. If the table column entries don't line up correctly in the worksheet, reopen **OXL_45.txt** in Word and correct the problem (probably the comma delimiters), and import the file again. Save the Excel file as **OXL_45.xls**.

4. Create another text document in Word similar to the one above, but use tabs instead of commas to separate the entries. Save it as **OXL_45A.txt**.

5. Arrange the Word window and the Excel window side by side on the desktop.

   a. Open Sheet2 in Excel.

   b. Select the text in the text document.

   c. Drag and drop the text into Excel.

5. Save the workbook and exit Excel.

Exercise 46

◆ **Critical Thinking**

You're the accountant who handles the bookkeeping for The Harvest Time Bread Company. Your Excel worksheet for June Sales indicates either that sales really jumped during June or there's a mistake in the sales figures given to you. You must send a memo to the company along with the worksheet so the figures can be confirmed. You also need a text document from the company showing the proposed price changes that you want to include in the worksheet.

Exercise Directions

1. Start Excel, if necessary.
2. Open ⊙ **46_HARVEST.xls**.
3. Save the file as **XL_46**.
4. Open Word and the file ⊙ **46_JUNESALES.doc**.
5. Save the file as **XL_46A.doc**.
6. In Excel, copy the range C4:F18 and paste link it into the Word memo, below the message. To center the table:
   a. Select the table and select Object on the Format menu.
   b. On the Layout tab, choose the Center alignment option.
7. Double-click the table and change the number of Honey Wheat Rolls sold to 3399 and the number of Butter White Rolls sold to 3310.
8. Return to Word to see if the changes are reflected.
9. Save the Word document, print one copy, and close Word.

10. In Excel, select the range C4:F18 and publish the selection as an interactive Web page.
    a. Change the file name to Harvest Time.htm.
    b. Change the title to *Harvest Time Bread June Sales Summary*.
    c. Select Open published Web page in browser, if it isn't already selected.
    d. Publish the selection.
11. In the browser, select the text *The Harvest Time Bread Company*.
    a. Click the Property Toolbox, the next-to-last button on the right end of the toolbar above the worksheet.
    b. Select Blue as the color for the font.
    c. Close the toolbox.
    d. Change the price of Honey Wheat Rolls to 0.60. Notice the total price change as you complete the entry.
    e. Close the browser.
12. In Excel, import the text file ⊙ **46_NEWPRICES.txt**.
    a. The file is delimited with tabs.
    b. Import the data beginning in cell C21.
    c. Format the new prices as numbers, two decimal places.
    d. Adjust column widths as necessary.
13. Save the workbook and exit Excel.

Lesson 8

Use Advanced Functions

Exercise 47

- ◆ **Understand IF Functions**
- ◆ **Enter an IF Function**
- ◆ **Nested IF Functions**
- ◆ **=SUMIF()**
- ◆ **=COUNTIF()**
- ◆ **Conditional Formatting**

Exercise 48

- ◆ **PMT Function**
- ◆ **What-If Data Tables**

Exercise 49

- ◆ **Solve a Problem with Goal Seek**
- ◆ **Use Solver to Resolve Problems**

Exercise 50

- ◆ **Conditional Sum Wizard**

Exercise 51

- ◆ **Audit Formulas**
- ◆ **Error Messages**

Exercise 52

- ◆ **Hide Data**
- ◆ **Save Different Views of the Workbook (Custom Views)**

Exercise 53

- ◆ **Scenarios**
- ◆ **Report Manager**

Exercise 54

- ◆ **VLOOKUP Function**
- ◆ **HLOOKUP Function**

Exercise 55

- ◆ **Lock/Unlock Cells in a Worksheet**
- ◆ **Protect a Worksheet**
- ◆ **Protect a Workbook**

Exercise 56

- ◆ **Share Workbooks**
- ◆ **Track Changes**
- ◆ **Merge Changes**

Exercise 57

- ◆ **Critical Thinking**

Exercise 47

◆ **Understand IF Functions** ◆ **Enter an IF Function**
◆ **Nested IF Functions** ◆ **=SUMIF()** ◆ **=COUNTIF()**
◆ **Conditional Formatting**

On the Job

IF functions allow you to test for values in your worksheet and then perform specific actions based on the result. For example, with an IF function, you could calculate the bonuses for a group of salespeople on the premise that bonuses are only paid if a sale is over $1,000. With the SUMIF function, you could total the sales in your Atlanta office, even if those sales figures are scattered all over the worksheet. And with the COUNTIF function, you could count the number of sales that resulted in a bonus being paid. If you want to highlight certain values in the worksheet, you can use conditional formatting.

As the manager of Pine Tree Apartments, you've been unhappy with the amount of time required to rent some of your apartments. So you're offering your staff a chance to earn some extra money, depending on the kind of apartments they rent. You've created a worksheet to help you keep track of everything, and now you want to use several IF, SUMIF, and COUNTIF functions to calculate the bonuses.

Terms

function A preprogrammed Excel formula for a complex operation. Functions take the form =FUNCTION(argument1, argument2, argumentn)

condition Values are tested against the IF condition to determine whether the condition is true or false, and as a result, a particular action (or no action) is taken.

argument A variable entered into a function. An argument can be a number, text, a formula, or a cell or range reference. Commas separate the arguments in a function.

conditional formatting Formatting that Excel automatically applies to cells when specified conditions are met.

Notes

Understand IF Functions

■ An IF statement is a logical **function** that defines a condition to test data.

■ If the result of the condition is true, one thing happens; if it's false, something else (or nothing) happens.

■ The format for an IF statement is as follows:

=IF(condition,x,y)

• The **condition** is a true/false statement.

• If condition is true, the result is **x**.

• If condition is false, the result is **y**.

■ For example, a teacher could use an IF statement to determine whether each student has passed or failed, based on the final average. The IF statement could use the following **arguments**:

• If a student's average is below 69, then he or she fails.

• If it's 69 or above, then he or she passes.

- The IF statement might look like this:

=IF(C3>=69, "PASS","FAIL")

- ✓ If the value in C3 is greater than or equal to 69, the word PASS would appear in the cell in which the formula was typed. Otherwise, the word FAIL would appear instead.

- ✓ To calculate a pass or fail for each student, you would copy this formula to the appropriate cells.

- ✓ In functions, labels such as PASS and FAIL must be enclosed in quotation marks (").

■ IF statements use the conditional operators below to state the condition:

=	Equals	<>	Not equal to
>	Greater than	>=	Greater than or equal to
<	Less than	<=	Less than or equal to
&	Used for joining text *(concatenating)*		

- ✓ IF statements can be used in combination with the Boolean operators OR, AND, and NOT to evaluate complex conditions.

Enter an IF Function

■ To help you enter an IF function, use the Formula palette.

Formula palette

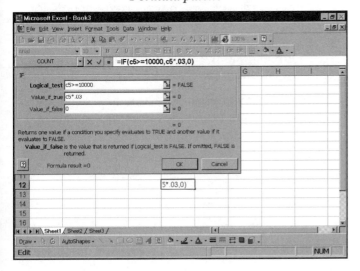

■ The Formula palette provides spaces for each part of the IF function: the condition, x, and y.

■ Each text box has a Collapse Dialog button at the end so that ranges can be selected from the workbook.

Nested IF Functions

■ You can use an IF function (or any other function, for that matter) as one of the arguments in another IF function.

■ For example:

=IF(C3>92, "A",IF(C3>83,"B",IF(C3>73,"C",IF(C3>65,"D","F"))))

- ✓ If the average score is greater than 92; the student gets an A if the score is less than or equal to 92 but greater than 83, the student gets a B if the score is less than or equal to 83 but greater than 73, the student gets a C, and so on.

=SUMIF()

■ A SUMIF statement is a logical function that uses a condition to add certain data.

■ If the result of the condition is true, data in a corresponding cell is added to the total; if it's false, the corresponding data is skipped.

■ The format for a SUMIF statement is as follows:

=SUMIF(range, condition, sum_range)

- Range is the range of cells you want to test.

- Condition is a true/false statement that defines which cells should be added to the total.

- If condition is true, the corresponding cell in sum_range is added to the total.

- If condition is false, the corresponding cell in sum_range is skipped (not added to the total)

■ For example, in a worksheet listing sales for several products, you might total the sales for widgets only by using this formula:

=SUMIF(D2:D55, "=Widget", G2:G55)

- ✓ Assume that column D contains the name of the product being sold, column E contains the quantity, column F contains the price, and column G contains the total amount for that sale.

- ✓ If column D contains the word Widget, the amount for that sale (located in column G) is added to the running total.

- ✓ Since Widget is a text label, you must enclose it in quotation marks (") in the formula.

■ You can leave the last argument off if you want to total the same range that you're testing. For example:

=SUMIF(G2:G10,<=500)

- ✓ Calculates the total of all values in the range G2:G10 that are less than or equal to 500.

=COUNTIF()

- A COUNTIF statement is a logical function that uses a condition to count the number of items in a range.

- If the result of the condition is true, the item is added to a running count; if it's false, the item is skipped.

- The format for a COUNTIF statement is as follows:

  =COUNTIF(range, condition)

  - Range is the range of cells you want to test.

  - Condition is a true/false statement that defines which cells should be counted.

- For example, to count the number of individual widget sales, you might use this formula:

  =COUNTIF(D2:D55, "=Widget")

  - ✓ *In this example, column D contains the name of the product being sold.*

  - ✓ *If column D contains the word Widget, that item is added to the running count.*

  - ✓ *Since Widget is a text label, you must enclose it in quotation marks (").*

- You can combine functions to create complex calculations, like this:

  =SUMIF(D3:D13,"PASS",C3:C13)/COUNTIF(D3:D13,"PASS")

  - ✓ *This computes the average score of all the students who passed the course.*

  - ✓ *Column D contains the words Pass or Fail, based on the student's final score. The final score is located in column C.*

  - ✓ *Excel counts the number of students who passed and calculates the total of their scores divided by the number who passed (notice the division operator, /) thus ending up with an average passing score.*

- You can also use these count functions for simple tasks:

  - COUNT() Counts the number of cells in a range that contain values.

  - COUNTA() Counts the number of cells in a range that are not empty.

  - COUNTBLANK() Counts the number of empty cells in a range.

Conditional Formatting

- To call attention to particular values, apply **conditional formatting**.

  - With conditional formatting, you specify whatever conditions you want, and then select formatting to apply when those conditions are met.

  - For example, with conditional formatting you could highlight expenses over $15,000 by adding a Blue fill, a Red text color, or both.

  - The formatting you choose is applied only to cells that meet the conditions you select.

  - Any formatting that's applied is added to existing formatting in the cell.

- You can choose up to three conditions for Excel to evaluate.

  - Excel evaluates the conditions in order. If a cell meets condition 1, the associated format is applied — and conditions 2 and 3 are not tested.

  - You can use multiple conditions to apply different formats, depending on the values in the cells. For example, you could add blue if the value is less than 200, green if the value is between 200 and 300, and red if the value is over 300.

- You can apply formatting based on the value in that cell, or on some other related result.

  - For example, if you have sales amounts for each store in column G and the total sales in cell G20, you could tell Excel to apply formatting to the cells in column G if they're greater than 15% of the total.

- You can copy conditional formatting with the Format Painter button, just as you would any other formatting.

Procedures

Enter an IF Function Using the Formula Palette

1. Click cell.
2. Type **equal (=)**.
3. Select **IF** function in Functions list.
4. Type condition in **Logical_test** box.
   - ✓ You can use the Collapse Dialog button and click cells in worksheet to insert cell references.
5. Click **Value_if_true** box ......
6. Type the argument if condition is true.
7. Click **Value_if_false** box..... Tab
8. Type the argument if condition is false.
9. Click **OK** .... Enter

Enter a SUMIF Function Using the Formula Palette

1. Click cell.
2. Type **equal (=)**.
3. Select **SUMIF** function in Functions list.
4. Type range to test in **Range** box.
   - ✓ You can use the Collapse Dialog button and click cells in worksheet to insert the range.
5. Click **Criteria** box .... Tab
6. Type the condition to test.
7. Click **Sum_range** box .... Tab
8. Type the range to sum if condition is true.
   - ✓ You can use the Collapse Dialog button and click cells in worksheet to insert the range.
9. Click **OK** .... Enter

Enter a COUNTIF Function Using the Formula Palette

1. Click cell.
2. Type **equal (=)**.
3. Select **More Functions** in Functions list.
4. Select **COUNTIF** in the **Function name** list ...... Alt + N

---

5. Click **OK** .... Enter
6. Type range to count in **Range** box.
   - ✓ You can use the Collapse Dialog button and click cells in worksheet to insert the range.
7. Click **Criteria** box .... Tab
8. Type the condition to test.
9. Click **OK** .... Enter

Apply Conditional Formatting

1. Select the cell or range to which you want to apply conditional formatting.
2. Click **Format** .... Alt + O
3. Click **Conditional Formatting** .... D
4. Select one of the following from the **Condition 1** list:
   - **Cell value is** if you want to use values as the formatting criteria. You can enter a value or a formula (a formula must start with an equal sign (**=**).
   - OR
   - **Formula is** if you want to use a formula as the formatting criteria. The formula must evaluate to a logical value of true or false.
5. Choose a compare operator from the second list.
6. Enter the value or cell reference or type the formula you want to use in the next box.
   - ✓ If you selected Cell value is in step 4, you can use a formula and the result of the formula is compared to the value in the cell(s) you selected in step 1. For example, you could enter =AVERAGE($F$3:$F$12), and compare the average of all the cells in column F with the value of the cell you selected in step 1.
   - ✓ If you selected Formula is in step 4, the formula you enter here is evaluated for a true/false condition. For example, you could enter =AVERAGE($F$3:$F$12)>1255 00, and format the cells you

---

selected in step 1 only if the average of the cells in column F is over $125,500.

7. Click **Format**................ Alt + F
8. Select the formats you want to apply if the conditions are met, such as font color, border(s), and color fill.
9. Click **OK** to return to the Conditional Formatting dialog box .... Enter
10. Add another condition if desired:
    a. Click **Add**............... Alt + A
    b. Repeat steps 4 to 9.
       - ✓ You can add up to three conditions, but the second and third conditions are ignored if the first condition is true, and so on.
11. Click **OK** .... Enter

Remove Conditional Formatting

1. Select the cells whose conditional formatting you wish to remove.
2. Click **Format**............... Alt + O
3. Click **Conditional Formatting**......................... D
4. Click **Delete** .... Alt + D
5. Select the condition you wish to remove.
6. Click **OK** .... Enter
7. Repeat steps 4 to 6 to remove other conditions.
8. Click **OK** .... Enter

Find Cells That Have Conditional Formatting

1. Click **Edit** .... Alt + E
2. Click **Go To**........................ G
3. Click **Special** .... Alt + S
4. Select **Conditional Format** .... T
5. Click **OK** .... Enter

Exercise Directions

1. Start Excel, if necessary.

2. Open 💿 **47_RENTED**.

3. Save the workbook as **XL_47**.

4. On the January Available worksheet, insert a column between columns H and I.
   - Use the column label *Rental Bonus*.

5. Enter formulas in column I that calculate the possible bonus to be paid if the apartment is rented.

   a. A bonus of $100 is paid for renting a 1 BR apartment, $150 for a 2 BR, and $225 for a 3 BR.
      - ✓ You'll need to use a nested IF function to create the formulas. Also, be sure to put "1 BR" "2 BR" and "3 BR" in quotes, since they're text labels.

   b. Format column I with Accounting format, two decimal places.

   c. Apply a conditional format to the range I12:I23 that applies Light Yellow fill if the value is equal to $225.

6. Type *Recap* in cell B26.

   a. Copy the format from cell B11.

   b. Adjust the height of the row so it looks more like row 11.

   c. In cell B27, type *Total Apartments Available*:

   d. In cell B28, type *Total Apartments Rented*:

7. In cell E27, enter a formula that counts the number of apartments in the listing.

   a. Use the =COUNTA() function.

   b. Use the range B12:B23.

8. In cell E28, enter a formula to calculate the number of apartments rented this month.

   a. Use the =COUNTIF() function.

   b. Be sure to put "Rented" in quotes, since it's a text label.

9. Calculate the bonuses:

   a. In cell C30, type *# of Units Rented*.

   b. In cell D30, type *Bonus*.

   c. In cell B31, type *Mark Brandon*.

   d. In cell B32, type *Pam Grier*.

   e. In cell B33, type *Tyrone Hill*.

   f. In cell B34, type *Kate Harper*.

   g. Copy the format from cell B11 to the range C30:D30.

   h. Adjust the height of the row.

   i. In the range C31:C34, enter formulas that calculate the number of apartments rented by each associate.
      - ✓ Use the =COUNTIF() function.
      - ✓ To specify the rental agent's name as a condition, you can either type the name in quotes ("Mark Brandon") or refer to the cell containing the name (B31). If you refer to the cell, however, you can copy the formula from one cell to another, which saves a lot of typing.

   j. In the range D31:D34, enter formulas that calculate the bonuses to be paid.
      - ✓ Use the =SUMIF() function.

   k. Format the range D31:D34 with Accounting format, two decimal places.

10. Apply conditional formatting to the cells D31:D34:

    a. Use a formula and the COUNTIF() function to highlight the people who have rented three or more units in a month.

    b. Apply Light Yellow fill to the cells if they meet the condition.

    c. Apply the conditional formatting to cell D31, and then copy it to the other cells in the range.
       - ✓ Be sure to change the reference to cell D31 in the COUNTIF function so that it's mixed — $D31, and not absolute — $D$31. That way, when you copy the formula, the reference will adjust to the row it's in.

11. Repeat steps 4–9 to calculate bonuses for apartments rented in February.
    - ✓ The apartments rented in February appear on the February Available worksheet.

12. Preview and print both worksheets.

13. Save the workbook.

14. Close the workbook and exit Excel.

Illustration A

PINE TREE APARTMENTS

Apartments available: January 1999

Unit	Available	Type	Fireplace?	Carpet Color	Status	Rented By	Rental Bonus	Rented To
102 B	12-Jan	2 BR	No	Beige	Available		$ 150.00	
404 C	30-Jan	1 BR	Yes	Blue	Rented	Pam Grier	$ 100.00	Jane Doe
104 D	10-Jan	2 BR	Yes	Beige	Available		$ 150.00	
103 D	21-Jan	2 BR	No	Tan	Rented	Pam Grier	$ 150.00	Tim Black
311 D	22-Jan	2 BR	Yes	Tan	Rented	Mark Brandon	$ 150.00	Sue Cooper
415 A	10-Jan	1 BR	No	Blue	Rented	Tyrone Hill	$ 100.00	Lu Xeng
316 C	29-Jan	3 BR	Yes	Tan	Rented	Mark Brandon	$ 225.00	Jenny Dell
310 A	12-Jan	1 BR	No	Tan	Rented	Pam Grier	$ 100.00	Mike Smith
311 B	29-Jan	3 BR	Yes	Gray	Rented	Kate Harper	$ 225.00	Joe Brown
412 C	10-Jan	1 BR	No	Tan	Available		$ 100.00	
412 D	21-Jan	2 BR	No	Tan	Rented	Tyrone Hill	$ 150.00	Larry Fitz
105 B	17-Jan	2 BR	Yes	Gray	Rented	Mark Brandon	$ 150.00	Sally Wilson

Recap

Total Apartments Available:	12
Total Apartments Rented:	9

	# of Units Rented	Bonus
Mark Brandon	3	$ 525.00
Pam Grier	3	$ 350.00
Tyrone Hill	2	$ 250.00
Kate Harper	1	$ 225.00

On Your Own

1. Start Excel, if necessary.
2. Open ⊙ **47_PETSALES**.
3. Save the worksheet as **OXL_47**.
4. Create a recap of the daily sales.
   a. Create formulas that show the total number (each) of dogs, cats, and fish sold that day, as well as the total amount of sales for each of those categories.
   b. Create a formula that shows the total dollar amount in sales (each) for pets, feed, and accessories.
   c. Display the sales totals for each salesperson.
5. Use conditional formatting to apply Tan fill to any sale over $100.
6. Print the worksheet.
   - Print the recap on a separate page.
7. Save the workbook and exit Excel.

Exercise 48

On the Job

What-if analysis allows you to play around with the figures and formulas in your worksheet to determine the optimal values for a given situation. For example, if you know that you can spend a maximum of $32,000 this year on new computers, you could adjust the monthly budget amount so you spend the total amount by the end of the year, and yet still remain within your department's monthly budgetary constraints.

You're thinking about buying a home, and you want to investigate the possibilities. In this exercise, you'll connect to the Internet, do a little research on current interest rates for 30-year mortgages, and, using a two-input data table, determine the largest amount you can comfortably borrow.

Terms

what-if analysis Excel's term for a series of tools that you can use to solve calculations that involve one or more variables.

variable An input value that changes depending on the outcome desired.

substitution values A special name given to the variables used in a data table.

input cell A cell in which a list of input values from a data table is substituted.

data table A range of cells that shows how changing certain values in your formulas affects the results of the formulas.

Notes

PMT Function

- The PMT (payment) function can be used to calculate a loan payment amount given the principal, interest rate, and number of payment periods.

- The arguments for the PMT function are as follows:

  =PMT(rate,nper,pv)

  - *rate*   Interest rate per period (for example, annual interest/12).
  - *nper*   Number of payment periods (for example, years*12).
  - *pv*   Present value — the total amount that a series of future payments is worth now (for example, the principal).

✓ The rate and the number of payment periods (nper) must be expressed for the same period, such as monthly or annually.

✓ For example, to calculate a monthly payment at a 9% rate of interest for 25 years, enter .09/12 as the monthly interest rate and enter 25*12 to get the number of monthly payment periods (nper) per year.

✓ The present value must be entered as a negative if you want the result to be displayed as a positive number.

- The PMT function can also be used to calculate the amount you need to invest in order to achieve a specific future amount, given the interest rate and number of payment periods.

- The arguments for the PMT function are as follows:

  =PMT(<u>rate</u>,nper,,fv)

  - *rate*   Interest rate per period (for example, annual interest/12).
  - *nper*   Number of payment periods (for example, years*12).
  - *fv*   Future value — the amount that a series of payments will be worth in the future, given a set interest rate.

  ✓ *The rate and the number of payment periods (nper) must be expressed for the same period, such as monthly or annually.*

  ✓ *Notice the "extra" comma in the syntax line above. If you're skipping part of a function (in this case, the present value argument), you still must supply the comma that normally would appear after it. For a PMT formula where you intend to create a future value rather than pay off a loan, the present value when you start is zero, so you can enter the zero as an argument: =PMT(rate,nper,0,fv) or just skip it by entering the comma without the zero: =PMT(rate,nper,,fv).*

  ✓ *The future value must be entered as a negative if you want the result to be displayed as a positive number.*

What-If Data Tables

- Excel's **what-if analysis** allows you to perform calculations that have more than one **variable**. Use a what-if data table to evaluate different situations based on certain variables and to find the best solution.

- For example, if you want to purchase a home and can only afford $1,000 per month, a data table can determine the maximum mortgage amount you can afford.

- The variables used in a data table are called **substitution values**.

- The **input cell** is the cell referred to by the what-if formula.

- Excel places each variable into the input cell as it solves each equation.

  ✓ *The what-if formula must refer to this input cell.*

- **Data tables** come in two types: one-input data tables and two-input data tables.

  ✓ *A one-input data table has one input cell; a two-input data table has two input cells.*

- In a one-input data table, you enter one series of variables, which are then substituted in a formula to come up with a series of answers.

  ✓ *For example, you could enter a series of loan rates to determine the varying payment amounts on 30-year fixed loan.*

One-input data table

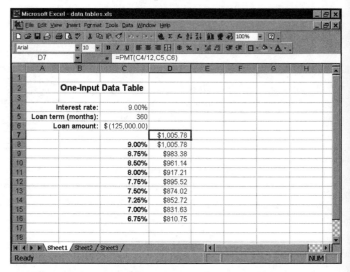

- In a two-input data table, you enter two series of variables, thus increasing the number of possible solutions.

  ✓ *For example, you can enter the loan rates and several loan terms (15, 20, 25, or 30 years) to determine what amount you can afford under varying plans.*

Two-Input data table

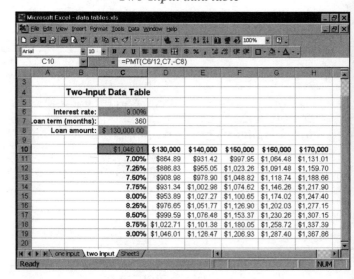

Procedures

Use the PMT Function

✓ *For example, to compute the monthly payment on a $100,000, 20-year loan at 6%, use this formula:*

=PMT(.06/12,20*12,-100000)

✓ *You can use cell references instead of typing values:*

=PMT(A1/12,A2*12,-A3)

1. Click cell where answer should appear.
2. Type **=PMT(** (opening parenthesis).
3. Type the rate divided by 12.

✓ *The rate is a percentage, so 9% would be entered as .09.*

4. Type **,** (comma).
5. Type the term times 12.

✓ *The term is the number of years.*

6. Type **,** (comma).
7. Type the principal.

✓ *The principal is the amount of the loan.*

✓ *If you want the answer expressed as a positive number, type a minus sign before the principal.*

8. Type **)** (closing parenthesis).
9. Press **Enter**.

Create a One-Input Data Table

1. Enter variables in a column.
2. Type the formula.

✓ *The formula must be entered in the cell one row above and one column to the right of the first column variable. For example, if you entered variables in cells C8:C16, type the formula in cell D7.*

✓ *The formula refers to a blank cell, which acts as an input cell.*

✓ *This procedure assumes that the data table has a column orientation rather than a row orientation. If you decide to enter the values for the data table across a row rather than down a column, place the formulas in the column to the left of the first value and one row below, rather than to the right and above.*

3. Select all cells in the data table range.

✓ *Select cells containing formula and substitution values. For example, select C7:D16.*

✓ *Don't select the input cell.*

4. Click **Data** .... Alt + D
5. Click **Table** .... T
6. Select **Column input cell** .... Alt + C

✓ *Select the input cell referred to by the formula in which the column variables should be used.*

7. Click **OK** .... Enter

Create a Two-Input Data Table

1. Enter one set of variables in a column.
2. Enter the second set of variables in a row.

✓ *Enter the first row variable one row above and one column to the right of the column of variables.*

✓ *For example, if you entered column variables in cells C11:C19, enter row variables in cells D10, E10, and so on.*

3. Click upper-left cell in table. ....

✓ *For example, click cell C10, just to the left of the first row variable.*

4. Type formula.

✓ *The formula refers to two blank (input) cells outside of the data table range, which act as input cells.*

5. Select all cells in the data table range.

✓ *Select cells containing formula and substitution values. For example, select C10:H19.*

✓ *Don't select the input cells.*

6. Click **Data** .... Alt + D
7. Click **Table** .... T
8. Select **Row input cell** .... Alt + R

✓ *Select the input cell referred to by the formula in which the row variables should be used.*

9. Select **Column input cell** .... Alt + C

✓ *Select the input cell referred to by the formula in which the column variables should be used.*

10. Click **OK** .... Enter

Exercise Directions

1. Start Excel, if necessary.
2. Open a new workbook and save it as **XL_48**.
3. In cell B2, type *Analysis for Home Loan*.
4. Format the title with Times New Roman, 18 points.
5. In cell B4, type *Rate:*
6. In cell B5, type *Principal:*
7. Apply bold, right-aligned formatting to cells B4 and B5.
8. In the range C8:H8, type the possible principal amounts: 150,000, 155,000, 160,000, and so on.
   a. Format the range with Accounting format, two decimal places, bold.
      ✓ *Adjust column widths, if necessary.*
   b. Apply this same format to cell C5.
   c. Type **150000** in cell C5.
9. In the range B9:B15, type the possible loan rates.
   a. Connect to the Internet and find out what the current home loan rates are for a 30-year fixed-rate loan.
      ✓ *Use www.bankrate.com or a search engine of your choice.*
      To use the DDC Internet simulation:
      • Click **Go**.
      • Click **Open**.
      • In the Address line, type the following: C:/Simulation/Ex48/Bankrate.htm
        ✓ *If you've copied the Internet simulation files to your hard drive or your CD-ROM drive is not C:, substitute the correct drive letter for C.*
      • Click **OK**.

   a. Use the lowest rate as your starting point; then add a **quarter** of a percent to each rate you enter in the range.
      ✓ *If the best rate you can get right now is 7.25%, enter that rate in cell B9, and enter 7.5% in cell B10, 7.75% in cell B11, and so on.*
      • In the simulation, click the *High five* link near the top of the page. In the Mortgages list, click the *30-year fixed* link.
   b. Format the range with Percent style, two decimal places, bold.
   c. Apply the same format to cell C4.
   d. Type the beginning rate in cell C4.
      ✓ *For example, if the best rate is 7.25%, type that in cell C4.*
10. In cell B8, enter a formula to calculate the monthly payment for a 30-year loan.
    a. Use cells C4 and C5 in the formula.
    b. Format cell B8 with Accounting format, two decimal places.
11. Select the range B8:H15.
12. Create a two-input data table using the selected range, cell C4 as the column input cell, and cell C5 as the row input cell.
    • Format the data table C9:H15 with Accounting format, two decimal places.
13. Print the worksheet.
14. Save the workbook and exit Excel.

Illustration A

Analysis for Home Loan

Rate:	6.00%
Principal:	$ 150,000

$899.33	$ 150,000	$ 155,000	$ 160,000	$ 165,000	$ 170,000	$ 175,000
6.00%	$ 899.33	$ 929.30	$ 959.28	$ 989.26	$ 1,019.24	$ 1,049.21
6.25%	$ 923.58	$ 954.36	$ 985.15	$ 1,015.93	$ 1,046.72	$ 1,077.51
6.50%	$ 948.10	$ 979.71	$ 1,011.31	$ 1,042.91	$ 1,074.52	$ 1,106.12
6.75%	$ 972.90	$ 1,005.33	$ 1,037.76	$ 1,070.19	$ 1,102.62	$ 1,135.05
7.00%	$ 997.95	$ 1,031.22	$ 1,064.48	$ 1,097.75	$ 1,131.01	$ 1,164.28
7.25%	$ 1,023.26	$ 1,057.37	$ 1,091.48	$ 1,125.59	$ 1,159.70	$ 1,193.81
7.50%	$ 1,048.82	$ 1,083.78	$ 1,118.74	$ 1,153.70	$ 1,188.66	$ 1,223.63

On Your Own

1. Start Excel, if necessary.

2. Create a new workbook and save it as **OXL_48**.

3. Create a one-input data table to help you analyze a possible investment.

   a. You want to invest some money each month in a money market fund.

   b. You want to end up with $25,000 at the end of five years.

4. Go online and get the current range of money market account rates.

   ✓ *Try www.bankrate.com or http://cnnfn.com/, or your favorite search engine.*

   • Use this range of possible rates as data for your input table.

5. Print the completed worksheet.

6. Save the workbook and exit Excel.

Exercise 49

◆ Solve a Problem with Goal Seek
◆ Use Solver to Resolve Problems

On the Job

Goal Seek and Solver provide additional ways in which you can solve "what if" problems. If you know some of the variables — that you wish to spend only $250,000 on new equipment, for example — you can use Goal Seek to help you determine which items and how many of each item you can buy. Solver could help you limit your budget to $40,000 a month while spending the total of $250,000 on equipment over the course of a year.

As the owner of a small but profitable toy company called Little Kids, you like to keep your employees happy. Everyone worked very hard during the holidays, and you hoped that by the end of the first quarter, you could afford to pay out a small bonus. With the help of Goal Seek, you'll meet your minimum profit goals while paying out the largest bonus possible.

Terms

Goal Seek A method of performing what-if analysis in which the result is known, but the value of a dependent variable is unknown.

Solver Another method of performing what-if analysis, in which the result is known but more than a single variable is unknown. There may also be additional constraints on the final result.

constraint A restriction placed on an adjustable variable in a Solver problem. For example, you can constrain Solver to spending a minimum or maximum amount in a particular category of monthly, quarterly, or annual expenses.

Notes

Solve a Problem with Goal Seek

- With **Goal Seek**, you can solve a problem when you know the desired result, but not one of the input variables.

- Goal Seek tests possible variables until it finds the input value that produces the desired result.

- For example, you can use Goal Seek to determine the exact amount you can borrow with a payment of $1,000 a month and a specific interest rate.

Use Solver to Resolve Problems

- With **Solver**, you can resolve problems involving more than one variable, with a known result.

- For example, you can adjust the amount you spend on new computers so that you don't go over an annual total of $100,000, while simultaneously limiting spending to $25,000 for any given month.

  ✓ *Another way to solve problems with multiple variables is with a PivotTable, which you'll learn how to use in Lesson 10.*

- Solver is more complicated to use than Goal Seek because the types of problems it solves tend to involve more than one variable—which is all that Goal Seek can handle.

- For example, suppose you want to deposit $600 in your savings account over the course of the next 12 months. You need an average of $50 per month to put toward savings (let's ignore for the moment any dividends or interest you earn on this money). Solver can figure out how best to adjust your regular expenses to accumulate the $50 each month. Some expenses are fixed amounts — rent or mortgage, insurance, and the like — but some may be adjustable — food, clothing, gifts/entertainment, and so on. Solver can adjust these amounts to find the optimal combination of amounts to give you the $100 for savings.

- When adjusting your expenses, you probably can't adjust most of them to zero — you need food, for example — so you use **constraints** to limit Solver to a minimum (or maximum) allowable amount for each adjustable expense.

- The advantage of using Solver is that you can usually make these types of calculation in minutes — and then, if the result isn't really workable, adjust the constraints and try again until Solver finds an appropriate solution.

- Solver isn't limited to solving money problems. For example, you might use Solver to calculate the optimal combination of staff, supplies, and animals bordered at your stables. For this type of problem, you might have the following types of adjustable variables:
  - Combination full-time and part-time grooms, trailer drivers, and trainers
  - Scheduled hours in a workday or workweek
  - Size of feed orders (assuming that larger orders get a better price break)
  - Rates for boarding geldings or mares versus stallions (which require individual enclosures away from other animals)
  - Rates for boarding racehorses or show animals (which require frequent loading and unloading as they travel to races or shows) versus riding animals or pets (which stay on your grounds full-time, or which might be groomed by their owners)

- Constraints might include some of the following:
  - Available stalls and enclosures; available storage space for feed; number of trailers; available tack
  - Hours required for feeding and grooming each animal
  - Maximum number of work hours per workday (you don't want to feed the horses at 3:00 in the morning)

Procedures

Use Goal Seek

1. Click **Tools** .... Alt+T
2. Select **Goal Seek** .... G
3. In the **Set Cell** box, select the cell that contains the formula you want to solve.
4. In the **To value** text box, type the result you want.
5. In the **By changing cell** box, select the cell that contains the value you want to adjust.
6. Click **OK** .... Enter

Use Solver

1. Click **Tools** .... Alt+T
2. Select **Solver** V

   ✓ If Solver isn't installed, you can install it with the **Tools, Add-Ins** command. (In the Add-Ins dialog box, scroll down in the **Add-Ins available** list and click **Solver Add-in**. Then click **OK**. When Excel indicates that it can't run this add-in and asks if you want to install it now, click **Yes**. You'll need the Office 2000 CD-ROM.)

3. In the **Set Target Cell** box, select the cell that contains the formula you want to solve.
4. Select an option:
   - Select **Max** .... Alt+M
   OR
   - Select **Min** .... Alt+N
   OR
   a. Select **Value of** .... Alt+V
   b. Type the value you want.
5. In the **By Changing Cells** box, select the cell(s) containing the values you want to adjust.

6. Add any constraints:

   a. Click **Add** ....

   b. Select a **Cell**
      Reference ....

   c. Select a comparison
      operator.

   d. Type or select a
      Constraint .... [Alt]+[C]

e. Click **OK** .... [Enter]

   ✓ To set multiple constraints,
     click **Add** instead of **OK**
     and add the next
     constraint. Repeat this
     step until you have added
     all the constraints, then
     click **OK**.

7. Click **Solve** .... [Enter]

8. Click **OK** .... [Enter]

   ✓ You can save the scenario,
     restore your previous values,
     or print reports from the dialog
     box that appears.

Exercise Directions

1. Start Excel, if necessary.

2. Open ⊙ **49_BONUS**.

3. Save the workbook as **XL_49**.

4. Bold and center the range, C9:F9.

5. Enter the figures for March:

Sales	$122,750.00
Salaries	$33,500.00
Operating Costs	$26,391.25

6. Use Goal Seek to find the largest bonus possible:

   a. The net profit for the quarter must equal $185,000.

   b. Change the proposed bonus percent in cell F3 until the goal is reached.

   ✓ *When Goal Seek adjusts the bonus percentage in cell F3, the values for the bonus formulas in row 12 change to use the new percentage, and cells F12 and C14:F14 show adjusted totals. Try using undo (Ctrl+Z) and redo (Ctrl+Y) repeatedly to watch the changes occur. Be sure to redo the goal seek before you continue to step 7.*

7. Create the bonus area:

   a. Type *Per Person* in cell C16.

   b. Type *Totals* in cell D16.

   c. Bold and center both cells.

   d. Type *Full Time Bonus* in cell B17.

   e. Type *Part Time Bonus* in cell B18.

   f. Apply italics right-align both cells.

8. Enter formulas to calculate the bonuses (even though there are no values to calculate at this point).

   a. There are nine full-time employees and four part-time employees.

   b. Create formulas in cells C17 and C18 to calculate the bonus per person.

   ✓ *For example, the formula for cell C17 divides the total shown in cell D17 by nine full-time employees.*

   c. The total bonus for the part-time employees is 33% of the total for the full-time employees.

   ✓ *Create a formula in cell D18 to calculate this amount.*

   d. Create a formula in D19 to total cells D17 and D18.

9. Use Solver to calculate the bonus payouts.

   a. With cell D19 as the target cell, have Solver change the amount in cell D17 until cell D19 has a value equal to cell F12, which is the total bonus payout that fits within your required bottom-line profit amount.

   b. Apply Accounting format, two decimal places to the range C17:D19.

10. Preview and print the worksheet.

11. Save and close the workbook and exit Excel.

On Your Own

1. Start Excel, if necessary.

2. Create a new workbook and save it as **OXL_49**.

3. Create a worksheet to help you determine the price you must charge for tickets to a one-night theatrical production, given the following information:

   a. Costumes cost $750.

   b. Scenery: $1,025.

   c. Theater rental: $1,500.

   d. Electrician: $225.

   e. Fee for the play: $1,350

   f. Playbills: $4.25 each (theater capacity is 1,420).

      ✓ *Assume that you'll always print 1,420 playbills.*

   g. You must make a profit of $1,200 as seed money for the next play.

4. Use Goal Seek to answer the following questions:

   a. What would be the lowest price you could charge for a ticket if the play were a sellout?

   b. How many seats would you have to fill if the ticket price were $9.00?

   c. What would be the lowest ticket price possible if you had an 80% sellout?

      ✓ *Hint: To solve the problems, set up tables like the one below:*

Tickets sold	
Ticket price	
Revenue	(formula)

   a. Enter a formula to calculate revenue. Use that cell for Goal Seek.

5. Save and close the workbook and exit Excel.

Exercise 50

Skills Covered:

◆ Conditional Sum Wizard

On the Job

With the Conditional Sum Wizard, you can quickly create a formula that totals only certain cells in a range, such as those cells that contain sales amounts for Indiana. The Conditional Sum Wizard takes the guesswork out of trying to use the IF function to perform the same task.

As the sales manager for Custom Made Closets and Cabinetry, you've been concerned about the store's recent expansion into cabinet sales and a broader selection of woods. You want to analyze the day's sales and see how the new products are doing. Luckily, with the Conditional Sum Wizard, your job's almost done!

Terms

Conditional Sum Wizard A series of dialog boxes that help you create an IF formula to total a given range, provided that the cells meet the criteria you set.

IF function A special function that performs a calculation only if the cell meets given criteria.

add-in An Excel feature that's not installed initially, but which you can easily add to the program when needed.

Notes

Conditional Sum Wizard

- Using the **Conditional Sum Wizard,** you can create a formula that uses **IF function** to total a given range of cells that meet the criteria you specify.
  - For example, if you have a list of sales totals, you can use the Conditional Sum Wizard to total all sales over $10,000.
- The Conditional Sum Wizard is an **add-in** that's not initially installed; it needs to be loaded on first use.
- You can apply multiple conditions to the IF formula.
  - For example, you could tell the Conditional Sum Wizard to total only those sales that are $10,000 or more for stores in Indiana.

Conditional Sum Wizard

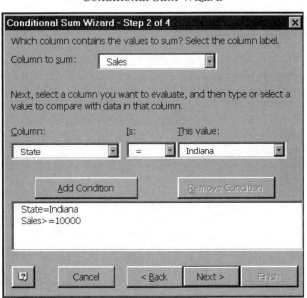

217

Procedures

Install the Conditional Sum Wizard

1. Click **Tools** .... `Alt`+`T`
2. Click **Add-Ins**. .... `I`
3. Click **Conditional Sum Wizard** .... `↓` `↑`, `Space`
4. Click **OK** .... `Enter`
5. When Excel asks whether to install the add-in, click **Yes** .... `Enter`

   ✓ You need the Office 2000 CD-ROM to install the add-in.

Use the Conditional Sum Wizard

1. Click inside the data range.

   ✓ The data range is the range that contains the worksheet data, and column row labels.

2. Click **Tools** .... `Alt`+`T`
3. Click **Wizard** .... `Z`
4. Click **Conditional Sum** .... `C`
5. Step 1: Click **Next >** .... `Enter`

   ✓ The proper data range should be selected automatically — if it's wrong, click the Collapse Dialog button and select the range yourself before clicking **Next >**.

6. Step 2: Select the **Column to sum**, if it's not already correct. .... `Alt`+`S`, `↕`
7. Select the **Column** to be checked for conditional values. .... `Alt`+`C`, `↕`
8. Select the **Is** condition operator .... `Alt`+`I`, `↕`
9. Select **This value** and select a label .... `Alt`+`T`, `↕`
10. Click **Add Condition** ... `Alt`+`A`

    ✓ You can repeat steps 7 to 10 to add additional conditions.

11. Click **Next >** .... `Enter`
12. Step 3: Specify how you want to copy the formula to the worksheet:

- **Copy just the formula to a single cell** .... `Alt`+`C`

  OR

- **Copy the formula and conditional values** .... `Alt`+`O`

13. Click **Next >** .... `Enter`
14. Step 4: Enter the cell location for the formula in the **Type or select a cell and then click Finish** box .... `Alt`+`T`

    OR

    Use the Collapse Dialog button to select the cell.

    ✓ If you're copying the formula and the conditional values, specify a cell where you want to place the conditional value and click **Next >**. Then specify the cell where you want to copy the formula.

15. Click **Finish** .... `Enter`

Exercise Directions

1. Start Excel, if necessary.
2. Open 💿 **50_CLOSET**.
3. Save the workbook as **XL_50**.
4. In cell D32, type *Totals*.
   a. Format the cell with Times New Roman, 14 points.
   b. Use AutoSum in cell F32 to create a formula that totals the sales for the day.
   c. Format cell F32 with Arial, 11 points, bold.
5. In cell E33, type *Total Closet Sales.*
   a. In cell E34, type *Total Cabinet Sales.*
   b. In cell E36, type *Total Pine Sales.*
   c. In cell E37, type *Total White Laminate Sales.*
   d. In cell E38, type *Total Oak Sales.*
   e. In cell E39, type *Total Maple Sales.*
   f. In cell E40, type *Total Cedar Sales.*
   g. In cell E41, type *Total Cherry Sales.*
   h. Apply italics and right-align cells E33:E41.
6. Use the Conditional Sum Wizard to calculate the following:
   a. In cell F33, total just closet sales.
   b. In cell F34, total just cabinet sales.
   c. In cell F36, total the pine sales.
   d. In cell F37, total the white laminate sales.
   e. In cell F38, total the oak sales.
   f. In cell F39, total the maple sales.
   g. In cell F40, total the cedar sales.
   h. In cell F41, total the cherry sales.
7. Preview and print the worksheet.
8. Save the workbook and exit Excel.

On Your Own

1. Start Excel, if necessary.
2. Open **OXL_47**, which you created in a previous exercise, or open 💿 **50_PETSALES**.
3. Save the file as **OXL_50**.
4. Since the highest profit is made on the sale of accessories and fish, the store owner wants to know the value of accessories and the value of fish each salesperson sold. Use the Conditional Sum Wizard to provide the answer. (You'll have to add two conditions in Step 2 of the wizard.)
5. Save the workbook and exit Excel.

Exercise 51

Skills Covered:

◆ **Audit Formulas** ◆ **Error Messages**

On the Job

If you have a problem with formulas in a large or complex worksheet, working through each formula to locate the values in the cells it references and to verify that everything is all right can be a tedious, complex job unless you use the Auditing feature.

As the accounting manager for Custom Made Closets and Cabinetry, you're pretty proud of the work you've just put in on creating a quarterly budget and income statement. But there's a problem, and you're not sure where to start, since the worksheet is full of complex calculations. In this exercise, you'll use Excel's auditing tools to help you locate the problem and fix it.

Terms

Auditing toolbar Contains buttons that help you quickly locate the source of any problem involving a formula.

precedent A cell referenced in a formula.

dependents Formulas whose results depend on the value in a cell.

Notes

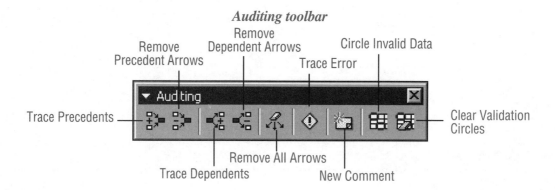

Auditing toolbar

Remove Precedent Arrows
Remove Dependent Arrows
Circle Invalid Data
Trace Error
Trace Precedents
Clear Validation Circles
Trace Dependents
Remove All Arrows
New Comment

Audit Formulas

- If you're having a problem with a formula, you can check its result with the buttons on the **Auditing toolbar**.
- With the Auditing toolbar, you can trace a formula's **precedents** — cells referred to by the formula.

- If you're worried about changing the value in a cell, you can trace its **dependents** with the Auditing toolbar.
  - A dependent is a formula whose result depends on the value in a given cell.
- When you trace precedents or dependents, arrows point to the related cells.

■ If a formula contains an error, you can use the Trace Error button on the Auditing toolbar to trace the problem.

■ While tracing precedents, dependents, or errors, you can add comments to cells with the Auditing toolbar.

  ✓ *As explained in Exercise 7, by default, a comment appears only when the mouse pointer is placed over the cell that contains the comment.*

■ You can trace errors caused by invalid data, and add circles around the errors you find with the Circle Invalid Data button on the Auditing toolbar.

  ✓ *You can later remove the circles with the Clear Validation Circles button.*

  ✓ *Invalid data is data in a cell that has a validation rule placed on it, but that doesn't meet with the validation requirements. See more on validation in Lesson 10.*

Tracing the precedents of a formula

	A	B	C	D	E	F
9	Commission Rate	0.06				
10	Bonus on sales over $40K	$200				
11						
12	Salesperson	Sales	Comm.	Bonus	Earnings	
13	Carl Jackson	$ 44,202.00	$2,652.12	$ 200.00	$ 47,054.12	
14	Ni Li Yung	$ 41,524.00	$2,491.44	$ 200.00	$ 44,215.44	
15	Tom Wilson	$ 43,574.00	$2,614.44	$ 200.00	$ 46,388.44	
16	Jill Palmer	$ 39,612.00	$2,376.72	$ -	$ 41,988.72	
17	Rita Nuez	$ 39,061.00	$2,343.66	$ -	$ 41,404.66	
18	Maureen Baker	$ 38,893.00	$2,333.58	$ -	$ 41,226.58	
19	Kim Cheng	$ 31,120.00	$1,867.20	$ -	$ 32,987.20	
20	Lloyd Hamilton	$ 41,922.00	$2,515.32	$ 200.00	$ 44,637.32	
21	Ed Fulton	$ 45,609.00	$2,736.54	$ 200.00	$ 48,545.54	
22	Maria Alvarez	$ 30,952.00	$1,857.12	$ -	$ 32,809.12	
23	Katie Wilson	$ 31,472.00	$1,888.32	$ -	$ 33,360.32	
24	Tim Brown	$ 44,783.00	$2,600.98	$ 200.00	$ 47,669.98	
25						

Sheet1 / Sheet2 / Sheet3 /

Error Messages

■ Following is a list of some error messages you might get if you enter data or formulas incorrectly.

  ● ####: The cell contains an entry that's wider than the cell can display. In most cases, you can widen the column to correct the problem.

● #VALUE: The wrong type of data was used in a formula. Possible causes are entering text when a formula requires a number or logical value, or entering a range in a formula or function that requires a single value.

● #DIV/0!: A formula is attempting to divide a value by zero. For example, if the value in cell B5 in the formula =A5/B5 is zero, or if cell B5 is empty, the result will be the #DIV/0! error.

● #NAME: Excel doesn't recognize text in the formula. Possible causes include a misspelling or using a nonexistent range name' using a label in a formula if the Accept labels in formulas option is turned off, or omitting a colon (:) in a range reference.

● #N/A: No value is available to the formula or function. Possible causes include omitting a required argument in a formula or function or entering an invalid argument in a formula or function.

● #REF: A cell reference is invalid. Possible causes include deleting cells referred to by formulas.

● #NUM: Indicates a problem with a number in a formula or function. Possible causes include using a nonnumeric argument in a function that requires a numeric argument, or entering a formula that produces a number too large or too small for Excel to represent.

● #NULL: The formula contains incorrect operators or cell references using ranges in formulas. For example, if you left the comma out of the following formula, a #NULL error would occur: SUM(A1:A6,C1:C6).

● Circular reference error: The formula references the cell it's in. For example, if you're adding the values of a group of cells and include the cell that contains the formula, you are creating an endless loop, which generates a circular error.

Procedures

Audit a Worksheet

✓ *These audit tools can be used to debug worksheet formulas. Tracer arrows are not saved with the workbook.*

Show Auditing Toolbar

1. Click **Tools**.................. Alt + T
2. Click **Auditing**.................... U
3. Click **Show Auditing Toolbar** .... S

Trace Dependents

1. Select the cell containing data used by a formula.
2. Click the **Trace Dependents** button 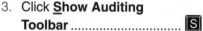 on the Auditing toolbar.

   ✓ *If tracer arrows don't appear, select Show all on the View tab in the Options dialog box (choose Tools, Options).*

Remove Dependent Tracer Arrows

1. Select the cell containing tracer arrows.
2. Click **Remove Dependent Arrows** button 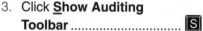 on the Auditing toolbar.

Trace Precedents

1. Select cell containing formula.
2. Click **Trace Precedents** button on Auditing toolbar.

Remove Precedent Tracer Arrows

1. Select cell containing tracer arrows.
2. Click **Remove Precedent Arrows** button on Auditing toolbar.

Remove All Tracer Arrows

Click **Remove All Arrows** button on Auditing toolbar.

Attach Comment to a Formula

1. Select cell to receive comment.
2. Click **New Comment** button on Auditing toolbar.
3. Enter comment.
4. Click **OK** .... Enter

Delete a Comment

1. Right-click the cell containing the comment you want to delete.
2. Click **Delete Comment**........ M

   ✓ *If you delete a comment accidentally, immediately choose Edit, Undo Delete comment.*

Edit a Comment

1. Right-click the cell containing the comment you want to edit.
2. Make changes as needed.
3. Click outside the cell to close the comment box.

Trace an Error in a Formula

1. Select cell that contains a formula with an error.
2. Click **Trace Error** button on the Auditing toolbar.

Exercise Directions

1. Start Excel, if necessary.
2. Open 💿 **51_BUDGET**.
3. Save the workbook as **XL_51**.
4. Display the Auditing toolbar.
5. List the dependents of the following cells:
   a. D16
   b. Dependent cell(s):_____
   c. C30
   d. Dependent cell(s):_____
   e. E21
   f. Dependent cell(s):_____

6. List the precedents of the following cells:
   a. C21
   b. Precedent cell(s):_____
   c. E35
   d. Precedent cell(s):_____
   e. E37
   f. Precedent cell(s):_____
7. Trace the error in cell E39 and correct it.
8. Trace the errors in cells D39 and D37 and correct the problem.
9. Trace the error in cell G21 and correct it.
10. Remove all arrows and hide the Auditing toolbar.
11. Save the workbook and exit Excel.

On Your Own

1. Start Excel, if necessary.
2. Open 💿 **51_EARNINGS**.
3. Save the workbook as **OXL_51**.
4. Create formulas in the empty columns of the table to make the calculations that the column labels indicate.
   a. In the commission column, use an absolute reference when referring to cell B9, where you will later enter a commission rate.
   b. In the bonus column, use an absolute reference when referring to cell B10, where you will later enter a bonus amount.
   c. Sales personnel receive a bonus on sales over $40,000.

5. Click any cell in the commission column and trace the precedents. Remove the arrows.
6. Click any cell in the bonus column and trace the precedents. Remove the arrows.
7. Click any cell in the total earnings column and trace the precedents. Remove the arrows.
8. Type *0.06* in cell B9 and type *$200* in cell B10.
9. Click cell B9 and trace its dependents. Remove the arrows.
10. Click cell B10 and trace its dependents. Remove the arrows.
11. Click any cell in the sales column and trace its dependents. Remove the arrows.
12. Save the workbook and exit Excel.

Exercise 52

Skills Covered:

◆ Hide Data ◆ Save Different Views of the Workbook (Custom Views)

On the Job

If you have data that's considered confidential or is needed strictly as supporting information, you can hide it from view. This helps you keep the displayed information to just the relevant data, or prevents you from accidentally printing that data.

You're the owner of Carella's Hair Design, and you need to prepare a month-end statement for each of your stylists. Although each stylist rents his or her booth, they all contribute to the cost of an accountant (who helps keep track of everyone's business records), several assistants, and a shampooist. You've prepared a single worksheet with all this data, but you want to print selected information from the report each month for each stylist, rather than printing the whole worksheet.

Terms

hide To prevent Excel from displaying or printing certain data. You can hide the contents of individual cells, whole rows or columns, and even worksheets or workbooks.

unhide To redisplay hidden data, worksheets, or workbooks.

view A saved arrangement of the Excel display and print settings that you can restore at any time.

Notes

Hide Data

- To prevent data from displaying or printing in a workbook, you can **hide** the data.

- You can hide the contents of individual cells, whole rows or columns, and even whole worksheets or workbooks.

  ✓ *Hiding data is useful for keeping important supporting or confidential information out of sight, but it won't prevent those who know Excel from exposing that data if they can get access to the workbook. If you need to keep data away from prying eyes, password-protect the workbook as described in Exercise 55.*

- You can hide multiple cells, rows, columns, and worksheets.

- When a row or column is hidden, the row number or column letter is missing from the worksheet frame. Hiding row 12, for example, leaves the row headings showing 11, 13, 14, and so on.

- Hiding a worksheet makes its tab disappear. If worksheets use a sequential numbering or naming scheme (such as Sheet1, Sheet2, Sheet3), the fact that a worksheet is hidden may be obvious.

- If you hide the contents of a cell, the cell appears to contain nothing, but the cell itself doesn't disappear from the worksheet.

■ Even if a cell's contents are hidden, you can still display the contents in the Formula bar by selecting the cell.

✓ *To prevent the data from displaying in the Formula bar, you can protect the worksheet, as described in Exercise 55.*

■ If you hide a workbook, its contents aren't displayed even when the workbook is open. This feature is useful for storing macros that you want to have available but not necessarily in view. (See Exercise 80 for more on Excel macros.)

■ If you copy or move hidden data, it remains hidden.

■ Hidden data doesn't print.

■ Because the data in hidden columns or rows doesn't print, you can use this feature to print noncontiguous columns or rows as if they were contiguous.

■ To edit, format, or redisplay the contents of hidden rows, columns, or worksheets, **unhide** the rows, columns, or worksheet.

Save Different Views of the Workbook (Custom Views)

■ You can set up the display of a workbook as you like, then save that setup in a custom **view** so you can switch back to it when needed.

■ For example, you could save one view of the worksheet with all cells displayed, another view with certain rows or columns hidden, and so on.

■ Before creating a view, set up the screen exactly as you want it to appear in the view.

■ Settings in a view include any selected cells, current column widths, how the screen is split or frozen, and window arrangements and sizes.

■ When creating a view, you can specify whether to save the settings for hidden columns and rows (hidden worksheets are always hidden in the view).

■ Because custom views can control print settings, you can create the same arrangement of printed data each time you print from that view (for example, printing just the tax deductible expenses from a monthly expense workbook).

■ The current view is saved with the workbook.

Procedures

Hide Cell Contents

1. Select cell(s) containing data to hide.
   a. Click **Format**..........`Alt`+`O`
   b. Click **Cells** ....`E`
   OR
   a. Right-click selection.
   b. Click **Format Cells** ....`F`
2. Click **Number** tab........`Ctrl`+`Tab`
3. Click the **Category** list box ....`Alt`+`C`
4. Select **Custom** in **Category** list box...............................`↕`
5. Click the **Type:** text box ....`Alt`+`T`
6. Replace the contents with ;;; (three semicolons) ....`;``;``;`
7. Click **OK**...........................`Enter`

Redisplay Hidden Cell

1. Repeat steps 1-4 in "Hide Cell Contents."
2. Select desired format ....`↕`
3. Click **OK** ....`Enter`

Hide Columns by Using the Format Menu

1. Select any cell in each column you want to hide.
2. Click **Format** ....`Alt`+`O`
3. Click **Column** ....`C`
4. Click **Hide**..........................`H`

✓ *A thick border appears in the worksheet frame where a column is hidden.*

Hide Columns by Dragging

Hide one column:

1. Point to the right border of column heading.

   ✓ *The pointer becomes* ↔ *.*

2. Drag ↔ left to column's left border.

   ✓ *A thick border appears in the worksheet frame where a column is hidden.*

Hide multiple columns:

1. Select columns.
2. Point to the right border of any selected column heading.

   ✓ *The pointer becomes* ↔ *.*

3. Drag ↔ left to column's left border.

Unhide a Hidden Column By Dragging

1. Point just right of column heading border.

   ✓ *The pointer becomes* ┽┝.

2. Drag ┽┝ right.

Unhide Hidden Column(s) by Using the Format Menu

1. Select surrounding columns.
2. Click **F**ormat .... `Alt`+`O`
3. Click **C**olumn .... `O`
4. Click **U**nhide .... `U`

Hide Rows by Using the Format Menu

1. Select any cell in each row you want to hide.
2. Click **F**ormat .... `Alt`+`O`
3. Click **R**ow .... `R`
4. Click **H**ide .... `H`

   ✓ *A thick border appears in the worksheet frame where a row is hidden.*

Hide Rows by Dragging

Hide one row:

1. Point to the bottom border of row heading.

   ✓ *The pointer becomes* ╪.

2. Drag ╪ up to row's top border.

   ✓ *A thick border appears in the worksheet frame where a row is hidden.*

Hide multiple rows:

1. Select rows.
2. Point to the bottom border of any selected row heading.

   ✓ *The pointer becomes* ╪.

3. Drag ╪ up to row's top border.

Unhide Hidden Row by Dragging

1. Point just below the bold row heading border.

   ✓ *The pointer becomes* ╪.

2. Drag ╪ down.

Unhide Hidden Rows by Using the Format Menu

1. Select surrounding rows.
2. Click **F**ormat .... `Alt`+`O`
3. Click **R**ow .... `R`
4. Click **U**nhide .... `U`

Hide a Workbook

1. Open workbook you wish to hide.
2. Click **W**indow .... `Alt`+`W`
3. Click **H**ide .... `H`
4. If asked, save the workbook when you close Excel.

Unhide a Workbook

1. Open workbook(s) you wish to unhide.
2. Click **W**indow .... `Alt`+`W`
3. Click **U**nhide .... `U`
4. Select workbook(s) you want to unhide.............................. `↑↓`
5. Click OK .... `Enter`

Hide Worksheet

1. Select the sheet(s) you wish to hide.
2. Click **F**ormat............... `Alt`+`O`
3. Click **Sh**eet........................ `H`
4. Click **H**ide .... `H`

Unhide Worksheet

1. Click **F**ormat............... `Alt`+`O`
2. Click **Sh**eet........................ `H`
3. Click **U**nhide .... `U`
4. Select sheet(s) you want to unhide.............................. `↓``↑`
5. Click OK .... `Enter`

Create Custom View

1. Set up the screen the way you want it to appear in the custom view. If desired, set up the print settings as well.
2. Click **V**iew.................... `Alt`+`V`
3. Click Custom **V**iews .... `V`
4. Click **A**dd .... `Alt`+`A`
5. Type a name for the view.
6. Change options, if desired.
7. Click OK.......................... `Enter`

Display a Custom View

1. Click **V**iew.................... `Alt`+`V`
2. Click Custom **V**iews .... `V`
3. Select view to display.
4. Click **S**how .... `Alt`+`S`

   ✓ *When you save the workbook, the view that's currently in effect is also saved. The next time you open the workbook, that view will still be in effect.*

Delete a View

1. Click **V**iew.................... `Alt`+`V`
2. Click Custom **V**iews .... `V`
3. In the **Vie**ws list, click the view you want to delete ..... `Alt`+`W`, `↑↓`
4. Click **D**elete .... `Alt`+`D`
5. Click **Y**es to confirm the deletion .... `Enter`
6. Click **C**lose .... `Enter`

Exercise Directions

1. Start Excel, if necessary.
2. Open ◈ **52_CARELLA**.
3. Save the workbook as **XL_52**.
4. Save the current display as a view called *Private*.
5. Hide the contents of cell C45.
6. Hide rows 15 to 38.
7. Save the view as *Susie Chen*.
8. Print the worksheet.
9. Redisplay the hidden rows, and then hide rows 10 to 15 and 22 to 39.
10. Save the view as *John Allen Bradley*.
11. Print the worksheet.
12. Redisplay the hidden rows, and then hide rows 9 to 20 and 28 to 39.
13. Save the view as *Allys Halverson*.
14. Print the worksheet.
15. Redisplay the hidden rows, and then hide 10 to 27 and 34 to 39.
16. Save the view as *Carrie Brook*.
17. Print the worksheet.
18. Redisplay the hidden rows, and then hide 10 to 33.
19. Save the view as *Deb Palmer*.
20. Print the worksheet.
21. Switch back to Private view.
22. Save the workbook and exit Excel.

On Your Own

1. Start Excel, if necessary.
2. Open a new workbook file and name it **OXL_52**.
3. Create a worksheet that calculates the new rate for each employee at Pete's Pets.
   - Enter some false employee information such as name, address, phone number, hire date, hire rate, current rate, Social Security number, tax filing status (married or single), and number of dependents.
4. Enter at least 15 hourly employees with various hire dates and current rates.
   a. Give everyone that's been there at least three years a $.55 per hour raise.
   b. Employees that have been there less than three years but more than one year get a $.35 per hour raise.
   c. All other employees get a raise of $.25 per hour.
5. Calculate the total cost of the raises, based on a 40-hour week, 52-week year.
6. Save the current view.
7. Hide information not directly related to the raise, such as Social Security number, address, phone number, and the like.
8. Save this view and print it.
9. Create another view that includes only the employee name, address, and phone number.
10. Print this new view.
11. Save the workbook and exit Excel.

Exercise 53

Skills Covered:

◆ Scenarios ◆ Report Manager

On the Job

With scenarios, you can create and save several versions of a worksheet based on "what-if" data. For example, you can create a best case, probable case, and worst case scenario for your company's annual sales. After you create your scenarios, you can use Report Manager to print the various versions of your data quickly.

As the owner of a cabinet shop, you're thinking of expanding, but first you need make some projections based on best, probable, and worst case scenarios. You'll do that in Excel and summarize the data by using Excel's Report Manager.

Terms

variable An input value that changes depending on the desired outcome.

scenario A what-if analysis tool you can use to create several versions of a worksheet, based on changing variables.

Report Manager A tool you can use to quickly print various scenarios, in combination with custom views.

add-in An extra program that (usually) comes with Excel and is designed for a specific purpose, such as Report Manager. Such programs don't open automatically when Excel starts to keep from wasting memory on programs you may not use. However, you can "add" these special programs to Excel whenever you need to use them.

Notes

Scenarios

- To help you deal with the outcome of an unpredictable future, you can create and save versions of your worksheet data based on changing **variables**.

- With **scenarios**, you can plug in the most likely values for several possible situations, and save the scenarios with the resulting worksheet data.
  - You can print and compare scenarios.
  - You can also create a summary worksheet to compare scenarios.

- After you save scenarios, you can switch between them easily.
  - When you switch to a particular scenario, Excel plugs the saved values into the appropriate cells in your worksheet, and then adjusts formula results as needed.

- You change from one scenario to another by using the Scenario Manager dialog box.
  - You can also create, summarize, delete, and merge scenarios with this dialog box.

Scenario Manager dialog box

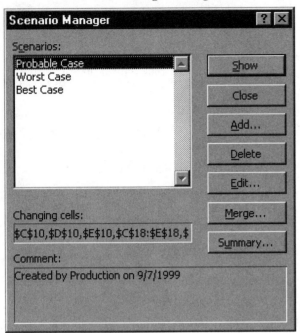

Report Manager

- With **Report Manager**, you can combine scenarios with custom views to create reports.
  - For example, suppose you created several scenarios detailing a budget: best case, worst case, and probable outcomes.
  - Suppose also that you created several custom views, such as details and summary.
  - With Report Manager, you can combine these scenarios with your views to create several reports, such as Best Case Summary or Probable Outcome Details.
- Because Report Manager is an **add-in**, it might not be available automatically when you start Excel.
  - ✓ *If Report Manager is ready to use, you'll find its command on the View menu.*
  - If Report Manager isn't currently available, you can install it with the Tools, Add-Ins command.

Procedures

Create a Scenario

1. Click **Tools**.................. `Alt`+`T`
2. Click **Scenarios**.................. `E`
3. Click **Add** .... `Alt`+`A`
4. In **Scenario name** box, enter a name for the scenario.
5. In **Changing cells** box, select or enter cell reference(s)................. `Alt`+`C`
6. Click **OK**.......................... `Enter`
7. In **Scenario Values** dialog box, enter values for changing cell(s).
8. Click **OK**.......................... `Enter`

Delete a Scenario

1. Click **Tools**.................. `Alt`+`T`
2. Click **Scenarios** .... `E`
3. In the **Scenarios** list, click the scenario you want to delete...... `Alt`+`C`, `↕`

4. Click **Delete**................. `Alt`+`D`
   - ✓ *Note that Excel doesn't require confirmation when deleting a scenario. Be sure that you want to do this before clicking the Delete button; deletions can't be undone.*
5. Click **OK** .... `Enter`

Edit a Scenario

1. Click **Tools** .... `Alt`+`T`
2. Click **Scenarios** .... `E`
3. In the **Scenarios** list, click the scenario you want to edit..........`Alt`+`C`, `↕`
4. Click **Edit**.................... `Alt`+`E`
5. Make changes to the scenario as needed.
6. Click **OK** .... `Enter`
7. Click **OK** again .... `Enter`

View a Scenario

1. Click **Tools** .... `Alt`+`T`
2. Click **Scenarios**.................. `E`
3. Select a scenario .... `Tab`, `↕`
4. Click **Show** .... `Alt`+`S`

Create a Scenario Summary

1. Click **Tools** .... `Alt`+`T`
2. Click **Scenarios**.................. `E`
3. Click **Summary**........... `Alt`+`U`
4. With **Scenario summary** selected, select the range of result cells............... `Alt`+`S`
5. Click **OK** .... `Enter`

Install Report Manager

1. Click **Tools** .... `Alt`+`T`
2. Click **Add-Ins** .... `I`
3. Select **Report Manager** in the **Add-Ins available** list .... `Alt`+`A`, `↕`, `Space`

4. Click **OK** .... `Enter`

5. If prompted, click **Yes** to install Report Manager .... `Enter`

   ✓ *This step requires the Office 2000 CD-ROM.*

Use Report Manager

1. Click **View** .... `Alt`+`V`

2. Click **Report Manager** .... `R`

3. Click **Add** .... `Alt`+`A`

4. Type a name for the report in the **Report Name** box.

5. In the **Sheet** box, select the worksheet that contains the data you wish to add to the report .... `Alt`+`S`

6. Select a **View** to use .... `Alt`+`V`, `↑↓`

7. Select a **Scenario** to use .... `Alt`+`N`, `↑↓`

   ✓ *A report can include scenarios, custom views, both, or neither.*

8. Click **Add** .... `Alt`+`A`

9. Repeat steps 5–8 to add more sections to the report.

   ✓ *Sections are printed in the order in which they appear in the Report Manager dialog box. To change the order of an item, select it and click either* **Move Up** *or* **Move Down**.

10. Select the **Use Continuous Page Numbers** option to print continuous page numbers with each section .... `Alt`+`C`

    ✓ *This feature is useful if the sections in the report are from various areas in the worksheet and aren't necessarily in order. The report will provide consecutive page numbering when you select this feature.*

11. Click **OK** .... `Enter`

12. Click **Print** to print the report now .... `Alt`+`P`

    OR

    Click **Close** to close the dialog box .... `Enter`

    OR

    Click **Add** and repeat steps 4–11 to create another report .... `Alt`+`A`, `↑↓`,

Delete a Report

1. Click **View** .... `Alt`+`V`

2. Click **Report Manager** .... `R`

3. In the **Reports** list, click the report you want to delete .... `Alt`+`R`, `↑↓`,

4. Click **Delete** .... `Alt`+`L`

5. Click **OK** .... `Enter`

6. Click **OK** again to confirm the deletion .... `Enter`

7. Click **Close** to close the Report Manager dialog box .... `Enter`

Edit a Report

1. Click **View** .... `Alt`+`V`

2. Click **Report Manager** .... `R`

3. In the **Reports** list, click the report you want to edit .... `Alt`+`R`, `↑↓`,

4. Click **Edit** .... `Alt`+`E`

5. Make changes in the report as needed.

6. Click **OK** .... `Enter`

7. Click **OK** again .... `Enter`

Exercise Directions

1. Start Excel, if necessary.

2. Open **XL_51**, created in Exercise 51, or open 🖝 **53_BUDGET**.

3. Save the workbook as **XL_53**.

4. Create a scenario called *Probable Case*, in which the values in these cells are saved as they currently appear:

   a. C10   445500
   b. D10   460000
   c. E10   455000
   d. C18   58750
   e. D18   52500
   f. E18   59500
   g. C25   72500
   h. D25   72500
   i. E25   72500
   j. C26   34850
   k. D26   34850
   l. E26   34850

5. Create another scenario called *Worst Case*, in which these values change:

   a. C10   425750
   b. D10   445000
   c. E10   445000
   d. C18   62500
   e. D18   62500
   f. E18   62500
   g. C25   75000
   h. D25   75000
   i. E25   75000
   j. C26   36200
   k. D26   36200
   l. E26   36200

6. Create another scenario called *Best Case*, in which these values change:

   a. C10   465750
   b. D10   475500
   c. E10   475500
   d. C18   55500
   e. D18   51500
   f. E18   55500
   g. C25   71500
   h. D25   71500
   i. E25   71500
   j. C26   34500
   k. D26   34500
   l. E26   34500

7. Display the Probable Case scenario.

8. Create a view called *Summary*, in which rows 10–11, 16–18, and 25–34 are hidden.

9. Create a view called *Details* in which all rows are displayed.

10. Create a report called *Best Case_Worst Case Summary*.

    a. In the first section of the report, combine the Best Case scenario and the Summary view.

    b. In the next section of the report, combine the Worst Case scenario and the Summary view.

    c. Use continuous page numbers throughout.

    d. Print the report.

11. Create another report called *Probable Case*.

    a. In the first section of the report, combine the Probable Case scenario and the Summary view.

    b. In the second section of the report, combine the Probable Case scenario and the Details view.

    c. Use continuous page numbers throughout.

    d. Print the report.

12. Save the workbook and exit Excel.

On Your Own

1. Start Excel, if necessary.
2. Open ⊛ **53_THEATER**.
3. Save the workbook as **OXL_53**.
4. In a previous exercise, you worked on a project to determine ticket prices for a theater production. Now you must offer some scenarios so the production committee can make some final decisions.
5. Create a scenario with the existing data and name it *Scenario 1*. Use cells C7:C8, F7:F8, F12:F13 as the changing cells.
6. Use the Auditing toolbar to become familiar with the formulas already entered in the worksheet. For example, trace the precedents of cell C12.

   ✓ *To locate cells with formulas quickly, press Ctrl+`. The ` is on the same key as the tilde (~). Press Ctrl+` again to return to the normal worksheet.*

7. Using Goal Seek and your knowledge of theater production, create a scenario named *Scenario 2* where tickets could be priced at $9.50 with only 85% of the seats sold, while still reaching the profit goal of $1,200. You won't be able to reach these goals without changing some of the estimated costs of the project. Think about the following as you make decisions:

   a. Theater capacity is 1420 seats.
   b. Certain costs are fixed and can't be reduced — theater rental, royalty fee, and the union electrician.
   c. Can you find a printer who can provide cheaper playbills? How much cheaper?
   d. Do you dare print fewer playbills than the capacity of the theater? How many could you get away with?
   e. Can you skimp a little on costumes and scenery? How much on each?
   f. You'll probably use Goal Seek several times as you change the variables.

8. Save the workbook and exit Excel.

Exercise 54

Skills Covered:
◆ VLOOKUP Function ◆ HLOOKUP Function

On the Job

With the VLOOKUP and HLOOKUP functions, you can look up information in a table based on a known value. For example, you could look up the salesperson assigned to a particular client. At the same time, you could look up that client's address and phone number. You can use the lookup functions in other ways as well. For example, you could look up the sales discount for a particular customer, or calculate the bonuses for a group of salespeople based on a hierarchical bonus structure.

As the payroll clerk for Marcus Furniture, you're tired of manually figuring out the commissions and bonuses each month for the sales associates. It's time to add a lookup feature to the worksheet so Excel will do the job for you.

Terms

table A method of organizing data in columns and rows. Each column typically represents a different field, and each row represents an entire record. For example, in one record you could have several fields (columns of data), such as name, address, phone number, and so on.

range name Name given to a set of adjacent cells. You might name a range in order to make it more convenient to reference that range in a formula or a function, such as VLOOKUP.

Notes

- The lookup functions (VLOOKUP and HLOOKUP) select a value from a **table**.
- There are two ways to look up data, depending on the way the data is arranged: vertically or horizontally.
  - VLOOKUP (vertical lookup) looks up data in a particular *column* in the table.
  - HLOOKUP (horizontal lookup) looks up data in a particular *row* in the table.
- The VLOOKUP function uses this format:

  =VLOOKUP(item,table-range,column-position)

  - *item* is text or a value that you're looking for.
    - ✓ The item must be located in the first column of the VLOOKUP table.

- ✓ Uppercase and lowercase are treated the same.
- ✓ If an exact match isn't found, the next smallest value is used.
- *table-range* is the range reference or **range name** of the lookup table.
  - ✓ Don't include the row containing the column labels.
  - ✓ If the lookup function is to be copied, the range should be expressed as an absolute reference.
- *column-position* is the column number in the table from which the matching value should be returned.
  - ✓ The far-left column of the table is one; the second column is two, etc.

- For example, to look up the mortgage payment for a $110,000 loan for 20 years at 9% in the following table, use this formula:

  =VLOOKUP(110000,C10:F22,3)

VLOOKUP Table

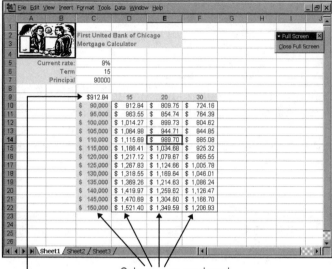

VLOOKUP table. Does not include column headings.

Columns are numbered from left to right beginning with 1.

- A similar formula could be used in a horizontal lookup table:

  =HLOOKUP(item,table-range,row-position)

  - *item* is text or a value that you're looking for.
  - *table-range* is the range reference or range name of the lookup table.

    ✓ Don't include the column containing the row labels.

  - *row-position* is the row number in the table from which the matching value should be returned.

- For example, to look up the mortgage payment for a $110,000 loan for 20 years at 9% in the same table, use this formula:

  =HLOOKUP(20,D9:F22,6)

Procedures

Insert a VLOOKUP or HLOOKUP Function

1. Click cell.
2. Type an equal sign (=) ....
3. Type the function name:
   - **VLOOKUP(**

   OR
   - **HLOOKUP(**

4. Click the Edit Formula button 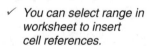.
5. Type item in **Lookup_value** box.

   ✓ Item can be an actual item or a reference to a cell containing the item.

   ✓ You can click a cell in the worksheet to insert a cell reference.

6. Type range in **Table_array** box .... Tab

   ✓ You can select range in worksheet to insert cell references.

7. Type row or column number in **Row_index_num** box or **Col_index_num** .... Tab
8. Click **OK** .... Enter

Exercise Directions

1. Start Excel, if necessary.
2. Open ⊘ **54_MARCUS**.
3. Save the file as **XL_54**.
4. Determine the commission rates for the associates:

   a. On the Comm-Bonus worksheet, select the table and name the range *table*. (Don't include the column headings in the range.)

   ✓ *If you don't remember how to name a range, refer to Exercise 14.*

   b. In cell E9 on the Jan Earnings worksheet, create a formula using the VLOOKUP function to look up the commission rate based on the sales figure in column D.

   ✓ *Remember that the columns in the lookup table are numbered 1, 2, and 3 from left to right.*

   c. Copy the formula to the rest of the column.

5. Determine the bonuses for the associates:

   a. In cell G9 on the Jan Earnings worksheet, create a VLOOKUP formula to look up the bonuses based on the sales figures in column D.

   b. Copy the formula to the rest of the column.

6. Use conditional formatting to make any bonus over $300 bold and Blue.

7. To prepare a worksheet for next month, copy the Jan Earnings worksheet and name the copy Feb Earnings.

   a. Delete the sales figures in column D.

   b. Change the title in row 5.

   c. Enter 12,000 in any cell in the sales column to see that the formulas work properly.

   d. Delete the 12,000 value.

8. Save the workbook and exit Excel.

On Your Own

1. Start Excel, if necessary.
2. Create a template to handle invoices for Midwest Candy Company.
3. Save the file as **OXL_54.xlt**.
4. At the top of column A (cells A1:A3), enter *Midwest Candy, Invoice date,* and *Order #.*
5. In column C (cells C1:C5), enter *Customer, Address, City-State, ZIP Code,* and *Ship Zone.*
6. In the body of the invoice, perhaps row 7 or so, enter the following column labels: *Description, Item #, Price/pound, Pounds Ordered, Total Cost.*
7. The shipping zone is based on the ZIP Code, so you want to use an HLOOKUP formula to enter the shipping zone when you type the ZIP Code.
   a. Create the lookup table on Sheet2.
   b. Create your own or use the one below as an example.
8. Create formulas in the invoice table to compute the values that the labels indicate.

9. Leave five or six rows for order input, and add the following in an area of your choice at the bottom of the order area:
   a. *Sub Total, Sales Tax (use % of your choice), Shipping Cost,* and *Total Cost.* You'll also need a cell for *Total Wt.* to use in computing the shipping cost.
   b. Enter appropriate formulas to calculate these entries.
   c. For Shipping Cost, you'll need a VLOOKUP table to find the costs for the different shipping zones.
   d. For the purposes of this exercise, create a simple VLOOKUP table on Sheet2 that gives the cost for shipping one pound of goods to each of the shipping zones included in the HLOOKUP table that you created in step 7.
      ✓ *To be realistic, you would create a large table with many columns of different pound labels similar to ones you would find in a UPS or U.S. post office.*
   e. Multiply the total weight of the order by the value the VLOOKUP table provides to arrive at the shipping cost.
10. Apply Accounting format to the appropriate cells, and other formatting as you wish.
11. Save the template.
12. Save the file as a workbook with the name **OXL_54.xls.**
13. Test your template by filling out a fictitious invoice with several entries.
14. Save the workbook and exit Excel.

Example of shipping zones if you shipped from the 50000 ZIP Code area.

ZIP Code	0	30000	40000	50000	60000	70000	80000	90000
Ship Zone	5	4	3	2	3	4	5	6

Exercise 55

◆ Lock/Unlock Cells in a Worksheet ◆ Protect a Worksheet
◆ Protect a Workbook

On the Job

If you design worksheets for others to use, or if you share a lot of workbooks, you may wish to protect certain areas of a worksheet from changes. In such a case, you can actually protect a cell to prevent it from accepting new data. You can also protect an entire worksheet or workbook so that others may only view its contents.

Your boss at the Little Kids Toy Shop appreciates your hard work on a net profit worksheet you created earlier, but he would like you to play around with the projected bonuses and create some scenarios he can look at. Once the final scenario is approved, you'll protect the worksheet to prevent accidental changes.

Terms

Protect To prevent changes to locked or protected areas or items.

Lock By default, all cells in a worksheet are locked. To prevent changes to locked cells, you must protect the worksheet.

Unprotect To remove protection from a worksheet or workbook.

Unlock To enable changes in areas of a protected worksheet, you must unlock those areas before turning on worksheet protection.

Notes

Lock/Unlock Cells in a Worksheet

- To prevent changes to selected cells or ranges in a worksheet, you can **protect** the worksheet.
  - All cells in an Excel worksheet are **locked** by default.
  - When you turn on worksheet protection, the locked cells can't be changed.
  - To allow changes in certain cells or ranges, **unlock** the cells before protecting the worksheet.
- If necessary, you can **unprotect** a protected worksheet so that you can change the data in locked cells.

- If someone tries to make a change to a protected cell, a message indicates that the cell is protected and considered read-only.
  - You can copy the data in a locked cell, but you can't move or delete it.
  - Data can't be copied to a part of the worksheet that's protected.
- You can protect charts and other objects in a worksheet by using this same process.
- You can move between the unlocked cells of a protected worksheet by pressing Tab.

Protect a Worksheet

■ When you activate worksheet protection, the cells you have unlocked are not protected.

- You can make changes to these cells.

■ You can also prevent changes to objects in the worksheet (such as clip art or drawn images), and scenarios (stored variations of a worksheet).

■ You can password-protect the sheet, so that no one can unprotect the worksheet accidentally.

- If you forget the password, you won't be able to unprotect the worksheet later on.

- However, you can copy the data to another, unprotected worksheet.

Protect a Workbook

■ You can protect an entire workbook against certain kinds of changes.

■ By applying this protection, you can prevent worksheets from being added, moved, hidden, unhidden, renamed, or deleted.

■ You can also prevent a workbook's window from being resized or repositioned.

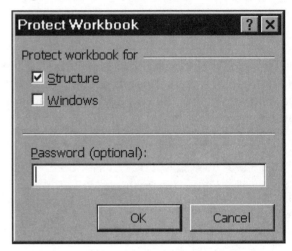

Procedures

Lock/Unlock Cells In a Worksheet

✓ *Locks or unlocks specific cells. By default, all cells in a worksheet are locked.*

1. If necessary, unprotect worksheet.

   ✓ *You can't lock or unlock cells if the worksheet is protected.*

2. Select cell(s) to unlock or lock.

3. Click **Format** .... `Alt`+`O`

4. Click **Cells** .... `E`

5. Click **Protection** tab.... `Ctrl`+`Tab`

6. Deselect or select
   Locked .... `Alt`+`L`

   ✓ *A gray check box indicates the current cell selection contains mixed (locked/unlocked) settings.*

7. Click **OK** .... `Enter`

8. Repeat steps for each cell or range to lock or unlock.

9. Protect worksheet.

Lock/Unlock Objects in a Worksheet

✓ *Locks or unlocks objects such as embedded charts, clip art, or drawn objects such as text boxes. By default, all objects in a worksheet are locked when a worksheet is protected.*

1. If necessary, unprotect worksheet.

   ✓ *You can't lock or unlock cells if the worksheet is protected.*

2. Click object to unlock or lock.

3. Click **Format** .... `Alt`+`O`

4. Click the appropriate command.

   ✓ *For example, if you selected a chart in step 2, choose the **Selected Chart Area** command here.*

5. Click **Protection** or
   Properties tab .... `Ctrl`+`Tab`

6. Deselect or select
   Locked .... `Alt`+`L`

   ✓ *A gray check box indicates the current cell selection contains mixed (locked/unlocked) settings.*

7. Click **OK** .... `Enter`

8. Repeat steps for each object to lock or unlock.

9. Protect worksheet.

Protect a Sheet

1. Lock or unlock cells, ranges, and objects as desired.

   ✓ *By default, all cells and objects in a worksheet are locked.*

2. Click **T**ools................... Alt + T
3. Click **P**rotection .... P
4. Click **P**rotect Sheet............. P

   To protect cell contents and chart items:

   Select **C**ontents .... Alt + C

   To protect graphic objects:

   Select **O**bjects .... Alt + O

   To protect scenarios:

   Select **S**cenarios......... Alt + S

   To password-protect sheet:

   Type a password in **Password (optional)** text box.

5. Click **OK** .... Enter
6. If a password was typed, retype password in text box.
7. Click **OK** .... Enter

Unprotect a Sheet

1. Click **T**ools................... Alt + T
2. Click **P**rotection .... P
3. Click **U**nprotect Sheet........ P

   If sheet is password-protected:

   Type password in **Password** text box.

4. Click **OK** .... Enter

Protect a Workbook

1. Click **T**ools................... Alt + T
2. Click **P**rotection .... P
3. Click **P**rotect **W**orkbook..... W

   To protect structure of worksheets:

   Select **S**tructure .... Alt + S

   To protect windows:

   Select **W**indows .... Alt + W

   To password-protect workbook:

   Type a password in **Password (optional)** text box.

4. Click **OK** .... Enter
5. If a password was typed, retype password in text box.
6. Click **OK** .... Enter

Unprotect a Workbook

1. Click **T**ools................... Alt + T
2. Click **U**nprotect **W**orkbook........................... W

   If workbook is password-protected:

   Type password in **Password** text box.

3. Click **OK** .... Enter

Exercise Directions

1. Start Excel, if necessary.
2. Open ⊙ **55_TOYS**.
3. Save the workbook as **XL_55**.
4. Save the current worksheet as a scenario called *Net Profit $185,000*.
   - Save the values currently in the cells F3 and D17.
5. Use Goal Seek to find a new bonus percentage (cell F3) based on a total net profit of 180,000 (cell F14).
6. Use Goal Seek to find a new bonus distribution based on the new total bonus amount.
   - Adjust cell D17 until the total in cell D19 equals the new bonus amount shown in cell F12.
7. Save these adjustments as a scenario called *Net Profit $180,000*.
8. Use Goal Seek to find a different bonus percentage based on a total net profit of 190,000.
9. Use Goal Seek to find a new bonus distribution based on the new total bonus amount.
10. Save these adjustments as a scenario called *Net Profit $190,000*.
11. Print all three scenarios.
12. Your boss has decided that he can live with the bonuses based on the net profit of $180,000, so change back to that scenario.
13. Protect the worksheet so it can't be changed.

    ✓ *If you use a password, write it down!*

14. Try making a change.
15. Unlock the worksheet.
16. Save the workbook and exit Excel.

On Your Own

1. Start Excel, if necessary.

2. Open ⊙ 55_MARCUS.

3. Save the workbook as OXL_55.

4. On the Feb Earnings worksheet, unlock the cells in the Sales column and cell A5.

5. Protect the worksheet, but don't enter a password.

6. Bill Mergenthal's base salary was raised to $850 and Mary Williams replaced Pat Kawalski at a base salary of $750. Try to make those changes on the worksheet.

7. Unprotect the worksheet and make the changes in step 6.

8. Protect the worksheet.

9. Copy the Feb Earnings worksheet and name it *Mar Earnings*.

10. Change the text in cell A5 to *March Earnings Report*.

11. Try to make an entry in any cell in the table other than in the Sales column to see if the cells are still locked.

12. Make an entry in the Sales column to see if the cells are unlocked, and then delete the entry.

13. Save the workbook and exit Excel.

Exercise 56

◆ **Share Workbooks** ◆ **Track Changes** ◆ **Merge Changes**

On the Job

If you create a workbook with data that's maintained by several people, you can use Excel to help you keep track of the simultaneous changes being made, and to automatically resolve them. For example, you may have a customer database that all your salespeople maintain. In other cases, you may want to track the changes made to a file passed around for review, and then later merge these changes into a single final version of the file.

You're a lawyer at Peterson, Barney, and Smith, and you need to enter the work hours for your associates, billable to one of your clients. You've enlisted the help of an assistant to enter some of the data, and later you plan on merging the data into a final billable invoice.

Terms

Shared workbook A workbook to which several people can make changes at the same time. Such a workbook is typically placed in a central directory on a company network, where the users can access it.

Track Changes A feature that records changes made to a file; you can review and accept or reject these changes.

Notes

Share Workbooks

- When you share a workbook, you make it possible for multiple users to make changes to the workbook simultaneously.

  ✓ *For example, you might wish to share a client database, project worksheet, inventory database, or department budget.*

- Typically, **shared workbooks** are located on a network, accessible to the people who need to use the workbook(s).

  - Everyone who needs to make changes to the workbook must have Excel 97 or Excel 2000.

- There are certain tasks you can't perform on a shared workbook:
  - Delete worksheets.
  - Delete chart sheets.

- Insert or delete a range of cells.

  ✓ *You can insert or delete entire rows and columns, however.*

- Merge cells.
- Use conditional formats.
- Set up data validation or passwords.
- Create or modify charts, clip art, drawings, hyperlinks, and other objects.
- Create or modify scenarios, outlines, PivotTables, subtotals, or data tables.
- Create or modify macros stored in the workbook.

- When you share a workbook, the **Track Changes** feature is automatically turned on; however, you can turn it off if you wish.
- You can also designate how you want Excel to handle simultaneous changes to the same cell.

Track Changes

- With the Track Changes feature, you can keep track of the changes made to a workbook by a group of people.
  - When you turn on the Track Changes option, the workbook is automatically shared.
  - However, this doesn't mean that you must allow users simultaneous access to the workbook in order for them to make changes to it.
  - You can route the workbook to people sequentially, allowing each person to make their changes individually.
  - You can also send the workbook to several people simultaneously, and later merge their changes to the workbook.
- Because the workbook is shared, you won't be able to make certain types of changes to it (see the previous section for more information).
- Each person's changes are highlighted in the workbook using a different color, so the author of the change is easy to determine.
- Some changes aren't tracked, including the following:
  - Formatting changes
  - Rows or columns that have been hidden or unhidden
  - Worksheets that have been inserted or deleted
  - New or changed comments
  - Cells whose values change because of a change made to another cell
- After changes are made to a workbook, you can easily review them, accept the ones you wish to make permanent, and reject the ones you wish to ignore.

Merge Changes

- If you distribute a shared workbook with Track Changes to multiple people for review at the same time, you can later merge the changes in these multiple copies.
  - Make copies of the shared workbook, each with a different file name, such as Share1, Share2, and so on.
  - These copies can later be merged into a single workbook.
- The history of changes made to the workbooks is used to create a single, final copy of the workbook.
  - This history is created using the Track Changes option.
- Data is merged into the starting workbook from the other workbooks you select to merge.
  - Changes are made in the order in which the workbooks appear in the Select Files to Merge into Current Document dialog box.

Procedures

Share a Workbook

1. Click **Tools**.................. Alt + T
2. Click **Share Workbook**........ H
3. Select **Allow changes by more than one user at the same time** .... Alt + A
4. Click the **Advanced** tab............ Ctrl + Tab
5. If you want, change the amount of time for which changes are tracked:

   ✓ *You must allow enough time to track changes and merge the workbooks later if you plan to do that.*

   a. Click **Keep change history for** box .... Alt + K
   b. Change the length of time for which the changes are tracked in the **days** box.
      OR
      Click **Don't keep change history** ...... Alt + D
6. Specify when changes are updated to the shared file:

   a. Click **When file is saved**.................. Alt + W
      OR
      Click **Automatically every** .... Alt + A
   b. Change the time period at which changes are saved in the **minutes** box.
   c. Select an option:
      • **Save my changes and see others' changes**............ Alt + C
         OR
      • **Just see other users' changes**............ Alt + J
7. Indicate how you want conflicting changes handled:
   • Click **Ask me which changes win** .... Alt + S
      OR

   • Click **The changes being saved win** .... Alt + T
8. Select any additional settings you want saved:
   • **Print settings** .... Alt + P
   • **Filter settings** .... Alt + F
9. Click **OK** .... Enter
10. When prompted, click **OK** again to save the workbook.

    ✓ *[Shared] appears in the title bar of the workbook to remind you that the file is now in shared mode.*

Unshare a Workbook

1. Click **Tools** .... Alt + T
2. Click **Share Workbook** .... H
3. Click the **Editing** tab .. Ctrl + Tab
4. Select **Allow changes by more than one user at the same time** .... Alt + A

   ✓ *This action turns the option off.*

5. Click **OK** .... Enter
6. To confirm, click **Yes** .... Enter

Track Changes

1. Click **Tools** .... Alt + T
2. Click **Track Changes**.......... T
3. Click **Highlight Changes**.... H
4. Click **Track changes while editing** .... Alt + T
5. Click **OK** .... Enter

Accept or Reject Changes

1. Click **Tools**.................. Alt + T
2. Click **Track Changes**.......... T
3. Click **Accept or Reject Changes** .... A
4. If prompted to save the workbook, click **OK**.......... Enter
5. Select which changes you want to review:

   a. Choose the timeframe for the changes to review from the **When** list.......... Alt + N, ↕

   b. Choose whose changes you wish to review from the **Who** list .... Alt + O, ↕
   c. Type or select the range for the part of the worksheet you wish to review in the **Where** box............. Alt + R
6. Click **OK** .... Enter
7. When a change is highlighted, select an option:
   • **Accept** the change.............. Alt + A
   • **Reject** the change.. Alt + R
   • **Accept All** of the remaining changes without reviewing them .... Alt + C
   • **Reject All** of the remaining changes without reviewing them .... Alt + J

Merge Changes

1. Open the workbook into which you want to merge the changes.
2. Click **Tools** .... Alt + T
3. Click **Merge Workbooks**..... W
4. If prompted, click **OK** to save the workbook.
5. Select the workbooks you wish to merge into the current workbook.
6. Click **OK** .... Enter

   ✓ *Data from the workbooks you selected is used to change the data in the current workbook.*

   ✓ *Only the data from the last workbook merged appears in the final, merged workbook. To review the changes made when the workbooks were merged, follow the steps in the procedure "Accept or Reject Changes." If multiple changes are shown for a particular cell in the Accept or Reject Changes dialog box, you must select one of the changes before clicking **Accept** or **Reject**.*

Exercise Directions

1. Start Excel, if necessary.
2. Open ⊚ **56_BILLING**.
3. Save the workbook as **XL_56A**.
4. Turn on Track Changes.
   - ✓ *Notice that this also puts the workbook in shared mode.*
   - Track all changes, by everyone.
5. Make an additional copy of the workbook, saved with the file name **XL_56B**.
6. Reopen **XL_56A**, and make the following changes:
   a. Change Mark's hours to 41.
   b. Change Sue's hours to 21.
   c. Change Michael's hours to 18.
   d. Change Che's hours to 25.
   e. Change Filing hours to 19.
7. Save the workbook.
8. Make the following changes to **XL_56B**:
   a. Change Sue's hours to 25.
   b. Change Che's hours to 45.
   c. Change Research hours to 98.
   d. Change Filing hours to 38.
   e. Change Copying hours to 27.
9. Save the workbook and close the file.
10. Merge the data from **XL_56B** into the **XL_56A** workbook.
11. Save the workbook and close it.
12. Exit Excel.

On Your Own

1. Start Excel, if necessary.
2. Open ⊚ **56_SALES**.
3. Save the workbook as **OXL_56A**.
4. Save two additional copies of the workbook as **OXL_56B** and **OXL_56C**.
5. Make the following changes to **OXL_56B**:
   a. For store 123, change Trees to $2,145.00.
   b. For store 123, change Flowers to $458.00.
   c. Save the workbook and close it.
6. Make the following changes to **OXL_56C**:
   a. For store 123, change Herbs to $225.00.
   b. For store 214, change Herbs to $256.00.
   c. Save the workbook and close it.
7. Open **OXL_56A** again.
8. Merge the changes from **OXL_56B** and **OXL_56C** into **OXL_56A**.
9. Create a history of the changes.
   - ✓ *Although you can review the changes one cell at a time with the Tools, Track Changes, Accept or Review Changes command, sometimes it's helpful to have a "history" of all the changes so that you can review them all at once. To create a history, click Tools, Track Changes, Highlight Changes, and select List changes on a new sheet. Excel adds a History worksheet with all the appropriate information about the changes tracked.*
10. Save the workbook and exit Excel.

Exercise 57

◆ **Critical Thinking**

As the training manager of CompuTrain, it's your job to schedule classes, trainers, and training rooms. Juggling your client demands with your limited resources can be quite a challenge, but you've done a pretty good job of it. To handle the schedule this month, you've been working hard on a new worksheet, and it's almost done. However, you've got some ideas you want to incorporate that will help automate the process a little — lookup tables, nested IF statements, and COUNTIF and SUMIF calculations — so your worksheet is not quite done yet.

Exercise Directions

1. Open 💿57_SCHEDULE.

2. Save the file as **XL_57**.

3. Change to Sheet2 and add a lookup table:

   a. Type the information shown in Illustration A.

   b. Format the row and column labels as bold.

   c. Select the range (excluding the column headings) and name it *Classes*.

4. Add references to the lookup table:

   a. In cell B11 on Sheet1, type a formula to look up the description for the class name shown in cell A11.

   b. Copy this formula to the range B12:B26.

   c. In cell G11, use a similar formula to look up the base cost for the class whose code is displayed in cell A11.

   d. Copy this formula to the range G12:G26.

   e. Apply Accounting format, two decimal places, to column G.

5. Add formulas to compute the cost of each class:

   a. In cell I11, type a formula that computes the extra charge, if any.

   ✓ *Companies that schedule more than 8 students in a class, but less than 12, are charged an additional $5 per student.*

   ✓ *Companies that schedule more than 12 students in a class are charged an additional $10 per student.*

   b. Copy this formula to the range I12:I26.

   c. Apply Accounting format, two decimal places, to column I.

6. Compute the total cost per class:

   a. In cell J11, type a formula that computes the total cost for the class.

   b. The cost is equal to the number of students times the base cost plus the extra charge, if any.

   ✓ *For example, if a class initially costs $45, but has an extra charge of $10, multiply $55 times the number of students in the class.*

7. Create a summary:

   a. In cell C29, type *May Totals by Trainer*.

   b. Set the font size to 14 points.

   c. In cells C31:E31, type *Trainer, Total Charges*, and *# of Classes*.

   d. In cells C32:C35, type the trainers' names: *Mark Bradley, Pat Brown, Susan Traywick*, and *Jenny Wilson*.

   e. In the range D32:D35, use =SUMIF() to create formulas that total the class charges attributable to each trainer. Apply Accounting format.

   f. In the range E32:E35, use =COUNTIF to create formulas that count the number of classes each trainer will teach.

8. Protect the lookup table and your formulas against any changes.

9. Print the worksheet.

   a. Use landscape orientation.

   b. Change the scale so that the worksheet prints on one page.

10. Save the workbook and exit Excel.

	Description	Base Cost
EXL2000	Excel 2000	50
EXL95	Excel 95	60
EXL97	Excel 97	55
OUT2000	Outlook 2000	60
OUT98	Outlook 98	55
PWR2000	PowerPoint 2000	60
PWR97	PowerPoint 97	55
WIN95	Windows 95	45
WIN98	Windows 98	45
WRD2000	Word 2000	50
WRD95	Word 95	60
WRD97	Word 97	55

Lesson 9

Create and Modify Charts

Exercise 58

- ◆ Chart Basics
- ◆ Select Chart Data
- ◆ Chart Elements
- ◆ Create a Chart
- ◆ Select a Chart
- ◆ Change the Chart Type
- ◆ Resize, Copy, Move, or Delete a Chart

Exercise 59

- ◆ Use the Chart Toolbar
- ◆ Select a Chart Object
- ◆ Resize, Move, or Delete a Chart Object
- ◆ Add a Chart Object
- ◆ Change Chart Text
- ◆ Change the Orientation of Chart Text

Exercise 60

- ◆ Enhance the Chart Background
- ◆ Format Category and Value Axes
- ◆ Change Color and Patterns of Data Series
- ◆ Add or Remove Data in a Chart

Exercise 61

- ◆ Preview a Chart
- ◆ Print a Chart Sheet
- ◆ Print an Embedded Chart
- ◆ Publish a Chart to the Internet/intranet

Exercise 62

- ◆ Change the Location of a Chart
- ◆ Change the Orientation of a Data Series

Exercise 63

- ◆ Create a Stock Chart
- ◆ Add a Secondary Value Axis to a Chart
- ◆ Change Data Marker Format

Exercise 64

- ◆ Create an Exploded Pie Chart
- ◆ Size the Plot Area or Legend in a Chart
- ◆ Create a Stacked Area Chart

Exercise 65

- ◆ Create a 3-D Chart
- ◆ Change the View of a 3-D Chart
- ◆ Display or Hide Gridlines or Data Labels

Exercise 66

- ◆ Map Excel Data with Microsoft Map
- ◆ Edit and Format a Map

Exercise 67

- ◆ Link a Chart and a Word Document
- ◆ Embed a Chart into a Word Document
- ◆ Edit a Linked or Embedded Chart

Exercise 68

- ◆ Critical Thinking

247

Exercise 58

◆ **Chart Basics** ◆ **Select Chart Data** ◆ **Chart Elements**
◆ **Create a Chart** ◆ **Select a Chart** ◆ **Change the Chart Type**
◆ **Resize, Copy, Move, or Delete a Chart**

On the Job

A chart presents your Excel data in a graphical format that's often easier to grasp than a lot of numbers. To present your data in the best format, you must select the proper chart type. For example, to wow your boss with your department's recent reduction in overtime, you might use a column or bar chart. To compare your division's sales with those of other divisions, you might use a pie chart instead.

You've been thinking about expanding your thriving business, Java Jungle Café, by adding several new stores around town. Unfortunately, expansion takes money, and that means convincing someone to give it to you. Luckily, you can use Excel to create some cool charts that show just how profitable your business is, and what a wise investment it would be.

Terms

embedded chart A chart placed as an object within a worksheet.

chart sheet A chart that occupies its own worksheet.

data series Typically, each column of the chart data represents a different data series.

legend Identifies each of the data series in a chart.

category Typically, each row of the chart data represents a different category.

y-axis The vertical axis of a chart; the value of each category is plotted along the y-axis.

x-axis The horizontal axis of a chart; categories are plotted along the x-axis.

Notes

Chart Basics

- Charts provide a way of presenting and comparing data in a graphic format.
- You can create **embedded charts** or **chart sheets**.
  - ✓ When you create an embedded chart, the chart exists as an object *in the worksheet with the data. All illustrations in this exercise are embedded charts.*

  - ✓ *When you create a chart sheet, the chart exists on a separate sheet in the workbook. You give these sheets names to describe the chart.*
- All charts are linked to the data they plot.
  - ✓ *When you change data in the plotted area of the worksheet, the chart changes automatically.*

Select Chart Data

■ To create a chart, you must first select the data to plot. Following are some guidelines for selecting chart data:

- The selection shouldn't contain blank columns or rows.

- Use the noncontiguous selection method to select chart data that's separated by blank cells, columns, or rows.

- You can also hide columns you don't wish to plot.

- The selection should include the labels for the data, when possible.

- A blank cell in the upper-left corner of a selection tells Excel that the data below and to the right of the blank cell contains labels for the values to plot.

- The selection determines the orientation of the data series (in columns or rows). However, orientation can be changed as desired.

■ The illustration below shows two selections: Example A depicts a contiguous data selection; Example B depicts a noncontiguous data selection.

Contiguous and noncontiguous selections

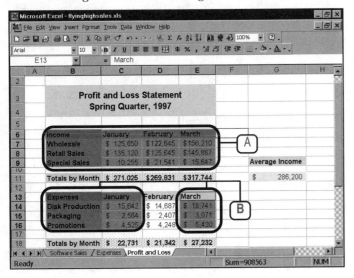

Chart Elements

■ The parts of a column chart are labeled in the illustration below.

■ As you move the mouse over each part of a chart, the name of the object displays.

■ Typically, each chart includes these parts:

• Data series	If you include more than one range of data for a single item (such as the 1997 *and* 1998 sales figures for off-road bikes), you'll create different **data series** for that item. Each series is represented on the chart by a different color bar, column, line, etc.
• Series labels	Labels identifying the charted values. These labels appear in the chart **legend**, which identifies each data series in the chart.
• **Category** labels	Labels identifying each data series shown on the horizontal axis (x-axis).

■ For charts that use axes (that's everything except pie charts):

- The **y-axis** is the vertical scale, except on 3-D charts. The scale values are based on the values being charted.

- The **x-axis** is the horizontal scale and typically represents the data series categories.

- The x-axis title describes the x-axis (horizontal) data.

- The y-axis title describes the y-axis (vertical) data.

Chart elements

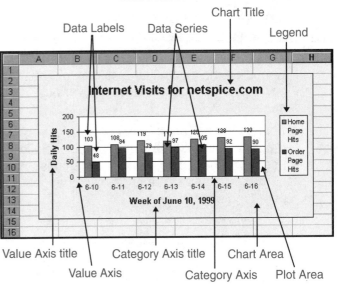

Create a Chart

- You can create charts quickly by using the Chart Wizard, which uses tabbed dialog boxes to step you through the process.

- As you make selections, the Chart Wizard shows you a miniature version of how the chart will look.

  ✓ *Previewing the chart enables you to select the format that best suits the data.*

- Each chart type includes chart subtypes — variations on the selected chart type.

- Excel offers several customized chart types for specialized data.

Select a Chart

- Prior to resizing, copying, moving, or editing a chart, you must first select it.

- When a chart is selected, it's surrounded by handles (small black squares). In addition, the Chart toolbar usually appears.

- You can click part of a chart to select it for resizing, copying, moving, deleting, or editing.

Change the Chart Type

- After creating a chart, you can easily change its chart type to another type.

- There are many chart types from which you can choose (some typical types are illustrated below):

  ✓ *All of the chart types listed here are available in a 3-D format.*

- *Column charts* compare individual values or sets of values. The height of each bar is proportional to its corresponding value in the worksheet.

- *Bar charts* are basically column charts, turned on their sides. Like column charts, use bar charts to compare values of various items.

- *Line charts* are another way of presenting data graphically. Line charts are especially useful when you plot trends, since lines connect points of data and show changes over time effectively.

- *Area charts* are like "filled in" line charts; you use them to track changes over time.

- *Pie charts* are circular graphs used to show the relationship of each value in a data range to the entire data range. The size of each wedge represents the percentage each value contributes to the total.

  ✓ *Only one numerical data range can be used in a pie chart. For example, if you have sales data for 1997 and 1998 for tricycles, off-road bikes, and helmets, you can only chart one year. The data for 1998 tricycles, off-road bikes, and helmets will be represented as individual pie slices.*

  ✓ *Pie charts can be formatted to indicate the percentage of the whole that each piece of the pie represents.*

- A chart can be copied and then edited to produce a different chart using the same worksheet data.

Different charts, but the same data

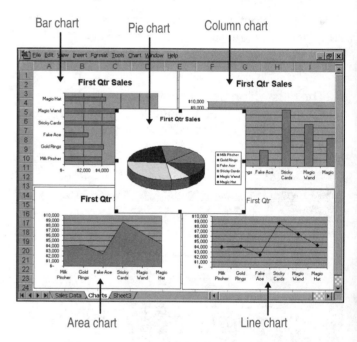

Resize, Copy, Move, or Delete a Chart

- You can resize, copy, move, or delete an embedded chart as needed.

- You can't resize or move a chart on a chart sheet; you can only copy it or delete the chart sheet.

- If you copy a chart, you can change its format to present data in a different way.

- You can select parts of a chart, such as the chart title or legend, and move, edit, or delete them.

Procedures

Select Contiguous Data

1. Click the blank cell in the upper-left corner of the data range.
2. Drag downward and to the right until you have selected the entire data range, including the label cells.

Select Noncontiguous Data by Using the Mouse

1. Click and drag over the cells in the first range you want to select.
2. Press **Ctrl** and drag over another range of cells .... `Ctrl`
3. Repeat step 2 for additional ranges.

Select Noncontiguous Data by Using the Keyboard

1. Select the first cell of the first range you wish to use .... `↕↔`
2. Press the **Shift** key as you use the arrow keys to select the rest of the first range. .... `Shift`
3. Still holding the **Shift** key, press **F8** .... `Shift`+`F8`

   ✓ *This locks the selection in place.*

4. Repeat steps 2 and 3 for each range you wish to select.

Create a Chart with the Chart Wizard

1. Select data to chart.
2. Start the Chart Wizard:
   - Click **Chart Wizard** button `📊` on Standard toolbar.

   OR
   a. Click **I**nsert .... `Alt`+`I`
   b. Click **Ch**art .... `H`

Chart Wizard Step 1 of 4

1. Select a standard or custom chart type:

   To select a standard chart type:

a. Select chart type in **Chart type** list box.... `Alt`+`C`, `📈`
b. Select sub-type for selected chart in **Chart sub-type** list box .... `Alt`+`T`, `↕↔`
c. If desired, click the **Press and Hold to View Sample** button and hold it down to display a preview .... `Alt`+`V`, `Space`

OR

To select a custom chart type:

a. Click **Custom Types** tab .... `Ctrl`+`Tab`
b. Select **U**ser-defined .... `Alt`+`U`

OR

a. Select **B**uilt-in........ `Alt`+`B`
b. Select desired custom chart in **Chart type** list................. `Alt`+`C`, `📈`

2. Click **Next >** .... `Enter`

Chart Wizard Step 2 of 4

1. If desired, change data range options on the **Data Range** tab:

   To change data range:
   - Type or select new worksheet range in **Data range** text box........ `Alt`+`D`

   To change orientation of data series:
   - Select **R**ows .... `Alt`+`R`

   OR
   - Select **Col**umns..... `Alt`+`L`

2. If desired, change series options on the **Series** tab:

   To add a series:
   a. Click **Add** button .... `Alt`+`A`
   b. Type new name for series in **Name** text box .... `Alt`+`N`
   c. Type or select range for new series (just the data) in **V**alues text box ...... `Alt`+`V`

To remove a series:

a. Select series to remove in **Series** list .... `Alt`+`S`
b. Click **R**emove......... `Alt`+`R`

To change range containing category labels:
- Type or select range containing labels in **Cat**egory (X) axis labels text box........ `Alt`+`T`

3. Click **Next >** .... `Enter`

Chart Wizard Step 3 of 4

1. If desired, from **Titles** tab, type title text:
   a. Type text for chart title in **Chart title** text box.................. `Alt`+`T`
   b. Type labels for category, series, and value axes.

      ✓ *Axis label options vary depending on the other chart settings.*

2. If desired, click **Axes** tab to set axis options.

   Axis display options vary depending on the other chart settings.

3. If desired, click **Gridlines** tab to set gridline options.

   Gridline options vary depending on the other chart settings.

4. If desired, click **Legend** tab to set legend options:
   a. Select **S**how legend.................... `Alt`+`S`
   b. Select a placement option:
   c. **Bottom**................... `Alt`+`M`
   d. **Corner**.................... `Alt`+`O`
   e. **T**op........................ `Alt`+`T`
   f. **R**ight .... `Alt`+`R`
   g. **L**eft........................ `Alt`+`L`

5. If desired, click **Data Labels** tab to set data label options:

   a. Select desired data-label display option:

      Available options vary depending on the other chart settings.

   b. Select or deselect **Legend key next to label** .... Alt + K

6. If desired, click **Data Table** tab to set data table options:

   To show data table:
   - Select **Show data table**...................... Alt + D

   To show legend keys:
   - Select **Show legend keys** .... Alt + L

7. Click **Next >** .... Enter

Chart Wizard Step 4 of 4

1. Place chart.

   To place chart as a new chart sheet:

   a. Select **As new sheet**...................... Alt + S

   b. Type name for sheet in **As new sheet** text box (optional).

   OR

   To place chart as an object in existing sheet:

   a. Select **As object in**.............. Alt + O

   b. Select or type name of the sheet in **As object in** text box ....

2. Click **Finish**...................... Enter

Select an Embedded Chart
- Click once on the chart area to select the entire chart.
- To deselect the chart, click anywhere in the worksheet.

Select a Chart Sheet
- Click the chart sheet's tab.
- To deselect the chart sheet, click a different worksheet tab.

Change a Chart's Type:

1. Select the chart or chart sheet.
2. Click **Chart**. .... Alt + C
3. Click **Chart Type**................. T
4. Select a standard or custom chart type.
5. Click **OK** .... Enter

Set the Default Chart Type

1. Select a chart or display a chart sheet.
2. Click **Chart** .... Alt + C
3. Click **Chart Type** .... T
4. Select the chart type you want to set as the default.
5. Click the **Set as default chart** button................ Alt + E
6. Click **Yes** to confirm..... Alt + Y

   OR

   Click **No** to cancel .... Esc

Resize an Embedded Chart

1. Select the chart you want to resize.
2. Move the mouse pointer to a handle.

   ✓ *The mouse pointer becomes ↔ when positioned correctly.*

   ✓ *To size object proportionally, point to a corner handle.*

3. Click the handle and drag it outward to make the chart bigger, or inward to make it smaller.

   ✓ *To align the edges of the chart to the worksheet gridlines, press **Alt** as you drag.*

   ✓ *To resize proportionally from the center of the chart outward or inward, hold down **Ctrl** as you drag.*

4. Release the mouse button and the chart is resized.

Move an Embedded Chart

1. Select the chart you want to move.
2. Click the chart anywhere except the handles, and drag it to its new location.

   ✓ *As you drag, the outline of the chart follows the mouse pointer.*

3. Release the mouse button and the chart is moved.

Copy an Embedded Chart

1. Select the chart you want to copy.
2. Click the **Copy** button .... Ctrl + C
3. Click elsewhere in the worksheet.
4. Click the **Paste** button .... Ctrl + P

   ✓ *You can change the format of the copied chart to view its data in a different way.*

Delete a Chart or Chart Sheet

1. Select the chart you want to delete.
2. Delete the chart.

   To delete an embedded chart:
   Press **Delete**...................... Del

   OR

   To delete a chart sheet:
3. Click **Edit** .... Alt + E
4. Click **Delete Sheet** L
5. Click **OK**......................... Enter

Exercise Directions

1. Start Excel, if necessary.

2. Open the file ⊛58_CHARTS.

3. Save the workbook as **XL_58**.

4. Select the range B11:E14.

5. Use the Chart Wizard to create a chart, using the following selections:

   a. Select the Stacked column with 3-D visual effect chart type and sub-type.

   b. Create the chart title *Total Income by Month*.

   c. Move the legend to the bottom.

   d. Add data labels that show the value.

   e. Save the chart as an embedded object.

6. Size and move the chart, so that the chart appears in A31:F48.

7. Create a second chart using the ranges B18:B25 and E18:E25.

   a. Select Pie with 3-D visual effect for the chart sub-type.

   b. Create the chart title *June Expenses*.

   c. Delete the legend.

   d. Add data labels that show the label and the percent.

   e. Save the chart as an embedded object.

8. Size and move the chart so that it appears in the range A51:F68.

9. Create a chart that displays this same data in a different format:

   a. Copy the second chart to the worksheet range beginning at H50.

   b. Change the sub-type of the copied chart to Clustered Bar.

   c. Resize the chart so that it fills the range H50:M67.

   d. Delete the chart.

10. Create another chart using the ranges C11:E11 and C29:E29.

    a. Select the chart sub-type called Line with markers displayed at each data value.

    b. Add the chart title *Net Profit - 2nd Qtr*.

    c. Add minor gridlines along the y-axis.

    d. Delete the legend.

    e. Add data labels that show the value.

    f. Include a data table as well.

    g. Save the chart as an embedded object.

    h. Resize and move the chart so that it appears in the range A71:H86.

11. Save and close the file and exit Excel.

On Your Own

1. Start Excel, if necessary.

2. Create a worksheet that tracks your television viewing for the past week.

3. Save the file as **OXL_58**.

4. Include these categories, or something similar:

   a. Sports

   b. News

   c. Situation Comedy

   d. Drama

   e. Science Fiction

   f. Movies

   g. Other

5. Include a column for each day of the week.

   • In the appropriate cells, type a value that equals the number of times you watched a program matching that category on that day.

6. Create totals for the number of programs watched each day, and also the number of programs watched in each category for the week.

7. Create a chart (on its own sheet) that best illustrates the proportion of time you spend watching programs of each category.

8. Create another chart (on its own sheet) that best illustrates the difference between the number of times each day you watch a news show versus a situation comedy.

9. Save the file and exit Excel.

Exercise 59

Skills Covered:

◆ **Use the Chart Toolbar** ◆ **Select a Chart Object**
◆ **Resize, Move, or Delete a Chart Object** ◆ **Add a Chart Object**
◆ **Change Chart Text** ◆ **Change the Orientation of Chart Text**

On the Job

Creating a chart by using the Chart Wizard is fairly easy, but often the process of chart creation doesn't stop there. For example, you may wish to resize the chart title, delete a legend, move the data labels, etc., to enhance the chart's appearance. By playing with the chart text, adding color, selecting an interesting font, increasing the font size, adding bold, and so on, you can give your chart a professional, finished appearance. Also, for an interesting look, you can play with the orientation of the title and chart labels.

Well, it's that time of year again — time to look back and access how well you've been doing. To help you analyze the trends in sales at Little Kids Toy Shop, you've decided to create a chart using the last three years' sales data. And since you'll be using this chart at your next employees' meeting, you want to dress it up a bit with some special formatting.

Terms

Chart toolbar A special toolbar that appears when you select any element of a chart. The Chart toolbar contains buttons that you can use to format the selected object or the chart itself.

Chart Objects A special box on the Chart Toolbar that enables you to select the chart object you wish to edit.

chart object Each chart element is an object that can be manipulated independently.

handles Small black squares that surround an object when it's selected.

orientation The direction (vertical or horizontal) of text.

Notes

Chart toolbar

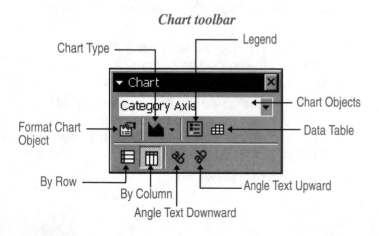

Chart Type — Legend
Chart Objects
Format Chart Object — Data Table
By Row
By Column
Angle Text Downward
Angle Text Upward

Use the Chart Toolbar

- Normally, when you select a chart or one of its parts, the **Chart toolbar** appears.

- If necessary, you can display the Chart toolbar by selecting Toolbars, Chart from the View menu.

- The Chart toolbar provides the following tools:
  - The **Chart Objects** box displays the name of the selected chart object. Click the arrow button to select other chart objects from the drop-down list.

- Format *Chart Object* formats the selected **chart object**. (The name in the ScreenTip changes to match the object that's currently selected.)

- Chart Type provides a drop-down palette of common chart types from which you can select.

  ✓ *The face of the Chart Type button changes to match the chart type most recently selected from the Chart Type palette. Clicking the button (rather than opening the palette) changes the current chart type to match the chart type displayed on the button face.*

- Legend hides or displays the chart legend.

- Data Table hides or displays the data table for the chart.

- By Row changes the orientation of the data series to rows.

- By Column changes the orientation of the data series to columns.

- Angle Text Downward angles selected text downward.

- Angle Text Upward angles selected text upward.

Select a Chart Object

- Prior to resizing, moving, copying, deleting, or editing a chart object, you must first select it.

- When an object is selected, it's surrounded by **handles** (small black squares). Also, the Chart toolbar usually appears.

- The name of the selected object appears in the Chart Objects box.

- You can select a different object from the drop-down list in the Chart Objects box on the Chart toolbar.

- To select individual data points, click any of the bars, columns, etc. representing the data series, and then click the specific data point you want. (Double-clicking the data point displays the Format Data Series dialog box.)

Resize, Move, or Delete a Chart Object

- By rearranging the parts of a chart, you can make it more attractive and easier to understand.

- To resize a chart element, select it and then drag one of the handles. Note that not every chart element can be resized.

- If you resize an object that contains text, the font size of the text may be changed accordingly.

- You can change the value represented by a column, line, bar, etc. in a chart by resizing the chart element. When you drag the chart element, the corresponding value in the worksheet changes to match.

- To move a chart element, select and drag it. (If the mouse pointer is a two-headed black arrow, you're dragging a handle and therefore resizing the object. You may need to undo the resizing operation before you continue.)

- To delete a chart element, select it and press Delete.

- When you delete an object from a chart, the remaining parts of the chart may be enlarged.

Add a Chart Object

- You may need to add an object to a chart — for example, data labels or axis titles — that you didn't include when creating the chart.

- To add a chart object to an existing chart, select the chart, open the Chart Options dialog box, and select the item(s) you need.

Change Chart Text

- You can edit chart text, or replace it with something else.

- Some text in a chart may be linked to worksheet data. For example, category axis labels are usually linked to column labels.

  ✓ *When you edit linked text in a chart, Excel removes the link to the worksheet data. Thus, if you later change the label within the worksheet data, that change will have no effect on the corresponding label within the chart.*

- Some text is unlinked to any worksheet data, such as axis and chart titles, text boxes, and trendline labels.

- You can edit chart text or change its formatting. For example, you can change the size, font, and attributes of chart text just as you might change a row or column label in your worksheet.

Change the Orientation of Chart Text

- You can change the **orientation** of (rotate) chart text just as you might change row or column labels.
  - Chart text includes the chart title, category axis labels, value axis labels, and data labels.
- Changing the orientation of text adds visual interest to charts. For example, you can angle the labels along the category axis, or use a vertical chart title in place of the normal horizontal title.
- The process for changing the orientation of any chart text is similar to changing the orientation of a row or column label, as you can see from the Format Axis dialog box.

- The dialog box shown here includes an option you don't see when formatting row or column labels: the Offset option. This option allows you to adjust the amount of space between the axis labels and the axis itself.
- When changing the alignment of chart titles and data labels, you can use the Horizontal and Vertical options to control the position of the text within its frame.
- In addition, you can change the placement of the data labels in relation to the data markers by using the Label Position option.

Alignment tab of the Format Axis dialog box

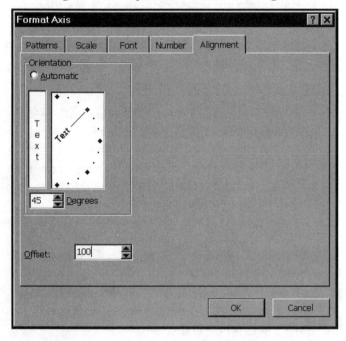

Procedures

Select a Chart Object

1. Display the Chart toolbar, if necessary.
2. Select the object from the **Chart Objects** list.

   ✓ *You can also click an object in the chart to select it. When an object is selected, handles appear around its perimeter.*

Resize a Chart Object

1. Select the object you want to resize.
2. Move the mouse pointer to a handle.

   ✓ *The mouse pointer becomes ↔ when positioned correctly.*

   ✓ *To size object proportionally, point to a corner handle.*

3. Drag the handle outward to make the object larger, or inward to make it smaller.
4. Release the mouse button and the object is resized.

Move a Chart Object

1. Drag the object to its new location.

   ✓ *As you drag, the outline of the object follows the mouse pointer.*

2. Release the mouse button and the object is moved.

Add a Chart Object to an Existing Chart

1. Select the chart.
2. Click **Chart** .... `Alt`+`C`
3. Click **Chart Options** .... `O`
4. Click the appropriate tab for the object you want to add .... `Ctrl`+`Tab`
5. Change the settings as needed.
6. Click **OK** .... `Enter`

Delete a Chart Object

1. Select the object you want to delete.
2. Press **Delete** .... `Del`

Change Chart Text

1. Click the chart object that contains the text you wish to change, or select that object from the Chart Objects list on the Chart toolbar.
2. Change the text:

   To replace existing text with new text:

   a. Select existing text.
   b. Type desired text.

      ✓ *What you type replaces selected text.*

   c. Click anywhere outside the text box.

   OR

   To edit existing text:

   a. Click desired character position in text.
   b. Insert and delete characters as desired.

      ✓ *To insert a line break, press **Enter**.*

   c. Click anywhere outside the text box.

Change the Orientation and Alignment of Chart Text

1. Click the chart object that contains the text you wish to change, or select that object from the Chart Objects list on the Chart toolbar.
2. Click the Format button on the Chart toolbar.

   ✓ *For example, click the Format Chart Title button.*

3. Click the **Alignment** tab............................... `Ctrl`+`Tab`
4. Change the orientation of text by performing one of the following:

   • Type the degree of rotation desired in the **Degrees** box .... `Alt`+`D`

   OR

   • Drag the pointer in the Orientation box.

   OR

   • Click the vertical box located to the left of the Orientation box.

5. Set additional options, if any:

   a. Select a horizontal alignment for the text within its text box from the **Horizontal** list .... `Alt`+`H`, `↑↓`, `Enter`

   b. Select a vertical alignment for the text within its text box from the **Vertical** list .... `Alt`+`V`, `↑↓`, `Enter`

   c. Select an **Offset** amount .... `Alt`+`O`, `↑↓`

   d. Select a **Label Position** .... `Alt`+`P`, `↑↓`, `Enter`

6. Click **OK** .... `Enter`

Exercise Directions

1. Start Excel, if necessary.
2. Open 💿 **59_SALES**.
3. Save the file as **XL_59**.
4. Select the range B9:E12.
5. Create a chart using the Chart Wizard.
   a. Select a Clustered bar chart.
   b. Enter the title *Yearly Sales*.
   c. Display a legend at the top of the chart.
   d. Include data labels that show the value.
   e. Place the chart as an embedded object in Sheet 1.
6. Resize and move the chart so that it fills the range A17:G33.
7. Change the text of the category axis labels, and the legend to Arial, 11 points.
8. Change the text of the value axis labels to Arial Narrow, 8 points, bold.
   - Change the orientation of the value axis label text to 15 degrees.
9. Select the "Children Toys" Data Labels object from the Chart Objects list.
   a. Using the Alignment tab, change the position of the labels to Inside End.
   b. Change the font to Arial, 8 points, bold.
10. Change the data labels for "Infant Toys" so that they're also positioned Inside End, and use Arial, 8 points, bold.
11. Change the font of the data labels for "Toddler Toys" to Arial, 8 points, bold.
    ✓ *Don't change the position of the Toddler Toys data labels.*
12. Change the text of the title to *Sales, 1997-1999*.
    - Apply the Impact font (or another font of your choice), 20 points, regular.
13. Save the workbook.
14. Close the workbook and exit Excel.

On Your Own

1. Start Excel, if necessary.
2. Open 💿 **59_PETS**.
3. Save the file as **OXL_59**.
4. Scroll down to the sales recap, and select the range C57:D59.
   a. Create a pie chart.
   b. Add the title *Pet Sales*.
   c. Include data labels that show the label and percent.
   d. Save the chart as an object in Sheet 2.
5. Resize and move the chart so that it fits in the range A1:G16.
6. Format the chart title:
   a. Edit the chart title to say, *Pet Sales - March 27, 1999*.
   b. Format the title using a font of your choice, 20 points.
   c. Change the vertical alignment to Bottom.
7. Apply Arial, 9 points, bold to the legend.
8. Apply Arial, 11 points to the data labels.
9. Resize the plot area to make the pie bigger.
   a. You'll probably need to move the plot area after you resize it.
   b. Feel free to move the legend and the chart title as well.
10. Save the workbook and exit Excel.

Exercise 60

◆ **Enhance the Chart Background**
◆ **Format Category and Value Axes**
◆ **Change Color and Patterns of Data Series**
◆ **Add or Remove Data in a Chart**

On the Job

A chart presents complex numerical data in a graphical format. Because a chart tells its story visually, you must make the most of the way your chart looks. There are many ways in which you can enhance a chart; for example, you can add color or pattern to the chart background, and format the value and category axes so that the numbers are easier to understand. In the end, you'll have a chart that tells the dynamic story of your company's increased sales and profit margins, your department's decreased overtime and increased productivity, and your rise from an obscure cubicle-slave to the company's latest vice president.

As the client services manager at Corporate Computer Solutions, you know that customer satisfaction is your number one concern. As a result, for the last few weeks, you've been tracking the number of calls taken by each of your technical representatives, and the customer satisfaction rating given to each rep in a recent survey. Now you want to create a nice-looking chart for your weekly meeting with the reps, so you can go over how each person has been doing.

Terms

chart area Encompasses all the elements of a chart.

plot area The area of the chart in which the data is plotted.

category axis The x-axis, usually the horizontal axis of the chart. Categories are plotted along this axis.

value axis The y-axis, usually the vertical axis of the chart. Data values are plotted along this axis.

tick marks Small marks that appear along the value axis to mark the location of gridlines. Tick marks also appear along the category axis to mark the placement of various data series.

Notes

Enhance the Chart Background

- A chart actually has two backgrounds: the larger **chart area** and the smaller **plot area**, as shown in the figure below.

Chart backgrounds

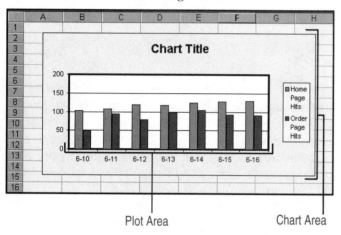

Plot Area   Chart Area

- You can format the chart area, the plot area, or both.

- To format either chart background, you can do any of the following:
  - Add a border around the background area.
  - Apply a color to the background.
  - Apply a fill effect, such as a *gradient* (which allows you to gradually blend up to two colors together), *texture* (such as marble), *pattern* (which uses two colors to form a pattern, such as diagonal stripes), or *picture* (which uses a graphic file as the background).
  - Add a shadow effect behind the border (chart area only).
  - Round the corners (chart area only).

Format Category and Value Axes

- The **category axis** (x-axis) is generally the horizontal axis for a chart. Categories and data series are plotted along the category axis.

- The **value axis** (y-axis) is usually a chart's vertical axis. The values of various categories or data series are plotted along the value axis.

- You can change the font, size, color, attributes, alignment, and placement of text or numbers along both the category and value axes.

- You can also change the appearance of the **tick marks**.

- In addition, you can adjust the scale used along the value axis.

Change Color and Patterns of Data Series

- When you create a chart, Excel automatically assigns a color to each series in the chart.

- You may want to change the color of a particular data series.

- Even if you're printing the chart in black and white, you may want to change the color of a data series to better distinguish it from other colors in the chart that translate to a similar gray tone.

- You can replace a color with a pattern (or add a pattern to a color) for a special effect.

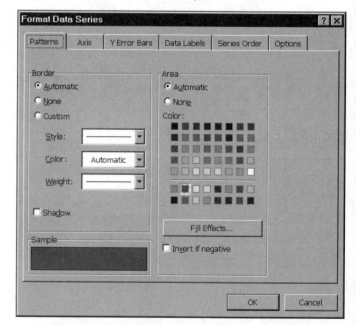

  - Patterns are especially effective on black-and-white printouts.

  - In addition to a set of standard patterns (such as diagonal), you can add special effects such as gradient fills, textures, shadows, and even images.

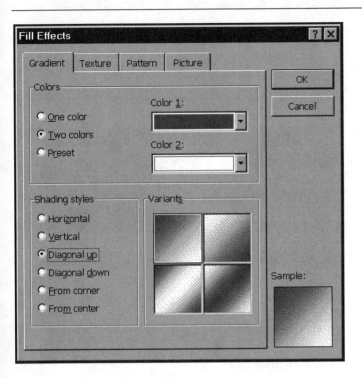

- When changing the color or pattern assigned to a particular data series, you can change the border style as well.

Add or Remove Data in a Chart

- After creating a chart, you can change the initial data range to add data to the chart.

- For example, you might add a data series to the chart for an additional store, salesperson, product, etc.

- You can remove data from a chart as well.

- When a chart is selected, the current data range is surrounded by colored Range Finder borders, as shown below.
    - You can drag the colored border to another range to select that range instead.
    - You can also use the drag handle on the Range Finder border to expand or contract the data range used by the chart.

- You can drag data onto a chart to add that data to the chart.
    - If the data and the chart are on different worksheets, you can use the Copy and Paste commands to add data to a chart.

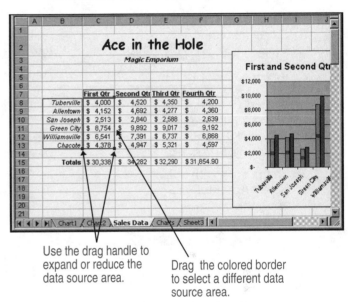

Use the drag handle to expand or reduce the data source area.

Drag the colored border to select a different data source area.

Procedures

Enhance the Chart Background

1. Select the chart area or the plot area.
2. Click the **Format** button [icon].
3. If desired, on the Patterns tab, select a **Border**:
   - Select **Automatic** to apply the normal border style .... [Alt]+[A]

   OR

   a. Select **Custom**.
   b. Select a border **Style** ... [Alt]+[S], [↗], [Enter]
   c. Select a border **Color** ....
      .... [Alt]+[C], [↕], [Enter]
   d. Select a border **Weight** (thickness).........................
      .... [Alt]+[W], [↗], [Enter]

To fill the area with color:

- Select **Automatic** to apply the normal background color (usually white) .... [Alt]+[U]

OR

- Select the desired color from the color palette ....
   .... [Alt]+[O], [↕], [Space]

OR

a. Click **Fill Effects** .... [Alt]+[I]
b. On the Gradient tab, choose the color option you want:

1. Select **One color** .... [Alt]+[O]
2. Choose the color you want to blend from the **Color 1** drop-down palette ....
   .... [Alt]+[1], [↕], [Enter]
3. Adjust the transition from **Dark** to **Light** ...... [Alt]+[K], [↗]

OR

1. Select **Two colors** ...... [Alt]+[T]

2. Choose the two colors you want to blend from the **Color 1** and **Color 2** drop-down palettes .... [Alt]+[1],
   .... [Alt]+[2], [↗], [Enter]

OR

1. Select **Preset** .... [Alt]+[R]
2. Choose the **Preset colors** option you want .... [Alt]+[E], [↗], [Enter]
   a. Select one of the **Shading styles**.
   b. Select one of the **Variants** .... [Alt]+[S]
   c. Click **OK** .... [Enter]

OR

To fill the area with a texture:

a. Click the **Texture** tab.
b. Select the texture you want:
   - Click the desired texture ...... [Alt]+[T], [↕]

OR

a. To import your own texture file, click **Other Texture** .... [Alt]+[O]
b. Select desired drive and folder from **Look in** text box list .... [Alt]+[I]
c. Double-click the texture file.

OR

To fill the area with a pattern:

a. Click the **Pattern** tab .... [Ctrl]+[Tab]
b. Select a **Foreground** color .... [Alt]+[F], [↕], [Enter]
c. Select a **Background** color .... [Alt]+[B], [↕], [Enter]
d. Click a **Pattern** .... [Alt]+[T], [↕]

OR

To fill the area with a picture:

a. Click the **Picture** tab .... [Ctrl]+[Tab]
b. Click **Select Picture** .... [Alt]+[L]
c. Select desired drive and folder from **Look in** text box .... [Alt]+[I]
d. Double-click the graphic file.

4. Click **OK** .... [Enter]
5. Click **OK** .... [Enter]

Format the Category or Value Axis

1. Select the axis.
2. Click the **Format** button [icon].
3. If desired, on the Patterns tab, select a **Lines** style:
   - Select **Automatic** to apply the normal line style .... [Alt]+[A]

   OR

   a. Select **Custom**.
   b. Select a border **Style** ... [Alt]+[S], [↗], [Enter]
   c. Select a border **Color** .. [Alt]+[C], [↕], [Enter]
   d. Select a border **Weight** (thickness) ....
      .... [Alt]+[W], [↗], [Enter]

4. If desired, change the **Major tick mark type** (location) .... [Alt]+[M], [↕]
5. If desired, change the **Minor tick mark type** (location) .... [Alt]+[R], [↕]
6. If desired, change the location of the **Tick mark labels** .... [Alt]+[T], [↕]
7. Click the **Scale** tab.

To change the scale for the category axis:

a. To change the point at which the y-axis intersects the category axis, enter a category number in the **Value (Y) axis c̲rosses at category number** text box .... Alt + C

b. To change the frequency of the category labels, enter a number in the **Number of categories between tick-mark l̲abels** text box (enter 2 to display every other label, and so on) ..... Alt + L

c. To change the frequency of the tick marks along the category axis, enter a number in the **Number of categories between tick mar̲ks** text box .... Alt + K

d. If you don't want the first category to be placed right against the y-axis, select **Value (Y) axis crosses b̲etween categories** .... Alt + B

e. If desired, select **Categories in r̲everse order** .... Alt + R

f. To place the y-axis on the right, select **Value (Y) axis crosses at m̲aximum category** .... Alt + M

To change the scale for the value axis:

a. Set the **Mi̲nimum** and **Maximum** values used on the y-axis .... Alt + N , Alt + X

b. Adjust the placement of the major and minor tick marks along the y-axis by changing the values in the **Maj̲or unit** and **Mi̲nor unit** text boxes .... Alt + A , Alt + I

c. To change the point at which the x-axis intersects the value axis, enter a value in the **Category (X) axis C̲rosses at** text box.................. Alt + C

d. If desired, adjust the **Display u̲nits** value. Normally, values are displayed in full, as in $6,000,000. You can tell Excel to display just "6" by selecting Millions from the Display units drop-down list........ Alt + U , ↕ , Enter

e. To display values as powers of 10, select the **L̲ogarithmic scale** option (values must be greater than zero, and **Maj̲or unit** and **Mi̲nor unit** values) must be at least 10.......... Alt + L

f. If desired, select **Values in r̲everse order** .... Alt + R

g. To move the category axis to the top of the plot area, select **Category (X) axis crosses at m̲aximum value** .... Alt + M

8. Click the **Font** tab and make whatever changes you want to the font, size, and other attributes of the value labels.

9. Click the **Number** tab and select the format you want for the axis labels.

10. Click the **Alignment** tab and angle the label text, if desired:

   • Drag the **Text** marker to set the degree of rotation.

   OR

   a. Enter a positive number in the **Degrees** text box to angle text from lower left to upper right, or a negative number to angle text from upper left to lower right.............. Alt + D

b. Select the amount of space you want between the axis labels and the axis by adjusting the **O̲ffset** value .... Alt + O

11. Click **OK** .... Enter

Change the Color and Patterns of Data Series

1. Click one item in the data series you wish to change, or select the data series from the Chart Objects list.

2. Click the **Format Data Series** button on the Chart toolbar.

3. If desired, use the Patterns tab to select a **Border**:

   • Select **A̲utomatic** to apply the normal border style .... Alt + A

   OR

   a. Select **Custom**.

   b. Select a border **S̲tyle**... Alt + S , ↕ , Enter

   c. Select a border **C̲olor** .. Alt + C , ↔ , Enter

   d. Select a border **Weight** (thickness) ....
   .... Alt + W , ↕ , Enter

4. If you wish, add a **Shadow** behind the data series .... Alt + D

To fill the data series with color:

   • Select **A̲utomatic** to apply the normal background color....................... Alt + U

   OR

   • Select the desired color from the color palette..........
   .... Alt + O , ↔ , Space

   OR

   a. Click **Fi̲ll Effects** .... Alt + I

   b. On the Gradient tab, choose the color option you want:

- Select **One**
  color................ `Alt`+`O`
- Choose the color you want to blend from the **Color 1** drop-down palette...........................
  .... `Alt`+`1`, `↕`, `Enter`
- Adjust the transition from **Dark** to
  Light......... `Alt`+`K`, `↔`

OR

- Select **Two**
  colors.............. `Alt`+`T`
- Choose the two colors you want to blend from the **Color 1** and **Color 2** drop-down palettes........
  .... `Alt`+`1`, `Alt`+`2`,
  .... `↕`, `Enter`

OR

- Select **Preset**.... `Alt`+`R`
- Choose the **Preset colors** option you want..
  .... `Alt`+`E`, `↕`, `Enter`
- Select one of the **Shading styles**.
- Select one of the **Variants**............ `Alt`+`S`
- Click **OK** .... `Enter`

OR

To fill the data series with a texture:

a. Click the **Texture** tab.

b. Select the texture you want:

  - Click the desired
    texture...... `Alt`+`T`, `↕`

  OR

  - To import your own texture file, click **Other Texture**. .... `Alt`+`O`

  - Select desired drive and folder from **Look in**
    list .... `Alt`+`I`

  - Double-click the texture file.

OR

To fill the area with a pattern:

a. Click the **Pattern**
   tab .... `Ctrl`+`Tab`

b. Select a **Foreground**
   color .... `Alt`+`F`, `↕`, `Enter`

c. Select a **Background**
   color .... `Alt`+`B`, `↕`, `Enter`

d. Click a
   Pattern.......... `Alt`+`T`, `↕`

OR

To fill the area with a picture:

a. Click the **Picture**
   tab .... `Ctrl`+`Tab`

b. Click **Select**
   Picture .... `Alt`+`L`

c. Select desired drive and folder from **Look in** text
   box.......................... `Alt`+`I`

d. Double-click the graphic file.

6. Click **OK** .... `Enter`

7. Click **OK** .... `Enter`

Add Data to a Chart

To add data by dragging:

1. Select the chart data you wish to add, including appropriate row and column labels.
2. Drag the selection into the chart area.
3. Release the mouse button to drop the selection onto the chart.

To add data with Copy and Paste:

1. Select the chart data you wish to add, including appropriate row and column labels.
2. Click the **Copy** button
   .... `Alt`+`C`
3. Click the chart to select it.
4. Click the **Paste** button
   .... `Alt`+`V`

To add data by using the Range Finder:

Drag the handle on a selection to expand it to include more data.

OR

Click and drag the outline of the selection to move it to another range.

Remove Chart Data

To remove an entire data series:

1. Click an item in the data series you wish to remove.
2. Press **Delete**...................... `Del`

To delete data by using the Range Finder:

Drag the handle up on a selection to reduce its size and remove selected data.

Exercise Directions

1. Start Excel, if necessary.
2. Open ⊚ **60_CALLS**.
3. Save the workbook as **XL_60**.
4. Add data to the chart:
   a. Click the chart to select it.
   b. Use the drag handle to expand the data range to C9:D13.
   c. Edit the chart title to say *Number of Calls - Wks 1 & 2.*
5. Edit the chart background:
   a. Select a two-color gradient fill.
   b. Choose Light Green as the first color, and Sea Green as the second color.
   c. Select the Diagonal up style, first variant.
   d. Add a shadow as well.
6. Add the Green marble texture to the plot area.

7. Format the data series:
   a. Select the Week 1 data series.
   b. Add a pattern fill effect, using Ivory as the foreground color and Sea Green as the background color.
   c. Use the Shingle pattern (located in the seventh column, fourth row).
   d. Select the Week 2 data series.
   e. Add a pattern fill effect here as well, using Ivory as the foreground color and Light Green as the background color.
   f. Use the Wide upward diagonal pattern (located in the third column, bottom row).
7. Select the chart title and add a Sea Green solid color fill.
   • Change the font color of the chart title to Ivory.
8. Change the scale of the value axis so that the maximum value is 250.
9. Save the workbook and exit Excel.

On Your Own

1. Start Excel, if necessary.
2. Open ⊚ **60_ANTIQUE**.
3. Save the workbook as **OXL_60**.
4. Add the February data to the chart.
5. Format the title:
   a. Change the chart title to *Jan-Feb Sales.*
   b. Add a solid color fill.
   c. Change the font to a light color, in a larger point size. You can also change the typeface if you like.
6. Apply a texture to the chart area, with a border of the heaviest weight.
7. Format the value axis:
   a. Set the display unit to Thousands and display the label.
   b. Change the font to something smaller.

   c. Change the point size on the Thousands label as well.
   d. Reduce the decimal places to zero.
8. Format the category axis:
   a. Change the font to something smaller.
   b. Adjust the orientation to display the category labels on a slant.
   c. Resize the chart and the plot area as needed so that all the category labels show.
9. Format the data series:
   a. Add a texture to one data series.
   b. Use a two-color gradient fill on the other data series.
10. Delete the data for end tables, china cabinets, and chairs from the chart.
11. Save the workbook and exit Excel.

Exercise 61

Skills Covered:

◆ **Preview a Chart** ◆ **Print a Chart Sheet**

◆ **Print an Embedded Chart** ◆ **Publish a Chart to the Internet/intranet**

On the Job

After creating a chart, you may want to print it out so you can share your data with others. You can print the chart with the rest of the worksheet data, or print just the chart. Another way to share information is to publish the chart to the Internet or your company's intranet. You can even make the published chart interactive, so that users can change the data in the chart as well as view it. This is especially useful when the data for the chart comes from several sources, such as several departments in the company.

The sales figures for the second quarter are in, and you're in charge of distributing the information throughout your company, Corporate Computer Solutions. You've decided to create a few fancy-looking charts and print them, some alone, and some with the corresponding data. These printouts will be distributed to managers in the company. For everyone else, you've decided to simply publish the data on the company's intranet.

Terms

intranet A private, Internet-like network whose data you view with a Web browser, just as you might view Internet data.

publishing The process of saving data to an intranet/Internet.

HTML Short for Hypertext Markup Language, HTML is the language of the World Wide Web. To publish a chart on the Internet/intranet, it must be converted to HTML.

static data Data that, once published, cannot be changed by the viewer.

interactive data Published data that can be changed by the viewer through his or her Web browser.

Notes

Preview a Chart

- Just as you can preview a worksheet prior to printing it, you can preview a chart as well.

- Previewing a chart before you print it allows you to envision how the chart will look when printed.

- Previewing the chart is especially important if you plan to print it on a black-and-white printer, since the preview is also in black and white.

- If you're printing on a color printer, the preview appears in color whether you're printing in color or black and white.

- If you want to print in black and white on a color printer, you may need to change the settings for the printer itself.

Preview a chart before you print it

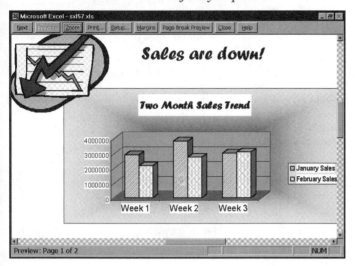

Publish as Web Page dialog box

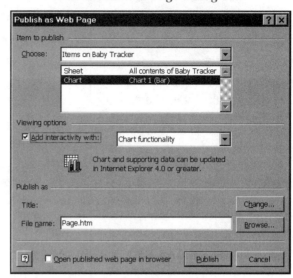

Print a Chart Sheet

- When you create a chart using the Chart Wizard, you have a choice of placing the chart on a separate chart sheet or embedding it as an object within an existing sheet.

- A chart sheet is a worksheet that contains only a chart.

- Chart sheets can be printed with the rest of the workbook or as separate sheets.

Print an Embedded Chart

- Embedded charts typically print with the worksheet in which they're located.

- This enables you to print a chart along with its corresponding data.

- You can print an embedded chart separately from its source worksheet.

Publish a Chart to the Internet/intranet

- The process of saving worksheet data to the Internet or your company's **intranet** is called **publishing**.

- To publish a chart on the Internet/intranet, Excel converts it to **HTML** format.

- Once the data is published, you can republish it as needed to update the data.

- The chart can be saved as **static data** (data that can be viewed, but not changed) or as **interactive data** (data that could be changed by the viewer).

- To publish interactive data, make the appropriate selections in the Publish as Web Page dialog box.

- From the user's standpoint, changing interactive data is similar to changing that data within Excel, so there's nothing new to learn.

- As you can see from the illustration below, many of the tools that normally appear in the Excel window are also available to the user of the published data.

Interactive chart

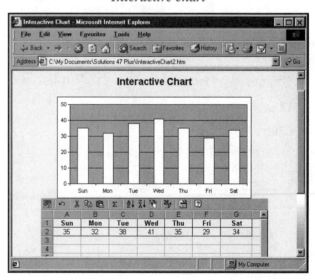

- To change interactive data through a Web browser, the user clicks in the individual cells and makes changes as usual.

- Prior to publishing data, you may want to save it to a local hard drive. Using an HTML editor, you can then make changes to the Web page to improve its appearance.

  - ✓ *After making any changes, you can republish the HTML file to its permanent location on your company's intranet or the Internet.*

267

Procedures

Preview a Chart

1. Select what you want to print:
   - Display the chart sheet or the worksheet containing the chart and data to print.

   OR

   - Click the embedded chart if you plan to print just the chart.

2. Click the **Print Preview** button ![btn].

3. When you're done previewing the chart, click **Print** to print it, or **Esc** to return to the worksheet............ `Alt`+`T`, `Esc`

   ✓ You can also change the page setup, as explained later in this section.

Print an Embedded Chart and Worksheet or a Chart Sheet

1. Select worksheet or chart sheet containing chart to print.

2. Click the **Print** button ![btn].

Print an Embedded Chart Separately

1. Select embedded chart.

2. Click the **Print** button ![btn].

Set Chart Print Options

1. Select the embedded chart or the chart sheet.

2. Click **File** .... `Alt`+`F`

3. Click **Page Setup** .... `U`

   ✓ From the Print Preview window, click **Setup**.

4. Click **Chart** tab .... `Ctrl`+`Tab`

5. Set printed chart size:
   - **Use full page** .... `Alt`+`U`
   - **Scale to fit page** ... `Alt`+`F`
   - **Custom** .... `Alt`+`C`

✓ Use the **Custom** option to print the chart at its actual size. Before printing, click the chart — whether embedded or on a chart sheet — and drag the selection handles to size the chart. After selecting **Custom** (and closing the Page Setup dialog box), preview the chart to be sure that the size is as you want it and that the chart is positioned correctly on the page.

6. If desired, select the **Draft quality** option to print the chart more quickly but at lower quality .... `Alt`+`Q`

   ✓ For some printers, you may need to change printer options to print at a lower resolution or with different color settings. Consult your printer manual, if necessary.

7. To print each data series using a pattern rather than color or shades of gray, select the **Print in black and white** option......................... `Alt`+`B`

8. Click **OK** .... `Enter`

Publish a Chart as Static Data

1. Select the embedded chart or chart sheet.

2. Click **File** .... `Alt`+`F`

3. Click **Save as Web Page** .... `G`

4. From the **Save in** list, select the Internet or intranet location where you want to save the chart .... `Alt`+`I`

   ✓ You can also save the HTML file to a local hard drive.

5. Type a name for the HTML file in the **File name** text box .... `Alt`+`N`

6. If desired, click **Change Title** and then type a title for the Web page (the HTML file)............. `Alt`+`C`

   ✓ The title appears in the title bar of the user's Web browser when the page is displayed.

---

7. Choose **Selection: Chart** .... `Alt`+`E`

8. Click **Publish** .... `Alt`+`P`

9. If desired, select **Open published web page in browser** to launch your Web browser so you can view the HTML file .... `Alt`+`O`

10. Click **Publish** .... `Alt`+`P`

Publish a Chart as Interactive Data

1. Select the embedded chart or the chart sheet.

2. Click **File** .... `Alt`+`F`

3. Click **Save as Web Page**..... `G`

4. From the **Save in** list, select the Internet or intranet location where you want to save the chart.................. `Alt`+`I`

   ✓ You can also save the HTML file to a local hard drive.

5. Type a name for the HTML file in the **File name** text box .... `Alt`+`N`

6. If desired, click **Change Title** and then type a title for the Web page (the HTML file)............. `Alt`+`C`

   ✓ The title appears in the title bar of the user's Web browser when the page is displayed.

7. Choose **Selection: Chart** .... `Alt`+`E`

8. Click **Publish** .... `Alt`+`P`

9. Choose **Add interactivity with**.............................. `Alt`+`A`

10. If desired, select **Open published web page in browser** to launch your Web browser so you can view the HTML file .... `Alt`+`O`

11. Click **Publish** .... `Alt`+`P`

Republish a Chart

1. Open the original workbook.
2. Make changes to the chart as needed.
3. Click **File** .... Alt + F

4. Click **Save as Web Page** .... G
   a. Click **Publish** .... Alt + P
   b. Open the **Choose** list and select **Previously published items** .... Alt + C , ↘
   c. Choose the item you want to republish from those listed.

OR
   a. Click **Republish: Chart** .... Alt + E
   b. Click **Publish** .... Alt + P
5. Click **Publish** .... Alt + P

Exercise Directions

1. Start Excel, if necessary.
2. Open ◉ **61_QTR2SALES**.
3. Save the file as **XL_61**.
4. Print the chart and its data from the Qtr 2 Sales sheet:
   a. Preview the worksheet.
   b. Notice that part of the chart is missing; it will print with some data on a second page. Use Page Setup to adjust the printout to print one page wide by one page tall.
   c. Print the worksheet and chart.
5. Print just the chart on the Qtr 2 Sales sheet.
   a. Select the chart only.
   b. Preview the chart.
   c. Use Page Setup to scale the chart to fit the page.
   d. Print the chart.
6. Print the chart sheet:
   a. Change to the Total Sales tab.
   b. Preview the chart.
   c. Print the chart.

7. Publish the Total Sales chart:
   a. Publish the chart to the DDC folder.
      ✓ *Your instructor may ask you to publish your chart to another folder.*
   b. Publish the chart as a static chart.
   c. Change the title of the Web page to *Total Q2 Sales.*
   d. Use the file name **XL_61CHART1.htm**.
8. Publish the chart on the Qtr 2 Sales worksheet:
   a. Publish the chart to the DDC folder.
   b. Publish the chart as an interactive chart.
   c. Change the title of the Web page to *Quarter 2 Computer Sales.*
   d. Use the file name **XL_61CHART2.htm**.
   e. Open the chart in your Web browser.
   f. Scroll down to the worksheet area and change the Maxima sales for George Billings to *$1,197,567.*
   g. Close the Web browser and return to Excel.
   h. Make the same change to data for George Billings in the workbook.
9. Save the workbook and exit Excel.

On Your Own

1. Start Excel, if necessary.
2. Open ⊙ **61_EXPENSES**.
3. Save the workbook as **OXL_61**.
4. Create a column chart using the range B7:H10.
5. Format the chart as you like, but include these elements:
   a. Include a title, such as *March Expenses*.
   b. Change the scale of the value axis so that the maximum is 500, and the minimum is 50.
   c. Display minor gridlines.
6. Print just the chart; then print it again with the worksheet data.
7. Publish the chart as an interactive chart.
   a. Use the file name **OXL_61MARCH.htm**.
   b. Open the chart in your Web browser.
   c. Change the hotel expense for March 29th to $121.32.

8. Create another chart using the ranges C7:H7 and C12:H12.
   a. Create a 3-D pie chart.
   b. Include a title, such as *Total Expense Distributions*.
   c. Add data labels that show the label and the percent.
   d. Include a legend.
   e. Apply formats to the chart background, title, legend, and other elements as you like.
9. Print the chart after previewing it.
10. Publish the chart as a static chart (non-interactive).
    • Use the file name **OXL_61EXPENSE.htm**.
11. Save the workbook and exit Excel.

Exercise 62

◆ **Change the Location of a Chart**
◆ **Change the Orientation of a Data Series**

On the Job

When you create a chart by using the Chart Wizard, you're asked where to place the new chart — on its own sheet, or as an embedded object in an existing sheet. After creating the chart, you may decide to move it. Perhaps during formatting you decide that the chart will look best on a sheet by itself; or maybe you decide that, by moving a chart from a chart sheet onto a worksheet, you can resize and format the chart more to your liking. Luckily, it's easy to change the location of a chart. After you settle on a location for the chart, you may still decide that something is wrong, such as the way in which the data series are oriented. Changing the orientation from columns to rows is a simple process that may help your chart tell its story more clearly.

As the owner of Movie Time Video, you've been thinking of expanding the business by carrying a wider variety of videos in the most popular categories. You've been tracking the video rental trends during June, and now you'd like to create a chart to help you sort out the data. You'll play with the chart location and data orientation until you get the exact format you want.

Terms

chart sheet A worksheet that contains only a chart.

embedded object In Excel, an object is an item that can be manipulated separately from the worksheet that contains it. A chart or other item that can be resized, moved, copied, and otherwise manipulated without affecting the worksheet data.

data series Typically, a row within the data range. If you include more than one row of data, your chart will have more than one data series. Data series may also consist of columns of data, rather than rows.

Notes

Change the Location of a Chart

- A chart can reside either on its own **chart sheet** or as an **embedded object** on an existing worksheet.

- Change a chart's location by switching a chart from a chart sheet to an embedded object on a worksheet, or vice versa.

Change the Orientation of a Data Series

- Normally, a chart's data is oriented around rows. If you select more than one row of data, you'll create a separate **data series** for each row.

- With the buttons on the Chart toolbar, you can quickly change a chart's orientation from rows to columns or vice versa.

Data series orientation

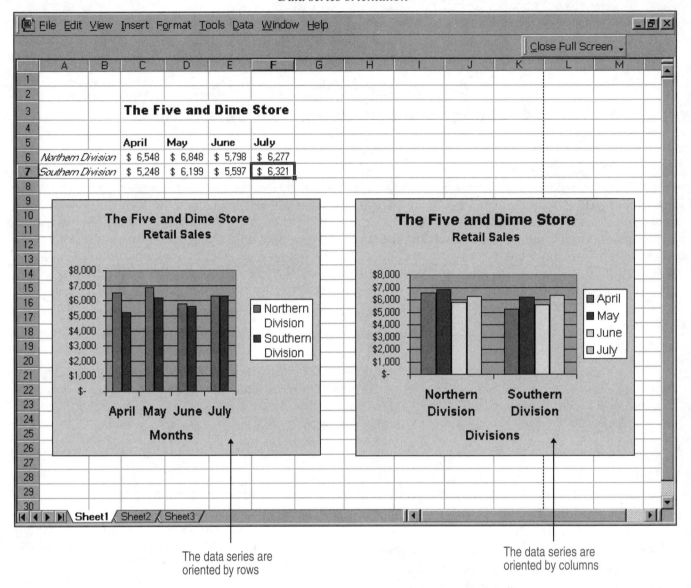

The data series are oriented by rows

The data series are oriented by columns

Procedures

Change the location of a chart

1. Select embedded chart or display the chart sheet.
2. Click **Chart** .... `Alt`+`C`
3. Click **Location** .... `L`
4. Change the location of the chart:
   a. Select
      As new sheet .... `Alt`+`S`
   b. Type name for the new sheet in text box.

OR

a. Select **As object in** ....
   .... `Alt`+`O`, `↗↓`, `Enter`
b. From drop-down list, select the sheet on which you want to place chart.
5. Click **OK** .... `Enter`

Change the Orientation of Data Series

1. Select the chart or display the chart sheet.

2. Click the appropriate button on the Chart toolbar:
   • To change to column orientation, click the **By Column** button `⊞`.

   OR

   • To change to row orientation, click the **By Row** button `⊟`.

272

Exercise Directions

1. Start Excel, if necessary.

2. Open ⊘ **62_MOVIES**.

3. Save the file as **XL_62**.

4. Using the Chart Wizard, create a chart using the range B10:G14.

   a. Use the Clustered Column chart type.

   b. Include the title *June Rentals - New Titles*.

   c. Save the chart as an embedded object in the *June New Rentals* worksheet.

   d. Move and resize the chart so that it fills the range A19:J38.

   e. Apply a 22-point font of your choice to the title.

   f. Change all other text to Arial, 9 points, bold.

5. Change the data orientation to column orientation.

6. Print the embedded chart only.

7. Change the data orientation back to row orientation.

8. Print the chart again, this time with its corresponding data.

9. Change the location of the chart so that it resides on its own chart sheet, called *June Chart*.

10. Print the chart sheet.

11. Save the file and exit Excel.

On Your Own

1. Start Excel, if necessary.

2. Save the file as ⊘ **OXL_62**.

3. Create a chart of air temperatures that you've tracked for one week.

   a. Use the column labels *Monday, Tuesday,* and so on.

   b. Use the row labels *6:00 AM, 12:00 PM*, and *6:00 PM.*

   c. Enter data in the corresponding cells.

4. Select all the data and create a line chart.

5. Format the chart as you like, but include these elements:

   a. Add a title, such as *June Temperatures*.

   b. Change the scale on the value axis so that the maximum is only slightly higher than the highest temperature, and the minimum is only slightly lower than the lowest temperature.

6. Print the chart.

7. Change to column orientation and print the chart again.

8. Change the location of the chart.

9. Make any needed adjustments to formatting and print the chart again.

10. Save the workbook and exit Excel.

Exercise 63

◆ **Create a Stock Chart**
◆ **Add a Secondary Value Axis to a Chart**
◆ **Change Data Marker Format**

On the Job

If you're like most people, you probably watch the stock market, and if you're lucky, you invest in it as well. And like most people, you worry about those investments and try to do what you can to make sure that they are wise ones. Excel can help you track the performance of a stock with its various stock charts. The stock charts don't eliminate the worry altogether, but by providing a helpful analysis, they can help you worry a little less.

You'll use your connection to the Internet to get the latest data on some stocks you've been watching. With that information you'll create a stock chart to help you analyze the data.

Terms

data marker A symbol that appears on a stock chart to mark a particular type of data, such as the stock close value.

Notes

Create a Stock Chart

- Charting stock data requires a special type of chart designed to handle standard stock information.
- Excel offers four different kinds of stock charts:
  - High-Low-Close
  - Open-High-Low-Close
  - Volume-High-Low-Close
  - Volume-Open-High-Low-Close
- Each chart handles a different set of data taken from this standard set of stock information:
  - Volume — The number of shares of that stock traded during the market day.

- Open — The value of the stock at the time when the market opened for the day.
- High — The highest value at which the stock was traded that day.
- Low — The lowest value at which the stock was traded that day.
- Close — The value of the stock when the market closed for the day.

- To create a stock chart, you must enter the data in columns, in the order specified by the type of stock chart you want.
  - ✓ *For example, if you select the Open-High-Low-Close chart, you must enter the data in four columns, in this order: Open, High, Low, and Close.*

- As row labels, you can use the stock symbol or name (if you're going to track more than one type of stock), or the date (if you're tracking one stock's trading pattern over several days).

■ A stock chart is also ideal for charting certain kinds of scientific data, such as temperature changes throughout the day.

Sample stock chart

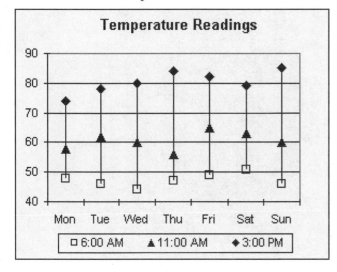

Chart with two value axes

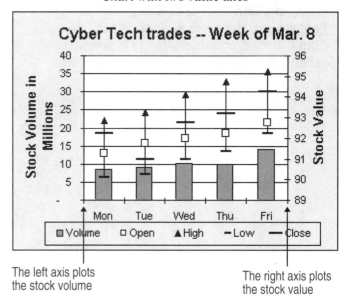

The left axis plots the stock volume

The right axis plots the stock value

Add a Secondary Value Axis to a Chart

■ To track two related but different values, use two value axes in the chart.

✓ *To create a chart with two value axes, turn on the Secondary axis option, located on the Axis tab of the Format Data Series dialog box.*

■ The value axes appear on opposite sides of the chart.

■ For example, use two value axes in a stock chart that includes both the volume of stock trading and the value of the stock.

- One axis plots the stock's trading volume.

- The other axis plots the stock's value at open, close, high, and low points in the day.

✓ *Secondary value axes are most common on stock charts, but you can add a secondary axis on other types of charts as well.*

Change Data Marker Format

■ When you create a stock chart, Excel uses a series of standard **data markers** for the open, close, high-low, volume, and close up and close down values.

■ Some of these markers may be too small, too dark, or too light to appear clearly on a printout.

■ To improve the appearance of your chart, you may want to adjust the data markers used by Excel.

Format Data Markers dialog box

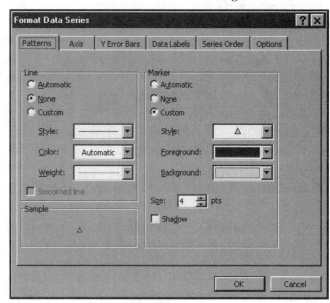

- Bars, columns, pie slices, and so on are also data markers. You can change many of the settings for the various types of data markers, but the most common change is adjusting the data markers on line charts or stock charts.

- You can change the color, size, and shape of each data marker used in a chart.

Procedures

Format Data Markers

1. Select the chart or display the chart sheet you wish to edit.
2. Select the series whose marker you wish to change.
   - ✓ *For example, select the High series.*
3. Click the **Format Data Series** button [icon] on the Chart toolbar.

   OR

   a. Click **Format** .... `Alt`+`O`
   b. Click **Selected Data Series** .... `E`
4. Click the **Patterns** tab ....`Ctrl`+`Tab`
5. Select the desired options:

Line
- Click **Automatic** ..... `Alt`+`A`

   OR

- **Click None**............. `Alt`+`N`

   OR

   a. Click **Custom** .... `Tab`
   b. Click **Style** ....
      .... `Alt`+`S`, `↑↓`, `Enter`
   c. Click **Color** ....
      .... `Alt`+`C`, `↕↕`, `Enter`
   d. Click **Weight**.......................
      .... `Alt`+`W`, `↑↓`, `Enter`
   e. Click **Smoothed Line** ..... `Alt`+`M`

Marker
- Click **Automatic** ..... `Alt`+`U`

   OR

- Click **None**............. `Alt`+`O`

   OR

   a. Click **Custom** .... `Tab`
   b. Click **Style** ....
      .... `Alt`+`L`, `↑↓`, `Enter`
   c. Click **Foreground**...............
      .... `Alt`+`F`, `↕↕`, `Enter`
   d. Click **Background**..............
      .... `Alt`+`B`, `↕↕`, `Enter`
   e. Click **Size**...........................
      .... `Alt`+`Z`, `↕↕`, `Enter`
   f. Click **Shadow** .... `Alt`+`D`
6. Click **OK**......................... `Enter`

Exercise Directions

1. Start Excel, if necessary.
2. Start Excel and open ⊙ **63_STOCKS**.
3. Save the workbook as **XL_63**.
4. Using your Internet connection, update each stock with the most current trading information.

   ✓ *You can use Yahoo! to get your stock information, or any site you prefer.*

   ✓ *If you're using the DDC Internet simulation:*

   - Click **Go**.
   - Click **Open**.
   - In the Address line, type the following: C:/Simulation/Ex63/Yahoo!.htm

   ✓ *If you've copied the Internet simulation files to your hard drive or your CD-ROM drive is not C:, substitute the correct drive letter for C.*

   a. Click the Stock Quotes link
   b. Type in the symbol MSFT.
   c. Click Get Quotes to get current information about the stock.
   d. Click the Detailed link for more information.
   e. Click Home to return to the Stock Quotes page.
   f. Repeat steps b-e for DELL, CPQ, and YHOO.

5. After entering the stock information into the worksheet, format the sheet as follows:

   a. Apply Comma Style, zero decimal places to the Volume column.
   b. Apply Fraction format, *Up to two digits (21/25)* to the Open, High, Low, and Close columns.

6. Using the range C8:H11, create a Volume-Open-High-Low-Close stock chart.

   a. On the Data Range tab in Step 2 in the Chart Wizard, select Columns to display the series by columns.
   b. On the Series tab, type the following names for the series by clicking the series number in the Series box and typing the corresponding name in the Name box.

   - Series 5: *Volume*
   - Series 1: *Open*
   - Series 2: *High*
   - Series 3: *Low*
   - Series 4: *Close*

   c. Use the title *Trading for April 2nd*

   ✓ *Use the current date in your title.*

   d. Add a value (y) axis title, *Stock Volume in Millions.*
   e. Add a second value (y) axis title, *Stock Value.*
   f. Embed the chart as an object in Sheet 1.
   g. Resize and move the chart so that it fits in the range B15:I30.

7. Format the chart as follows:

   a. Change all text to Arial, 11 points, bold.
   b. Enlarge the chart title to 14 points.
   c. Change the scale of the value axis so that it uses Millions as its display unit. Don't show the units label.
   d. Format the secondary value axis with Currency format, zero decimal places, $ symbol.
   e. Add the Newsprint texture to the plot area.

8. Change each data marker as indicated:

   a. Change the Open series marker to 4 points, with a Teal background color.

   ✓ *Hint: Select Series "Open" in the Chart Objects drop-down list on the Chart toolbar and then click the Format Data Series button.*

   b. Change the High series marker to a triangle, 4 points, with a foreground color of Dark Teal, and a background color of Yellow.
   c. Change the Low series marker to 4 points, with a background color of Dark Teal.
   d. Change the Close series marker to an X with a vertical line, 6 points, with a foreground color of Teal.
   e. Add an Ivory solid color fill to the bars that mark the Volume series.

   ✓ *If ScreenTips don't appear for the colors in the Area section of the Patterns tab, Ivory should be the third color on the next-to-last row.*

9. Preview and print the chart.
10. Save the workbook.
11. Exit Excel.

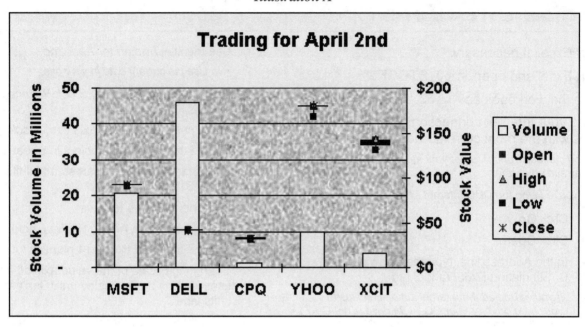

On Your Own

1. Start Excel, if necessary, and open **OXL_62**, created in Exercise 62.

2. Save the workbook as **OXL_63**.

3. Create a stock chart using the temperature data. Choose a High-Low-Close stock chart.

4. Format the data markers as needed to produce an attractive chart that is easy to understand.

5. Use lines to connect the daily readings.

6. Add formatting to the chart background, plot area, legend, value axis, and category axis as desired.

7. Print the chart.

8. Save the workbook and exit Excel.

Exercise 64

Skills Covered:

◆ **Create an Exploded Pie Chart**
◆ **Size the Plot Area or Legend in a Chart**
◆ **Create a Stacked Area Chart**

On the Job

Although a pie chart may be a great chart type for emphasizing your data, an exploded pie chart may be better. In an exploded pie chart, one or more pieces are "pulled away" from the pie in order to better emphasize them. When creating an exploded pie chart, you may wish to resize the plot area to provide more room in which to explode a pie piece or two. In addition, you may want to reduce the size of the legend to provide a larger area in which to plot data. If an exploded pie chart isn't right for your data, a stacked area chart, which emphasizes the difference between data series, may be a better choice.

As the manager of a custom cabinetry franchise called Custom Made Closets and Cabinetry, you must prepare several charts for an upcoming meeting with your loan officer. In this exercise, you'll create several pie charts illustrating your gross profit and expenses for July.

Terms

exploded pie chart A chart in which one or more pieces are separated from the rest of the pie for emphasis.

plot area The area within a chart in which the data is plotted.

legend An optional part of a chart, the legend displays a description of each data series included in the chart.

stacked area chart A special type of area chart in which the values for each data series are stacked on one another, creating one large area.

Notes

Create an Exploded Pie Chart

- If an ordinary pie chart doesn't tell all of the story about your data you can use an **exploded pie chart**.

- In an exploded pie chart, one or more pieces of the pie are separated from the rest of the pie, enabling you to emphasize certain data.

- Excel offers two different exploded pie types, one 2-D, and the other 3-D.
  - In both chart types, all pieces of the pie are exploded (separated from each other).

- You can create a customized exploded pie by dragging one or more pieces of a pie chart outward.
  - In a pie of pie chart, which is similar to an exploded pie chart, a data series is taken from the first pie and illustrated in a second, smaller pie.
  - You might use this type of chart to better illustrate a small series of values in the larger pie.

Exploded pie and pie of pie

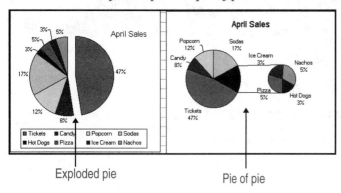

Exploded pie   Pie of pie

- After creating the pie of pie chart, you can adjust the values displayed in the second pie as needed.

- Anther way to illustrate a subgroup is a bar of pie chart which uses a vertical bar chart instead of a second pie chart to illustrate the data.

Size the Plot Area or Legend in a Chart

- Often, when creating an exploded pie chart, you may need to resize the **plot area** to create a larger space in which to work.

- To expand the plot area, you may need to reduce or resize the **legend**.

- You resize the plot area or legend as you might any other object, by dragging one of the handles.

Resizing the plot area

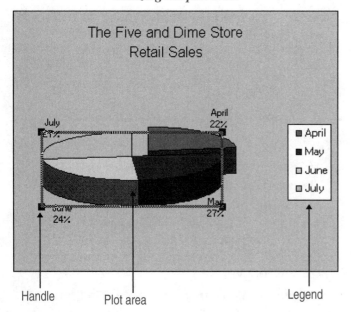

Handle   Plot area   Legend

Create a Stacked Area Chart

- In a **stacked area chart,** the values in each data series are stacked on top of each another, creating a larger area.

- Use a stacked area chart to emphasize the difference in values between two data series, while also illustrating the total of the two.

Stacked area chart

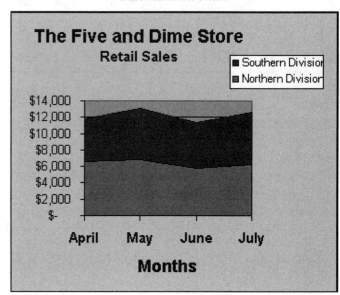

Procedures

Explode a Pie Section

1. Select the pie chart or display the chart sheet you wish to change.
2. Click a pie section to select it.

   You may need to click the section twice (not a double-click) to select a single pie slice instead of the entire pie.

3. Drag the pie slice to the desired position.

Create a Pie of Pie or Bar of Pie from an Existing Pie Chart

1. Select the pie chart or display the chart sheet you wish to change.
2. Click the **Chart Wizard** button .
3. Click the **Pie of Pie** or **Bar of Pie** button in the **Chart sub-type** list .... Alt+T, ↕
4. Click the **Finish** button ..... Enter

   Excel automatically decides which data should appear in the secondary pie (or bar) and which belongs in the primary pie. If necessary, adjust the grouping as shown in the next step.

5. Drag and drop the data points as needed between the pie (or pie and bar) charts.

Adjust a Pie of Pie or Bar of Pie Chart

1. Select the chart or display the chart sheet you wish to change.
2. Click the pie slice in the larger pie that represents the total of the values displayed in the smaller pie.
3. Click the **Format Data Point** button on the Chart toolbar.
   OR
   a. Click **Format** .... Alt+O
   b. Click **Selected Data Point** ...... E
4. Click the **Options** tab .. Ctrl+Tab
5. Choose the desired options:

Choose how you wish to select the values that appear in the second pie:

a. Open the **Split series by** list .... Alt+P
b. Select an option ... ↕, Enter

To split the series by position:

a. Click **Position** in the **Split series by** box.
b. Select or type a number in the **Second plot contains the last: xx values** box ...... Alt+E, ↔, Enter

To split the series by value:

a. Click **Value** in the **Split series by** box.
b. Type a number in the **Second plot contains all values less than** box ...... Alt+E, ↔, Enter

To split the series by percentage of the total:

a. Click **Percent Value** in the **Split series by** box.
b. Type a number in the **Second plot contains all values less than %** box ...... Alt+E, ↔, Enter

To split the series manually:

- Click **Custom** in the **Split series by** box.

   After choosing any additional options, you'll need to drag slices from the primary pie chart and drop them on the secondary pie or bar to create the custom pie or bar chart. If you accidentally drag the wrong slice, just drag it back to the primary pie.

Adjust the size and position of the second pie:

a. Select a size from the **Size of second plot** list .... Alt+I, ↕
b. Adjust the distance between the first pie and the second with the **Gap width** list. .... Alt+G, ↕

Select from additional options:

a. Display or hide the lines connecting the two pies with the **Series lines** option .... Alt+S
b. Format all pie slices with the same color or vary the colors with the **Vary colors by slice** option .... Alt+V

6. Click **OK** .... Enter

Resize Plot Area or Legend in a Chart

1. Select the chart or display the chart sheet you wish to change.
2. Select plot area or legend.

   Handles appear on border of the object.

3. Point to handle on side or corner of object to resize.

   Use a corner handle to resize the object proportionally.

4. Drag object's outline to size.
5. Release mouse button when object is desired size.

   Text associated with the object — such as data labels or legend text — is automatically resized as well.

Create a Stacked Area Chart from an Area Chart

1. Select the area chart you wish to change to a stacked area chart.
2. Click **Chart** .... Alt+C
3. Click **Chart Type** .... T
4. Click **Standard Types** tab .... Ctrl+Tab
5. In **Chart type** list, select **Area** .... Alt+C, ↕
6. In **Chart sub-type** list, select **Stacked Area** ..... Alt+T, ↕
7. Click **OK** .... Enter

Exercise Directions

1. Start Excel, if necessary.
2. Open 🖸 **64_PROFIT**.
3. Save the workbook as **XL_64**.
4. Create a pie chart with the range B24:C33.
   a. Add the title *July Expenses.*
   b. Add a legend to the right of the chart.
   c. Display data labels that show the percent.
   d. Create the chart as an embedded object in Sheet 1.
   e. Resize and move the chart so that it occupies the range A40:F55.
   f. Change the font of all chart text to Arial, 8 points.

      To change the point size or font for all text on the chart, select the chart or display the chart sheet and use the Size or Font buttons on the Formatting toolbar.

   g. Change the chart title font to Bookman Old Style (or a font of your choice), 11 points, bold.
5. Explode the Sales Salaries and Advertising pie slices by dragging them outward.

6. Resize the plot area to enlarge the pie chart by about 25%.
7. Print the chart.
8. Create a pie of pie chart with the two ranges B9:C11 and B16:C18.
   a. Add the title *July Gross Profit.*
   b. Add a legend to the bottom of the chart.
   c. Display data labels that show the percent.
   d. Create the chart as an embedded object in Sheet1.
   e. Resize and move the chart so that it occupies the range A58:F73.
   f. Change the font of all chart text to Arial, 8 point.
   g. Change the chart title font to Bookman Old Style (or another font or your choice), 14 points, bold.
9. Change the options for the second pie:
   a. Split the series by position.
   b. Set the second plot display to the last three values.
   c. Set the size of the second plot to 50.
10. Print the chart.
11. Save the workbook and exit Excel.

On Your Own

1. Start Excel, if necessary.
2. Open 🖸 **64_CATER**.
3. Save the workbook as **OXL_64**.
4. Create a 3-D pie chart with the ranges C5:F5 and C11:F11.
   a. Create the chart as an embedded object in Sheet 1.
   b. Resize and move the chart as needed.
   c. Format the chart as you like, adding data labels and a legend if desired.
   d. Resize the plot area to create as large a chart as possible.
   e. Explode the Food pie slice.
5. Print the chart.

6. Create a stacked area chart with the range B5:F9.
   a. Create the chart as an embedded object on Sheet 2.
   b. Resize and move the chart as needed.
   c. Display the data series by columns.
7. Format the chart as you like, but make these changes as well:
   a. Format the chart background and plot area.
   b. Format each series in the chart with a fill effect instead of a solid color.
8. Print the chart.
9. Save the workbook and exit Excel.

Skills Covered:

◆ **Create a 3-D Chart** ◆ **Change the View of a 3-D Chart**
◆ **Display or Hide Gridlines or Data Labels**

On the Job

When you're creating a chart for a big presentation or printed report, you want that chart to look as good as possible. Sometimes, changing from a flat 2-D chart to a 3-D chart is all you need to do. Using a 3-D chart adds a high-tech look to an otherwise ordinary presentation of the facts. When creating a 3-D chart, you may want to change its perspective to enhance the presentation of data. You also may want to display or hide gridlines and/or data labels to make the values easier to understand.

As the accountant for Magnolia Steel Bearings and Fittings, you'd like to make a visual comparison of quarterly sales and actual cash collections. A 3-D column chart seems to be the best choice to represent this data.

Terms

3-D chart A chart in which the data is presented in three dimensions: width, height, and depth.

z-axis An axis that appears on 3-D charts. In a two-dimensional chart, the x-axis represents the category (usually horizontal or width) axis, and the y-axis represents the value (usually vertical or height) axis. In a 3-D chart, the z-axis becomes the value axis, and, where applicable, the y-axis becomes the series (depth) axis.

gridlines Horizontal lines that appear on a chart, extending from the value axis. You can also display vertical gridlines from the category axis, although that's less common. Gridlines come in two varieties: major gridlines and minor gridlines (which fall between major gridlines).

data labels Labels giving information about a data marker in a chart. Data labels might display values, names, percentages, and so on.

Notes

Create a 3-D Chart

- Excel provides a 3-D version of nearly every category of chart: bar, column, pie, and so on.

- To create a **3-D chart**, select that type from the Chart sub-type list in the Chart Type dialog box or Step 1 of the Chart Wizard.

Select a 3-D chart type

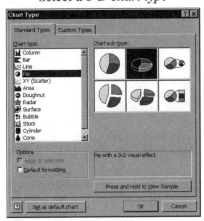

- 3-D charts have an additional axis, called the series or depth axis.
  - The former y-axis (value axis) becomes the series axis on the chart.
  - The value axis is called the **z-axis**.
- Some charts, while listed as 3-D charts, aren't truly three-dimensional, but are simply 2-D charts with some perspective added.
  - A true 3-D chart has three axes: x, y, and z.
  - A 2-D chart with perspective added has only two axes, x and y.

Two different types of 3-D charts

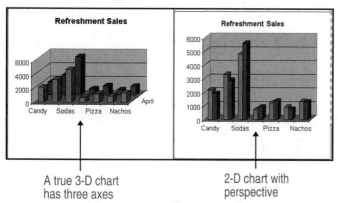

A true 3-D chart
has three axes

2-D chart with
perspective

Change the View of a 3-D Chart

- After creating a 3-D chart (or a 2-D chart with perspective), you may wish to change that perspective or view.
- You can tilt the floor of the chart up or down.
- You can rotate the chart floor right or left.
- If you choose not to lock the axes at right angles, you can change the chart's 3-D perspective.

Changing the 3-D view

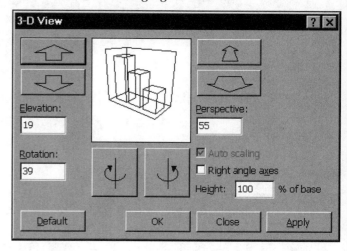

- You can change the depth of the chart and increase or decrease the gaps between series.

Display or Hide Gridlines or Data Labels

- On a 3-D chart, **gridlines** become a bit more important than on a 2-D chart, since they help to guide the eye along the axis.
  - ✓ *You can add or remove gridlines for any chart type.*
  - You can increase the number of major gridlines by changing the point at which the gridlines recur.
  - You can also display minor gridlines.
- **Data labels** display the value, percentage, or name (or combinations of value, percentage, and name) at each data point.
  - Data labels help to identify the significance of the elements (the bars, columns, lines, pie slices, and so on) in the plot area.
  - You can adjust where data labels appear — on top of, behind, or in front of the data point.

Procedures

Label the Series in a Chart

1. Select the chart or display the chart sheet you wish to change.
2. Click **Chart**.................. Alt + C
3. Click **Source Data** .... S
4. On the Series tab, select a series from the **Series** list................... Alt + S , ↓ ↑
5. Type a name in the **Name** box .... Alt + C
6. Repeat steps 4 and 5 to name other series.
7. Click **OK** .... Enter

Change the View of a 3-D Chart

1. Select the chart or display the chart sheet you wish to change.
2. Click **Chart**.................. Alt + C
3. Click **3-D View** V
4. Set 3-D options:

   To change elevation:
   • Click **Elevation** button ⬆ or ⬇ .

   OR

   a. Click desired **Elevation** button........................... Tab
   b. Press **Spacebar** until you reach desired elevation .... Space

   OR

   a. Click **Elevation** text box .... Alt + E
   b. Type desired elevation number.

   To rotate chart:
   • Click **Rotation** button right ↺ or left ↻ .

   OR

   a. Click desired **Rotation** button........................... Tab
   b. Press **Spacebar** until you reach desired rotation..................... Space

   OR

a. Click **Rotation** text box.................. Alt + R
b. Type desired rotation number.

To change perspective:
✓ This option will not be available when **Right angle axes** is selected.

• Click **Perspective** button ⬳ or ⬆ .

OR

a. Click desired **Perspective** button .... Tab
b. Press **Spacebar** until you reach desired perspective............... Space

OR

a. Click **Perspective** text box.................. Alt + P
b. Type desired perspective number.

To lock axes at right angles:
• Click **Right angle axes** .... Alt + X

To scale chart to fit better in the plot area:
✓ This option will be available only when **Right angle axes** is selected.

• Select **Auto scaling** .... Alt + S

To set height as a percentage of base of chart:
a. Click **Height % of base** text box.................. Alt + I
b. Type number (5-500).
   ✓ This option is not available if **Auto scaling** is selected.

To preview chart with current settings:
a. Move dialog box to display chart.
b. Click **Apply** .... Alt + A

To return to default settings:
• Click **Default** .... Alt + D
5. Click **OK** .... Enter

Change the 3-D View with the Mouse

1. Select the chart or display the chart sheet you wish to change.
2. Click a corner of the plot area.
   OR
   Select **Corners** from the Chart Objects list on the Chart toolbar.
3. Drag a corner to adjust the 3-D view (in wireframe).
   ✓ If you want to see the data markers as well as the axes of the chart in the wireframe view, press and hold **Ctrl** as you drag.
4. Release the mouse button when the chart is in position.
   ✓ If you make a mistake or don't like the results, click **Undo** or use the **3-D View** dialog box to reset the chart to the default settings.

Change the Depth and Gap Width of a 3-D Chart

1. Select the chart or display the chart sheet you wish to change.
2. Click one of the data series.
3. Click the **Format Data Series** button on the Chart toolbar.
   OR
   Click **Format** .... Alt + O
4. Click **Selected Data Series** .... E
5. Click the **Options** tab ... Ctrl + Tab
6. Enter the amount of space you want between data markers in the **Gap depth** box.................. Alt + G , ↓ ↑
7. Enter the amount of space you want between categories in a series in the **Gap width** box.................. Alt + W , ↓ ↑

8. Enter the depth desired for the 3-D chart (relative to the width) in the **Chart depth** box .... `Alt`+`C`, `↓``↑`

9. Click **OK** .... `Enter`

Display or Hide Gridlines

1. Select the chart or display the chart sheet you wish to change.

2. Click **Chart** .... `Alt`+`C`

3. Click **Chart Options** .... `O`

4. Select **Gridlines** tab.... `Ctrl`+`Tab`

5. Select or deselect options:

   ✓ *The options available depend on the selected chart type.*

6. If desired, give a 2-D look to the walls, floor, and gridlines of a 2-D chart with perspective by selecting the **2-D walls and gridlines** option .... `Alt`+`2`

7. Click **OK** .... `Enter`

Change the Frequency of Gridlines

1. Select the chart or display the chart sheet you wish to change.

2. Select the **value axis**.

3. Click the **Format Axis** button on the Chart toolbar.
   OR

   a. Click **Format** .... `Alt`+`O`

   b. Click **Selected Axis** .... `E`

4. Click the **Scale** tab ..... `Ctrl`+`Tab`

5. Set the frequency of major gridlines by typing a value in the **Major unit** text box....................... `Alt`+`J`

6. Set the frequency of minor gridlines by typing a value in the **Minor unit** text box....................... `Alt`+`I`

7. Click **OK** .... `Enter`

Display or Hide Data Labels

1. Select the chart or display the chart sheet you wish to change.

2. Click **Chart** .... `Alt`+`C`

3. Click **Chart Options** .... `O`

4. Click **Data Labels** tab .... `Ctrl`+`Tab`

5. Select display options:

   • **None** .... `Alt`+`O`

   • **Show value** .... `Alt`+`V`

   • **Show percent** .... `Alt`+`P`

   • **Show label** .... `Alt`+`L`

   • **Show label and percent** .... `Alt`+`A`

   • **Show bubble sizes** .... `Alt`+`U`

   ✓ *Only the options available for each chart type display.*

6. Click **OK** .... `Enter`

Exercise Directions

1. Start Excel, if necessary.

2. Open ◉ **65_BUDGET**.

3. Save the workbook as **XL_65**.

4. Create a 3-D Column chart with the ranges B4:E4, B7:E7, and B15:E15.

   a. Give Series 1 the name *Total Sales*.

   b. Give Series 2 the name *Cash Collections*.

   c. Use the title, *Fiscal Budget - 2002*.

   d. Display both major and minor gridlines for the value (Z) axis only.

   e. Hide the legend.

   f. Display data labels to show values.

   g. Move and resize the chart to fit in the range A20:E37.

5. Format the chart as follows:

   a. Apply Arial, 9 points, bold to the value axis.

   b. Change the major unit of the value axis to *75000* and the minor unit to *25000*.

   c. Change the number format along the value axis to display zero decimal points.

d. Change the style of the minor gridlines to a dashed line format.

e. Apply Arial, 11 points, bold to the category and series axes.

f. Apply Bookman Old Style (or the font of your choice), 14 points, bold to the chart title.

g. Apply Arial, 8 points, bold to the data labels.

h. Apply Accounting format, zero decimal places, no symbol to the data labels.

   ✓ *Select the data labels with the Chart Objects drop-down list on the Chart toolbar. Then click the Format Data Labels button and use the settings on the Number tab to set this format.*

6. Change the 3-D view:

   a. Set the Elevation to 18 degrees.

   b. Set the Rotation to 35 degrees.

7. Set the chart depth to 110, the gap depth to 150, and the gap width to 180.

8. Print the chart.

9. Save the workbook and exit Excel.

On Your Own

1. Start Excel, if necessary, and open
   ⊘ **65_TICKETS**.

2. Save the file as **OXL_65**.

3. Create a Clustered Bar chart with a 3-D visual
   effect with the range A6:F7.

   a. Display minor gridlines for the value (Z) axis.

   b. Display your choice of data labels.

4. Format the chart as you wish, but include
   these changes:

   a. Format the minor gridlines using a style you like.

   b. Change the 3-D perspective by dragging the
      corners of the chart.

   c. Increase the distance between bars.

5. Print the chart.

6. Create a pie chart with a 3-D visual effect
   using the ranges B6:F6 and B9:F9.

   • Display your choice of data labels.

7. Format the chart as you wish, but include
   these changes:

   a. Change the 3-D perspective using the 3-D View
      dialog box.

   b. Explode the pie piece representing the
      production of *Romeo and Juliet*.

8. Print the chart.

9. Create a 3-D Column chart using the ranges
   A6:F7 and A9:F9.

10. Format the chart as you wish, but include
    these changes:

    a. Change the 3-D perspective by dragging the
       corners of the chart.

    b. Apply the pyramid shape (#2) to the Tickets Sold
       data series.

       ✓ *To change the shape of bars and columns in 3-D
         charts, select the data series to change, open the
         Format Data Series dialog box, click the Shape
         tab, and select the shape you want.*

    c. Apply a fill effect to the walls of the chart.

11. Print the chart.

12. Save the workbook and exit Excel.

Exercise 66

◆ Map Excel Data with Microsoft Map ◆ Edit and Format a Map

On the Job

If your data is geographically related, what better way to present it than with a map? For example, if a worksheet contains sales data for Illinois, Indiana, and Ohio, you could display the sales total on a map of these states, making your data instantly understandable and much more dynamic.

The annual stockholders meeting is coming up, and the boss has put you in charge of creating the graphics for his presentation. Today's challenge is to create a map showing the states in which the various Custom Made Closets and Cabinetry stores are located, colored by region, with small dots representing the sales volume in each state.

Terms

map labels Text labels you can add to a map. Excel can provide labels for every state or country displayed on a data map with Microsoft Map.

Microsoft Map Control A special dialog box that you can use to change the analysis of the data on a data map.

dot density A method used for displaying data on a map in which the frequency of dots matches the value displayed.

Notes

Map Excel Data with Microsoft Map

- The Office 2000 software includes a mapping program, Microsoft Map, that you can use to enhance worksheet data by displaying the appropriate map.

  ✓ *Microsoft Map isn't installed by default, so you may need to install it before using this feature. Insert the Office CD-ROM, select Add or Remove Features, then select the Microsoft Map option under Microsoft Excel for Windows and choose Run from My Computer. Click Update Now to begin the installation.*

- You can display data on a map by U.S. state or by country.

- You can format data maps in much the same way as charts: adding data labels, patterns and colors, and a legend.

- To create a data map, the worksheet must contain a column with the names of states or countries.

- Excel includes demographic data such as population and income statistics that you can use to enhance a map.

Edit and Format a Map

- Unlike charts, to edit a map, you must first double-click it.

- In edit mode, the Microsoft Map toolbar replaces the Standard and Formatting toolbars.

Microsoft Map toolbar

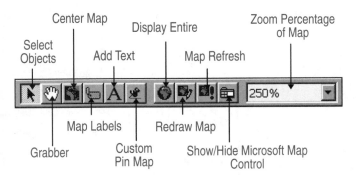

- Use the Microsoft Map toolbar to center the map, add **map labels**, and change the relative size, among other options.

Microsoft Map Control

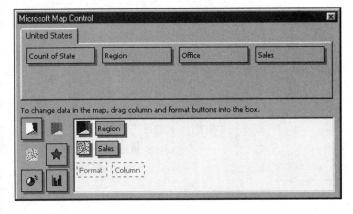

- With the **Microsoft Map Control**, you can change the analysis of a data map — for example, you can change the **dot density** or add map labels.

- When you drag a category from the top of the box onto the Column area, and then drag a format button on top of the Format area, Excel analyzes the data in the column, formats it as instructed, and places it on the map.

- The map you create sits directly on the worksheet. If you want to place it in a frame, draw a rectangle or a similar object on top of the map.

  - Use the Draw button on the Drawing toolbar to send the rectangle object to the back.

  - Fill the rectangle object with color and add a border, if you like.

  - You can also group the map and rectangle object so they can be moved and resized as one object.

Procedures

Edit a Data Map

- Double-click the map.
  - ✓ *The Microsoft Map Control opens and the Microsoft Map toolbar appears.*

Create a Map

1. Select geographic data.

   a. Click the **Map** button 🌐.
      - ✓ *The mouse pointer becomes ✛.*

   b. Drag rectangle to define map area.

   OR

   a. Click **Insert** .... `Alt`+`I`

   b. Click **Object** .... `O`

   c. Click the **Create New** tab .... `Ctrl`+`Tab`

   d. Click **Microsoft Map** in the **Object type** list .... `Alt`+`O`, `↕`

   e. Click **OK** .... `Enter`

2. If necessary, select desired map from those listed and click **OK** .... `Enter`

Change Map Analysis Settings

1. Double-click the map to open it.

2. If necessary, display the Microsoft Map Control by clicking the **Show/Hide Microsoft Map Control** button 📇.

3. To add a column of data to the map for analysis, drag the name of the column from the top of the Microsoft Map Control box to the **Column** area.
   - ✓ *You may need to remove the current category from the Microsoft Map Control to add something else.*

4. Microsoft Map supplies a format for the category you just added. To change the format to something else, select a Format button from those on the left, and drag it in front of the column name you just added.
   - ✓ *To remove a column's data from the map, drag the column name out of the box in the lower-right corner of the Microsoft Map Control.*

Change Shading for Categories

1. Click **Map** .... `Alt`+`M`

2. Click **Category Shading Options** .... `T`

3. Select category from **Categories** list .... `↕`

4. Click **Color** .... `Alt`+`O`

5. Select new color .... `↕`

6. Click **OK** .... `Enter`

Change Dot Density

1. Click **Map** .... `Alt`+`M`

2. Click **Dot Density Options** .... `D`

3. Change dot size (**Small** or **Large**) .... `Alt`+`M` or `Alt`+`L`

4. Change summary function (**SUM** or **AVERAGE**) .... `Alt`+`S` or `Alt`+`A`

5. Change the number of units each dot represents ..... `Alt`+`U`

6. Click **OK** .... `Enter`

Add Map Labels

1. Click **Map Labels** button 🏷 on Map toolbar.

2. Select the part of the map you want to label from the **Map feature to label** drop-down list .... `↕`

3. Choose the type of label you want to display:
   - Select **Map feature names** .... `Alt`+`M`

   OR

   a. Select **Values from** .... `Alt`+`V`

   b. Choose a column from which you want to pull values for the labels........ `↓`

4. Click **OK** .... `Enter`

5. Click the map where you want to add a label.

6. When you're done adding labels, click the **Select Objects** button ➤.

Exercise Directions

1. Start Excel, if necessary.
2. Open 🖴 **66_CLOSETS**.
3. Save the workbook as **XL_66**.
4. Create a map using the range C6:F22.
   a. Draw the map within the range A24:G39.
   b. When prompted, select the map option United States in North America.
5. Format the map as follows:
   a. Using the Microsoft Map Control, set up category shading by region, and dot density by sales amount.
   b. Change the category shading for Midwest to Navy.
   c. Change the title of the map to *Custom Made Cabinetry - July Sales.* Apply Comic Sans MS (or a font of your choice), 18 points.
      ✓ *Double-click the title to replace the existing text with the new title.*
      ✓ *Right-click the title and select Format Font to change the font.*

d. Double-click the legend and change the title to *CMCC.* Change the subtitle to *Sales Regions.* Apply Comic Sans MS (or the font of your choice), 9 points, bold to the title.
e. Double-click the dot density legend and change the title to *Custom Made Closets & Cabinetry.* Change the subtitle to *July Sales.* Apply Comic Sans MS (or the font of your choice), 9 points, bold to the title.
6. Drag the dot density legend to the left edge of the map area.
7. Resize the legend to make it larger and easier to read.
8. Change the zoom to 250%.
9. Print the map.
10. Save the workbook and exit Excel.

On Your Own

1. Start Excel, if necessary.
2. Create a worksheet listing August sales for the Fulton Computer stores:
   a. Texas: $455,043
   b. Oklahoma: $399,363
   c. Tennessee: $433,538
      ✓ *Use abbreviations for the states.*
3. Save the workbook as **OXL_66**.
4. Create a map.
5. Zoom in on the Texas, Oklahoma, and Tennessee region.
   ✓ *Zoom the map, then use the grabber to drag the map to show the central and eastern parts of the U.S.*

6. Using the Microsoft Map Control, change to a graduated symbol format.
   • Change the graduated symbol to a diskette, which you'll find in the Wingdings font.
7. Add map labels for each of the three states.
8. Add a title to the map, and format the title as you like.
   • Format and change the legend text as well.
9. Print the map.
10. Save the workbook and exit Excel.

Exercise 67

Skills Covered:

◆ **Link a Chart and a Word Document**
◆ **Embed a Chart into a Word Document**
◆ **Edit a Linked or Embedded Chart**

On the Job

You're trying to convince your boss that the new reorganization is working and that profits are up, and a chart just might be the clearest evidence. And when you're overseeing this year's stock report, a few charts here and there are certainly expected, if not required. But if the source data is likely to change, you shouldn't just copy it into a Word document for a report or memo. Instead, you can link the data to its source, so that your chart will update automatically. This is especially useful when the source data is updated by several people in an organization. If you want to create a static report, however, you can embed the chart in the Word document to ensure that any changes you make to the Word document later will not affect the Excel data.

You're the Client Services Manager at Corporate Computer Solutions, and you've got a big presentation on Monday. The boss is concerned with last month's client survey results, and he wants to know what you've been doing to improve customer satisfaction. You've got some good results from the most recent survey; now all you have to do is to create a few good-looking charts in a report to convince your boss that you're doing your job well.

Terms

link A reference in a destination document to an object (such as a chart) in a source document. When a linked object is changed, the object is updated in the other document through the link. A link can be manual or automatic.

embed Insert an object into a second document in such a way that it can still be edited by the source application. When you double-click an embedded object, the source application (or its tools) appear, so you can edit the object. However, the original data is unchanged by this process.

Notes

Link a Chart and a Word Document

- When you link an Excel chart to a Word document, the chart isn't copied into the document. Instead, a **link** to the chart is created.

- When the chart is changed in Excel and the Word document is opened again, the link causes the data displayed in the document to be updated as well.

- For the link to be maintained, the source file must remain in its original location.

- A link can be manual or automatic.
  - If manual, you control when the source data is updated in the destination document.
  - If automatic, the destination document is updated with each change to the source data (even if the destination document is already open).
- You can create a link to an embedded chart or a chart sheet.
- When you link or embed a chart, you use the Paste Special dialog box.

Paste Special dialog box

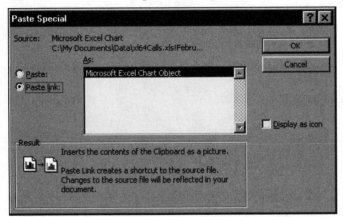

- Instead of inserting a linked object (chart), you can create a hyperlink to the worksheet that contains the chart.
  - A hyperlink looks like text underlined in blue.
  - When you point to a hyperlink with the mouse, the cursor changes to a hand.
  - When you click the hyperlink within your Word document, Excel starts, and the worksheet opens.

    ✓ *See Lesson 11 for help in creating a hyperlink.*

Embed a Chart into a Word Document

- When you **embed** an Excel chart into a Word document, the data is copied into the Word file.
- Unlike linked data, you can edit an embedded chart from within the Word document.

  ✓ *To edit the embedded chart, just double-click it.*

- When you edit an embedded chart, the Chart toolbar appears, along with the Excel Standard and Formatting toolbars.
- Making changes to an embedded chart doesn't affect the original data.

Edit a Linked or Embedded Chart

- Since linked data is stored in the source document, you simply open the source workbook in Excel to edit a linked chart.
  - Change the worksheet data, and the Excel chart is updated.
  - Save the workbook, and the link is updated.
  - Open the Word document, and the chart can be updated automatically or when you manually update the link.
- Embedded data is stored within the Word document.
  - To edit the embedded chart, you work within the Word document.
  - When you open the chart for editing, Excel toolbars appear.
  - When you edit embedded data, the source data is *not* changed.

Procedures

Link an Excel Chart to a Word Document

1. Select the chart or display the chart sheet.
2. Click the **Copy** button .
3. Switch to the Word document, and position the insertion point where you want to insert the chart.
4. Click **Edit** .... `Alt`+`E`
5. Click **Paste Special** .... `S`
6. Click **Paste link** .... `Alt`+`L`
7. Select **Microsoft Excel Chart Object** in the **As** list .... `Alt`+`A`, `⤓`
8. If you want to display the chart as an icon in the Word document, select the **Display as icon** option .... `Alt`+`D`
9. Click **OK** .... `Enter`

   ✓ When you create a link, it's updated automatically. However, if you create a link to an icon, the link is updated manually.

Update a Link Manually

1. Open the destination file (the Word document).
2. Click **Edit** .... `Alt`+`E`
3. Click **Links** .... `K`
4. Select the link(s) you want to update .... `⤓`
5. Click **Update Now** ...... `Alt`+`U`

   ✓ If you want to update one linked chart quickly, select it in the Word document and press F9.

Change Link Information

1. Click **Edit** .... `Alt`+`E`
2. Click **Links** .... `K`
3. Select the link you want to update.
4. To change the location of the linked file, click **Change Source...** .... `Alt`+`N`

   a. From the **Look in** list, select the drive and folder in which the file is currently located .... `Alt`+`I`
   b. Type the name of the source file in the **File name** text box................. `Alt`+`N`
   c. Click **Open** .... `Enter`
5. To remove the link, click **Break Link** .... `B`
   • Click **Yes** .... `Enter`
6. To change how the link is updated, select an option:
   • Select **Automatic**... `Alt`+`A`
   OR
   • Select **Manual** .... `Alt`+`M`
   OR
   • Select **Locked** .... `Alt`+`K`

     ✓ The **Locked** option prevents a linked object from being updated.
7. Click **OK** .... `Enter`

Embed a Chart in a Word Document

1. Select the chart or display the chart sheet.
2. Click the **Copy** button .
3. Switch to the Word document and position the insertion point where you want to embed the chart.

4. Click **Edit** .... `Alt`+`E`
5. Click **Paste Special** .... `S`
6. Click **Paste** .... `Alt`+`P`
7. Select **Microsoft Excel Chart Object** in the **As** list .... `Alt`+`A`, `⤓`
8. If you want to display the chart as an icon in the Word document, select the **Display as icon** option.............. `Alt`+`D`
9. Click **OK** .... `Enter`

Edit a Linked Chart

1. Double-click the linked chart or icon.

   ✓ Excel starts and displays the source workbook.
2. Make whatever changes you want.
3. Click **File** .... `Alt`+`F`
4. Click **Exit** .... `X`
5. When prompted, select **Yes** to save your changes........... `Enter`

Edit an Embedded Chart

1. Double-click the embedded chart or icon.

   ✓ The chart is surrounded by a thick gray border, and Excel's menus and the Chart toolbar appear.
2. Make changes as needed.

   ✓ To change the chart data, click the tab for the worksheet that contains the data, and make your changes.

   ✓ Be sure to redisplay the chart tab before you end the editing session, so the chart will be visible in the Word document.
3. Click outside the chart border.

Exercise Directions

1. Start Excel, if necessary.
2. Open ⊙ **67_CALLS**.
3. Save the workbook as **XL_67**.
4. Select the *Number of Calls* chart.
5. Make the following changes to the chart:
   a. Using the drag handle on the Range Finder, change the data range to B8:F13.
   b. Change the chart title to *Number of Calls - February.*
   c. Change the chart type to a line chart with markers displayed at each data value.
   d. Change the scale along the value axis to 140 minimum, 250 maximum
   e. Display data series by row.
6. Open the Word document ⊙ **67_REPORT.doc**.
7. Save the document as **XL_67.doc**.
8. Return to Excel and copy the chart.
9. Switch to Word and paste the chart as a link, in the spot marked *[link chart 1 here].*
   ✓ After inserting the chart, delete the placeholder text.

10. Switch back to Excel, and select the chart *Client Satisfaction.*
11. Copy the chart.
12. Switch back to Word and paste the chart on page two as an embedded object in the spot marked *[embed chart 2 here].*
13. Double-click the first chart and change the plot area to the preset gradient color Moss.
14. Save the Excel workbook.
15. Close the file and exit Excel.
16. In Word, double-click the second chart and change Kate Wilson's February satisfaction rating from 7.3 to 6.0.
    ✓ You'll find the source data in Sheet1 of the embedded workbook.
17. Click the Chart sheet to see whether the chart reflects the change you made.
18. Save and print the letter.
19. Close the file and exit Word.

On Your Own

1. Start Excel, if necessary.
2. Start a new worksheet and save the workbook as **OXL_67**.
3. Enter sales data for your new company, FastGrow.Com.
   ✓ FastGrow is the fastest growing medical supply company in the Midwest.
   ✓ FastGrow operates in four cities — Indianapolis, Indiana; Columbus, Ohio; Cincinnati, Ohio; and Chicago, Illinois.
   a. Enter some revenue figures for the last three months for each of the four offices.
   b. Enter some expenses as well.
   c. Compute the net income.
4. Create a 3-D exploded pie chart that shows the net income. Format the chart as you like.

5. Start Word, and create a letter to a possible investor, NewGrowth Investments, asking for funding for your latest project, a Web-based drug store that can fill prescriptions.
6. Save the letter with the file name, **OXL_67.doc**.
7. Embed the chart in the letter.
8. Proofread the letter. Before you print it, change the revenue figures for Chicago to reflect a recent report from your Accounting department.
9. Print the letter.
10. Close all files, saving all changes, and exit Word and Excel.

Exercise 68

◆ **Critical Thinking**

As the V.P. of Accounting for Magnolia Steel, you need to prepare for an upcoming shareholders meeting. In this exercise, you'll create a few charts and a map that illustrate the expected and actual revenues from your various plants over the last quarter.

Exercise Directions

1. Start Excel, if necessary.
2. Open 📀 68_MAGSTEEL.
3. Save the file as **XL_68**.
4. Create a clustered column chart with 3-D visual effect, using the ranges B4:E4 and B7:E7.
   a. Add the title *Difference Between Expected and Actual Revenues*.
   b. Add minor gridlines on the value (z) axis.
   c. Hide the legend.
   d. Add data labels that show the values.
   e. Save the chart as an embedded object in Sheet2.
   f. Resize and move the chart so that it occupies the range A1:H17.
5. Format the chart as follows:
   a. Select a font and font size for the title so that it fits on one line.
   b. Apply Arial Narrow, 9 points, bold to the value axis, and change the scale to a minimum of -750000, a maximum of 3250000, and a minor unit of 250000.
   c. Apply Arial Narrow, 10 points, bold to the Category axis.
   d. Apply Arial, 8 points, bold to the data labels.
   e. Format Series 1 with a one-color gradient fill using Periwinkle, with a slightly dark cast (adjust the Dark-Light setting), vertical shading style, the last variant.
   f. Format the walls with the Fog preset gradient fill, set in horizontal shading style.

   g. Format the chart area with a Sphere pattern (next-to-last pattern on the bottom row, Pattern tab) using Gray-25% foreground color and Periwinkle background color. Add a heavy weight border in Blue-Gray.
6. Create a line-column custom chart, using the range A4:E6 on Sheet1 as the data source.
   a. Add the title *Expected vs. Actual Sales*.
   b. Add major gridlines on the value (y) axis.
   c. Display the legend at the bottom.
   d. Save the chart as an embedded object in Sheet1.
   e. Resize and move the chart so that it occupies the range A10:E27.
7. Format the chart as follows:
   a. Reverse the order of the data series.
      ✓ To do this, change the chart type to a column chart temporarily. Then select one data series and use the Format Data Series dialog box to move the Actual Sales series above the Expected sales series (on the Series Order tab). Then select the Expected sales series and change it to a line chart.
      ✓ Make sure that Apply to selection is turned on in the Options section of the dialog box, so that the change in chart type will apply only to the selected data series.
   b. Format the chart area with a two-color gradient fill, blending Blue-Gray and Violet in a diagonal up shading style, first variant.
   c. Apply Haettenschweiler (or another font of your choice), 16 points, Light Yellow to the chart title.
   d. Apply Arial, 8 points, bold, Light Yellow to the value axis, and use millions as the display unit.

e. Use Arial, 9 points, Light Yellow for the Millions label. Center the Millions label vertically.

f. Apply Arial, 9 points, bold, Light Yellow to the category axis.

g. Format the Actual Sales series with the graphic ☉ **GEAR.bmp**, stacked.

   ✓ *On the Picture tab in the Fill Effects dialog box, select **GEAR.bmp** to insert when the graphic appears in the Picture box, select Stack in the Format section of the dialog box and then click OK.*

h. Format the Expected sales series with an Indigo line of medium weight. Add a Blue-Gray foreground and Yellow background to the marker. Use a square marker style, 5 points.

i. Add a White marble texture to the plot area.

j. Change the location of the chart to Sheet2.

k. Move the chart and resize it to fill the range A20:H37.

8. Print both charts.

9. Start Word and create a memo to the shareholders explaining both charts. Save the file as **XL_68.doc**.

   a. Include one chart as an embedded chart.

   b. Link the other chart to the memo.

   c. Try making a change to one of the charts.

   d. Save the file and exit Word.

10. Create a map:

   a. Select the range A4:E6 on Sheet1.

   b. Copy the selection and use Paste Special to paste and transpose the data to a range beginning in cell A11.

c. In cell A11, type *State*.

d. Right-align the list of states and the column heading.

e. Bold the labels in row 11.

f. Widen column B to 14.57.

g. Create a map using the range A11:C15.

h. Draw the map in the range A17:E32 on Sheet1. Use the United States in North America map.

i. Zoom to 700% and center the subject states with the grabber tool.

j. Use value shading to illustrate actual sales. In addition, add a column chart with expected and actual sales.

   ✓ *Click the Column Chart button in the Microsoft Map Control and drag it into the box. Drag the column button for Actual Sales into the box in line with the Column Chart icon. Drag the column button for Expected sales into the box to the right of the Actual Sales icon.*

k. Change the map title to *Actual and Expected Sales*. Apply Arial, 15 points, and center the title near the top of the map.

l. Change the legend title to *Magnolia Steel*, Arial, 9 points.

m. Change the legend subtitle to *Actual Sales*, Arial, 6 points.

11. Print the map with the data.

   • Adjust page breaks as needed to print the results on one page.

12. Save the workbook and exit Excel.

Lesson 10

Analyze Data

Exercise 69

- Create a List/Database
- Name a List/Database
- Use a Data Form to Add Records
- Adding Fields to a List

Exercise 70

- Modify a Record
- Find a Record
- Delete a Record

Exercise 71

- Control Data Entry
- Copy and Paste Validation Rules
- Circle Invalid Data

Exercise 72

- Sort Records in a List
- Rules for Sorting
- Undo a Sort
- Restore the Record Order

Exercise 73

- AutoFilter a Database

Exercise 74

- Advanced Filters
- Guidelines for Entering Criteria
- Examples of Advanced Criteria
- Remove an In-place Advanced Filter
- Edit Extracted Records

Exercise 75

- Use Database (List) Functions
- Excel's Database Functions

Exercise 76

- Subtotal a List
- Create Nested Subtotals
- Remove a Subtotal
- Copy a Subtotal
- Outline a Worksheet

Exercise 77

- Create PivotTables and PivotCharts
- Publish a PivotTable or PivotChart
- Use PivotTable Toolbar

Exercise 78

- Data Consolidation
- Create Consolidation Tables

Exercise 79

- Critical Thinking

Exercise 69

Skills Covered:

◆ **Create a List/Database** ◆ **Name a List/Database**
◆ **Use a Data Form to Add Records** ◆ **Adding Fields to a List**

On the Job

Although Excel is generally used for accounting purposes, performing complex calculations, and analyses, it can perform another function as well — that of a database manager. Using Excel, you can organize many types of information, such as client addresses and phone numbers, product inventory, equipment inventory, and so on, without learning a completely new program. And Excel makes it so easy!

You're the new owner of a beauty salon called Carella's Hair Design. Since this is your first business, you're feeling a bit overwhelmed. But one thing you know you can accomplish fairly quickly (and which you need desperately) is an inventory of the hair styling products you offer for sale.

Terms

database An organized collection of records.

record A collection of data relating to a specific item or person. A record is composed of two or more fields. For example, a record containing information on a particular person might include first and last name, address, city, state, and so on. In an Excel database, each row makes up one record.

field One part of a record, such as an item description, item number, or unit cost. In an Excel database, each field is placed in its own column.

data form A special dialog box that Excel provides for adding, deleting, editing, and locating records in a database.

Notes

Create a List/Database

- An Excel list, or **database**, is an organized collection of records.

  ✓ *In Excel, a list and a database are the same thing.*

- A **record** is a row of data, composed of two or more fields (columns).

Excel database

Field names

Store	Salesperson	Computer	Model	Price
Glendale	George Billings	Maxima	M1245	$ 775.50
Carmel	Ginny Byer	Maxima	M1245	$ 778.45
Carmel	Sue Cooper	Maxima	M1245	$ 780.90
Carmel	John Poole	Maxima	M1245	$ 787.50
Glendale	Sally Kyte	Maxima	M1245	$ 789.75
Carmel	John Poole	Maxima	M1245	$ 792.56
Carmel	Ginny Byer	Ultima	U4654	$ 1,545.90
Glendale	Sally Kyte	Ultima	U4654	$ 1,560.80
Carmel	John Poole	Ultima	U4567	$ 1,591.40
Glendale	Bob Smith	Ultima	U3334	$ 1,670.90
Carmel	Ginny Byer	Ultima	U4654	$ 1,675.80

Record

Field

■ When you create a database, keep these things in mind:

- Create a new **field** (column) for any data you may want to sort or search by later.

    ✓ *For example, if your database is a list of people, you may want to separate first and last names into different columns, so you can sort by last name.*

- Enter the field names (column labels) at the top of the database.

    ✓ *It's a good idea to make the column labels bold or unique in some other way, so they are easily distinguished from the records in the database.*

    ✓ *You can use spaces in field names.*

- Don't leave any blank rows between the column labels and the first record in the database.

- If a column label is long, you can enter it on two lines.

    ✓ *This improves the appearance of the data form.*

    ✓ *To enter data on two lines, press Alt+Enter to begin a second line of data in the same cell.*

- You can use formulas in data records.

- To create multiple databases within a workbook, place each on its own worksheet.

- If the worksheet contains other data in addition to the database, separate the two by at least one row and one column.

■ After creating a database, you can add, change, or delete records. You also can sort, filter, and print the database.

Name a List/Database

■ After creating a list/database, you may wish to name the range containing the data.

✓ *Using the range name DATABASE allows Excel to automatically expand the range when you add new records using the data form.*

■ Naming a database makes it simpler to manipulate.

■ When naming a database, be sure the range includes the row containing the column labels (field names).

Use a Data Form to Add Records

■ To make entering data into a database a simple process, Excel provides a special dialog box called a **data form**.

Data form

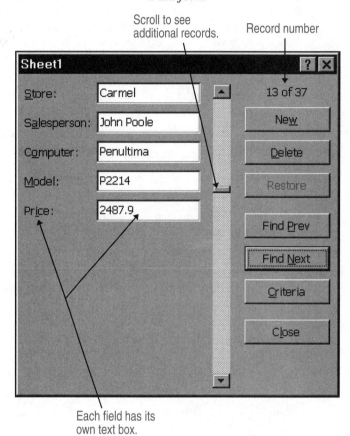

Scroll to see additional records.

Record number

Each field has its own text box.

■ The data form displays the information for a single record.

- Each field in the record is displayed in its own text box.

    ✓ *This makes it easier for you to enter all the data you need to complete a particular record.*

    ✓ *If the data in a field is the result of a calculation, the data form prevents you from accidentally entering other data into that field.*

- The number of the current record and the total number of records in the database is displayed in the data form.

    ✓ *This helps you keep track of where you are.*

- The data form allows you to enter new records, delete records, edit records, and find records.

- The easiest way to add a record is using the data form.
  - ✓ An alternative method is to insert a row between any of the existing rows in the database, and type information into the new row.
  - ✓ You can also enter data into the row directly below the last row in the database; Excel expands the database automatically to include this row. (This only works if you've named the range Database.)
  - ✓ If you're entering several record with repetitive information (such as the same city, warehouse number, etc.), use the data form to enter the unique fields only. Use the fill handle in the worksheet to enter the repetitive data.

Adding Fields to a List

- You can insert a new field into a list/database by simply inserting a column between existing columns in the database.
  - ✓ When you insert a field into an existing database, remember to fill in the data in that field for each of the existing records.
- You can also create a new field by typing a column label in the column to the right of the last column in the database.
  - ✓ This only works if you've named the range Database.

Procedures

Create a List (Database)

1. Start by typing the field names (column labels) in a row.
   - ✓ Don't skip columns — field names must occupy adjacent columns.
   - ✓ If a label doesn't fit in a cell, insert a line break by pressing **Alt+Enter**.
   - ✓ Remember to format the column labels so they're distinguishable from the data.
2. Enter data for the first record in the row below the field names.
   - ✓ Don't skip a row between the field names and the first row of data.
   - ✓ If a field doesn't apply to a particular record, leave that cell blank.
3. Enter data for the second record in the next row.
   - ✓ Continue until all records are entered.
   - ✓ Don't skip any rows.

Scroll Records by Using the Data Form

1. Select any cell in list.
2. Click **Data** .... Alt + D
3. Click **Form** .... O
4. Scroll through the records using scroll bar.
   OR
   a. To view next record, click **Find Next** .... Alt + N
   b. To view previous record, click **Find Prev** .... Alt + P
5. Click **Close** .... Alt + L

Add a Record by Using the Data Form

1. Select any cell in list.
2. Click **Data** .... Alt + D
3. Click **Form** .... O
4. Click **New** .... Alt + W
5. Type data in the first text box (field).
   - ✓ Remember that you can't enter data into a calculated field.
6. Press **Tab** .... Tab
   - ✓ You can also press **Shift+Tab** to move back to a previous field.

7. Type data in the next field.
8. Repeat steps 6 and 7 until the record is complete.
   - ✓ You can skip a field if it doesn't apply to this record.
9. Press **Enter** .... Enter
10. Repeat steps 4–8 to add another record.
11. Click **Close** .... Alt + L

Name a List (Database)

1. Select the database range.
   - ✓ Be sure to include the row containing the field names.
2. Click **Insert** .... Alt + I
3. Click **Name** .... N
4. Click **Define** .... D
5. Type a name for the database.
   - ✓ You'll probably want to use the name **database**.
6. Click **OK** .... Enter
   - ✓ To quickly add a range name, select the range and click in the **Name** box to the left of the Formula bar. Type the name you want to use and press **Enter**.

Exercise Directions

1. Start Excel, if necessary.
2. Open ⊚ **69_SALON**.
3. Save the file as **XL_69**.
4. Select the range B9:E9.
5. Format the range as follows:
   a. Change the font to Arial, 9 points, bold.
   b. Add a Light Turquoise fill.
6. Click in any cell within the database and open the data form.
7. Add the following records:
   ✓ *You don't need to type the $ when entering the price per item.*

8. Insert a column called *Cost per Box* between *Qty per Box* and *Cost per Item*.
9. In cell D10, type a formula to compute the cost per box.
   ✓ *Hint: Multiply the cost per item by the number of items in a box.*
10. Copy the formula to the other cells in column D.
11. Select cells B9:F27.
12. Name the selected range *database*.
13. Print the worksheet.
14. Save the workbook and exit Excel.

Item	Qty per Box	Cost per Item	Items in Inventory
Hair Gold Conditioner - Xtra D	12	$3.50	12
Hair Gold Hot Oil Conditioner	32	$4.50	32
Beauty Time Curling Brush	4	$4.50	8
Beauty Time Hair Pick	10	$3.25	10
Hair Gold Shampoo - Color	12	$4.50	24
Hair Gold Conditioner - Color	12	$4.50	24
Hair Gold Spritz	10	$5.25	10
Hair Gold Xtra Hold	10	$5.50	20
Hair Gold Gel	10	$5.60	20

On Your Own

1. Start Excel, if necessary.
2. Your insurance agent has suggested that you make a list of important household items in the event of loss or theft. Create a database to list these items.
   ✓ *Possible field names might include Description, Location (Room), and Replacement Cost.*
3. Save the file as **OXL_69**.
4. Format the column labels as you like.
5. Enter at least 15 sample entries.
   ✓ *Make sure you include items in various rooms of the house, including at least two in the kitchen, and three in the living room.*
   ✓ *Don't worry about organizing the entries as you enter them; you'll learn how to sort a database in Exercise 72.*

6. Add columns called *Original Cost* and *Purchase Date*.
7. Complete the information needed to fill in the additional columns.
8. Select the database range and name it *database*.
   ✓ *Be sure to include the field names in the range.*
9. If you haven't already done so, be sure to add the finishing touches to your worksheet, such as a nice title, some formatting, clip art or drawn art, and so on.
10. Print the worksheet.
11. Save the workbook and exit Excel.

Exercise 70

◆ Modify a Record ◆ Find a Record ◆ Delete a Record

On the Job

The purpose of a good database is to organize information. To keep your database current, you need to make changes to various records, add new records, and delete old ones. If the database is large, it may be difficult to find the exact record you need. And if you're using the database to provide information to some type of service-related position (such as client services, sales, or technical help), time is of the essence. Luckily, Excel makes the process of locating the exact item you need quite simple.

You're the new training manager for a computer training company called CompuTrain. Although business is booming, the records are a mess! To organize your training resources, you're going to use Excel to create an employee database for the trainers at CompuTrain.

Terms

search criteria Specifications you provide that help Excel locate exact item(s) in the database.

wildcard A symbol that substitutes for one or more characters within the search criteria. For example, using wildcards, you could search for any person whose last name begins with *S*, or *Sm.* Valid wildcards include an asterisk, * (which can replace any number of characters in a word), and a question mark, ? (which replaces a single character).

operator A symbol such as < (less than) that is used to specify a condition within the search criteria. Valid operators include < (less than), > (more than), = (equal to), <= (less than or equal to), >= (greater than or equal to), and <> (not equal to).

Notes

Modify a Record

- To maintain the accuracy of a database, you'll probably have to modify records from time to time.

- You can modify records using the data form or by making changes within the cells.

- Changing a record is as simple as locating the record, typing the new information, and then moving to the next record or closing the data form.

- You can search for the records you want to modify, and then step through only those records.

  ✓ *This saves you from scrolling through the entire database to locate the records you want to change.*

Find a Record

- You can locate specific records by entering **search criteria** into the data form.

  - For example, entering *Ohio* in the State field of a data form would retrieve only those records that contain the word *Ohio* in the State column.

  - The criteria you enter must match what's in the database exactly.

  - Case doesn't matter in search criteria, however. Entering *ohio* is the same as entering *Ohio*.

- After you enter search criteria, the data form searches the database and displays the first matching record.

  - You can use the data form to scroll through any additional matching records.

  - Records that don't match aren't accessible from the data form until you close it and then redisplay it.

    ✓ *You can also delete the search criteria to redisplay all records in the data form.*

- You can use **wildcards** when entering search criteria into a field.

  - An asterisk can be used to replace multiple characters in a word.

    ✓ *For example, if you want to search for Joan Phillips, and you aren't sure whether her name is spelled with one l or two, enter as much as you know for sure, followed by the asterisk: Phil*.*

    ✓ *You can type characters after the asterisk as well. For example, typing* Sm*h *will match* Smith, Smyth, *and* Smythe, *while* Sm* *will match* Smith, Smyth, Smothers, Smile, Smythe, *and so on.*

- A question mark can be used to replace a single character.

    ✓ *For example, you could enter* Fl?nn *to get both* Flynn *and* Flinn.

    ✓ *You can use multiple question marks when needed, as in* Sm?th?.

    ✓ *Typing* Fl*n *may produce different results than* Fl??n, *which limits the match to words with five characters exactly.*

    ✓ *As another example, you could* type 314-475-???? *to find phone numbers in the* 314 *area code that use the prefix* 475.

  - To search for a field that contains a question mark or an asterisk, precede it with a tilde (~), as in *2178~?SN* (which will find the entry *2178?SN*).

- You can use **operators** when entering search criteria.

  - Operators allow you to search for records that contain data higher than, lower than, or equal to a particular value.

    ✓ *You can use operators with both numeric and alphanumeric data.*

  - Valid operators include < (less than), > (greater than), = (equal to), <= (less than or equal to), >= (greater than or equal to), and <> (not equal to).

    ✓ *For example, type* >=1/1/98, *to find records that contain a date on or after January 1st, 1998.*

Delete a Record

- When a record is deleted, its row is removed from the worksheet, and the remaining rows move up.

- If you accidentally delete a record, you can't use Undo to restore it.

    ✓ *Prior to deleting records from a database, save the workbook. Then, if you accidentally delete the wrong record(s), you can close the file without saving the changes and open it again.*

Procedures

Find Records by Using the Data Form

1. Click any cell in list.
2. Click **Data**.................... `Alt`+`D`
3. Click **Form** .... `O`

   ✓ *For the best results, scroll to the first record in the database before entering criteria.*

4. Click **Criteria**............... `Alt`+`C`
5. Select the text box for the field you wish to search .... `Tab`
6. Type the search criteria.

   ✓ *If you need to remove previous criteria, click **Clear**.*

7. To add criteria for additional fields, repeat steps 5 and 6.
8. Click **Find Next**........... `Alt`+`N`

   OR

   Click **Find Prev**........... `Alt`+`P`
9. Repeat step 8 to display each matching record.

To Clear Search Criteria

1. Click **Criteria** .... `Alt`+`C`
2. Click **Clear**.................. `Alt`+`C`
3. Click **Form**.................. `Alt`+`F`

Delete Records by Using the Data Form

   ✓ *Deleted records can't be restored.*

1. Click any cell in list.
2. Click **Data** .... `Alt`+`D`
3. Click **Form** .... `O`
4. Display record to delete.
5. Click **Delete** .... `Alt`+`D`
6. Click **OK** to confirm .... `Enter`

   ✓ *The remaining records are automatically renumbered.*

7. Repeat steps 4-6 to delete any additional records.

Exercise Directions

1. Start Excel, if necessary.
2. Open ⊙ **70_EMPLS**.
3. Save the file as **XL_70**.
4. Add the following employees:
   a. Beth Cooper, 2/21/99, ID #46978, Sr. Intern, South Street, $22.50.
   b. Mike Bailey, 3/1/99, ID #55213, Intern, South Street, $16.25.
   c. Meghan Byer, 3/1/99, ID #55234, Intern, Northland Lake, $17.00.
5. Make the following changes in the database:
   a. Apply any necessary formatting to the three newest records to make them consistent with the existing records.
   b. Delete the record for Mike Willis.
   c. Widen the columns as necessary to display all data and column labels completely.
6. All employees in the South Street store are moving to a store on Cumberland Ave. Change their records to reflect the move.
   a. Search for employees who have *South Street* in the Store field, and then make your changes one by one.
   ✓ *Press Enter after making a change to a record. Then click Find Next or Find Prev to search for the next record.*
   ✓ *Scroll to the first person in the database before entering your search criteria — this will help you avoid missing anyone when you start making changes.*
   b. Widen the column, if necessary.

7. All employees with an hourly rate less than $20 are getting a $1 per hour increase — even those who were just hired.
   ✓ *Search for employees who have less than $20.00 in the Hourly Rate field.*
   ✓ *Press Enter after making a change to a record. Then click Find Next or Find Prev to search for the next record.*
8. Someone named *Pat* something (you remember it begins with *B*) wants his name changed to *Patrick*. Find the record and change it with the data form.
9. By the way, how many employees have a last name that begins with B?
   ✓ *Hint: If you're searching for an initial letter only, you don't need to type a wildcard.*
   a. How many begin with Br?
   b. How many begin with A, B, or C?
   ✓ *Hint: Try searching for <=d.*
   c. How many have an annual salary above $65,000 and work in the Cumberland Ave. store?
   d. How many interns earn more than $40,000 per year?
10. Print the worksheet.
11. Save the workbook and exit Excel.

On Your Own

1. Start Excel, if necessary.
2. Open **OXL_69**, the workbook you created in Exercise 69, or open ⊙ **70_HOUSEHOLD**.
3. Save the workbook as **OXL_70**.
4. Use the data form to add at least ten household items to the database (perhaps some in the garage or office/den).
5. Use the data form to:
   a. Update the items in the bedroom, since you just replaced all of them with new purchases.
   b. Reevaluate the replacement cost of all the items and change some of the entries.
   c. Delete any items whose replacement cost is less than a certain amount, say $200.
6. Print the worksheet.
7. Save the workbook and exit Excel.

Exercise 71

Skills Covered:

◆ **Control Data Entry** ◆ **Copy and Paste Validation Rules**
◆ **Circle Invalid Data**

On the Job

After creating a database and adding, changing, and deleting records, you soon realize just how easy it is to enter incorrect information. This is especially true when several people maintain a database. Since the accuracy of your data is often critical — especially if the data tells you what to charge for a product or what to pay someone — controlling the validity of the data is paramount.

You're the manager of Pine Tree Apartments, and you want to make sure that no one makes any mistakes when updating your apartment availability database. You've decided to use data validation to provide some help for new staff members and some restrictions to ensure data accuracy.

Terms

validation A process that enables you to maintain the accuracy of a database by specifying acceptable entries for a particular field.

input message A message that appears when a user clicks in a cell providing information on how to enter valid data.

Paste Special A variation of the Paste command that allows you to copy part of the data relating to a cell — in this case, the validity rules associated with that cell — and not the data in the cell itself.

Notes

Control Data Entry

- With data **validation**, you can control the accuracy of the data entered into a database.

  ✓ Data validation is designed for entering data directly into cells in the worksheet, not for using the data form. Data validation also doesn't apply if the cell entry results from using the fill handle, pasting or moving data from another location, or a formula. However, you can find invalid entries created by these methods with the Circle Invalid Data button on the Auditing toolbar.

- By specifying the type of entries that are acceptable, you can prevent invalid data from being entered.

  ✓ For example, you could create a list of valid department numbers.

  ✓ You can set other rules as well, such as whole numbers only; numbers less than or greater than some value; or data of a specific length, such as five characters only.

  ✓ With the Custom option, you can enter a formula that compares the entry value with a value in another field (column). For example, if one cell contains the word Rented, then a second cell must have a value greater than zero.

308

Data Validation dialog box

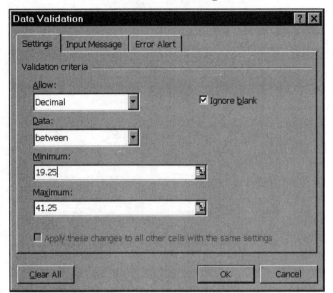

- If you restrict entries to a specified list, a down-arrow button appears when the cell is selected. Clicking the button displays a drop-down list of the acceptable entries, from which you can select.

- Entries in a restricted list are case-sensitive. If the list specifies *Yes* and the user instead types *yes*, for example, Excel will reject the entry. Whenever possible, use lowercase letters for list entries to prevent case-sensitivity problems and speed up data entry.

- Excel's AutoComplete feature can complicate data entry in an Excel database. AutoComplete can alter the case of an entry or complete an entry in a manner the user doesn't intend.

  - For example, if a previous entry in the field is *Westlane* and the user is entering only *West*, AutoComplete will nonetheless fill in *Westlane*.

  - To turn off the AutoComplete feature, choose Tools, Options, click the Edit tab, and deselect Enable AutoComplete for cell values.

- Data validation can prevent incorrect entries and speed up data entry, but other methods can be faster for entering some types of data. To enter data for a set of new parts at a particular warehouse, for example, enter only the unique data for each part. Then fill in all the cells in the Warehouse field at once — select the cells, type the entry, and press Ctrl+Enter. Or type the entry in the first cell and use the fill handle to complete the remaining cells.

- After entering the criteria for what constitutes a valid entry, you can also specify a particular error message to appear when an incorrect entry is typed.

Error message

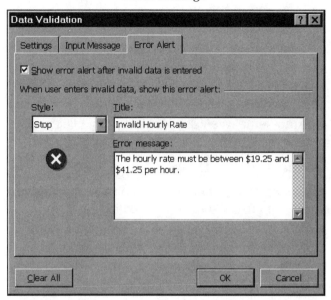

- In addition, you can create an **input message** that displays when you click a cell to help the user enter the right type of data.

  ✓ *This message only appears when a user inputs data directly into the worksheet, bypassing the data form.*

Input message

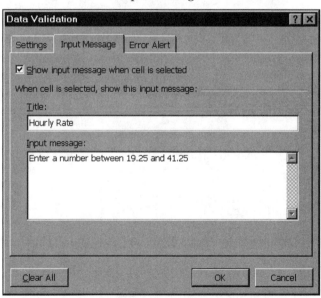

Copy and Paste Validation Rules

- After creating rules that limit the valid entries for a cell, you can use the **Paste Special** command to copy the rules to the other cells in the same column.

  ✓ *This allows you to create one set of rules for an entire field (column).*

- Another way to apply the same validation rule to an entire field is to select the column before creating the validation rule. The new rule applies to all cells in the selection.

- If the same rule will apply to multiple fields, select all those fields before creating the rule.

Circle Invalid Data

- To locate and correct invalid data in a database, you can use the Auditing toolbar.

- With the Circle Invalid Data button on the Auditing toolbar, data that violates specified validation rules is identified quickly with a red circle.

Invalid data appears in a red circle

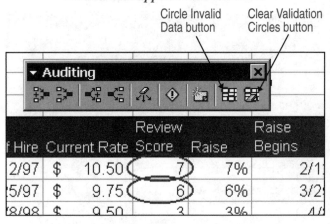

- As you correct the data, the circle in that cell automatically disappears.

  ✓ *You can remove any remaining circles (for errors you want to ignore) by clicking the Clear Validation Circles button.*

Procedures

Set Data Validation for a Cell

1. Select the cell(s) to receive validation settings.
2. Click **Data** .... Alt +D
3. Click **Validation** L

   To restrict entries to a number:

   a. Select **Whole number** or **Decimal** in the **Allow** list .... Alt +A, ⬜, Enter

   b. Select a **Data** operator .... Alt +D, ⬜, Enter

   c. Specify the **Minimum** and **Maximum** acceptable numbers, if necessary .... Alt +M, Alt +X

   To restrict entries to a data or time:

   a. Select **Date** or **Time** in the **Allow** list........ Alt +A, ⬜, Enter

   b. Select a **Data** operator .... Alt +D, ⬜, Enter

   c. Specify acceptable **Start date** and **End data** or **Start time** and **End time** settings, if necessary........... .... Alt +S, Alt +N

   To restrict text entries to a certain length:

   a. Select **Text length** in the **Allow** list........ Alt +A, ⬜, Enter

   b. Select a **Data** operator .... Alt +D, ⬜, Enter

   c. Specify the **Minimum** and **Maximum** acceptable lengths, if necessary........... .... Alt +M, Alt +X

   To restrict entries to text:

   a. Select **Text length** in the **Allow** list........ Alt +A, ⬜, Enter

   b. Select **greater than or equal to** in the **Data** list .... Alt +D, ⬜, Enter

   c. Type **0** (zero) in the **Minimum** box .... Alt +M

   To display a drop-down list of acceptable entries in the cell:

   a. Select **List** in the **Allow** list .... Alt +A, ⬜, Enter

   b. Click in the **Source** box and type a list of acceptable entries, separated by commas .... Alt +S

   ✓ *For example, type* Living Room, Kitchen, Office/Den, Bedroom.

   OR

   Click the **Collapse Dialog** button and select the cell or range in the worksheet that contains the entry list. (Use an absolute reference.)

   ✓ *The entry list can be a range of cells with one item per cell or a single cell with a list of items separated by commas.*

OR

Type = (equal sign) followed by the address of the cell or range containing the entry list. (Use an absolute reference.)

c. Select **In-cell dropdown** .... `Alt`+`I`

To create a custom restriction based on a formula:

a. Select **Custom** in the **Allow** list .... `Alt`+`A`, `↕`, `Enter`

b. Type the formula in the **Formula** box, using appropriate absolute, mixed, and relative references.............. `Alt`+`F`

✓ *Formulas must evaluate to TRUE or FALSE.*

OR

Click the **Collapse Dialog** button and select a cell in the worksheet that contains the formula.

OR

Type = (equal sign) followed by the address of the cell containing the formula.

To enter an input message:

a. Select **Input Message** tab.......... `Ctrl`+`Tab`

b. Click **Show input message when cell is selected** .... `Alt`+`S`

c. Enter **Title**............... `Alt`+`T`

d. Enter **Input message**................. `Alt`+`I`

To customize error message:

a. Select **Error Alert** tab .... `Ctrl`+`Tab`

b. Click **Show error alert after invalid data is entered** .... `Alt`+`S`

c. Select alert **Style**.... `Alt`+`Y`, `↕`, `Enter`

✓ *A stop* alert *refuses the entry. A* warning *alert asks whether the reader wants to proceed with the entry despite the validation rule. An* information *alert presents the error message.*

d. Enter **Title** .... `Alt`+`T`

e. Enter **Error message** .... `Alt`+`E`

4. Click **OK** .... `Enter`

Copy Validation Rules

1. Select cell(s) whose validation rules you wish to copy.

2. Click the **Copy** button .... `Ctrl`+`C`

3. Select the destination range.

4. Click **Edit**................ `Alt`+`E`

5. Click **Paste Special** .... `S`

6. Select **Validation** .... `Alt`+`N`

7. Click **OK** .... `Enter`

Find All Cells with Validation Rules

1. Click **Edit**................ `Alt`+`E`

2. Click **Go To** .... `G`

3. Click **Special** .... `Alt`+`S`

4. Select **Data validation** .... `Alt`+`V`

5. Select **All**.................... `Alt`+`L`

Find Cells with Similar Validation Rules

1. Select a cell with the validation rule you want to find.

2. Click **Edit** .... `Alt`+`E`

3. Click **Go To** .... `G`

4. Click **Special** .... `Alt`+`S`

5. Select **Data validation**................... `Alt`+`V`

6. Select **Same** to find cells with the same validation rule(s) as selected the cell........... `Alt`+`E`

Display the Auditing Toolbar

1. Click **Tools** .... `Alt`+`T`

2. Click **Auditing** .... `U`

3. Click **Show Auditing Toolbar**............................ `S`

Circle Invalid Data

1. Display the **Auditing** toolbar.

2. Click the **Circle Invalid Data** button ⊞.

✓ *Excel displays red circles around all data that doesn't meet the specified validation rules. Cells without validation rules are ignored.*

Correct Invalid Data

1. Display validation circles.

2. Select a cell containing a validation circle.

3. Correct the entry in the cell to a valid entry.

Clear Validation Circles

1. Display the **Auditing** toolbar.

2. Click the **Clear Validation Circles** button ▨.

✓ *All validation circles disappear.*

Exercise Directions

1. Start Excel, if necessary.

2. Open ⊙ **71_PINETREE**.

3. Save the file as **XL_71**.

4. Click in cell F9.

5. Create the following data validation criteria:

   a. Create a drop-down list of acceptable entries.

   b. In the Source text box, type *Beige, Gray, Tan, Blue*.

      ✓ *Be sure to use commas as separators. A comma isn't required after the last entry.*

      ✓ *You could also type the list in the worksheet and then select it using the Collapse Dialog button. (Make sure that the address is absolute.)*

   c. Create a stop error message with the title *Invalid data* and the message *Enter either beige, gray, tan, or blue.*

6. Copy the validation rules to the other cells in column F using Paste Special. Copy the rules through cell F35.

   ✓ *Copying the validation rules beyond the existing list/database allows you to add new records that will still be covered by the rules.*

7. Click in cell I9.

8. Create the following data validation criteria:

   a. Require a whole number between 380 and 720.

   b. Create an input message called *Current rental rates* that reminds the user that 1 BR apartments rent for $420, 2 BR for $520, and 3 BR for $690. A fireplace is $10 more per month.

   c. Create a stop error message with the title *Invalid rent amount* and the message *Please check the current rental chart for the proper charge.*

9. Copy the validation rules to the other cells in column I through cell I35.

10. Add the following records by typing the entries in the worksheet in the rows following the database.

    ✓ *Some may cause error messages. Correct as indicated.*

    a. 4, 404A, 1, No, Tan, Joe Smithe, Mike Cooper, 420, 4/16/99, Rented.

    b. 4, 412B, 2, Yes, Blue, Jenny Byer, Peggy Smith, 530, 5/31/99, Rented

    c. 11, 110C, 2, No, Green, Joe Hooper, Mike Callen, 520, 9/12/99, Rented.

       ✓ *Carpet should be listed as gray, not green.*

    d. 11, 110B, 2, Yes, Tan, Julie Smithe, blank (no second entry) 275, 6/19/99, Rented.

       ✓ *The rent on this apartment should be 525, not 275.*

    e. 3, 311A, 3, Yes, Brown, skip the next two cells, 700, 2/12/99, Available.

       ✓ *Carpet should be listed as blue, not brown.*

11. Using the Edit, Go To command, locate all cells in the worksheet that have validation rules.

12. Save the workbook and exit Excel.

On Your Own

1. Start Excel, if necessary.

2. Open ⊚ **71_RAISE**.

3. Save the file as **OXL_71**.

4. Add a new column called *Raise Begins*.

   ✓ *Insert the new column between the existing columns F and G.*

   a. Create a formula in cell G8 that computes the date when the raise will begin, which occurs annually from the date of hire.

      ✓ *You could take the date of hire plus 365 (or 365.25 if you prefer), and then format the cell so that it displays only the month and day. The formula would look like this:*

      =C8+365

      ✓ *To show the complete date with the current year, you could use this formula:*

      =DATE(YEAR(*TODAY*()),MONTH(C8),DAY(C8))

      ✓ *Using the YEAR function, you get 1999 from today's date; using the MONTH function, you get 2 from the hire date in cell C8; and using the DAY function, you get 12 from the hire date in cell C8. Put them all together using the DATE function, and you get (1999,2,12) which is displayed in the cell as 2/12/99.*

   b. Copy the formula to the other cells in column G (G9:G12).

5. Add data validation to column E questioning any raises above the average of 5%.

   ✓ *Use Custom, with a formula such as =H8<D8+(D8*.06).*

   ✓ *Issue a warning alert, not a stop alert.*

   ✓ *Add an input message that instructs the user to enter a whole number between 1 and 10.*

6. In column F, add a formula that computes the new raise.

   a. A person receiving a score of 5 gets a 5% raise.

      ✓ *Divide the review score by 100.*

   b. Format column F with Percent Style.

7. In column H, add a formula that computes the new rate.

   ✓ *Multiply the old rate by 1 plus the rate percent.*

8. Create a text box warning users that raises must be entered into the worksheet (they shouldn't use the data form).

   a. Format the text box however you like.

   b. Position it in column A to the left of the database.

   c. Widen column A if necessary.

9. Give everyone a raise rating; be sure to try some numbers that will trigger the error message. Accept some of the incorrect entries.

10. Use the Circle Invalid Data button on the Auditing toolbar to locate invalid entries.

11. Correct the entries or clear the validation circles.

12. Save and close the workbook.

13. Exit Excel.

Exercise 72

◆ **Sort Records in a List** ◆ **Rules for Sorting**
◆ **Undo a Sort** ◆ **Restore the Record Order**

On the Job

Entering data in random order makes the job a bit easier, since you don't have to organize the information first. But trying to find information in a disorganized database is time-consuming. So, after entering data into a database, the first order of business is ordering (sorting) the data.

You're an accountant with Corporate Computer Solutions, and it's time for the end-of-the-month inventory. To make the process of entering the current inventory numbers easier, you're going to sort the database first. As an added incentive, you've decided that sorting the database will help you perform a better analysis of February sales.

Terms

ascending order An arrangement of items in alphabetical order (A to Z) or numerical order (1, 2, 3, and so on). Dates are arranged from oldest to most recent.

descending order An arrangement of items in reverse alphabetical order (Z to A) or reverse numerical order (10, 9, 8, and so on). Dates are arranged from most recent to oldest.

key One level within a sort. For example, you might sort a list by last name (one key) and then sort duplicate last names by first name (another key).

Notes

Sort Records in a List

- After entering data into an Excel database (list), you can arrange the items however you wish.

- You might want to sort a list in alphabetical order (for example, a list of names), or numerical order (a price list), or date order (a list of employees and their hire dates).

- Lists can be sorted in **ascending order** or **descending order**.
  - Ascending order will arrange labels alphabetically (A to Z), numbers from smallest to largest, and dates from oldest to most recent.

- Descending order is simply the reverse of ascending order.

- You can sort any contiguous data in the worksheet; it doesn't have to be a database. For example, you might want to sort an expense report to list all the expenses in order by account number.

- A list can be sorted using more than one **key**.
  - A key is a single sort level.
  - In the example below, a list of employees has been sorted by state. Employees with duplicate states are then sorted by last name, and those with duplicate last names are sorted by first name for a total of three keys.

Sort example

First Name	Last Name	City	State
Alan	Smith	Phoenix	Arizona
Tom	Smith	Flagstaff	Arizona
Alice	Sook	Scottscale	Arizona
Mark	Smith	Denver	Colorado
Matthew	Smith	Boulder	Colorado
Jenny	Stone	Longmont	Colorado
Glenda	Sothby	St. George	Utah
Grace	Sothby	Ogden	Utah
Jerry	Stone	Price	Utah

- You can sort on a maximum of three keys in a single sort.

■ You can sort a list by using the sort buttons on the Standard toolbar, or with the Sort dialog box.

Sort buttons

Sort dialog box

Rules for Sorting

■ Excel sorts data based on the actual cell content, not the displayed results.

■ If you choose to sort in ascending order, items are arranged as follows:

- *Numeric sort.* Numbers are sorted from the largest negative number to the largest positive number.

  ◆ For example, -3, -2, -1, 0, 1, 2, and so on.

- *Alphanumeric sort.* Labels (text or text/number combinations) are sorted first by *symbols*, then by *letters*.

  ◆ Symbols are arranged in this order: (space) ! " # $ % & ( ) * , . / : ; ? @ [\ ] ^ _ ` { | } ~ + < = >

  ◆ Letters are arranged alphabetically, A to Z.

- Hypens (-) and apostrophes (') are ignored in alphanumeric sorts, except when sorting cells whose contents are identical apart from a hyphen or apostrophe. In those situations, the cell containing the symbol is placed last.

- If names in the database contain spaces (*de Lancie*), the sort results may differ from what you expect. Because spaces sort to the top of the list, *de Lancie* lands above *Dean* and *Debrazzi*.

- Alphanumeric sorts on number/text combination may also surprise you. Combinations like 1Q through 11Q, for example, sort like this *10Q, 11Q, 1Q, 2Q, 3Q,* and so on.

- Dates are sorted chronologically.

  ◆ For example, 1/10/99 would come before 2/12/99.

- If a cell in the sort column is blank, that record is placed at the end of the list.

  ✓ *This is true whether the sort is ascending or descending.*

■ As an example of sorted records, consider this list:

Jay's Grill	1256 Adams Ave.
CompuTrain	12 Brown Street
Central Perk	
Carriage Club	Carriage Center
Giving Tree	? Mark Building

■ If the list is sorted by address (ascending order), you'll end up with:

CompuTrain	12 Brown Street
Jay's Grill	1256 Adams Ave.
Giving Tree	? Mark Building
Carriage Club	Carriage Center
Central Perk	

■ Notice that the record that doesn't contain an address is placed last.

- Using the Sort dialog box, you can sort left to right (across a row) rather than top to bottom (down a column). This option is useful if your database is organized with a horizontal rather than a vertical orientation.

- You also can sort with case sensitivity. In a case-sensitive sort, capital letters are sorted above lowercase letters, so *Kit* appears above *kit*.

Undo a Sort

- You can undo a sort if you click the Undo button immediately after completing the sort.

- If you don't undo a sort immediately, the original sort order is lost.

- To protect your data, always save the workbook prior to sorting.

✓ *If something goes wrong, simply close the workbook without saving changes, and open the saved version from disk.*

Restore the Record Order

- If you want to keep your original sort order as well as the new, sorted list, copy the original list to another sheet in the workbook and then sort.

- Another way to restore the original record order at any time is to include a unique field in every record.
  - For example, you could include a field called *Record number*, and fill in unique numbers for each record. (Make sure all numbers are the same length.)
  - To restore the original order, simply sort by this column.

Procedures

Sort with the Default Sort Settings

1. Select cell in the column you want to sort by.
2. Click **Sort Ascending** button [A↓].
   OR
   Click **Sort Descending** button [Z↓].

Sort a List

1. Select any cell in list.
2. Click **Data**.................. [Alt]+[D]
3. Click **Sort** .... [S]
4. Specify any field headings in the selected database.
   - If the first row contains field headings, select **Header row** .... [Alt]+[R]
   OR
   - If there are no field headings, select **No header row** ...... [Alt]+[W]
     ✓ *If you indicate that the database has a header row, Excel will use the field headings in the drop-down lists in the Sort dialog box.*

5. Select sort options:
   To set the first key sort order:
   a. Select a field or column in the **Sort by** list.... [↑↓], [Enter]
   b. Select **Ascending** .. [Alt]+[A]
      OR
      Select **Descending** .... [Alt]+[D]

   To set second key sort order (optional):
   a. Select a field or column in the **Then By** list.................
      .... [Tab], [↑↓], [Enter]
   b. Select **Ascending** .. [Alt]+[C]
      OR
      Select **Descending** .... [Alt]+[N]

   To set third key sort order (optional):
   a. Select a field or column in the **Then By** list.................
      .... [Tab], [↑↓], [Enter]
   b. Select **Ascending** .. [Alt]+[I]
      OR
      Select **Descending** .... [Alt]+[G]

6. If desired,
   click **Options** .... [Alt]+[O]
   To select a custom sort order for first key:
   - Select desired sort order from the **First key sort order** list ....
     .... [Alt]+[F], [↑↓]+[Enter]
   To set a case-sensitive sort:
   - Select **Case sensitive** .... [Alt]+[C]
   To change orientation of sort (from columns to rows):
   - Select **Sort left to right** .... [Alt]+[L]
7. Click **OK** to return to the Sort dialog box .... [Enter]
8. Click **OK**........................... [Enter]

Undo a Sort

✓ *It's best to undo a sort immediately.*

1. Click **Edit** .... [Alt]+[E]
2. Click **Undo Sort**.................. [U]
   ✓ *You can also simply click the Undo button on the Standard toolbar.*

Exercise Directions

1. Start Excel, if necessary.

2. Open ✆ **72_COMPUTER**.

3. Save the file as **XL_72**.

4. In cell I8, type a formula to compute the sales for February.

   ✓ *Subtract the inventory on March 1 (to be added later) from the inventory on Feb 1 to create the formula.*

5. Copy the formula down to cell I24, (you'll add records in the next step).

6. Add the following new products to the inventory:

   a. Maxima, M2314, 920, 775, 21, 16.

   b. Penultima, P4665, 2798, 2130, 12, 9.

   c. Ultima, U3343, 1495, 1235, 9, 5.

7. To simplify entering the rest of the inventory numbers, sort the database:

   a. Open the Sort dialog box.

   b. Select March 1, Ascending as the first sort key.

   c. Select Model #, Ascending as the second key.

8. After sorting the database, select column E and freeze the panes. Scroll the right pane so that column H is adjacent to column D. This allows you to check your work as you complete the next step.

9. Complete the rest of the inventory, adding the totals for March:

   a. M1245, 12.

   b. M2245, 16.

   c. M2314, 16.

   d. M3456, 16.

   e. M4488, 11.

   f. M4565, 18.

   g. P1145, 13.

   h. P2214, 21.

   i. P3154, 16.

   j. P4564, 18.

   k. P4665, 9.

   l. U1234, 11.

   m. U3334, 13.

   n. U3343, 5.

   o. U3654, 5.

   p. U4567, 13.

   q. U4654, 9.

10. Unfreeze the panes.

11. Sort the inventory again to find out which product sold the most in February:

    a. Open the Sort dialog box.

    b. Select Number Sold, Descending as the first key.

    c. Select Model #, Ascending as the second key.

    d. Which model sold the most?

    e. How many units were sold?

    f. Which model sold the least?

12. Format columns E and F with Accounting format, zero decimal places.

13. Widen columns E and F as necessary.

14. Print the worksheet.

15. Save and close the workbook.

16. Exit Excel.

On Your Own

1. Start Excel, if necessary.

2. Design a database to track homes for sale in your area.

   ✓ *You're thinking about putting your own house up for sale, and you want to check out the competition.*

   ✓ *Include columns for the asking price, address, neighborhood or association, square footage, number of bedrooms, and extras, like a family room, bonus room, study, basement, fenced yard, and so on.*

3. Save the file as **OXL_72**.

4. Format the worksheet attractively, adding a title, some clip art, and some color.

5. Connect to the Internet to find data for your database.

   a. Enter at least 15 homes into the database.

   b. Use the real estate listings on-line to make your database realistic.

      ✓ *Be sure to add your own home to the database as well, along with what you think your asking price will be. (If you don't own a home, make one up!) To make your home easier to spot in the database, type an asterisk (*) at the end of its address. Sort the database by neighborhood (key 1), and then by asking price (key 2).*

6. Answer some key questions using the information in your database:

   a. Which house is the most expensive in each neighborhood?

   b. Which house is the least expensive?

   c. Which neighborhood has the highest number of houses for sale?

7. Sort the database by square footage.

   a. Which house has the most square footage? What is its asking price?

   b. Which house has the least? What is its asking price?

8. Sort the database by the number of bedrooms (key 1) and by square footage (key 2).

   a. Which houses have the same number of bedrooms as yours? What are their asking prices?

   b. Which house has square footage closest to the amount in your own home? What is its asking price?

   c. Do the houses that are similar to yours have features that yours doesn't?

9. Now that you have more information, adjust the asking price of your own house, if necessary.

   ✓ *How close was your original asking price to reality?*

10. Print the worksheet.

11. Save and close the workbook.

12. Exit Excel.

Exercise 73

◆ AutoFilter a Database

On the Job

It doesn't take much time before a database gets too large to view completely on the screen without having to do a lot of scrolling. When you're looking for particular records, such as all the salespeople who work in the Grand Ave. office, you can use AutoFilter to filter (reduce) the number of records to just the ones you want to view right now. With AutoFilter, even large databases become manageable.

You're a database specialist, and you've been hired by Dr. Benjamin Child and Associates to help them with a case study that they are doing on premature infant development. They've given you a raw database of information, but you need to organize it and then filter it to answer some of their questions.

Terms

filter Reduce the total number of records displayed on the screen to a selected few.

AutoFilter A tool for filtering a database automatically.

Notes

AutoFilter a Database

- Excel has a **filter** tool called **AutoFilter** that you can use to select which records in your database you wish to view.

  ✓ *Filtering a database doesn't delete records or alter the database in any way.*

- In the example below, AutoFilter was used to display only the records for the Penultima computer models.

AutoFilter example

Type	Model #	Retail Price	Cost	Feb 1 Inv.	Mar 1 Inv.	# Sold in Feb
Penultima	P3154	$ 3,210	$ 2,345	36	16	20
Penultima	P2214	$ 2,598	$ 1,895	32	21	11
Penultima	P4564	$ 3,568	$ 2,456	28	18	10
Penultima	P1145	$ 2,054	$ 1,868	21	13	8
Penultima	P4665	$ 2,798	$ 2,130	12	9	3

Excel hides rows not in the AutoFilter selection (note missing row numbers).

Penultima was selected from the drop-down list.

- As you can see in the figure, AutoFilter adds an arrow button to the right of each field name in the AutoFiltered database.

  - When you click the arrow button, a drop-down list displays.

- This list contains one of each kind of entry from that column.

  ✓ *For example, if a database contains records from three states, Indiana, Illinois, and Ohio, the drop-down list will contain the entries Indiana, Illinois, and Ohio.*

- Select an item from the drop-down list, and only records that match that item are displayed.

  ✓ *For example, if you select Ohio from the list, only records with Ohio in that field will display.*

- After you make a selection, the arrow button turns blue to remind you which filter is controlling the display. The row numbers of the filtered records also appear in blue.

■ Each AutoFilter list contains these common entries:

- (All) This option displays all records again.

  ✓ *To redisplay all records in the database, select the (All) option from the list with the blue arrow.*

- (Top 10…) This option displays the top (or bottom) 10 records in that category.

  ✓ *Despite the name, you can select the actual number of items to display. The number must be between 1 and 500.*

- (Custom…) This option allows you to specify up to two conditions, such as records with sales greater than $1,000 or a sale date between 2/15/99 and 2/22/99.

- (Blanks) This option allows you to display only the records with no value in this field (column).

- (NonBlanks) This option allows you to display only the records that contain a value in this field (column).

  ✓ *The Blanks and NonBlanks options only appear for fields that contain at least one blank cell.*

  ✓ *Use the Blanks filter to locate and correct records with missing data.*

■ You can make selections from more than one AutoFilter list in order to create a small subset of records.

  ✓ *For example, you might select Ohio from the State list and then (Top 10) from the Sales list to display the top ten sales records in the Ohio region.*

  ✓ *If you select criteria from more than one AutoFilter list, only records that match both criteria are displayed.*

■ The AutoFilter feature is an option on the Filter submenu of the Data menu. Click the option to turn AutoFilter off.

Procedures

AutoFilter a List

1. Select any cell in list.
2. Click **Data** .... `Alt`+`D`
3. Click **Filter**.......................... `F`
4. Click **AutoFilter** .... `F`

   ✓ *Arrow buttons appear next to each field name.*

5. Click the down-arrow button of the field you wish to filter.
6. Select an item from the list............. `↑↓`, `Enter`

Customize the AutoFilter

1. Select **(Custom)** from the AutoFilter list.
2. Select an operator in the first list .... `Shift`+`Tab`, `↑↓`, `Enter`
3. Select or type a value in the second list .... `Tab`, `↑↓`, `Enter`
4. To specify other criteria for the column:

   - Select **And** .... `Alt`+`A`
   OR
   - Select **Or** .... `Alt`+`O`

5. Select second operator .... `Tab`, `↑↓`, `Enter`
6. Select or type the second value .... `Tab`, `↑↓`, `Enter`
7. Click **OK** .... `Enter`

Redisplay All Records in List

1. Click **Data** .... `Alt`+`D`
2. Click **Filter** .... `F`
3. Click **Show All**.................... `S`

   ✓ *You can also click the blue arrow(s) and select (All) to redisplay all records.*

Remove the AutoFilter

   ✓ *This process will redisplay all records and remove the AutoFilter arrows and drop-down lists.*

1. Click **Data** .... `Alt`+`D`
2. Click **Filter** .... `F`
3. Click **AutoFilter**.................. `F` to deselect it.

Exercise Directions

1. Start Excel, if necessary.

2. Open 73_CHILD.

3. Save the file as **XL_73**.

4. Display only records involving multiple births:

   a. Turn on the AutoFilter.

   b. Select Y from the AutoFilter list in column D.

5. Sort the displayed records by birth weight (column E).

6. Of the babies born in a multiple birth (Y in column D), who had the lowest birth weight?

   Who had the highest birth weight?

7. Redisplay all the records; then hide any records of babies who didn't gain at least four ounces in their first month:

   a. Select Custom from the AutoFilter list in column G.

   b. Select *is greater than* as the operator.

   c. Type *4* into the second text box.

   d. Click OK.

8. How many records are still displayed?

   How many are boys (guess by the names)?

   How many are girls?

9. Redisplay all records.

10. In cell R11, type the label *Total Weight Gained*.

    a. If necessary, use the Format Painter to format the cell to match the other field names.

    b. Widen the column, if necessary.

    c. In cell R12, enter a formula to compute the total weight gained for this baby.

    d. Copy the formula to the other cells in column R.

11. Turn off the AutoFilter and turn it on again to include the new column.

12. Sort on another column (your choice).

13. Hide the records that don't contain entries for the sixth month.

    • Select (NonBlanks) from the AutoFilter list in column P.

14. Redisplay all the records; then display only those records where the baby gained at least two pounds, but no more than three pounds. (32 oz. to 48 oz.).

    a. Select Custom from the AutoFilter list in column R.

    b. Select *is greater than or equal to* as the first operator.

    c. Type *32* into the text box.

    d. Select *And*.

    e. Select *is less than or equal to* as the second operator.

    f. Type *48* into the text box.

    g. Click OK.

15. How many records remain?

    How many boys?

    How many girls?

16. Redisplay all records.

17. Save and close the workbook.

18. Exit Excel.

On Your Own

1. Start Excel, if necessary.

2. Open **OXL_72**.

   ✓ *You're going to use AutoFilter to refine the research you've begun in preparation for selling your home. But first, you'll make some additions to the database you created in Exercise 72.*

3. Save the file as **OXL_73**.

4. Add a column called *Curb Appeal* to the database:

   a. Go back and rate each house, on a scale from 1–5, on how appealing it looks from the curb.

   b. Using AutoFilter, display only the houses with a rating of 4 or 5.

   c. What are their asking prices?

      ✓ *You may want to sort the filtered database by asking price to make your analysis easier.*

   d. How do they compare to your house?

5. Add a column called *Number of Weeks on Market*.

   ✓ *Turn off the AutoFilter before adding the column.*

   a. Go back and add the proper information for each house.

      ✓ *You may not find this information on the Internet. If not, simply make up some information to complete the database.*

   b. Use the AutoFilter to display only houses that have been on the market for longer than three months (12 weeks).

   c. Why do you think they haven't sold?

      ✓ *You may want to sort by asking price to help with your analysis.*

   d. How do they compare to your house in price?

6. Use the AutoFilter to display only the houses whose asking price is greater than or equal to yours.

   a. Filter the list further, eliminating houses that aren't in your neighborhood.

   b. How does your house compare?

7. You've just found out that five more houses have recently been put on the market. Add them to the database. (Make up the data.)

8. Four houses were sold.

   a. Add a column that lists the sales price.

   b. Enter the sales prices for these houses.

   c. Use the AutoFilter to display only the houses that have been sold.

   d. How many sold for within 5% of their asking price?

   e. How do they compare with your home's asking price?

9. Redisplay all records.

10. Sort the database by asking price.

11. Print the worksheet.

12. Save and close the workbook.

13. Exit Excel.

Exercise 74

Skills Covered:

◆ **Advanced Filters** ◆ **Guidelines for Entering Criteria**
◆ **Examples of Advanced Criteria**
◆ **Remove an In-place Advanced Filter** ◆ **Edit Extracted Records**

On the Job

Although AutoFilter allows you set up some custom criteria to control which records are displayed on the screen, it can't do all the things that an advanced filter can. With an advanced filter, you can extract the matching records and then format, sort, and make other changes to them without affecting the records in the database. This is handy when you want to print or format a subset of the database, or delete a few records from the subset that you don't want to use (even if they match the criteria). With this technique, you can create a custom list even if you can't specify the exact criteria for it. In addition, advanced filters let you create complex criteria using formulas, multiple conditions applied to a single field, and so on to filter the database.

You've just been hired as the new accounts payable manager for Women's Physicians Network, and you need to organize the outstanding debts. You've already created a list of accounts with outstanding invoices; now you're going to use an advanced filter to help you analyze it.

Terms

filter Display the records in a database that match particular criteria.

extract Copy records that match specified criteria to another place in the worksheet where they can be changed, sorted, formatted, printed, and so on.

criteria range Area of the worksheet in which you specify criteria for selecting records from the database.

extract range Area where Excel copies the database records that result from an advanced filtering process.

Notes

Advanced Filters

- With an advanced filter, you can **filter** database records in one of two ways:
  - You can hide records that don't match certain criteria — in much the same way as with AutoFilter.
  - You can **extract** (copy) records to another place in the worksheet.
- Although an advanced filter can hide records just like AutoFilter, it's different in many ways.

- An advanced filter allows you to enter more complex criteria than AutoFilter.
- Instead of selecting criteria from a drop-down list, you enter it in a special area in the worksheet that you have set aside for that purpose.
- After setting up a **criteria range**, you type the criteria you want to match in cells within this range.

- You then open a dialog box in which you specify the range where the database is contained, the range containing the criteria, and the range to which you want records copied/extracted (if applicable).

Advanced Filter dialog box

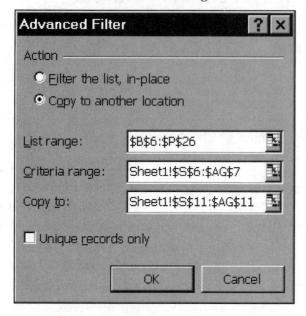

- To set up the criteria range, you simply copy the field names from the top of the database to another area of the worksheet.

  - Usually you create the criteria range several rows above or below the database.

  - The criteria range must be copied to the same worksheet.

  - The labels in the criteria range must exactly match the labels used in the database, which is why you should copy them rather than typing them.

  - After the criteria range is established, you type the criteria under the appropriate field name(s).

    ✓ *For example, to display only records belonging to Smith, you might type* Smith *under the Last Name field name in the criteria range you've established.*

- To make the correct range references appear automatically in the Advanced Filter dialog box, assign the range names Database, Criteria, and Extract.

  - You're not required to assign all three range names — just assign the ranges you want to use with the database.

- Remember to redefine the range names as necessary to include any rows and/or columns you've added to the database, criteria, or extract ranges.

Guidelines for Entering Criteria

- You enter criteria in the criteria range, below the field names you copied.

  ✓ *The following examples are strictly for purposes of demonstration; the field names and contents of your database will likely differ from those shown here.*

- If you want to establish an AND condition, where two or more criteria must be true for a record to match, then type the criteria under their proper field names in the same row.

  ✓ *For example, to display records where the quantity on hand is over 25 AND the cost is less than $10, type both criteria in the same row.*

- If you want to establish an OR condition, where any of two or more criteria will qualify a record as a match, then type the criteria under their proper field names, but in separate rows.

  ✓ *For example, to display records where the quantity on hand is over 25 OR the cost is less than $10, type the criteria in different rows.*

- When you enter text, Excel looks for any match beginning with that text.

  ✓ *Typing* Sam *under the First Name label would match records such as* Sam, Samuel, *and* Samantha.

- You can use wildcards when entering text criteria.

  - A question mark (?) can be used to replace a single character in a specific position within the text.

    ✓ *For example, type* Sm?th *under the Last Name label to get* Smith *and* Smyth.

  - An asterisk (*) can be used to replace none or several characters within the text.

    ✓ *For example, type* Sm*th *under the Last Name label to get* Smith, Smyth, Smouth, *and* Smaningfith.

  - Because ? and * are assumed to be wildcards, if you want to find records that actually contain those characters, you must precede them with a tilde (~).

    ✓ *For example, type* RJ4~?S2 *to get* RJ4?S2.

- You can use operators to compare text, numbers, or dates.
  - Operators include < (less than), > (greater than), <= (less than or equal to), >= (greater than or equal to), <> (not equal to) and = (equal to).
  - For example, enter *>256000* under the *Annual Salary* label to get all records that contain an annual salary over $256,000.
  - You can use operators with dates as well. For example, enter *>=01/01/99* under the *Hire Date* label to get all records with a hire date on or after January 1, 1999.
  - You can also use operators with text, as in *<M*, which will display all records beginning with the letters *A* through *L*.
- You can use formulas to specify criteria.
  - For example, to display only records where the total sale (stored in column G) is greater than the average of column G, you could enter something like this for cell G5:

    =G5>AVERAGE($G$5:$G$21)

  - G5 in this example is the first cell in the database in column G.
  - You could also use the label cell (G4) or the label itself, as in this formula:

    ="Total Sales">AVERAGE($G$5:$G$21)

  - The comparison cell address uses relative cell addressing, while the rest of the formula must use absolute cell addresses (preceded by $).
  - To use a formula to specify criteria, type it in a cell that *doesn't* have a label above it.
    - ✓ For this reason, it's usually best to type a formula in the first column to the right of the criteria range you originally established.
  - Be sure to redefine the criteria range to include the cell that contains the formula and the blank cell above it.
  - You can use more than one formula by typing the second formula in the next column, and adjusting the criteria range again.
    - ✓ If you need to use two formulas, and either one may be true in order to get a match, then type them in the same column, in different rows.
    - ✓ See examples below for placement of formulas in the criteria range.

Ace Computer Sales

Salesperson	Computer	Sale Amt.	
Smith	Maxima	$ 1,230.00	
Parker	Ultima	$ 1,505.00	
Jones	Ultima	$ 1,495.00	
Parker	Maxima	$ 1,280.00	
Smith	Maxima	$ 1,280.00	
Jones	Maxima	$ 1,340.00	← Database
Parker	Ultima	$ 1,590.00	
Parker	Ultima	$ 1,620.00	
Smith	Maxima	$ 1,320.00	
Jones	Ultima	$ 1,580.00	

Salesperson	Computer	Sale Amt.	
Smith	Maxima	>1250	← Criteria Range

Salesperson	Computer	Sale Amt.	
Smith	Maxima	$ 1,280.00	← Result List
Smith	Maxima	$ 1,320.00	

Examples of Advanced Criteria

- To display records for Smith and Jones, type these criteria, in two rows, under the Name field.
  - ✓ As on the preceding pages, the following examples show some typical database field names. Be sure to copy the field names from your own database to the criteria range.

Name	Computer	Sale Amt.
Smith		
Jones		

- To display records for Smith where the total sale amount is over $1,200, type these criteria in one row under the appropriate field names:
  - ✓ You could also display these records with the proper selections from two AutoFilter lists.

Name	Computer	Sale Amt.
Smith		>1200

- To display Smith's sales records of Maxima computers with a total sales amount more than $1,250, type this in one row:
  - ✓ Again, you could display these records using the AutoFilter.

Name	Computer	Sale Amt.
Smith	Maxima	>1250

- To display records for both Smith and Jones that have a sale amount over $1,250, type this in two rows:

Name	Computer	Sale Amt.
Smith		>1250
Jones		>1250

- To display records that have a sale amount over $1,250 or that involve Maxima computers (no matter what amount), type this in two rows:

Name	Computer	Sale Amt.
	Maxima	
		>1250

- To display records of sales of Maxima computers over $1,250, type this in one row:

Name	Computer	Sale Amt.
	Maxima	>1250

- To display records of sales of Maxima or Ultima computers over $1,250, type this in two rows:

Name	Computer	Sale Amt.
	Maxima	>1250
	Ultima	>1250

- To display records whose sale amount is greater than or equal to the average, type this in a cell without a label:

  ✓ *Be sure to name the criteria range to include the cell in which you type the formula and the blank cell above it.*

Sale Amt.	
	=C2>AVERAGE($C$2:$C$17)

- To display records whose sale amounts are between $1,250 and $2,000, type this in two cells without a label in the same row, but in different columns:

  ✓ *Don't type this in the cell below the* Sale Amt. *label — it won't work.*

Computer	Sale Amt.		
		=C2>1250	=C2<2000

- To display records whose total sale is greater than the average OR over $2,000, type this in two rows, but in the same column:

Sale Amt.	
	=C2>AVERAGE($C$2:$C$17)
	=C2>2000

Remove an In-place Advanced Filter

- Unlike the AutoFilter, an advanced filter applied in-place to the database isn't easily detectable.
  - When you open the Data, Filter submenu, there's no check mark next to Advanced Filter to indicate that an advanced filter has been applied.

    ✓ *Notice that the Show All option is available, however.*

  - If the row numbers in the database are blue and the AutoFilter down-arrow buttons aren't visible, an advanced filter is in place.

- To remove an in-place advanced filter, click in the database and choose Data, Filter, Show All.

Edit Extracted Records

- If you elect to copy (extract) **extract range** records to another area of the worksheet (called the results list), you can edit them as needed.

- You can change, format, print, sort, delete, and otherwise manipulate the extracted records as needed.

- Even if you alter the extracted records, it won't affect the original records stored in the database.

- This allows you to create a customized, professional-looking report with the extracted records.

- You can even delete some of the extracted records if you don't want to work with them.

Procedures

Set Up a Criteria Range

✓ *After setting up a criteria range, you're ready to perform filtering using the Advanced Filter dialog box.*

1. Select the range that contains the database labels.

2. Click the **Copy** button 🖺 .... `Ctrl`+`C`

3. Click in the worksheet where you want to establish the criteria range.

   ✓ *The criteria range must be located in the same worksheet as the database.*

   ✓ *Typically, you create a criteria range below the database, separated from it by a few rows.*

4. Click the **Paste** button 🖺 .... `Ctrl`+`V`

5. Enter criteria in row(s) directly below the appropriate criteria labels.

   ✓ *Remember that formulas, if you use them, must be entered in cells that don't have a label above them.*

Set Up an Advanced Filter

1. Set up the criteria range as described in the earlier procedure.

2. Click in any cell within the database.

3. Click **Data** .... `Alt`+`D`

4. Click **Filter** .... `F`

5. Click **Advanced Filter** .... `A`

6. If necessary, in the **List range** text box, type or select the range containing the database .... `Alt`+`L`

7. Click **Criteria Range** .... `Alt`+`C`

8. Type or select the criteria range.

   ✓ *Include the criteria label(s) with the criteria.*

   ✓ *If the criteria includes a formula, include the blank cell(s) above the cell(s) containing the formula.*

9. Select **Filter the list, in-place** .... `Alt`+`F`

   OR

   Select **Copy to another location** .... `Alt`+`O`

10. If you wish to copy (extract) the matching records, click **Copy to** .... `Alt`+`T`

11. Type or select the range to which you want the results list copied.

    ✓ *The range must be located in the same worksheet as the database.*

    ✓ *If you indicate a single cell as the Copy to range, Excel copies the filtered results to cells below and to the right of the cell, overwriting existing data without warning.*

12. If you don't want to display/extract duplicate records, select **Unique records only** .... `Alt`+`R`

13. Click **OK** .... `Enter`

Show All Records in a Filtered List

1. Click **Data** .... `Alt`+`D`

2. Click **Filter** .... `F`

3. Click **Show All** .... `S`

Exercise Directions

1. Start Excel, if necessary.

2. Open ✏️74_ACCTPAY.

3. Save the file as **XL_74**.

4. Select the range D7:J7 (the column labels).

5. Copy the range to row 27.

6. Extract the records for April Carroll to row 31:

   a. Type *April Carroll* in cell E28.

   b. Click a cell in the database.

   c. Open the Advanced Filter dialog box.

   d. Select Copy to another location.

   e. Select the criteria range D27:J28.

   f. Select the copy to range D33:J33.

7. Create an invoice for April:

   a. Type the word *Total* in cell I37.

   b. In cell J37, type a formula to compute the total balance that April owes.

   c. Format the invoice however you like. For example, you might format cell I37 with bold, and add a title to the invoice.

   d. Select the invoice range.

   e. Open the File menu and select Print.

   f. Choose Selection and click OK to print the invoice.

8. Extract all the records for Big M insurance where no payment has been made:

   a. Clear cell E28 and type *Big M* in cell H28.

   b. Type *0* (zero) in cell I28.

   c. Click a cell in the database.

   d. Open the Advanced Filter dialog box.

   e. Select Copy to another location.

   f. Select the criteria range D27:J28.

   g. Select the copy to range D33:J33.

   h. Sort the records by invoice amount.

   i. Select the invoice range and print it.

9. Extract the records for Big M, Med One, and Med First where no payment has been made.

   a. Type *Med One* in cell H29, and type *0* in cell I29.

   b. Type *Med First* in cell H30, and type *0* in cell I30.

   c. Click a cell in the database.

   d. Open the Advanced Filter dialog box.

   e. Select Copy to another location.

   f. Select the criteria range D27:J30.

   g. Select the copy to range D33:J33.

   h. Sort the results list by invoice date so that the most recent invoices are on top.

   i. Type a formula in cell G38, to compute the total of the unpaid insurance claims.

   j. Select the extract range and its total and print it.

10. Extract only the records with an outstanding amount over 25% of the original amount:

    a. Delete the old criteria in the range H28:I30.

    b. Type this formula in cell K28:
       =J8>$G$8*.25

    c. Click a cell in the database.

    d. Open the Advanced Filter dialog box.

    e. Select Copy to another location.

    f. Select the criteria range K27:K28.

    g. Select the copy to range D33:J33.

    h. Sort the list by invoice date so that the oldest invoices are on top.

    i. Select the extract range and print it.

11. Extract only the records with an invoice date in February:

    The formula in this example uses the DATE function, which returns the value of a date (the number of days from 1/1/1900 until the date entered). This value can then be compared to the values (the dates) in column F.

    a. Type this formula in cell K28:
       =F8>=DATE(1999,2,1)

    b. Type this formula in cell L28:
       =F8<=DATE(1999,2,28)

    c. Click a cell in the database.

    d. Open the Advanced Filter dialog box.

    e. Select Copy to another location.

    f. Select the criteria range K27:L28.

    g. Select the copy to range D33:J33.

    h. Sort the extracted records by medical insurance company (key 1), and then by invoice date (key 2).

    i. Select and print the extract range.

12. Save and close the workbook.

13. Exit Excel.

On Your Own

1. Start Excel, if necessary.

2. Open ✑ **74_PETS**.

3. Save the file as **OXL_74**.

4. Use an advanced filter to create a list of items that need to be reordered.

   ✓ *An item needs to be reordered if its current inventory is below the Reorder When value.*

   ✓ *Use the formula =F6<G6.*

5. Modify the extract range so you can use it as your order form.

   a. Order 10 cases of each pet food product.

   b. Order 2 cases each of the larger items, like dog beds and scratching posts.

   c. Order 4 cases of the smaller items, like bones, leashes, and toys.

6. Compute the total cost of the order.

   a. First, calculate the cost per product by multiplying the cases ordered by the price per case.

   b. Total the cost of the order.

   c. Add in extra costs like tax (6%) and the $100 delivery fee.

7. Format the "order form" however you like.

   a. Make sure you include the company name (Pete's Pets) and its address (214 Main Street, Cumberland, Ohio 45678) on the order form.

   b. Add borders and patterns to make the order form look professional.

8. Print the "order form."

9. Save and close the workbook.

10. Exit Excel.

Exercise 75

◆ **Use Database (List) Functions** ◆ **Excel's Database Functions**

On the Job

Functions can perform many wonderful, automatic calculations such as totaling a range of cells or finding the minimum value. With a database, you may wish to perform these same functions on selected records that meet specific criteria, such as totaling the sales amounts for all the records with the name Bill Barker in the Salesperson field. With database functions, you can perform all sorts of calculations and analyses on your database.

You're the owner of a small toy store called Little Kids Top Shop. You're putting together a big order for goods from various vendors, and you want to use Excel's database functions to help you organize and analyze the data.

Terms

function A preprogrammed calculation. You give a function a particular set of parameters, such as a range of cells, and it calculates the result for you.

argument The parameters for a particular function. All database functions use three arguments: the database/list range, a field from the database, and the criteria you want to use to qualify the function.

database range The range that includes all the database records and the field name row.

field The name of the field you wish to use in the function.

criteria range The range that contains the criteria.

Notes

Use Database (List) Functions

- Excel provides several **functions** specifically designed to be used with a database.

- With one of these functions, you can perform a calculation on records in your database that meet particular criteria.

- You enter the criteria you want to use with the database function by typing the criteria in the worksheet, just as you do with advanced filters.

- All database functions have three **arguments**:
  - The **database range** is the range that includes all the database records and the field name row.

- The **field** is the name of the field you wish to use in the function. Instead of the field name, you can also specify a number that represents the field's *database column* (not the worksheet column).

- The **criteria range** is the range that contains the criteria.

- Each database function follows this format:

  =dfunction(database range, field, criteria range)
  - For example:

    =DSUM(B3:G16, F3, B20:G20)
  - This function totals the values in column F that meet the criteria in the range B20:G20.

- As with other functions, the simplest way to enter a database function is to use the Function Wizard.

■ You can use named ranges in your functions.

- For example, you can name the database and the criteria range.

- This saves you the trouble of typing the range(s) manually.

- It also provides a margin of safety if you copy the functions to other places in the workbook.

■ After you enter a database function, a result is displayed immediately.

- If you change the criteria in the criteria range, the result of the function will also change.

- If you don't want to change the original result but you want to reference the same field in a new function, just make a copy of the field label.

Excel's Database Functions

■ Excel has many functions that are designed specifically to be used with a database.

■ Many of these functions are similar in purpose to functions you've seen before, such as SUM, AVERAGE, and so on.

■ Here's a list of Excel's database functions:

DAVERAGE	Finds the average value in the selected field for records meeting the criteria.
DCOUNT	Counts the cells containing numbers in the selected field for records meeting the criteria.
DCOUNTA	Counts only nonblank cells in the selected field for records meeting the criteria.

DGET	Returns the value in the selected field for the single record meeting the criteria. Displays the error message #NUM! if more than one record meets the criteria.
DMAX	Finds the maximum value in the selected field for records meeting the criteria.
DMIN	Finds the minimum value in the selected field for records meeting the criteria.
DPRODUCT	Multiplies the values in a field times the values in the field used in the criteria.
DSTDEV	Estimates the standard deviation of a sample of the values in the selected field for records meeting the criteria.
DSTDEVP	Calculates the standard deviation for all the values in the selected field for records meeting the criteria.
DSUM	Finds the sum of values in the selected field for records meeting the criteria.
DVAR	Estimates variance based on a sample of the values in the selected field for records meeting the criteria.
DVARP	Calculates variance based on all the values in the selected field for records meeting the criteria.

Procedures

Insert a Database Function by Using the Function Wizard

1. Set up the criteria range in the worksheet.

   ✓ *Follow the steps in Exercise 74 in the procedure "Set Up a Criteria Range."*

2. Select the cell in which you want to display the results of the function.

3. Type an equal sign **(=)** .... ▣

4. Select **More Functions** in the **Functions** list.

5. In the **Function category** list, select

   Database .... `Alt`+`C`, `▼`

6. Select the desired database function in the **Function name** list .... `Alt`+`N`, `▼`

7. Click **OK** .... `Enter`

8. Type or select the database range.

9. Click in the **Field** box .... `Tab`

10. Type or select the field name you want to use in the function.

11. Click in the **Criteria** box ...... `Tab`

12. Type or select the criteria range.

13. Click **OK** .... `Enter`

   ✓ *If you prefer, you can type the database function directly into the cell, rather than using the Function Wizard.*

Exercise Directions

1. Start Excel, if necessary.

2. Open 🖭 **75_TOYS**.

3. Save the file as **XL_75**.

4. Select the range C7:O25 and give it the range name *Database*.

5. Enter the formula for the cost analysis of Wooden Toys, Incorporated:

   a. Type *Wooden Toys, Incorporated* (Don't forget the comma!) in cell E3, under the Vendor label in the criteria range.

   ✓ *Note that the column labels for the criteria range have been copied for you; normally, you would need to do this yourself to create the criteria range, as explained in an earlier exercise.*

   b. In cell F30, enter a formula to compute the total order for Wooden Toys, Incorporated.

   ✓ *Hint: Use the DSUM() function, Database as the database range, O7 as the field, and E2:E3 as the criteria range.*

   ✓ *O7 is the Total Cost field.*

   ✓ *When you type the Database range name in the Formula palette, notice that Excel displays the first few characters from the upper-left corner of the range (the field names) to the right of the Collapse Dialog button. When you enter the address for the field, the Formula palette displays the contents of that field. When you finish the function by specifying the criteria range, the bottom half of the Formula palette displays the result of the function.*

   c. In cell F31, enter a formula to compute the total number of items ordered from Wooden Toys, Incorporated.

   ✓ *Hint: Use the DSUM() function again, but this time, use N7 as the field.*

   ✓ *N7 is the Total # Items field.*

   d. In cell F32, type a formula to calculate the average cost per item ordered from Wooden Toys, Incorporated.

   ✓ *Hint: Use DAVERAGE() this time, and J7 as the field.*

   ✓ *J7 is the Cost per Item field.*

6. Repeat step 4 to compute the totals for JB Toy Warehouse.

   ✓ *Don't change the value in cell E3; that would change the formulas you created in step 5. Instead, type JB Toy Warehouse in cell P3.*

   ✓ *Use the range P2:P3 as the criteria range for your formulas.*

   ✓ *You can continue to use the cells O7, N7, and J7 in your formulas.*

7. Compute the totals for International Imports.

   ✓ *Type International Imports in cell Q3 and use the range Q2:Q3 in your formulas.*

8. In cell F42, enter a formula to display the name of the highest priced item you're ordering.

   ✓ *To get this formula to work, you'll use a combination of the MAX() and the DGET() functions.*

   ✓ *MAX() is a function that finds the maximum value in the given range.*

a. In cell J3, type a formula to compute the maximum price in the Cost per Item field.

  ✓ *Use the MAX() function, and the range J8:J25.*

b. In cell F42, use the DGET() function to create your formula.

  ✓ *Use D7 as the field and J2:J3 as the criteria range.*

  ✓ *The DGET() function returns the value in the field you indicate (in this case, the Description field) for the first record in the database that matches the criteria you typed (in this case, the result of your MAX() formula).*

9. In cell F43, enter a formula to display the name of the lowest priced item you're ordering.

  ✓ *Follow a process similar to the one you used in step 8.*

a. In cell R3, type a formula to compute the minimum price in the Cost per Item field.

  ✓ *Use the MIN() function and the range J8:J25.*

  ✓ *You can't type the formula in cell J3, because you'll change the result of the formula you created in step 8.*

b. In cell F43, use the DGET() function to create your formula.

  ✓ *Use D7 as the field again, and R2:R3 as the criteria range.*

10. Format cells F30, F32, F34, F36, F38, and F40 with Currency format, two decimal places. If desired, widen column F to make the results of the cost analysis look a little better.

11. Print the worksheet.

12. Save and close the workbook.

13. Exit Excel.

On Your Own

1. Start Excel, if necessary.

2. Open ⊛ **75_CATER**.

3. Save the file as **OXL_75**.

4. Insert a column called *Total Weight* and enter a formula that computes the total weight of the cases ordered.

5. Select the database range and name it (use the name *Database*).

6. Prepare the criteria range:

   a. Copy the Vendor label to the range C1:H1.

   b. Copy the name of each vendor underneath one of the labels, in row 2.

7. Create an area at the bottom of the worksheet where you can compute the following for each vendor:

   a. Number of cases ordered.

   b. Average cost per case.

   c. Total weight.

   d. Cost of the order.

   e. Shipping charge.

     ✓ *Calculate $20 for every 50 lbs. of weight.*

   f. Total cost.

     ✓ *This is the cost of the order plus the shipping cost.*

8. Print the worksheet.

9. Save and close the workbook.

10. Exit Excel.

Exercise 76

Skills Covered:

◆ Subtotal a List ◆ Create Nested Subtotals ◆ Remove a Subtotal ◆ Copy a Subtotal ◆ Outline a Worksheet

On the Job

With the Subtotals feature, you can create automatic totals within the records of a database to help you perform more complex analyses. For example, if the database contains sales records for various stores, you can create totals for each store or each salesperson. If the database lists employee information, you can create totals for weekly and annual salaries at each location. With the Subtotals feature, you can total numeric data instantly without having to insert rows, create formulas, and copy data. Instead, it all happens with a few simple clicks.

You're the sales manager of Corporate Computer Solutions, and you've created a worksheet listing the computers sold for today in your various stores. Using Excel's Subtotals feature, you plan to create a thorough analysis.

Terms

function A preprogrammed calculation. For example, the SUM() function totals the values in a specified range.

database function A specialized type of function for databases/lists. For example, the DSUM() function totals the values in a given range, but only for the database records that match criteria you supply.

Notes

Subtotal a List

- With the Subtotals feature, you can quickly insert subtotals between records in a database without having to create custom **functions**.
  - Instead of entering DSUM() formulas to total a field for particular records, you can use the Subtotals feature.
  - For example, you can subtotal a sales database to compute the amount sold by each salesperson on a given day.
  - You can also use the Subtotals feature to insert other **database functions**, such as DCOUNT(), DAVERAGE(), and so on.

- To learn more about using database functions, see Exercise 75.

- The Subtotals feature does the following:
  - Calculates subtotals for each change in the field you indicate.
    - ✓ *For example, if you select the field Salesperson, Excel will create subtotals for each person.*
  - Inserts the totals in a row just below that group of data.
  - Calculates a grand total.
  - Inserts labels so you know what's being totaled/subtotaled.

- Displays the outline controls.

  ✓ *The outline controls allow you to control the level of detail that's displayed.*

Subtotals view

	B	C	D	E	F	G
7		Store	Salesperson	Computer	Model	Price
8		Carmel	Ginny Byer	Maxima	M1245	$ 778.45
9		Carmel	Ginny Byer	Maxima	M1245	$ 799.75
10		Carmel	Ginny Byer	Maxima	M4565	$ 1,180.90
11				**Maxima Total**		$ 2,759.10
12		Carmel	Ginny Byer	Penultima	P2214	$ 2,614.80
13		Carmel	Ginny Byer	Penultima	P2214	$ 2,614.75
14		Carmel	Ginny Byer	Penultima	P3154	$ 3,157.90
15		Carmel	Ginny Byer	Penultima	P4564	$ 3,617.80
16				**Penultima Total**		$12,005.25
17		Carmel	Ginny Byer	Ultima	U1234	$ 1,845.90
18		Carmel	Ginny Byer	Ultima	U4654	$ 1,675.90
19				**Ultima Total**		$ 3,521.80
20			**Ginny Byer Total**			$18,286.15
21		Carmel	John Poole	Maxima	M1245	$ 787.50
22		Carmel	John Poole	Maxima	M1245	$ 792.56
23		Carmel	John Poole	Maxima	M2245	$ 912.80
24				**Maxima Total**		$ 2,492.86
25		Carmel	John Poole	Penultima	P2214	$ 2,487.90
26		Carmel	John Poole	Penultima	P4564	$ 3,613.70
27				**Penultima Total**		$ 6,101.60
28		Carmel	John Poole	Ultima	U4567	$ 1,591.40
29		Carmel	John Poole	Ultima	U4654	$ 1,560.80
30				**Ultima Total**		$ 3,152.20
31			**John Poole Total**			$11,746.66
32		Carmel	Sue Cooper	Maxima	M1245	$ 780.90
33				**Maxima Total**		$ 780.90

\Sheet1 / Sheet2 / Sheet3 /

- Before you use the Subtotals feature, sort the database by the fields you wish to total.

- When you select Subtotals from the Data menu, a dialog box displays, from which you can make several choices:

Subtotals dialog box

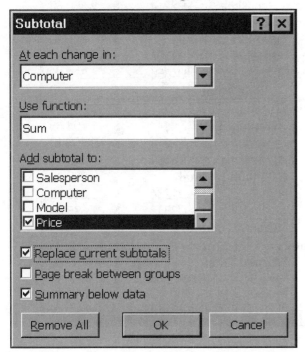

- *At each change in.* Select the field name by which you want to total.

- *Use function.* Select a database function.

- *Add subtotal to.* Select one or more fields to use with the database function you selected.

- *Replace current subtotals.* Select this option to create a new subtotal within a database, leaving the current subtotals intact.

- *Page break between groups.* Places each subtotaled group on its own page.

- *Summary below data.* Inserts the subtotals/grand total below each group, rather than above it.

- *Remove all.* Removes all subtotals.

■ Subtotals act just like any other formula; if you change the data, the total will recalculate automatically.

■ You can use the Subtotals feature on a filtered database.

  - The totals are calculated based only on the displayed records.

  - To learn more about filtering a list with AutoFilter, see Exercise 73.

Create Nested Subtotals

■ You can create subtotals within subtotals (nested subtotals).

■ For example, you could create a subtotal for each salesperson, and for each store (including the entire sales staff for that store).

■ To create nested subtotals:

  - Sort the database by both of the fields you wish to total.

    ✓ *For example, sort by Store (key 1), and then by Salesperson (key 2).*

  - Create the first subtotal using Store as the field.

  - Create the second subtotal using Salesperson as the field, but this time turn off the option to replace the current subtotals (thus keeping the subtotals for the salesperson field intact).

Remove a Subtotal

- You can remove the subtotals from a database by clicking the Remove All button in the Subtotal dialog box.

- You can also remove subtotals by creating new subtotals that replace old ones.

- If you just created the subtotals and you don't like the results, choose Edit, Undo Subtotals to remove the subtotals, and then start over.

Copy a Subtotal

- You can copy the subtotals created by the Subtotals feature to another part of the worksheet.

  ✓ *You could do this to create a custom report, for example.*

- Use Paste Special and select the Paste Values option in the Paste Special dialog box.

Outline a Worksheet

- The Subtotals feature displays the outline controls around the worksheet frame.

- With the outline controls, you can hide or display the records within any given group.

  - For example, you could hide the details of each salesperson's individual sales, and show only his or her subtotal.

  - You could also show details for some salespeople while hiding the details for others.

- To show the detail within a group, click its Show Detail button **+**.

- To hide the detail for a particular group, click the Hide Detail button **–**.

- To show a particular level of detail within a database, click the appropriate outline level button **1** **2** **3**.

  - If you click the highest level button (3 in the illustration), all details are displayed.

  - If you click the lowest level button (1 in the illustration), all detail is hidden — only the grand total is displayed.

Outline level buttons

Outline controls

	B	C	D	E	F	G
48		Glendale	George Billings	Maxima	M1245	$ 775.50
49		Glendale	George Billings	Maxima	M4565	$ 1,250.00
50				**Maxima Total**		$ 2,025.50
51		Glendale	George Billings	Penultima	P2214	$ 2,610.10
52		Glendale	George Billings	Penultima	P2214	$ 2,560.80
53		Glendale	George Billings	Penultima	P3154	$ 3,334.85
54				**Penultima Total**		$ 8,505.75
55		Glendale	George Billings	Ultima	U1234	$ 1,745.60
56		Glendale	George Billings	Ultima	U4654	$ 1,675.80
57				**Ultima Total**		$ 3,421.40
58			**George Billings Total**			$ 13,952.65
61				**Maxima Total**		$ 1,702.35
62		Glendale	Sally Kyte	Penultima	P2214	$ 2,456.10
63		Glendale	Sally Kyte	Penultima	P4564	$ 3,612.30
64				**Penultima Total**		$ 6,068.40
65		Glendale	Sally Kyte	Ultima	U1234	$ 1,810.40
66		Glendale	Sally Kyte	Ultima	U334	$ 1,675.80
67				**Ultima Total**		$ 3,486.20
68			**Sally Kyte Total**			$ 11,256.95
69				**Grand Total**		$ 69,480.33
70			**Grand Total**			$ 69,480.33
71						

Show Detail button

Hide Detail button

Sheet1 / Sheet2 / Sheet3 /

Outline controls

Procedures

Subtotal a Database

✓ *Create subtotals for groups of data in specified fields with a grand total that appears at the bottom of the database. Excel will apply outlining to the resulting subtotals.*

✓ *You can also subtotal a filtered database.*

1. Sort database by the column(s) you want to subtotal.

   ✓ *Items you want to subtotal should be grouped together.*

2. Select any cell in list.
3. Click **Data** .... Alt + D
4. Click **Subtotals** .... B
5. Click **At each change in** .... Alt + A
6. Select field you wish to subtotal .... ⬆⬇, Enter
7. Click **Use Function** ..... Alt + U
8. Select desired function .... ⬆⬇, Enter
9. Select **Add Subtotal to** .... Alt + D
10. Click field(s) containing the values to calculate .... ⬆⬇, Space

To replace current subtotals:
- Select **Replace current subtotals** .... Alt + C

To insert page breaks between subtotaled groups:
- Select **Page break between groups** ... Alt + P

To place subtotals and grand totals above data:
- Deselect **Summary below data** .... Alt + S

11. Click **OK** .... Enter

Remove Automatic Subtotals

1. Select any cell in subtotaled database.
2. Click **Data** .... Alt + D
3. Click **Subtotals** .... B
4. Click **Remove All** .... Alt + D
5. Click **OK** .... Enter

Create Nested Subtotals

1. Sort database by all the fields you wish to subtotal.
2. Subtotal first group in database.

3. Follow steps to subtotal second group in database, but deselect **Replace current subtotals** .... Alt + C
4. Click **OK** .... Enter

Collapse or Expand Outline Levels

Show group details:
- Click the **Show Detail** button **+** for the group you want to expand.

Hide group details:
- Click the **Hide Detail** button **−** for the group you want to collapse.

Show all outline groups for a level:
- Click the row level button 1 2 3 for the lowest level you want to show.

   ✓ *Lower numbers show less detail.*

Exercise Directions

1. Start Excel, if necessary.

2. Open 🖸 **76_SALES**.

3. Save the file as **XL_76**.

4. Sort the database.

   ✓ *Use Store as the first key, Salesperson as the second key, and Computer as the third.*

5. Create subtotals for each store:

   a. Open the Data menu and select Subtotals.

   b. Select Store from the At each change in list.

   c. Select Sum from the Use function list.

   d. Select Price from the Add subtotal to list.

   e. Click OK.

6. If necessary, adjust the width of column G to display the new subtotals.

7. Create subtotals for each salesperson:

   a. Open the Data menu and select Subtotals.

   b. Select Salesperson from the At each change in list.

   c. Select Sum from the Use function list.

   d. Select Price from the Add subtotal to list.

   e. Select the Replace current subtotals option to turn it off.

      ✓ *This will create subtotals for each salesperson within each store.*

   f. Click OK.

8. Create subtotals for each computer type sold by a salesperson:

   a. Open the Data menu and select Subtotals.

   b. Select Computer from the At each change in list.

   c. Select Sum from the Use function list.

   d. Select Price from the Add subtotal to list.

   e. Make sure that the Replace current subtotals option is off.

      ✓ *This will create an additional total for each computer type sold by each salesperson.*

   f. Click OK.

9. Click outline level button 3 to display only the subtotals and the grand total.

10. Print the worksheet.

11. Display the details for Ginny Byer and Sue Cooper.

    ✓ *Hint: Click the plus signs in the rows containing their totals.*

12. Click outline level button 2 to display only the subtotals for the two stores and the grand total.

13. Print the worksheet.

14. Click outline level button 5 to redisplay all records.

15. Remove all subtotals.

    a. Open the Data menu and select Subtotals.

    b. Click Remove All.

16. Create a subtotal that shows the number of computers sold at each store:

    a. Open the Data menu and select Subtotals.

    b. Select Store from the At each change in list.

    c. Select Count from the Use function list (deselect Price).

    d. Select Computer from the Add subtotal to list.

    e. Click OK.

17. Add a subtotal that displays the sales volume at each store.

    a. Open the Data menu and select Subtotals.

    b. Select Store from the At each change in list (deselect Price).

    c. Select Sum from the Use function list.

    d. Select Price from the Add subtotal to list (deselect Computer).

    e. Make sure that the Replace current subtotals option is off.

    f. Click OK.

18. Click outline level button 3 to display the new subtotals.

19. Print the worksheet.

20. Save and close the workbook.

21. Exit Excel.

On Your Own

1. Start Excel, if necessary.

2. Open ☺ 76_APPLIANCE.

3. Save the file as OXL_76.

4. Create subtotals for each state and each store.

   ✓ *Hint: Sort the database first, using State as key 1 and Store as key 2.*

   ✓ *After sorting, use the Data, Subtotals command to create each subtotal.*

   ✓ *Use the Sum function and the Price field.*

   ✓ *After subtotaling the states, create subtotals for the stores. Remember to deselect the Replace current subtotals option so you don't lose the state subtotals.*

5. Display only the subtotals.

   ✓ *If necessary, widen the columns so you can see all the numbers.*

6. Print the worksheet.

7. Clear all subtotals.

8. Create new subtotals for each store, totaling the dollar volume and count for each appliance.

   a. Sort the database by Store and Appliance.

   b. Create a subtotal for each store showing the dollar volume.

   c. Create another subtotal for each appliance type displaying the number of appliances sold. (Retain the dollar subtotals as well.)

9. Print the worksheet.

10. Clear all subtotals.

11. Sort the database again, and create some subtotals of your own choice.

12. Print the worksheet.

13. Save and close the workbook.

14. Exit Excel.

Exercise 77

Skills Covered:

◆ **Create PivotTables and PivotCharts**
◆ **Publish a PivotTable or PivotChart** ◆ **Use PivotTable Toolbar**

On the Job

If you want to analyze complex data, a PivotTable can make the whole process a lot easier. For example, if you have a database containing information such as sales data by product, store, region, and salesperson, you can summarize it in a PivotTable. With the table, you can display totals by region for each product, and then quickly rearrange the table to display sales totals by office and individual salesperson. Or you can combine the tables to display totals by region, office, salesperson, and product. The flexibility of a PivotTable is its greatest asset.

As the sales manager at Java Jungle Café, you keep track of a lot of different sales figures. In this exercise, you'll create a PivotTable and a PivotChart to help you analyze your on-line coffee sales, comparing those sales to the business you do in the store. When the PivotTable is complete, you'll publish it to the Internet and make some additional changes on-line to test the system.

Terms

PivotTable A flexible table that allows you to analyze complex data in a variety of ways.

PivotChart A chart based on PivotTable data.

AutoFormat A set of predesigned formats applied to a worksheet or a PivotTable. Using AutoFormat allows you to format your work quickly, with a more professional look.

Page field A field from an Excel database that's used to create different pages or views within the PivotTable.

Notes

Create PivotTables and PivotCharts

- A **PivotTable** allows you to summarize complex data, such as your company's sales records, accounting records, and so on.
- The advantage of the PivotTable is that it lets you quickly change how the data is summarized.
  - For example, you could change a report that summarizes sales data by region and office to one that summarizes the same data by salesperson and product.

Sample PivotTable

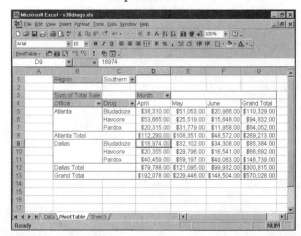

- The source data for a PivotTable may be a text file, a query file, or even a database (list) within an Excel workbook.

- Typically, you lay out the data in the PivotTable after it's created; however, you have the option of letting the PivotTable Wizard create the layout.

  ✓ *You might want to use the wizard to lay out the report when you're dealing with a large amount of data that's difficult to manipulate.*

- After creating a PivotTable report, you can create a matching **PivotChart** as well.

  ✓ *You can also choose to create the PivotChart first.*

- You can format a PivotTable quickly by applying an **AutoFormat**.

Publish a PivotTable or PivotChart

- You can publish a PivotTable to the Internet or your company's intranet.

- The process of publishing a PivotTable or PivotChart is similar to the process of publishing a worksheet, as explained in Lesson 7.

- You can publish a PivotTable or PivotChart with interactivity, which means that others can make changes to it on-line.

- When an interactive PivotTable or PivotChart is viewed in a Web browser, a toolbar appears at the top of the area, providing the tools for making changes.

Changing a PivotTable in a Web browser

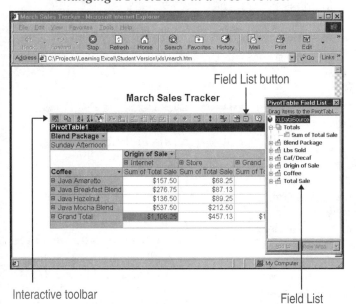

Interactive toolbar

Field List

- The interactive toolbar contains a button that displays the Field List, which enables you to drag and drop fields onto the PivotTable just as you would within Excel.

- Use the Property Toolbox button on the interactive toolbar to display the Property Toolbox, which you can use to change the properties of a cell within the PivotTable (its formatting and such), or some element of a PivotChart.

- Certain characters in column labels of PivotTables, such as decimal points and periods, may cause an error when the published table is opened in a browser. If you get such an error message, change the offending label as noted in the message and republish the table.

Use the PivotTable Toolbar

- After you create a PivotTable, the PivotTable toolbar appears. Use the toolbar to arrange the data in the table.

PivotTable toolbar

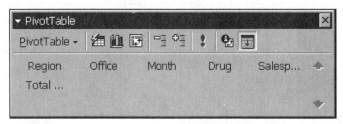

- At the top of the toolbar are typical toolbar buttons that allow you to set table options, refresh data, format the table, create a chart, and so on.

- Under the toolbar buttons are buttons for each column used in the Excel database.

  ✓ *By dragging these buttons into various parts of the table, you can instantly change how the table data is summarized.*

- Items you drag into the body of the table are summarized. Typically, you'll drag numerical items, such as sales amounts, gross revenue, and so on.

  ✓ *In the earlier figure, the item Total Sales was used in the body of the table.*

  ✓ *If you want a count of a body item, right-click its button, select Field Settings, and then select Count.*

- Items you drag into the row area appear in the rows of the table. Items you drag into the column area appear in the columns of the table.

- Initially, all the items under a particular button are displayed and summarized in the table.

  ✓ You can limit the display to one or two items by clicking the down arrow on the appropriate button and selecting the item(s) you want to display.

- In addition to dragging buttons into the body, row, and column areas of the table, you can drag them into the **page fields** area.

  ✓ This allows you to create pages in which only the items relating to a particular category are displayed.

  ✓ In the earlier figure, items for the Southern region only are displayed. You would switch to the Northern region by clicking the down arrow on the Region button and selecting Northern. Or display both regions by selecting (All).

PivotTable drop areas

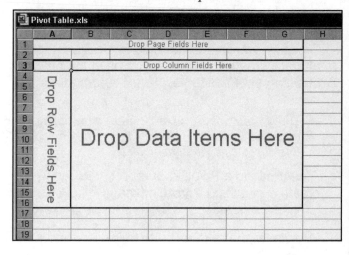

Procedures

Create a PivotTable with an Excel Database

1. Click within the Excel database.

   ✓ If the database has subtotals, remove them before attempting to create a PivotTable.

2. Click **Data**.................... Alt + D

3. Select **PivotTable and PivotChart Report** .... P

4. Select **Microsoft Excel list or database**.......... Alt + M

5. If necessary, click **PivotTable** .... Alt + T

6. Click **Next >** .... Enter

7. Click **Next >** .... Enter

   ✓ The wizard should automatically select the range for the database. If the selection is wrong, you can select the correct range yourself.

8. Select **New worksheet** .... Alt + N
   OR
   Select **Existing worksheet** .... Alt + E

   ✓ If you select this option, you'll need to specify the target location for the PivotTable.

9. Click **Finish** .... Alt + F

   ✓ The PivotTable toolbar appears, with buttons representing each of the columns (fields) in the database.

10. Drag the button for the field you want to show in the table body into the area marked **Drop Data Items Here**.

    ✓ This item is typically a numerical item, such as total sales.

    ✓ The titles of the drop areas may disappear after you drop one button on a certain area. Refer to the drop areas illustration above, if necessary.

11. Drag the button for the item(s) you want to show in separate rows of the table into the area marked **Drop Row Fields Here**.

12. Drag the button for the item(s) you want to show in separate columns of the table into the area marked **Drop Column Fields Here**.

13. If you wish to display only the items related to a particular category, add a page field by dragging the button for that item into the area marked **Drop Page Fields Here**.

    ✓ To remove an item from the table, drag its button outside the table area.

    ✓ To format a PivotTable, click the **Format Report** button on the **PivotTable toolbar** and select a format you like.

Create a PivotChart from a PivotTable

1. Click inside the PivotTable.

2. Click the **Chart Wizard** button on the **PivotTable toolbar** to create the PivotChart automaticlly.

3. Make any adjustments you like.

   • To remove a field from the chart, drag its button off the chart area.

   • To add a field to the chart, drag its button from the **PivotTable toolbar** onto the chart area.

- To change the chart type, click the **Chart Type** button on the **Chart toolbar** and select the chart type you want to use, or use the **Chart** menu.

Apply an AutoFormat to a PivotTable

1. Click inside the PivotTable.
2. Click **Format** .... `Alt`+`O`
3. Click **AutoFormat** .... `A`
4. Click the format you wish to apply.
5. Click **OK** .... `Enter`

Preview a PivotTable or PivotChart Before Publishing

1. Click **File** .... `Alt`+`F`
2. Click **Web Page Preview** .... `B`
3. If necessary, change to the worksheet that contains the PivotTable or PivotChart.
4. When you're finished previewing, close the Web browser.

Publish a Static PivotTable or PivotChart

1. Select the PivotTable or PivotChart you want to publish.
   To select a PivotTable:
   a. Click a cell in the table.
   b. Click **PivotTable** on the PivotTable toolbar ... `Alt`+`P`
   c. Click **Select** .... `S`
   d. Click **Entire Table** .... `T`
   To select a PivotChart:
   - Click the chart sheet.
2. Click **File** .... `Alt`+`F`
3. Click **Save as Web Page** ..... `G`
4. Click **Selection: PivotTable** .... `Alt`+`E`
   OR
   Click **Selection: Chart** .... `Alt`+`E`
5. Click **File name** text box .... `Alt`+`N`
6. Type file name.

To change the title for the Web page:
   a. Click **Change Title** .... `Alt`+`C`
   b. Type new title.
   c. Click **OK** .... `Enter`
7. Click **Publish** .... `Alt`+`P`
8. Click **Open published web page in browser** .... `Alt`+`O`
9. Click **Publish** .... `P`

   ✓ *The Web page is complete and automatically displays in the browser. It will be published as a static page without interactive functionality.*

Publish an Interactive PivotTable or PivotChart

1. Select the PivotTable or PivotChart you want to publish.
   To select PivotTable:
   a. Click a cell in the table.
   b. Click **PivotTable** on the PivotTable toolbar... `Alt`+`P`
   c. Click **Select** .... `S`
   d. Click **Entire Table** .... `T`
   To select a PivotChart:
   - Click the chart sheet.
2. Click **File** .... `Alt`+`F`
3. Click **Save as Web Page** .... `G`
4. Click **Selection: PivotTable** .... `Alt`+`E`
   OR
   Click **Selection: Chart** .... `Alt`+`E`
5. Click **Add interactivity** .... `Alt`+`A`
6. Click **Publish** .... `Alt`+`P`

   ✓ *The Publish as Web Page dialog box displays publishing options.*
7. Select item to publish:
   a. If necessary, click **Choose** and select a worksheet or chart sheet .... `Alt`+`C`
   b. If necessary, click **PivotTable** or **Chart** ...... `↗`

8. If necessary, click **Add interactivity with** .... `Alt`+`A`
   - Select **Chart functionality** or **PivotTable functionality** in the drop-down list.
9. To change the title of the resulting Web page:
   a. Click **Change** .... `Alt`+`H`
   b. Type title.
   c. Click **OK** .... `Enter`
10. To change name of resulting HTML file:
    a. Click **File name** text box .... `Alt`+`N`
    b. Type path and file name.

    ✓ *You can save the file to a temporary location on your hard drive until you are ready to publish it to your assigned Web address.*
11. Click **Open published web page in browser** .... `Alt`+`O`

    ✓ *You can open the file in the browser at another time, if you prefer.*
12. Click **Publish** .... `Alt`+`P`
13. View the file.
14. Close the browser when you've finished.

Republish a Web Report

1. Open the Excel file.
2. Select the range of cells to publish.
3. Click **File** .... `Alt`+`F`
4. Click **Save as Web Page** .... `G`
5. Click **Republish: Chart** or **Republish:PivotTable** .... `Alt`+`E`
6. Select desired publishing options.
7. Click **Publish** .... `Alt`+`P`

Exercise Directions

1. Start Excel, if necessary.
2. Open the file ⊙ **77_COFFEE**.
3. Save the workbook as **XL_77**.
4. Create a PivotTable using the range B10:G89.
   a. Place the PivotTable on Sheet2 in the range beginning in cell B3.
   b. Drag the Coffee button into the area marked Drop Row Fields Here.
   c. Drag the Origin button into the area marked Drop Column Fields Here.
   d. Drag the Lbs Sold button into the area marked Drop Data Items Here.
   e. Drag the Blend button into the area marked Drop Page Fields Here.
5. Display only the Adventurer blend coffees.
   - Print the resulting PivotTable.
6. Add a row to the PivotTable for Caf/Decaf sales.
   ✓ *Drop the Caf button on the right half of the Coffee button.*
7. Display the data by total sale, instead of by pounds sold.
   ✓ *Drag the Lbs Sold button off the table, then drag the Total Sale button into the Drop Data Items Here area.*
8. Display information about the Coffee Lovers blends.
9. Format the sales amounts with Currency format.
   a. Click in cell D5.
   b. Click the Field Settings button on the PivotTable toolbar.
   c. Click the Number button.
   d. Click Currency and click OK.
   e. Click OK again.
10. Print the resulting report.
11. Create a PivotChart and then make these changes:
    a. Remove the Caf/Decaf breakdown.
    b. Change to a Clustered Column chart.
    c. Display the Sunday Afternoon blends.
    d. Print the resulting chart.
12. Save and close the file and exit Excel.

PivotTable

	A	B	C	D	E	F
1		Blend Package	Sunday Afternoon ▼			
2						
3		Sum of Total Sale	Origin of Sale ▼			
4		Coffee ▼	Internet	Store	Grand Total	
5		Java Amaretto	$157.50	$68.25	$225.75	
6		Java Breakfast Blend	$276.75	$87.13	$363.88	
7		Java Hazelnut	$136.50	$89.25	$225.75	
8		Java Mocha Blend	$537.50	$212.50	$750.00	
9		Grand Total	$1,108.25	$457.13	$1,565.38	
10						
11						
12		PivotTable ☒				
13		PivotTable ▼				
14						
15						

PivotChart

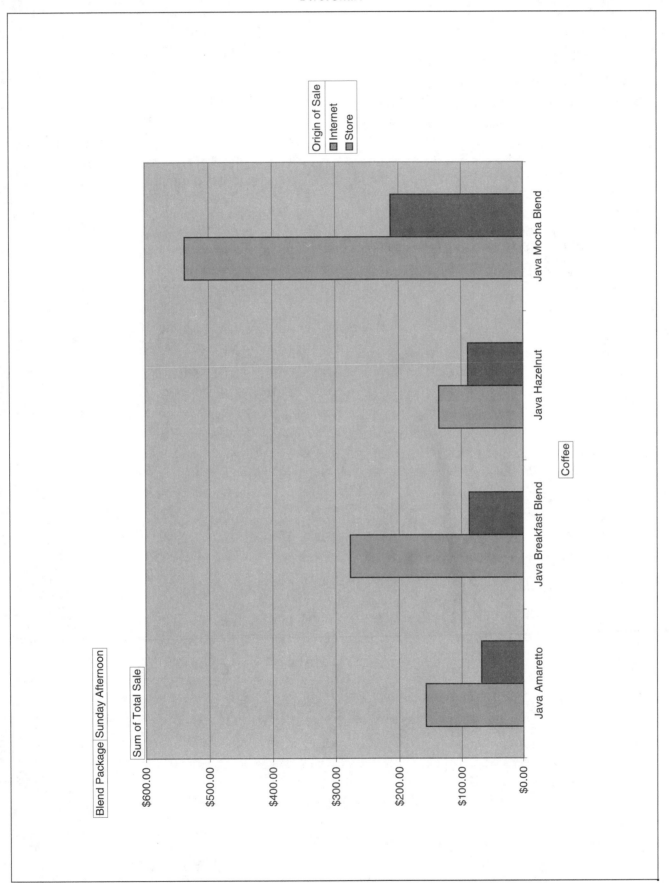

On Your Own

1. Start Excel, if necessary.
2. Open the file ⊘ **77_PETS**.
3. Save the workbook as **OXL_77**.
4. Create a PivotTable with the range B9:F49.
   - ✓ *Before creating the PivotTable, sort the database by the fields you intend to use for the PivotTable. (See step 5.)*
   - • Save the PivotTable on Sheet2.
5. Organize the information in the table however you like.
   - ✓ *For example, you might use Salesperson as a row heading and Description as a column heading. You might also add Product Type as a page field. Use Cost as the body of the table.*
6. Format the table using the Format Report button on the PivotTable toolbar.
7. Print the resulting table.
8. Create a PivotChart.
   a. Change the chart type.
   b. Adjust the display of data until you like the result.
   c. Print the chart.
9. Save and close the file and exit Excel.

Exercise 78

◆ **Data Consolidation**
◆ **Create Consolidation Tables**

On the Job

Excel's data-consolidation feature allows you to consolidate the data from similar worksheets into a single worksheet. For example, you may have a workbook that contains separate worksheets for three months' worth of sales. After consolidation, you have a single worksheet that contains the totals for the three-month period. Of course, you can use other database functions, too; for example, you could consolidate the three sales worksheets to find the average sales per month.

You're the sales director of Corporate Computer Solutions, and you've just received the last figures you need to complete the March sales worksheet. Your boss has asked you to compile the totals for the first quarter. After the totals are compiled, you'll create a pie chart to help you analyze the sales trends for the quarter.

Terms

consolidation by category Consolidating data from worksheets that are designed similarly into a single worksheet.

consolidation by position Consolidating data from worksheets that aren't set up as databases.

consolidation table The table of consolidated data that results from using the Data, Consolidate command.

Notes

Consolidate Data

■ With Excel's Data, Consolidate command, you can consolidate data from separate ranges into a single worksheet.

- The data can come from the same worksheet, separate worksheets, and even separate workbooks.

- You can consolidate similarly structured databases using the **consolidate by category** option.

- Consolidate non-database data using the **consolidate by position** option.

■ You consolidate data by completing the Consolidate dialog box.

Consolidate dialog box

Select function

Data to consolidate

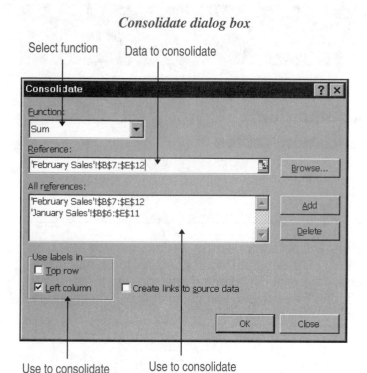

Use to consolidate by category

Use to consolidate multiple workbooks

Create a Consolidation Table

- Follow these general guidelines when making choices in the Consolidate dialog box to create your **consolidation table**:
  - Select the function you want to use, such as SUM, AVERAGE, COUNT, and so on.
  - Add as many ranges as needed to the All References list.
  - Copy the column and row labels from the database with the options in the Use labels in area of the dialog box.
  - If the data you want to consolidate is located in different workbooks, use the Create links to source data option to have Excel update the table automatically whenever the source data changes.

Procedures

Consolidate Data by Category

✓ *Consolidate by category with databases, when all source data appears in the same order and uses the same category labels.*

1. If data comes from separate workbooks, open and arrange the workbooks on the screen.
2. Change to the destination worksheet.
3. Click in the upper-left cell of the range in which you want the consolidated data to appear.

4. Click **Data** .... `Alt`+`D`
5. Click **Consolidate** .... `N`
6. Click **Function** .... `Alt`+`F`
7. Select function you want to use .... `↕`, `Enter`
8. Click **Reference** .... `Alt`+`R`
9. Select or type the first range you want to consolidate.
10. Click **Add** .... `Alt`+`A`
   ✓ *The range is added to the **All references** list.*

11. Repeat steps 8 to 10 for each range you wish to consolidate.
12. To create a link to the source data, select **Create links to source data** .... `Alt`+`S`
   ✓ *You can't link the data if the destination range and the source data are on the same worksheet.*

13. Click **OK** .... `Enter`

348

Exercise Directions

1. Start Excel, if necessary.
2. Open ✺ 78_SALES.
3. Save the file as **XL_78**.
4. Switch to the March Sales worksheet.
5. Complete the worksheet by entering the data in the table below:

	Lexton Laser 1100e	Lexton ColorJet 345	Lexton All in 1
George Billings	$131,547	$56,784	$131,456
Sally Kyte	$91,457	$87,541	$75,847
Bob Smith	$75,984	$75,847	$124,156
John Poole	$81,456	$66,879	$134,578
Ginny Byer	$139,478	$75,147	$98,147

- Add formulas in row 14 to total the new data.

6. Insert a new worksheet behind the March Sales worksheet.
7. Rename the worksheet *Qtr 1 Sales*.
8. Copy the graphic and the title from the March Sales worksheet to the new worksheet.

   ✓ *Place the graphic and the title in approximately the same spot on the Qtr 1 Sales worksheet as on the March Sales worksheet.*

9. Click in cell B7 of the Qtr 1 Sales sheet.
10. Click Data and select Consolidate.
11. Select the SUM function.
12. Select the range B7:H12 in the January Sales worksheet and click Add.
13. Add the range for the February Sales worksheet.

14. Add the range for the March Sales worksheet.

    ✓ *Make sure to click the Add button each time.*

15. Select the options to use both the Top row and Left column labels.
16. Click OK to create the consolidation table.
17. Format the new table in a manner similar to that of the tables on the other worksheets:

    a. Select the range B7:H7.

    b. Format it with Arial, 9 points, centered, with White text and a Violet fill.

    c. Select the range B8:B14.

    d. Format it with Arial, 10 points, bold with a Gray-25% fill.

       ✓ *Hint: Since you're duplicating existing formats, you can use the Format Painter to save time.*

    e. Adjust the width of the columns to fit the data.

18. Type *Totals* in cell B14, and format it as Arial, 10 points, bold, Dark Blue.
19. Type a formula in cell C14 to total the sales for Maxima computers.
20. Copy the formula to the range D14:H14.
21. Select the range C7:H7. Then hold down Ctrl and select the range C14:H14 as well.
22. Click the Chart Wizard button and create a pie chart using the data you just selected.

    a. Place the chart on the Qtr 1 Sales worksheet.

    b. Format the chart however you like.

23. Print the chart and the Qtr 1 Sales worksheet.
24. Save the workbook and close it.
25. Exit Excel.

On Your Own

1. Start Excel, if necessary.
2. Open 🖫 78_APPLIANCE.
3. Save the file as **OXL_78**.
4. Consolidate the sales data from Monday to Sunday into a single table.
   a. Use the SUM function.
   b. Place the consolidated table on Sheet2.
   c. Format the table however you like.
5. Create a chart that depicts the number of appliances sold by each salesperson.
   a. Use the Clustered column chart type with 3-D visual effect.
   b. Place the chart on its own worksheet.
   c. Format the chart as you wish.
   d. Print the chart.
6. On Sheet2, create a second consolidation table to show the average sales per day.
   a. Use the same ranges.
   b. Choose the AVERAGE function.
   c. Format the table however you like.
7. Create another chart, this one depicting the average sales by salesperson.
   a. Use an exploded pie chart.
   b. Place the chart on its own worksheet.
   c. Format the chart however you like.
   d. Print the chart.
8. Name all the worksheets appropriately.
9. Move the sheet with the consolidated data to the front, just behind the original worksheet (Jan 4 – 10).
10. Save and close the workbook.
11. Exit Excel.

Exercise 79

◆ **Critical Thinking**

You're a legal secretary for the law firm of Peterson, Barney, and Smith, and your boss, Mark Brandon, has asked you to go over his expense report before he turns it in to the Accounting Department.

Exercise Directions

1. Start Excel, if necessary.
2. Open ✆79_EXPENSES.
3. Save the file as **XL_79**.
4. Format the Expense column with Currency format, two decimal places.
5. Mr. Brandon wants a quick listing of his private charges from February 1st to the 10th:
   a. Open the Data menu, select Filter, and then select AutoFilter.
   b. Open the AutoFilter list in the Date column and select Custom.
   c. Set the first criterion to *is greater than or equal to 2/1/99*.
   d. Select And.
   e. Set the second criterion to *is less than or equal to 2/10/99*.
   f. Select Private from the Expense Type AutoFilter list.
6. Print the report.
7. Mr. Brandon wants a report detailing his expenses, sorted from the most expensive to the least expensive, excluding any private expenses:
   a. Use the Data, Filter, Show All command to show all records.
   b. Open the AutoFilter list in the Client column and select NonBlanks. (Private expenses don't list a client, so those expenses have a blank cell in the Client column.
   c. Click in the Expense column and then click the Sort Descending button to sort the database.

8. Print the report.
9. Turn the AutoFilter off.
10. Mr. Brandon wants a quick summary of expenses per client, with subtotals for each type of expense.
    a. Sort the database by Client (key 1) and Expense Type (key 2).
    b. Open the Data menu and select Subtotals.
    c. For each change in Client, create a Sum of Expense.
    d. Create additional subtotals for each change in Expense Type.
       ✓ *Don't replace the first subtotals.*
11. Hide the detail for the private expenses.
12. Print the report.
13. Remove all subtotals.
14. Mr. Brandon also needs a report detailing his average expenses by type.
    a. Sort the database by Expense Type (key 1) and by Expense (key 2).
    b. Open the Data menu and select Subtotals.
    c. For each change in Expense Type, create an Average of Expense.
15. Print the report.
16. Remove all subtotals.
17. Save and close the workbook.
18. Exit Excel.

Lesson 11

Create Macros and Hyperlinks

Exercise 80

- ◆ Record a Macro
- ◆ Stop Recording
- ◆ Run a Macro

Exercise 81

- ◆ Open a Workbook Containing Macros
- ◆ Edit a Macro
- ◆ Delete a Macro
- ◆ Assign a Macro to a Toolbar Button
- ◆ Assign a Macro to a Graphic Control

Exercise 82

- ◆ Link Documents with Hyperlinks
- ◆ Add a Hyperlink to a Worksheet

Exercise 83

- ◆ Critical Thinking

Exercise 80

Skills Covered:

◆ **Record a Macro** ◆ **Stop Recording** ◆ **Run a Macro**

On the Job

A macro is a recorded series of actions. If you perform certain tasks frequently — such as opening a workbook, moving to a particular page, and inserting the current date — you can record these actions and play them back quickly and easily so that Excel performs the commands for you.

It's time again to recap the monthly income and expenses from your business, the Java Jungle Café. This time around, however, you're going to use your new knowledge of macros to help speed up an otherwise boring and repetitive task — formatting the worksheet.

Terms

macro A series of recorded actions that can be replayed when needed. The recorded actions are carried out automatically for the user.

play a macro Execute the macro commands.

absolute reference Refers to a specific location in an Excel worksheet.

relative reference Refers to a location that's relative to the original cell used in the macro.

Notes

Record a Macro

- A **macro** is a series of actions that are recorded and saved in a file.

  ✔ *You might record a series of actions you perform routinely, such as searching for an item in a worksheet, copying or moving data, entering company or personal information, inserting common formulas, and so on.*

- When you **play a macro**, the recorded actions are performed automatically, without any intervention from you.

- Before recording a macro, you should plan the steps you want to record.

  ✔ *You may even want to write down the steps so you don't do something out of order.*

- You also need to decide whether you will use **absolute references** or **relative references** in the macro.

- Suppose you record a relative macro with B7 as the active cell.

- During the macro recording, you click cell B2, type your name, and apply bold formatting to the text.

- You later play the macro with D9 as the active cell.

- The data and formatting will be entered in cell D4, which is located in the same column, five rows up. This cell has the same relationship to the active cell (D9) as cell B2 had to the active cell during recording process (B7).

- If you record the same macro with absolute referencing, your name and the bold formatting will always be entered in cell B2.

- By default, macros are recorded in absolute mode.
  - You can change to relative mode before recording any actions.
  - You can also change to relative mode during the recording process.
- You need to select a name for the new macro.
  - The name can't include spaces, but you can use an underscore instead, as in Format_Red.
  - The name should be descriptive enough to help you identify the purpose of the macro later.
  - For example, for a macro that inserts and formats a company header at the top of worksheet, you could use the name CoHeader.
- Another decision you need to make before recording a macro is where to save the macro.
  - If you save the macro in the current workbook, you can use it within any of that workbook's worksheets.
  - If you save the macro in the Personal Macro Workbook, you can use the macro within any Excel workbook.
  - You can also save the macro in a new workbook if you would like to use the macro with certain workbooks, but not all workbooks.
    - ✓ You'll need to open this "macro workbook" prior to using the macros with any other Excel workbook.
- Finally, you should decide on a keyboard shortcut (such as Ctrl+J) you can use to start the macro.
  - Although not required, a keyboard shortcut allows you to test and then later run the macro quickly and easily.
  - If you don't assign a keyboard shortcut to the macro, you can run the macro by selecting it from the Macro dialog box.
  - The shortcut key you select is paired with the Ctrl key to create the keyboard shortcut, as in Ctrl+J. You can also press Shift when selecting a key to get the key combination Ctrl+Shift, as in Ctrl+Shift+J.

- Avoid using the standard shortcut combinations Ctrl+X (cut), Ctrl+C (copy), Ctrl+V (paste), Ctrl+P (print), Ctrl+S (save), etc. for macros.
- You can assign a macro to a toolbar button at any time, regardless of whether it already has a shortcut key assigned.

Stop Recording

- When you begin to record a macro, the Stop Recording toolbar appears.
- Use this toolbar to stop the recording process.
- The toolbar also contains a button that you can use to change between absolute and relative recording modes.

Stop Recording toolbar

Stop Recording button → ■   ← Relative Reference button

- Click the Stop Recording button at any time to stop recording the macro.
- Click the Relative Reference button to change from absolute to relative cell referencing.
  - ✓ You can switch between relative and absolute cell referencing as many times as needed during the macro recording.
  - ✓ The Relative Reference button is a toggle. When the button is selected (pressed), it sets relative references. When deselected (raised), which is the default setting, it sets absolute references.

Run a Macro

- To run a macro after you've recorded it, you need to open the workbook in which the macro was saved.
  - ✓ If you saved the macro in the Personal Macro Workbook, this workbook is opened for you automatically.
- You can run the macro by pressing the keyboard shortcut or by selecting the name of the macro from the Macro dialog box.

Macro dialog box

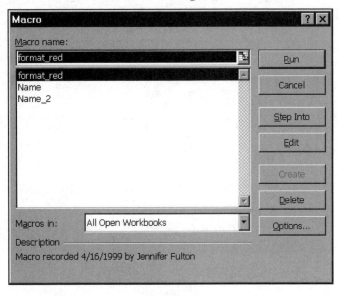

- If you have assigned a macro to a toolbar button, you can click that button to run the macro.
  - ✓ You'll learn how to assign a macro to a toolbar button in Exercise 81.

Procedures

Record a Macro

1. Click **Tools**................. `Alt`+`T`
2. Click **Macro**........................ `M`
3. Click **Record new macro** ... `R`
4. Click in the **Macro name** text box....................... `Alt`+`M`
5. Type macro name.
   - ✓ The macro name can't contain spaces.
6. Click **Description**........ `Alt`+`D`
7. Type macro description (optional).
8. If you want, assign a shortcut key to the macro:
   a. Select **Shortcut key** .... `Alt`+`K`
   OR
   Click in **Ctrl+** box .... `Tab`
   b. If you want, press.......... `Shift`
   c. Type the letter you want to use as the shortcut.

   - ✓ If the letter is already in use, Excel will notify you when you click OK in step 10.

9. Specify where you want the macro stored:
   a. Select **Store macro in** box......................... `Alt`+`I`
   b. Select a location.............. `↕`, `Enter`
10. Click **OK** .... `Enter`
11. To set recording references to relative or absolute:
    - Click the **Relative Reference** button 🔳 on the Stop Recording toolbar to select or deselect this option.
12. Perform the actions you want recorded.
    - ✓ Toggle the **Relative Reference** button as needed while you're recording.

13. Click the **Stop Recording** button ■ on the Stop Recording toolbar to end recording.

Run a Macro

- Press assigned keyboard shortcut .... `Ctrl`+*letter*
OR
- If Shift was used in the shortcut ...... `Ctrl`+`Shift`+*letter*
OR
1. Click **Tools** .... `Alt`+`T`
2. Click **Macro** .... `M`
3. Click **Macros** .... `M`
   OR
   Press **Alt+F8** .... `Alt`+`F8`
4. Select macro in **Macro name** list .... `Tab`, `↓` `↑`
5. Click **Run** .... `Alt`+`R`

Exercise Directions

1. Start Excel, if necessary, and open ⊙80_COFFEE.

2. Save the workbook as **XL_80**.

3. Create a macro called *CoName*.

   ✓ *You'll use this macro in the next part of this exercise, which you'll complete in Exercise 81.*

   a. Save the macro in this workbook.

   b. Assign the shortcut Ctrl+Shift+C.

   c. Use absolute reference mode.

4. Record the following actions:

   a. Type the name *Java Jungle Cafe* in cell C5.

   ✓ *Click the Enter button on the formula bar to complete the entry, rather than pressing Enter. This saves you from having to return to cell C5 — an additional step that would be recorded in the macro.*

   b. Apply Impact font, 24 points. Merge and center the title in cells C5:F5, and add a Light Yellow solid color fill.

   c. In cell C6, type *Coffee Shop Income*.

   d. Apply Arial, 10 points, bold. Merge and center the subtitle in cells C6:F6, and add a Tan solid color fill.

   e. Stop the macro recording.

5. Click in cell B11, and create a macro called *Std_Format*.

   a. Save the macro in this workbook.

   b. Assign the shortcut Ctrl+Shift+F.

   c. Add a macro description, if you like.

   d. Use relative reference mode.

6. Record the following actions:

   a. Hold down the Shift key as you press End, release End, and press the right-arrow key to select the range B11:D11.

   ✓ *Use the arrow keys and End-and-arrow combinations to record the macro so that it can be used to format areas of varying size. The End key is a toggle, so you must press and release it before you press an arrow key.*

   b. Apply Arial, bold, centered, 9 points. Add a Light Yellow solid color fill.

   c. Press the left-arrow key, and then the down-arrow key, so the cell pointer is in cell A12.

   d. Hold down the Shift key. Then press and release End and press the down-arrow key so that the range A12:A24 is selected.

   e. Apply Arial, 10 points, italic, right-aligned. Add a Tan solid color fill.

   f. Press End, press the down-arrow key, press End, and press the down-arrow key so that cell A26 is selected.

   g. Apply Arial, 10 points, bold. Add a Tan solid color fill.

   h. Press End and press the right-arrow key so that cell C26 is selected. Hold down the Shift key as you press and release End and then press the right-arrow key to select cell D26 as well.

   i. Apply Arial, 10 points, bold. Add a Light Yellow solid color fill.

   j. Press End and then press the right-arrow key to select cell D26 only, and apply Accounting format, two decimal places.

   k. Press the up-arrow key twice to move to cell D24. Press End and then press the up-arrow key to jump to cell D11, and then press the down-arrow key to move to cell D12.

   l. Hold down the Shift key as you press and release End and then press the down-arrow key so that the range D12:D24 is selected.

   m. Apply Accounting format, two decimal places.

   n. Press End and then the left-arrow key, and then the right-arrow key to move to cell B12. Then hold down the Shift key as you press and release End and then press the down-arrow key so that the range B12:B24 is selected.

   o. Apply Number format, two decimal places.

   p. Stop the macro recording.

7. Test your formatting macro by clicking in cell B28 and pressing Ctrl+Shift+F.

8. Repeat the test with cell B37.

9. Adjust column widths as needed to display the data fully.

10. Preview and print the Income worksheet.

11. Save and close the workbook and exit Excel.

On Your Own

1. Start Excel, if necessary, and open ☉ **80_APPLIANCE**.

2. Save the workbook as **OXL_80**.

3. Create a macro called *Sort_DB* that sorts the database on the August Sales worksheet by state, and then by appliance.

   a. Begin recording the macro in cell B8.

   b. Assign a shortcut key combination such as Ctrl+Shift+S.

   c. Store the macro in this workbook.

   d. Use relative reference mode.

4. Test the macro by sorting the database on the September Sales sheet.

5. Create a second macro called *Zoom_Out* that adjusts the zoom percentage to 55%, changes to Full Screen view, and then scrolls down, if necessary, so that the database is fully displayed.

   a. Begin recording the macro in cell B8.

   b. Assign a shortcut key combination such as Ctrl+Shift+O.

   c. Store the macro in this workbook.

   d. Use absolute reference mode.

6. Create a third macro called *Zoom_In* that returns to Normal view, restores the zoom percentage to 80%, and moves the cell pointer back to cell B8, if necessary.

   a. Assign a shortcut key combination such as Ctrl+Shift+I.

   b. Store the macro in this workbook.

   c. Continue to use absolute reference mode.

7. Test the two zoom macros.

8. In the range J7:L13, create a recap area for Illinois sales.

   a. List each appliance type on a separate line.

   b. Next to each type, use a formula to display the total sales.

9. Create a similar area for Indiana sales in the range J15:L21.

10. Copy the clip art and the title, JJ Appliances, to the range I1:N6.

11. Create a similar recap area on the September Sales worksheet.

12. Save and close the workbook and exit Excel.

Exercise 81

◆ **Open a Workbook Containing Macros** ◆ **Edit a Macro**
◆ **Delete a Macro** ■ **Assign a Macro to a Toolbar Button**
◆ **Assign a Macro to a Control**

On the Job

After creating a macro, you may want to make minor changes to it, or you may decide that you no longer need the macro and you want to remove it. If the macro proves useful, on the other hand, you may want to assign it to a toolbar button or control to make the macro easier to use.

You did a good job on your monthly income and expenses worksheet, and everything seems to be going much faster. However, you're not quite satisfied with the macros' ease of use. In this exercise, you'll refine the workbook you created in Exercise 80, adding macros to toolbar buttons and controls, and deleting macros you no longer need.

Terms

Visual Basic for Applications A special version of the Visual Basic programming language used by Office to record macros.

Visual Basic A programming language that can be used to construct Windows programs.

control List boxes, option buttons, and so on that are displayed on the worksheet itself. These controls are similar in appearance to their dialog box counterparts, but are controlled by macros or programs that you create and assign.

Notes

Open a Workbook Containing Macros

■ Macros can be helpful, useful tools or they can wreak havoc on your system by performing actions that prove harmful to Excel, your workbooks, or your computer.

■ Because macros of unknown origin may prove damaging to your computer, Excel prompts you to consider disabling macros whenever you attempt to open a workbook that contains macros.

Macro Warning dialog box

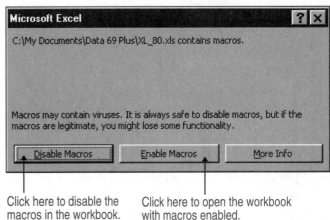

Click here to disable the macros in the workbook.

Click here to open the workbook with macros enabled.

- If you know the origin of the workbook and trust its source, you can ignore the warning message that appears, open the workbook, and activate its macros.

- If you're unsure of the workbook's source, you can still open it, and disable the macros at the same time.

  ✓ *Disabling the macros in a workbook may prevent you from being able to use it effectively.*

Edit a Macro

- Excel macros are recorded in a programming language called **Visual Basic for Applications** (VBA).

  ✓ *VBA is an offshoot of the programming language* ***Visual Basic***.

- To edit a macro you've recorded, you need to know something about the VBA programming language.

  ✓ *You can learn about VBA through Excel's Help system.*

- If you don't know anything about programming and don't want to learn, you can simply re-record the macro.

  - However, there are some changes you can't make unless you actually edit the macro.

  - For example, if you change the display so that gridlines don't appear while recording a macro, Excel will record the command this way:

    ActiveWindow.DisplayGridlines = False

  - If you want the macro to act as a toggle — that is, turn the gridlines off if they're on, and turn them on if they're off — this command won't work.

  - However, if you change the command to read as follows, it will act as a toggle:

    ActiveWindow.DisplayGridlines = Not ActiveWindow.DisplayGridlines

    ✓ *This command must be typed on one line in the Visual Basic module with a space between Not and the remainder of the command.*

Delete a Macro

- If a macro has outlasted its usefulness, you can delete it.

- To delete a macro, you use the Macro dialog box.

- In the Macro dialog box, select the workbook that contains the macro.

- If you've assigned a macro to a toolbar button or graphic control, you'll need to delete that, manually.

Assign a Macro to a Toolbar Button

- If a macro proves useful, and you want to make it easy to use that macro often, assign it to a toolbar button.

  ✓ *It usually makes sense to add a button to a toolbar only if the macro is placed in the Personal Macro Workbook. Otherwise, you'll have a button on a toolbar that won't do anything unless a particular workbook is open.*

- The button can be placed on any toolbar, such as the Standard or Formatting toolbars, or a custom toolbar that you create. You can even add a button to the menu bar.

- After you add the Custom Button to a toolbar, you can change the image that appears on it (which is normally a happy face).

- You can also change the name of the button, which is displayed on the button face, and supplies the ScreenTip that appears when the mouse pointer rests on the button.

Assign a Macro to a Control

- If you want to keep the macro close at hand, you can assign it to a **control**.

- A control looks like the kind of graphical item you typically find in a dialog box: command buttons, list boxes, option buttons, check boxes, and so on.

- For most macros, a simple control, such as the OK button you often see in a dialog box, is usually best.

  - To run the macro, you just click the control to which you've assigned it.

- To assign a macro to a control, you must first draw the control on the worksheet by using the Forms toolbar.

  - You then assign the macro to the control.

  - You can change the text that appears on the control to something descriptive of the macro's purpose.

- After the control is assigned a macro, the mouse pointer changes to a hand when it's moved over the button.

- You can move, resize, and change the button's appearance as needed.

- To make changes to the control, you select it.

  ✓ *Since clicking the button activates the macro, you must use the Select Object tool on the Drawing toolbar to select the control button before making changes to it.*

Procedures

Edit a Macro

1. Click **Tools**.................. `Alt`+`T`
2. Click **Macro**...................... `M`
3. Click **Macros**.................... `M`
4. Select macro in **Macro name** list............................ `Tab`, `↓``↑`

   ✓ *If the macro is in a different workbook or the Personal Macro Workbook (listed in the dialog box as PERSONAL.xls), select the workbook from the **Macros in** list.*

5. Click **Edit** .... `Alt`+`E`

   ✓ *The Visual Basic Editor displays.*

   ✓ *If the macro is in the Personal Macro Workbook, you must unhide the workbook before you can edit the macro. Choose Window, Unhide, select PERSONAL.xls from the list, and click OK. (Remember to hide the Personal Macro Workbook again later.)*

6. Make changes to the macro commands as needed.
7. When you're finished making changes, click **File** .... `Alt`+`F`
8. Click **Close and Return to Microsoft Excel** .... `C`

Change Shortcut Key or Description for an Existing Macro

1. Click **Tools**.................. `Alt`+`T`
2. Click **Macro**...................... `M`
3. Click **Macros**.................... `M`
4. Select macro in **Macro name** list............................ `Tab`, `↓``↑`
5. Click **Options**.............. `Alt`+`O`

6. Click **Shortcut key**...... `Alt`+`K`
7. Press the key you want to use as a shortcut.

   ✓ *You can press Shift to create a shortcut key, such as Ctrl+Shift+letter.*

8. Click **Description**........ `Alt`+`D`
9. Type a new description.
10. Click **OK** .... `Enter`

Delete a Macro

1. Click **Tools**.................. `Alt`+`T`
2. Click **Macro**...................... `M`
3. Click **Macros**.................... `M`
4. Select macro in **Macro name** list............................ `Tab`, `↓``↑`
5. Click **Delete**.................. `Alt`+`D`
6. Confirm the deletion by clicking **Yes**............. `Alt`+`Y`

Assign a Macro to a Toolbar Button

1. Click **Tools**................. `Alt`+`T`
2. Click **Customize** .... `C`
3. Click **Commands** tab .. `Alt`+`C`
4. Select Macros from the **Categories** list .... `Tab`, `↓``↑`
5. Select Custom Button from the **Commands** list .... `Alt`+`D`, `↓``↑`
6. Drag Custom Button onto the toolbar you want to customize.

   ✓ *Drop the button where you want to position it on the toolbar.*

7. Click **Modify Selection**........ `Alt`+`M`
8. Click **Assign Macro**............ `M`

9. Select macro........... `Tab`, `↓``↑` in **Macro name** list.
10. Click **OK** .... `Enter`
11. Change the toolbar button picture (optional):
    a. Click **Modify Selection** .... `Alt`+`M`
    b. Click **Change Button Image** .... `B`
    c. Click new image.
12. Change the button's name (optional):
    a. Click **Modify Selection** .... `Alt`+`M`
    b. Click **Name**.................... `N`
    c. Type new button name.

       ✓ *Type an ampersand (&) in front of the letter you want underlined in the button name. If you display text on the button (with or without the image), pressing Alt plus this letter will activate the button.*

       ✓ *Avoid using a letter that's already in use on an Excel menu or toolbar.*

       ✓ *The button name is also used for its ScreenTip.*

    d. Press **Enter** .... `Enter`
13. Click **Close** .... `Enter`

Display the Forms Toolbar

1. Click **View**.................. `Alt`+`V`
2. Click **Toolbars**.................... `T`
3. Click **Forms** .... `↓``↑`, `Enter`

Assign a Macro to a Control

1. Click **Button** button ☐ on Forms toolbar.

   ✓ The pointer becomes +.

2. Click in the worksheet to establish the upper-left corner of the control button.

   ✓ Don't release the mouse button yet.

3. Drag downward and to the right, drawing the button on the worksheet.

4. Select macro in **Macro name** list.......................... Tab , ↓ ↑

5. Click **OK** .... Enter

6. Edit button text as desired.

7. Click anywhere in worksheet.

Select a Control Button Without Running the Macro

   ✓ If you need to change the text, size, or position of a control later, you need to select the button without running the associated macro.

1. Click **Drawing** button 🖉 on Standard toolbar to display Drawing toolbar.

2. Click **Select Objects** button ⬚ to activate it.

3. Click any part of the control.

   ✓ Excel marks the control with a selection outline and handles.

4. Make change(s) to the button as needed.

   ✓ When you're finished making changes to the control, be sure to click the **Select Objects** button again to stop selecting. You can then run the macro assigned to the control as usual.

Exercise Directions

1. Start Excel, if necessary.

2. Open **XL_80**, created in Exercise 80, or open 💿**81_COFFEE** instead.

   • When prompted, click Enable Macros.

3. Save the workbook as **XL_81**.

4. Assign the macro CoName to a toolbar button on the Standard toolbar.

   a. Place the button to the left of the Help button, at the right end of the toolbar.

   b. Assign the name *Co Heading* to the button.

   c. Change the image to the cup of coffee graphic.

5. Assign the other macro, Std_Format, to a toolbar button as well.

   a. Place the button at the right end of the Formatting toolbar.

   b. Assign the name *Std Format* to the button.

   c. Change the image to the magic eight ball.

6. Try out the new buttons:

   a. Change to the Expenses worksheet.

   b. Click the Co Heading button on the Standard toolbar.

   c. Edit the subtitle to read *Coffee Shop Expenses*.

   d. Copy the heading (C5:F6) to the range K5:N6.

   e. Edit the subtitle to read *Coffee Shop Expense Recap*.

   f. Click in cell B11.

   g. Use the Std Format button on the Formatting toolbar to format the associated range.

   h. Repeat these steps to format the ranges beginning with cells B28 and B37.

7. Create a macro to format the recap areas of the workbook:

   a. Before you begin the macro, type *Expense Recap* in cell H12.

   b. Use the macro name *Recap_Format*.

   c. Don't assign a shortcut key.

   d. Save the macro in the workbook.

   e. Use relative reference mode.

8. Record the following actions, beginning with the cursor in cell H12:

   ✓ As before, you'll use the arrow keys and End-and-arrow combinations so that the macro will work with ranges of different sizes. Remember to release the End key before you press another key.

   a. Apply Impact, 14 points to cell H12.

   b. Hold down the Shift key as you press the right-arrow key so that the range H12:I12 is selected.

   c. Apply a Light Yellow solid color fill.

   d. Press the down-arrow key and the right-arrow key to move to cell I13.

   e. Hold down the Shift key as you press and release End and then press the down-arrow key to select the range I13:I20.

f. Apply Arial, 10 points, italic, right-aligned. Apply a Tan solid color fill.

g. Press the right-arrow key, then hold down the Shift key as you press and release End and then press the down-arrow key to select the range J13:J20.

h. Apply Accounting format, two decimal places.

i. Press End, press the down-arrow key, press End, and press the down-arrow key to move to cell J22.

j. Apply Accounting format, two decimal places.

k. Press End and then press the left-arrow key to move to cell H22.

l. Apply Arial, 10 points, bold.

m. Hold down the Shift key as you press the right-arrow key to select the range H22:I22.

n. Apply a Lime solid color fill.

o. Adjust column I to fit its data.

p. Stop recording.

> ✓ *It's wise to save a workbook before recording a macro (in case you eventually need to give up and start over from scratch) and save it again immediately after you complete the macro (in case of power loss, so you won't have to re-record the macro).*

9. Assign the macro to a button on the Formatting toolbar.

a. Place the button to the left of the Std Format button at the right end of the Formatting toolbar.

b. Assign the name *Recap Format* to the button.

c. Change the image to the fish.

10. Complete the recap area on the Recap sheet.

a. In cells E13:E15, enter formulas to display the total coffee sales, and so on.

b. Add the company page headings using the new toolbar button.

c. Using the Recap Format button, format the ranges beginning with cells C12 and C19.

11. Create a print macro:

a. Change to the Expenses worksheet.

b. Create a macro that sets the print range equal to A1:G50 and prints the resulting page.

c. Name the macro *Print_Expense_Totals*.

d. Use absolute reference mode.

e. Create a control button on the worksheet to run the macro.

> ✓ *When creating a control button, you can drag to create the size you want, or just click in the worksheet to create a standard-sized button at the location. Resize the button as needed.*

f. Place the button under the subtitle and change the text to read *Print Expense Totals*.

g. Use 8-point text for the button title.

12. Create another print macro:

a. Create a macro that sets the print range equal to G1:O24 and prints the resulting page.

b. Name the macro *Print_Expense_Recap*.

c. Use absolute reference mode.

d. Create a control button on the worksheet to run the macro.

e. Place the button to the right of the other button and change the text to read *Print Expense Recap*.

f. Use 8-point text for the button title.

13. Print all the worksheets.

- When printing the Expenses worksheet, use the control buttons to print the totals and the recap separately.

14. Delete the CoName macro.

15. Remove the macro buttons from the Standard and Formatting toolbars.

16. Save and close the workbook and exit Excel.

On Your Own

1. Start Excel, if necessary.
2. Open **OXL_80**, created in Exercise 80, or open ⊙**81_APPLIANCE**.
   - When prompted, click Enable Macros.
3. Save the workbook as **OXL_81**.
4. Create a chart macro:
   a. Use the macro name *Pie_Chart*.
   b. Save the macro in the workbook.
   c. Don't assign a shortcut.
   d. Use relative reference mode.
5. Record your actions as you create a pie chart using the range K8:L13 on the August Sales worksheet.
   ✓ *Plan the type of formatting you want to use before you record the macro.*
   a. Select a pie chart subtype of your choice.
   b. Save the chart on its own worksheet.
   c. Format the chart however you like, adding a colorful chart background, title, legend, data labels, and so on.
   d. After you finish recording the macro, assign it to a button on the Standard toolbar.
6. Use this toolbar button to create a similar pie chart using the range K16:L21.
   a. Notice that the macro didn't work correctly. Although you recorded it relatively, the pie chart keeps using the original source data rather than the currently selected data. To fix this problem, open the macro in the Visual Basic Editor.
   b. Select and then delete the following command:
      - ActiveChart.SetSourceData Source:=Sheets("August Sales").Range("K8:L13") _,PlotBy:=xlColumns.

c. Close the Visual Basic Editor.
d. Delete the chart sheet you just created with the macro.
e. Reposition the cell pointer as needed and run the new version of the macro to create the pie chart for the range K16:L21.
f. Using the toolbar button, create similar charts with the ranges K8:L13 and K16:L21 on the September Sales worksheet.
g. Add or correct chart titles and sheet names so you can tell the difference between all the charts at a glance.
7. Edit the Zoom_Out macro so that gridlines are turned off when the macro is activated.
   ✓ *Add this line to the macro:*
     ActiveWindow.DisplayGridlines = False
   ✓ *Don't use this macro on a chart sheet (which doesn't have gridlines). It will cause an error.*
8. Edit the Zoom_In macro to turn the gridlines back on.
   ✓ *You can copy the gridlines command from the Zoom_Out macro; just change False to True.*
9. Add two control buttons to the August Sales worksheet.
   a. Assign the Zoom_Out macro to one button.
   b. Assign the Zoom_In macro to the other button.
   c. Use whatever button names you want.
   d. Copy the buttons to the September Sales worksheet as well.
10. Test the new buttons to make sure they work.
11. Save and close the workbook and exit Excel.

Exercise 82

◆ Link Documents with Hyperlinks ◆ Add a Hyperlink to a Worksheet

On the Job

A hyperlink can connect a worksheet to specific locations within any worksheet in any workbook, or to information on the Internet or the company intranet. Using a hyperlink is a convenient way to provide quick access to related information. For example, in a sales worksheet, you could provide a hyperlink to an area in the workbook (or in another workbook) that provides product cost or other revenues.

As the owner of the Java Jungle Café, you wear many hats. And today you're a "Sales Analyst." To analyze recent sales trends, you've decided to compare September and October sales figures with some pricing information from the Internet. Because you'll need to move between documents a lot as you make comparisons, you've decided to add hyperlinks to make the whole process easier. This will also make the process easier for your accountant, who'll be using the workbooks after you're finished with them.

Terms

hyperlink Text or graphics linked to related information in the same workbook, another workbook, or another file.

Internet A global collection of interconnected networks.

intranet A private Internet-like network, typically used to link the various parts of a company.

Web pages Documents (frequently including multimedia elements) that can be accessed with a Web browser.

hotspot An area within a graphic which, when clicked, acts as a hyperlink.

HTML Short for Hypertext Markup Language, the language used to display information on a Web page.

URL Short for *uniform resource locator*. The location of the page or file on the Internet.

Notes

Link Documents with Hyperlinks

- A **hyperlink** is text (frequently formatted in blue and underlined) or a graphic object that, when clicked, connects the user to related information elsewhere in the worksheet or in another file.
  - You can link to information in the same worksheet, another worksheet in the same workbook, another workbook, or anywhere on the Internet.

- On the **Internet** or an **intranet**, similar hyperlinks are used to connect related documents.

- Documents on the Internet that use HTML format are called **Web pages**.

- Web pages frequently have multimedia capabilities such as sound, movies, animations, and so on, as well as providing controls such as forms, dialog boxes, and buttons.

- When you move the mouse pointer over a hyperlink, it changes to a pointing hand.
  - This is to help you distinguish hyperlinks from regular text.
  - Because the mouse pointer changes to a hand when over a hyperlink, you must use special techniques to select the link for editing.
- A hyperlink can also be represented by a graphic image.
  - A hyperlink that's embedded within a graphic creates a **hotspot** — a spot or area within the graphic that, when clicked, acts as a link.
- Usually, when a hyperlink is represented as text, that text appears in a blue underlined font.
  - ✓ *You can change the default color of hyperlink text.*
  - When you click a hyperlink and then later return to it, you'll probably notice that it has changed to purple underlined text.
  - This change helps you quickly identify the links you've used (and those you haven't).
- Clicking a hyperlink moves you to the associated location.
  - If the hyperlink involves another file, that file is opened automatically.
  - If you want the user to move to a particular place within a worksheet, you might want to create a range name so that you can use that name in the link. Clicking the hyperlink takes the user to that range within the worksheet.
    - ✓ *If you don't want to create a range name, you can still link to a specific place within a worksheet by typing its cell address.*
  - If you link to other types of documents, such as Word documents, you can create bookmarks that act the same way as range names — they allow you to link to a particular place within the document.
- You can create hyperlinks that connect a user to data in the current workbook or workbooks located on a company intranet.
- You can also connect to data on the Internet.
  - You can connect to Excel files or to **HTML** documents, since Excel can display either.
  - This capability allows you to include links to related Web pages (since they're coded in HTML) within your worksheets.

- You can include hyperlinks in ordinary Excel worksheets.
  - You can also include hyperlinks in workbooks that you have converted to HTML format.

Add a Hyperlink to a Worksheet

- If you want to create a hyperlink from text, enter the text before you follow the steps to create the hyperlink.
- Likewise, if you want to create a hyperlink from a graphic image, insert the image into the worksheet first.
- Normally, you insert a hyperlink using the Insert Hyperlink dialog box.

Insert Hyperlink dialog box

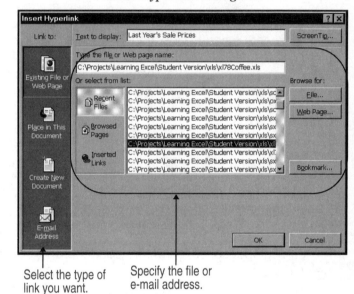

Select the type of link you want.

Specify the file or e-mail address.

- If you want to create a hyperlink to a Web page or an intranet document, you can bypass the Insert Hyperlink dialog box and simply type the Web page address (**URL**) or intranet location into a cell.
  - Excel will instantly recognize the address as a URL, and create a hyperlink from it automatically.
  - A Web address might look like this:
    http://www.ddcpub.com/newpage.html
- With your Internet or intranet connection, you can include a hyperlink to an e-mail address within a worksheet.
  - When a user clicks this type of hyperlink, an e-mail form opens with the recipient's address included.

Procedures

Insert a Hyperlink to a File

1. Select the text or graphic you want to use for the link.
2. Click the **Insert Hyperlink** button 🔗 on the Standard toolbar.
   OR
   a. Click **I**nsert .... Alt + I
   b. Click **Hyperl**ink I
3. If prompted, click **Y**es to save the workbook .... Alt + Y
4. Click the **Existing File or Web Page** button in the Places bar .... Alt + X
5. Enter the path to the file in the **Type the fil**e **or Web page name** text box .... Alt + E
   OR
   a. Click **F**ile .... Alt + F
   b. Select drive and/or directory from **Look i**n list ..... Alt + I
   c. Select file .... Tab , ↓ ↑
   d. Click **OK** .... Enter
   OR
   a. Click **Rec**ent Files .... Alt + C
   b. Select a file you've used recently from those listed .... ↓ ↑
   ✓ If you're linking to an Excel workbook, you can link to a specific range, or you can select a sheet from those listed and type a cell address.
6. To link to a specific location within the file:
   a. Click **B**ookmark ..... Alt + O
   b. Select the name from those listed .... ↓ ↑
   c. Click **OK** .... Enter

7. To change the ScreenTip that appears when the mouse pointer rests on the hyperlink:
   a. Click **ScreenTi**p ..... Alt + P
   b. Enter the description you want to display.
   c. Click **OK** .... Enter
   ✓ This option isn't supported in older browsers.
8. Click **OK** .... Enter

Insert a Hyperlink to a Web Page

1. Select the text or graphic you want to use for the link.
2. Click the **Insert Hyperlink** button 🔗 on the Standard toolbar.
   OR
   a. Click **I**nsert .... Alt + I
   b. Click **Hyperl**ink I
3. If prompted, click **Y**es to save the workbook ...... Alt + Y
4. Click the **Existing File or Web Page** button in the Places bar .... Alt + X
5. Enter the address of the Web page in the **Type the fil**e **or Web page name** text box .... Alt + E
   OR
   a. Click **W**eb Page ..... Alt + W
   b. Using your Web browser, change to the page you want.
   c. Switch back to Excel.
   OR
   a. Click **B**rowsed Pages .... Alt + B
   b. Select a page you've visited recently from those listed .... Tab , ↓ ↑

6. To link to a specific location within the page:
   a. Click **B**ookmark ..... Alt + O
   b. Select the name from those listed .... ↓ ↑
7. To change the ScreenTip that appears when the mouse pointer rests on the hyperlink:
   a. Click **ScreenTi**p ..... Alt + P
   b. Enter the description you want to display.
   c. Click **OK** .... Enter
8. Click **OK** .... Enter

Insert a Hyperlink to a Location in the Current Workbook

1. Select the text or graphic you want to use for the link.
2. Click the **Insert Hyperlink** button 🔗 on the Standard toolbar.
   OR
   a. Click **I**nsert .... Alt + I
   b. Click **Hyperl**ink I
3. If prompted, click **Y**es to save the workbook .... Alt + Y
4. Click the **Place in This Document** button in the Places bar .... Alt + A
5. Enter the cell address in the **Type the c**ell **reference** text box .... Alt + E
   OR
   • Select a location from the **Or select a place in this document** list .... Alt + C , ↓ ↑
6. To change the ScreenTip that appears when the mouse pointer rests on the hyperlink:
   a. Click **ScreenTi**p ..... Alt + P
   b. Enter the description you want to display.
   c. Click **OK** .... Enter
7. Click **OK** .... Enter

Insert a Hyperlink to a New Workbook

1. Select the text or graphic you want to use for the link.
2. Click the **Insert Hyperlink** button 🔗 on the Standard toolbar.
   OR
   a. Click **Insert** .... `Alt`+`I`
   b. Click **Hyperlink** .... `I`
3. If prompted, click **Yes** to save the workbook .. `Alt`+`Y`
4. Click the **Create New Document** button in the Places bar .... `Alt`+`N`
5. Type a name for the new workbook in the **Name of new document** text box ..... `Alt`+`D`
6. If necessary, change the drive and directory in which you want the new workbook saved:
   a. Click **Change** .... `Alt`+`C`
   b. Select drive and/or directory from **Save in** list ..... `Alt`+`I`
   c. Click **OK** .... `Enter`

7. Indicate when you want to edit the new workbook:
   • **Edit the new document later** ..... `Alt`+`L`
   OR
   • **Edit the new document now** ...... `Alt`+`W`
8. To change the ScreenTip that appears when the mouse pointer rests on the hyperlink:
   a. Click **ScreenTip** ..... `Alt`+`P`
   b. Enter the description you want to display.
   c. Click **OK** .... `Enter`
9. Click **OK** .... `Enter`

Insert a Hyperlink to an E-mail Address

✓ *This type of link will open an e-mail form with the recipient's e-mail address included.*

1. Select the text or graphic you want to use for the link.
2. Click the **Insert Hyperlink** button 🔗 on the Standard toolbar.
   OR

   a. Click **Insert** .... `Alt`+`I`
   b. Click **Hyperlink** .... `I`
3. If prompted, click **Yes** to save the workbook .... `Alt`+`Y`
4. Click the **E-mail Address** button in the Places bar .... `Alt`+`M`
5. Enter the address for e-mail messages in the **E-mail address** text box .... `Alt`+`E`
   OR
   • Select an address from the **Recently used e-mail adresses** list .... `Alt`+`C`, `↓``↑`
6. Type a description for the messages in the **Subject** box .... `Alt`+`S`
7. To change the ScreenTip that appears when the mouse pointer rests on the hyperlink:
   a. Click **ScreenTip** ...... `Alt`+`P`
   b. Enter the description you want to display.
   c. Click **OK** .... `Enter`
8. Click **OK** .... `Enter`

Edit a Hyperlink

1. Right-click the hyperlink.
2. Click **Hyperlink** .... `H`
3. Click **Edit Hyperlink** .... `H`
4. Make your changes.
5. Click **OK** .... `Enter`

Exercise Directions

1. Start Excel, if necessary, and open ⊚ **82_SALES**.

2. Save the workbook as **XL_82**.

3. Create some range names:

   a. Give cell J12 on the Sept Sales worksheet the name *Sales_Recap*.

   b. Give cell A47 on the Sept Sales worksheet the name *Sept_Chart*.

   c. Give cell A46 on the Oct Sales worksheet the name *Oct_Chart*.

4. Add some hyperlinks on the Sept Sales worksheet:

   a. In cell G12, type *Sept Chart*.

   b. Create a link from cell G12 to the September sales chart.

   c. In cell G13, type *Oct Chart*.

   d. Create a link from cell G13 to the October sales chart.

   e. In cell G14, type *Price Comp*.

   f. Create a link from cell G14 to the workbook ⊚ **82_PRICES** Sheet1, cell C12.

   g. In cell G15, type *Sept-Oct Comp*.

   h. Create a link from cell G15 to the sales recap (use the Sales_Recap range).

   i. Format cells G12:G15 as Arial, bold, 9 points, centered.

      ✓ Use the Shift key and the arrow keys to select the cells for formatting.

5. If necessary, adjust the width of column G to fit the size of the link text.

6. Copy these links to the range, G12:G15 of the Oct Sales worksheet.

   a. Select the cells without clicking the links.

   b. Adjust the width of column G, if necessary, after you paste the links in place.

7. Add some other links:

   a. In cell A47 of the Sept Sales worksheet, type *To Sept*.

   b. Create a link from cell A47 to cell C12 of the Sept Sales worksheet.

   c. In cell B47 of the Sept Sales worksheet, type *To Oct*.

   d. Create a link from cell B47 to cell C12 of the Oct Sales worksheet.

   e. Format the range A47:B47 with Arial, bold, 9 points.

   f. Copy the range A47:B47 to A46:B46 in the Oct Sales worksheet and M12:N12 of the Sept Sales worksheet.

8. Test all the links by clicking them one by one.

   ✓ When you open the Price Comparison worksheet using the hyperlink, the Web toolbar appears. You can use this toolbar to access other files or Web pages by typing their addresses in the large text box.

   ✓ Close the Price Comparison Workbook after opening it with the hyperlink.

9. Save and close the **XL_82** workbook and exit Excel.

On Your Own

1. Start Excel, if necessary, and open **OXL_73**, created in Exercise 73.

2. Save the workbook as **OXL_82**.

3. Add links in the file to the Web sites of the various realtors from which you originally located homes for sale.

   ✓ You'll probably want to link to each realtor's search page so you can conduct updated searches from there when needed.

4. After you create the links, use them to conduct another search for new homes in your area.

5. Update the listing with the new information.

6. Save and close the workbook and exit Excel.

Exercise 83

◆ **Critical Thinking**

You're getting more comfortable with using Excel, and you wish that you could say the same thing about your boss at Corporate Computer Solutions. Unfortunately, he's a bit slow when it comes to computers, so in this exercise, you'll use your new skills with macros to make a couple of computer sales databases easier for him to use.

Exercise Directions

1. Start Excel, if necessary.

2. Open ◈ **83_COMPUTERS**.

3. Save the file as **XL_83**.

4. Create a macro called *Sort_Type* that sorts the database by type of computer: Penultima, Maxima, or Ultima.

   a. Save this macro in the workbook.

   b. Don't assign a shortcut key.

   c. Use absolute reference mode.

   d. Record your actions as you sort the database by type and model number.

5. Create a second macro called *Sort_Sold* that sorts the database by the number of computers sold.

   a. Save this macro in the workbook.

   b. Don't assign a shortcut key.

   c. Use absolute reference mode.

   d. Record your actions as you sort the database by number sold in February, type, and model number.

6. Create a third macro called *Sort_Cost* that sorts the database by the cost of each computer.

   a. Save this macro in the workbook.

   b. Don't assign a shortcut key.

   c. Use absolute reference mode.

   d. Record your actions as you sort the database by retail price, type, and model number.

7. Create a macro called *Top_Sellers* that uses advanced filters to generate and print reports of the top sellers for each type of computer.

✓ *A top seller is any model that sold six or more units in a month.*

a. Select the database and assign it the range name *Database*.

   ✓ *Naming the database isn't required, but it can save steps when running multiple database operations.*

b. Copy the database field labels from the range C7:I7 to cell C29. Then select the range C29:I30 and name it *Criteria*.

c. Start recording the macro. Save the macro in this workbook, with no shortcut key. Use absolute reference mode.

d. Enter the first type of computer, *Ultima*, in cell C30. Then enter the restriction >=6 in cell I30.

e. Use an advanced filter to create the report.

   ✓ *In the Advanced Filter dialog box, select the option Copy to another location.*

   ✓ *Select cell C35 as the Copy to range. The advanced filter will place the column labels in row 35 and the extract results in rows 36 and following.*

f. Switch to relative reference mode, select the extract range, and print it.

   ✓ *When selecting the extract range, use the arrow keys and End-and-arrow combinations as you did with the formatting macro in Exercise 80.*

g. Switch back to absolute reference mode and click in cell C30.

h. Type *Maxima*.

i. Run the advanced filter to create a new report.

j. Return to relative reference mode and then select and print the extract range.

k. Repeat steps g–j for Penultima computers.

8. Create four control buttons and assign a macro to each one.

   a. Place the buttons in the range A8:B17.

   b. Use the labels *Sort Type*, *Sort No. Sold*, *Sort Retail Cost*, and *Print Report* on the control buttons.

9. Test the buttons to make sure that each macro works as desired.

   ✓ *Hint: When testing the sort buttons, click a cell in the database first.*

10. Add a hyperlink to another database:

    a. Type the link in cell A19: *Click here to view weekly sales.*

    b. Merge and wrap the text within the range A19:B20.

       ✓ *Open the Format Cells dialog box and click the Alignment tab. In the text control section, select the Wrap text and Merge cells options.*

    c. Add a Light Yellow fill and a Thick Box border.

    d. Link the text to cell C8 on Sheet1 of the file ✆**83_SALES**.

    e. Apply bold formatting to the hyperlink text.

11. Test the link.

12. When the link opens **83_SALES**, save the workbook as **XL_83A**.

13. Create a macro in **XL_83A** called *Sort_Store* that sorts the database by store sales.

    a. Save this macro in the workbook.

    b. Don't assign a shortcut key.

    c. Use absolute reference mode.

    d. Record your actions as you sort the database by store, computer, and model.

14. Create a second macro called *Sort_Person* that sorts the database by salesperson, computer, and model.

    a. Save this macro in the workbook.

    b. Don't assign a shortcut key.

    c. Use absolute reference mode.

    d. Record your actions as you sort the database by salesperson, computer, and model.

15. Create a macro called *Sales_Report* that uses advanced filters to generate and print reports of each person's sales.

    a. Select the database and assign it the range name *Database*.

    b. Copy the database field labels from the range C7:G7 to cell C47. Then select the range C47:G48 and name it *Criteria*.

    c. Start recording the macro. Save the macro in this workbook, with no shortcut key. Use absolute reference mode.

    d. Enter the first person, *Bob Smith*, in cell C48.

    e. Use an advanced filter to create the report.

       ✓ *In the Advanced Filter dialog box, select the option Copy to another location.*

       ✓ *Select cell C51 as the Copy to range. The advanced filter will place the column labels in row 51 and the extract results in rows 52 and following.*

    f. Switch to relative reference mode, select the extract range, and print it.

       ✓ *When selecting the extract range, use the arrow keys and End-and-arrow combinations.*

    g. Switch back to absolute reference mode and click in cell C48.

    h. Type *George Billings.*

    i. Run the advanced filter to create the new report.

    j. Return to relative reference mode and then select and print the extract range.

    k. Repeat steps g–j for the remaining salespeople: *Ginny Byer*, *John Poole*, *Sally Kyte*, and *Sue Cooper*.

16. Create three control buttons and assign a macro to each one.

    a. Place the buttons in the range A8:B14.

    b. Use the descriptions *Sort Store*, *Sort Salesperson*, and *Print Report* on the control buttons.

17. Test the buttons to make sure each macro works as desired.

    ✓ *Hint: When testing the sort buttons, click a cell in the database first.*

18. Save both workbooks and exit Excel.

Index

T

X

Y

Z

Quick Reference Guides find software answers faster because you read less

$12 ea.

Did We Make One for You?

Find it quickly and get back to the keyboard—fast

The index becomes your quick locator. Just follow the step-by-step illustrated instructions. We tell you what to do in five or six words.

Sometimes only two.

No narration or exposition. Just "press this—type that" illustrated commands.

The spiral binding keeps pages open so you can type what you read. You save countless hours of lost time by locating the illustrated answer in seconds.

The time you save when this guide goes to work for you will pay for it the very first day

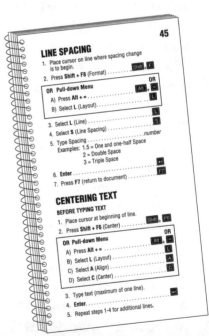

To order call 800-528-3897 fax 800-528-3862

275 Madison Ave., New York, NY 10016

7/99 Q

The Visual Reference Series

VISUAL REFERENCE BASICS

TEACHES 100 BASIC FEATURES

Microsoft Windows 98
Includes Tips for Windows 95 & Windows 3.1 Upgrades

Karl Schwartz

VISUAL REFERENCE BASICS

TEACHES 100 BASIC FUNCTIONS

Microsoft Outlook 2000

Diana Rain

G54

$15 ea.

Each book shows you the 100 most important functions of your software programs

We explain your computer screen's elements—icons, windows, dialog boxes—with pictures, callouts, and simple, quick "Press this—type that" illustrated commands. You go right into software functions. *No time wasted.* The spiral binding keeps the pages open so you can type what you read.

Did we make one for you?

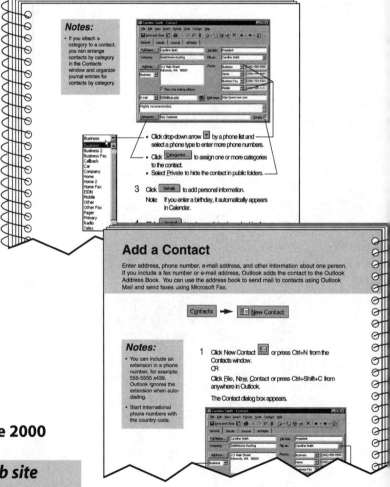

Preview any of our books at our Web site
http://www.ddcpub.com

To order call 800-528-3897 or fax 800-528-3862

7/99 V

DDC *Publishing*

275 Madison Avenue, New York, NY 1001...

Fast-teach Learning Books

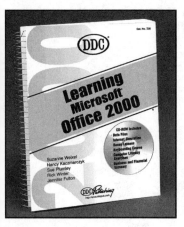

How we designed each book

Each self-paced hands-on text gives you the software concept and each exercise's objective in simple language. Next to the exercise we provide the keystrokes and the illustrated layout; step by simple step—graded and cumulative learning.

Did we make one for you?

FREE CATALOG
AND
UPDATED LISTING

We don't just have books that find your answers faster; we also have books that teach you how to use your computer without the fairy tales and the gobbledygook.

We also have books to improve your typing, spelling and punctuation.

Return this card for a free catalog and mailing list update.

275 Madison Avenue,
New York, NY 10016

❏ Please send me your catalog and put me on your mailing list.

Name

Firm (if any)

Address

City, State, Zip

Phone (800) 528-3897   *Fax (800) 528-3862*

SEE OUR COMPLETE CATALOG ON THE INTERNET @: http://www.ddcpub.com

---

FREE CATALOG
AND
UPDATED LISTING

We don't just have books that find your answers faster; we also have books that teach you how to use your computer without the fairy tales and the gobbledygook.

We also have books to improve your typing, spelling and punctuation.

Return this card for a free catalog and mailing list update.

275 Madison Avenue,
New York, NY 10016

❏ Please send me your catalog and put me on your mailing list.

Name

Firm (if any)

Address

City, State, Zip

Phone (800) 528-3897   *Fax (800) 528-3862*

SEE OUR COMPLETE CATALOG ON THE INTERNET @: http://www.ddcpub.com

---

FREE CATALOG
AND
UPDATED LISTING

We don't just have books that find your answers faster; we also have books that teach you how to use your computer without the fairy tales and the gobbledygook.

We also have books to improve your typing, spelling and punctuation.

Return this card for a free catalog and mailing list update.

275 Madison Avenue,
New York, NY 10016

❏ Please send me your catalog and put me on your mailing list.

Name

Firm (if any)

Address

City, State, Zip

Phone (800) 528-3897   *Fax (800) 528-3862*

SEE OUR COMPLETE CATALOG ON THE INTERNET @: http://www.ddcpub.com